KINGMAKER

ALSO BY SONIA PURNELL

Just Boris: A Tale of Blond Ambition

Clementine: The Life of Mrs. Winston Churchill

A Woman of No Importance: The Untold Story of the American Spy Who Helped Win World War II

KINGMAKER

PAMELA HARRIMAN'S ASTONISHING LIFE OF POWER, SEDUCTION, AND INTRIGUE

Sonia Purnell

VIKING

VIKING
An imprint of Penguin Random House LLC
penguinrandomhouse.com

Simultaneously published in hardcover in Great Britain by Virago Press,
an imprint of Hachette UK Limited, London, in 2024

First United States edition published by Viking, 2024

Copyright © 2024 by Sonia Purnell
Penguin Random House supports copyright. Copyright fuels creativity, encourages diverse voices, promotes free speech, and creates a vibrant culture. Thank you for buying an authorized edition of this book and for complying with copyright laws by not reproducing, scanning, or distributing any part of it in any form without permission. You are supporting writers and allowing Penguin Random House to continue to publish books for every reader.

Grateful acknowledgment is made for permission to reprint the extract on page 175 from "Black-Ass Poem After Talking to Pamela Churchill" in Nicholas Gerogiannis, *Ernest Hemingway: 88 Poems* (New York: Harcourt Brace Jovanovich, 1979). Copyright © 1979 by The Ernest Hemingway Foundation and Nicholas Gerogiannis.

Epitaph on p. 406 from John Maxwell Edmonds,
"Four Epitaphs," *The Times*, 6 February 1918.

Picture credits may be found on pages 485–86.

Library of Congress Cataloging-in-Publication Data
Names: Purnell, Sonia, author.
Title: Kingmaker : Pamela Harriman's astonishing life of power, seduction, and intrigue / Sonia Purnell.
Other titles: Pamela Harriman's astonishing life of power, seduction, and intrigue
Description: New York : Viking, [2024] | Includes bibliographical references and index.
Identifiers: LCCN 2024024225 (print) | LCCN 2024024226 (ebook) |
ISBN 9780593297803 (hardcover) | ISBN 9780593297810 (ebook) |
ISBN 9780593834572 (international edition)
Subjects: LCSH: Harriman, Pamela, 1920–1997. |
Ambassadors—United States—Biography. | Philanthropists—United States—Biography. |
Harriman, Pamela Digby Churchill Hayward, 1920–1997—Relations with men. |
Aristocracy (Social class)—Great Britain—Biography. |
Great Britain—Social life and customs—20th century. |
United States—Social life and customs—20th century.
Classification: LCC E840.8.H27 P87 2024 (print) | LCC E840.8.H27 (ebook) |
DDC 973.9/092 [B]—dc23/eng/20240603
LC record available at https://lccn.loc.gov/2024024225
LC ebook record available at https://lccn.loc.gov/2024024226

Printed in the United States of America
1st Printing

Designed by Cassandra Mueller

To the Otaries, with love

À demain!

We know what we are, but know not what we may be.

> Ophelia in Act IV, Scene V, *Hamlet*
> by William Shakespeare

Contents

Prologue 1

ACT ONE
War
7

ACT TWO
Peace
141

ACT THREE
Power
237

Acknowledgments 449

Notes 455

Selected Bibliography 475

Picture Credits 485

Index 487

Prologue

At four in the afternoon on Monday, February 3, 1997, a uniformed chauffeur in an armored Cadillac drives the Honorable Pamela Harriman from her Paris residence on rue du Faubourg Saint-Honoré. Fifteen minutes later he pulls up outside the Hôtel Ritz. As Harriman climbs the red-carpeted steps past the boutiques selling diamonds and into the lobby, she looks her usual stately self. The staff greet her as one of their most distinguished visitors, and the semi-mythical "seductress of the century" rewards them with her regal smile. The onetime daughter-in-law of Winston Churchill rarely sets foot outside her bedroom without full *maquillage*. Her leonine hair is artfully swept out and up. Her wardrobe reflects regular appearances on the fashion front row. A rigid diet and exercise regime—and a remarkable facelift—means she looks two decades younger than her seventy-six years. The effect is immaculate but subtle as befits President Clinton's handpicked envoy to France.

Pamela is almost forgotten now—and if she is remembered at all, it is with disdain or condescension—but on this day she is arguably the most famous diplomat in the world and the most powerful courtesan in history. Even so, few know how Her Excellency daringly used sex to cement the vital Special Relationship between Britain and America during the Second World War. Or how she helped landmark figures—some of the political or industrial "kings" of the twentieth century—to achieve and wield power. Or how she even played a part in ending the Cold War.

She commands the respect of politicians, spies and diplomats who have worked with her across two continents and five decades, with an unrivaled address book and instant access to the leaders of the United States and France. Once she was barred from mixing with royalty and banned from embassies as "that red-headed tart," but now she presides over the grandest embassy of all. Her eminence is remarkable given that as a British-born aristocrat without a single paper qualification, this is her first formal job. Yet as many loathe her as love her, and she is the subject of multiple blood feuds, four excoriating books and a litany of lawsuits. A chorus of critics dismiss her as a lightweight, but why, if a B-movie actor can become President Reagan, cannot such a woman become *Madame l'ambassadeur*?

Pamela is nursing a crushing headache as she descends the marbled hotel stairs to the Ritz Health Club and peers through the curtains of the balcony to see who is in the pool below. Often it is cleared for her to swim in private, but she has come without notice today at the urging of her deputy, who is concerned about his boss. He knows she has recently asked a saddened president to be relieved of her duties, bringing her remarkable reign in Paris to an end.

Pamela changes into a figure-sculpting swimsuit and steps down into the most elegant indoor pool in the city, flanked by Egyptian-style pillars under a *trompe l'œil* sky. Younger men still fall for her glamour—including, rumor has it, one of the handsome pool attendants young enough to be her grandson. They are beguiled by her mesmerising eyes, seductive laugh and the way she makes each feel he is the most important man in the world. She starts to swim, head proud above the water to protect her coiffure, but after twenty lengths she groans and goes limp in the water. Someone rushes to pull her out and a member of the hotel security team, Henri Paul, tries to revive her with an oxygen mask. (Seven months later his quick response will earn him the honor of driving Princess Diana, and the world's opprobrium when she meets her death in a Paris tunnel.)

This foggy February day he is urgent yet professional as a tear rolls down Pamela's face and she slips into unconsciousness. An ambulance roars into the Place Vendôme with siren blaring and a distressed President Jacques Chirac orders the best doctors in Paris to try to save the woman he owes so much. In Washington, President Bill Clinton gives an emotional statement about his great friend who made his own once improbable ascent possible.

These are not the only leaders to have paid court to her—Kennedy was her intimate friend; Nixon, Eisenhower and Ford sought her counsel and her company; Franklin Roosevelt demanded news of her; Nancy Reagan *wanted* to be her friend; the Gorbachevs *were* her friends; de Gaulle doted on her; the wartime Australian prime minister Robert Menzies protected her; and her onetime father-in-law Churchill depended on her. She was not a woman, as former Secretary of State Madeleine Albright observed, to "let her century pass her by." She seized it and left an indelible mark.

Hers is a story of virtually everyone who was anyone in the twentieth century, from Nelson Mandela to Joe Biden, Truman Capote to Dennis Hopper, Ed Murrow to Gloria Steinem, the Rothschilds to the Mitfords. She counted as friends Martha Gellhorn, Max Beaverbrook, Frank Sinatra, Christian Dior and the Duke and Duchess of Windsor. Hers was a life born of a pandemic, forged by world war and defined by haute couture, palaces and jewels, but also by love, jealousy, fortitude, heartache, illness, daredevilry and betrayal. She received dozens of proposals of marriage and took hundreds of lovers, enjoyed countless thrills on superyachts and private jets. She hungered for the trappings of wealth, but what excited her most was power. She learned to muster her privilege and fame to try to win it on behalf of those who did not have what she had. And, most of all, to bring peace.

Narrowly missing death time and again in the Blitz, she lost precious friends to the war, and while living at Downing Street bore intimate witness to Churchill's desperate struggle to save Britain from Hitler. Such visceral experiences left her with a compulsion to try to stop future conflict, yet her efforts were often belittled and misread. Few understand just how she became one of the twentieth century's most influential political players. Most of what she did was kept secret by Pamela herself or ignored by others; her papers were locked away, others classified; her surviving friends were reluctant to speak.

Only through four years of intense research in Britain, America and France was I able to unearth astonishing new testimony that allows us finally—three decades after her death—to appreciate the achievements of a woman whose name was trashed by the presumptions of her time. Just as I discovered when writing about her mother-in-law, Clementine Churchill—another formidable yet woefully underrated woman—history has reduced Pamela to a distorted stereotype, in her case a conniving and ridiculous gold digger obsessed by sex. And yet, struck by how both Winston and Clementine Churchill prized her very special contribution throughout the Second World War and the global significance of the demands they made of her, I was driven to find out the truth.

Perhaps only against the background of today's perilous tensions between West and East—and the bloody invasion of Ukraine—can we begin to register the sacrifices of a twenty-year-old woman hell-bent on waging war against tyranny. Perhaps only as more evidence comes to light can we take in the full scope of the roles she played at the pinnacle of power in three countries half a century apart—a reach and longevity unmatched by virtually anyone in modern times. Or recognize how the grit of one woman of astonishing skill but little education could help lay the groundwork for, and later revive, transatlantic alliances once again being put to the ultimate test.

Newly discovered papers, private letters and diaries, fresh accounts—and the transcripts of extensive interviews with her released for the first time—reveal how the real Pamela bore only passing resemblance to her reputation. Together they paint a nuanced character whose obvious faults were outweighed by an exceptional zest for life and reinvention, combined with experience and gifts unlikely to be seen in one person again. And yet her star sometimes shone too brightly; her access to power drew unfriendly fire. She had the temerity to succeed when failure should—in her critics' eyes—have been her due.

When her son Winston phoned a family friend to announce her death, he spoke of how her "extraordinary and dramatic exit" befitted his "extraordinary, dramatic mother." News of her demise was marked by an outpouring of grief but also, in some quarters, uncontained pleasure. Pamela was portrayed throughout her life, including in two weighty biographies, *Life of the Party* and *Reflected Glory*, as a scheming adjunct to her men. Her death began a reappraisal that can only now be completed. One of her closest friends, Richard Holbrooke, a tough-nut diplomat stricken by sorrow at her passing, cited the philosopher Søren Kierkegaard to observe that while life is lived forward it is best understood backward. And so the thrilling and astonishing "arc that Pamela Harriman traveled" should start, Holbrooke advised us, "by beginning at its end with her ambassadorship to France." For the evening of her life—when she finally achieved her seemingly impossible dreams—gave a "different meaning" to everything that had gone before. After half a century of being defined by powerful men, this was when she proved herself a singular force on her own account. And yet few appreciated what she managed to do. Or how it ultimately led an exceptional figure of the twentieth century to a lonely death.

ACT ONE
War

1

"Daddie & I were *sure* you would be a boy!" Constance told her first born. She and her husband, Kenny, had chosen the breezy name of Robin for the eagerly awaited heir to a proud and noble dynasty, so the arrival of Pamela Beryl on March 20, 1920, had come as a shock. "We were not a bit disappointed,"[1] Constance insisted but the lottery of being born a girl meant that Pamela would be denied education, expectations and a large inheritance. The rest of her life would be spent making up for it.

That Pamela had been born at all was a minor miracle. When the Honorable Constance Bruce married Captain Kenelm Digby of the Coldstream Guards in London in July 1919, the world outside was soaked in death. Twenty million had perished in the First World War, the gaunt and pale young groom very nearly among them. Then the Spanish flu scythed up to a hundred million more souls and the latest wave of the pandemic was only now receding.*

Within a month, twenty-four-year-old Constance was pregnant, but her excitement was tinged by fear. Expectant women were particularly vulnerable to the flu, some falling dead in the street, thick blood frothing from their nostrils.[2] The young had been the chief casualties of a plague spread through victory parades and church services

---

* Exact figures are impossible but recent estimates of the global death toll from Spanish flu vary from fifty to one hundred million.

just like her wedding. The healthier the patient the more likely they were to die.

As the child quickened within her, Constance was cheered by the fact that fewer friends and family were falling ill. And yet many seemed unable to shake off a feeling of impending doom. Pamela's mother—known as Pansy because her handsome face was shaped like the flower—refused to be one of them. Blessed with self-belief and physical vigor—Pamela remembered her as a "very, *very* strong woman"[3]—Pansy did not do self-pity. She had worked as a nurse during the war but now illness was not to be discussed in her presence and she flung open windows to expel unwelcome thoughts.

Pamela arrived three weeks before her time—"Like all things in my life," she observed, "I was in a hurry when I was born"—and Pansy was still with her husband on his army base at Farnborough when she went into labor. "You were the only baby I was allowed to keep on my bed, wrapped in my housemaid's flannel petticoat," Pansy told her daughter, as the cot and hand-embroidered swaddling prepared for the event were thirty miles away in London. "I had twelve hours to adore you at close range—until your things arrived."

Pamela's family had enjoyed four hundred years of wealth and aristocratic entitlement but now faced a pressing shortage of cash. Within a few months Kenny would become the 11th Baron Digby and master of the Dorset mansion of Minterne in southwest England, a house in Belgravia in central London and Geashill Castle with 34,000 acres near Dublin. Yet the £50,000 (£1.8 million today) that also came his way was not enough to maintain all the estates and pay the necessary taxes.[4] Wanting to join the post-pandemic exodus from city life to healthy open spaces, the Digbys opted to sell their London residence. Within a couple of years they also lost Geashill Castle, when nationalists burned it down during the Irish Civil War, having taken an uncle and aunt prisoner, telling each of them the other had been shot. In the face of such turmoil (and the much-feared socialist forces unleashed by the 1917 revolution in Russia), they clung to a rigid English class system softened by a *noblesse oblige* to the less fortunate.

Nevertheless, Kenny did what few in his class expected to do and when Pamela was four months old took a job—even if it was a nice sinecure as military secretary to the Governor General of Australia, living in the manicured grounds of Government House in Melbourne. Despite the additional income, Pansy was obliged to sell some of her jewels to fund their lifestyle. Money was shorter still when another daughter, Sheila, was born in 1921. Thankfully Kenny (an expert on equestrian form) won handsomely on the horses at Melbourne's Flemington Racecourse but Pansy envied her two sisters back home, with their supremely wealthy husbands and grander titles. As a mere baron, Kenny occupied the lowest rung of the English peerage, and the Minterne estate ran to just 1,500 acres (down from 40,000). Pansy determined that Pamela would become a rich countess or even a duchess to avoid the Digbys' inevitable social and financial retreat.

Precocious and spirited, Pamela was doted on by her mother almost as if she had been the desired son. She became a powerful voice at a tender age when, according to family folklore, she learned her first words from a loquacious pet cockatoo. When she was three, Pansy promised to take Pamela out in the family's first car but was unable to open the gate and informed her daughter that the outing was canceled. The Honorable Pamela (elevated since her father became a baron) stamped her small foot in fury and declared through her tears, "Man will come and man will fix." A few moments later a policeman, alerted by the kerfuffle, arrived to assist and as Pamela liked to relate, "my faith in men started with that day because I decided whenever I needed anything they would be there to help."[5]

Shortly afterward, the Digbys sailed back to England, although the two girls were dispatched on a less luxurious ship under the care of Nanny Hall. Sheila was a handful during six weeks at sea but Pamela occupied herself with the most powerful and handsome man on board, the captain, an imposing figure with flamboyantly twirled mustaches. She had watched him squire a series of besotted women around deck and so "obviously, I thought that was the chic thing to do." Her vivid red curls coyly tied with ribbons, she walked up to the captain, tugged at his sleeve and asked, "Can we go walkies too?" Thereafter he escorted her solemnly each day and she won a silver napkin ring for the best baby on board[6] despite displaying a nascent ruthless streak: "According to Nanny I shouldn't have gotten that napkin ring because I had a terrible habit of waiting until the other children turned their backs and then throwing their toys into the sea."[7]

After the sun and bustle of Melbourne, cold and uncomfortable Minterne was a readjustment for Pamela. Kenny and Pansy adored the quintessentially English country life ten miles from the nearest town—an isolation enforced by steep tree-topped slopes encircling the house. On wet days a penumbra of cloud closed in, smothering the view from the nursery windows entirely. The only way out was by winding unpaved roads that played havoc with cars' suspensions. London was a long day's journey away and the Digbys rarely went. While the twenties were roaring in town, Pansy and Kenny preferred the otherworldliness of their home—the inspiration for Great Hintock in Thomas Hardy's *The Woodlanders*—even if their elder daughter quickly resented it. Early on Pamela knew she wanted more than a closeted life revolving around horses, labradors and Kenny's beloved rhododendron collection. The family crest—an ostrich supported by two monkeys with a horseshoe in its beak—suggested the allure of faraway lands.

The house was barely twenty years old, built by the 10th Baron Digby to replace an older house plagued by dry rot, big rats and bad drains. There were fifty rooms but, eccentrically, no bathrooms, as Kenny's father had considered them "disgusting."[8] A seamstress came once a year for a whole month to redo the slipcovers for the chairs in the billiard room, dining room, study, drawing room, tapestry room and Pansy's private sitting room. She brought fabrics of every conceivable pattern and color, yet Pansy chose ones that "reflected what had been there for centuries," rejecting anything Pamela thought "fresh and exciting." Minterne life "had to be the way it had always been."[9]

Until they were fourteen, Pamela and Sheila were confined to the nursery rooms on the second floor where Kenny and Pansy rarely ventured; it was a children's world presided over by Nanny and two nursery maids. Lessons finished before lunch, leaving the afternoon free for mischief. Once, Pamela brought her black Shetland pony up in the back lift to join them. "All hell broke loose," she remembered, and "quite rightly as the pony could have panicked . . . and kicked us to pieces." Four stable boys had to carry the poor creature down three floors to the basement and Pamela was sent to bed for the rest of the day. Usually, however, misdemeanors were rarely mentioned beyond the playroom and, having been bathed and brushed, the girls would be delivered downstairs to take afternoon tea with their mother, before being packed off again for supper with Nanny. It was a regime run by women; men were unreachable figures. Kenny was not a "big thing" in her life and Pamela had to ask permission to enter his study. Most days she saw him only briefly, when she passed through her parents' room at eight to bid them good morning while they had tea and biscuits in bed. Pamela was her mother's "favourite" and Sheila her father's. "He was quite severe," she said, and so "Mummy was the big influence in our lives."[10] Pamela loved to join Pansy in her boudoir to play bezique, a card game rewarding quick wits and good memory.

The Digbys' money worries did not stop them in those early days from employing a huge retinue of staff that Pamela looked back on as "mind-boggling." "Everybody in the village worked for Daddy," including twenty retainers in the stables, gardens and dairy. In the house, the butler ruled over a valet, two footmen (in livery with gold buttons engraved with the Digby ostrich), a chauffeur, a carpenter, a hall boy and a pantry boy. It was unthinkable that Pansy would not have a lady's maid, several chambermaids and a cook assisted by two kitchen and three scullery maids, with a still-room maid just to prepare desserts.[11] "We ate a lot in those days"[12] and soon it showed: while Sheila was called "Miss Thin" by staff, to her horror Pamela became known as "Miss Fat."[13] Secure in her mother's favor, however, Pamela was a show-off, especially in the saddle in front of her parents' guests from London or, even better, abroad. Pamela set out to entrance while Sheila was "shy and couldn't be bothered."[14] Most often, though, the Digbys' entertaining was local and snobbish. Only rather dreary nobles were welcome for games of bridge—middle-class doctors and lawyers who worked for a living were below the salt.[15]

The arrival in 1924 of Edward, known as Eddie, usurped Pamela in the pecking order. From a tender age, she understood that his status as the eldest son assured him the family estate and title under the ancient system of primogeniture. Pamela could not contain the occasional flash of resentment at such injustice and was punished for it. "Jealousy was the absolutely worst sin," she remembered. "They got really angry with me then."[16] Uncomplaining stoicism was drilled into Digby women as an essential virtue.

Eddie was mesmerized by his big sister's fizzing energy, conceding that she was the natural leader despite her sex and that she kept him "well in order."[17] His presence spurred her on to ever greater competitiveness on horseback and she won her first show-jumping prize at the age of seven. Sheila outrode her with the hunt, however, and determined to prove her own fearlessness, Pamela attempted a particularly high gate and hit her head as she fell. The shock left her with a white streak in her hair for the rest of her life.

It was not just the thrill of the chase that captivated Pamela but an American neighbor who was joint master of the Cattistock Hunt, and his actress wife. It was then daring to be an actress in English society, even more so that both were divorced, and shocking that their house had so many bathrooms. Their "jazzier" clothing—especially their preference for top hats for hunting over traditional bowlers—also suggested a forbidden world outside Dorset that electrified her. "It was the first time I was aware of the difference between the English and Americans," Pamela recalled. "I had an enormous crush on her."[18]

In the spring, Pamela's parents would depart on a round of aristocratic house parties, where they refrained from the rampant games of bed-swapping. "Mummy" frequently told her eldest daughter "how lucky" she had been to marry Kenny and that they had always "adored each other." Pamela recalled that it "never occurred to one that there could be anything like a divorce."[19] If home life was reassuringly stable, what was missing were other children. Pamela was most envious of Eddie's masculine privilege when at the age of eight in 1932 he was sent to boarding school in preparation for Eton. Girls of Pamela's class were educated at home by governesses and not allowed out unchaperoned. Although about to enter her teens, she rarely saw a boy, let alone spoke to one.

Pamela made little academic progress with her Scottish governess who was barely educated herself and replaced by a brainy Swiss woman who had worked for the family of the art historian Kenneth Clark. Her attempts to introduce Pamela to an enticing world of paintings, history, music and literature did not endear her to Kenny, however. A man of decided intellectual incuriosity, he was concerned that "over-educated" girls might deter suitors. The three Digby daughters (the youngest, Jacquetta, was born in 1928) had only modest dowries but the notion of a career outside the home was unthinkable. Marriage would be their vocation; scholarly pursuits were not only unnecessary but undesirable.

Kenny took up his hereditary seat in the House of Lords as a staunch Conservative but at home discouraged all talk of politics and politicians—a diktat that made both infinitely more exciting to his eldest child. His forebear Sir Everard Digby, a convert to Catholicism, had in 1605 become embroiled in the Gunpowder Plot to blow up Parliament and restore the Catholic monarchy and was hanged, drawn and quartered for his folly. This cautionary tale, combined with the horrors of war and the flu pandemic, had reinforced Kenny's faith in the unchanging rhythms of upper-class country life. The Digby motto was *Deo non Fortuna*—not through luck but by God—and on Sundays the family attended the tiny medieval church at the gates to Minterne. Each week they walked past plaques commemorating the Churchill family—who had sold the estate to the Digbys in 1768—including the first Sir Winston, who had been born at Minterne in 1620. Eight generations back, a Digby had married a previous Churchill, so the current Winston Churchill was also descended from Digbys.[20] To Kenny, though, the Churchills were political chancers who belonged in London and nowhere near his daughters.

The walls of Minterne's wood-paneled picture gallery were hung with comforting family portraits and seascapes of Digbys under sail, including a famous admiral. Of more interest to Pamela was a painting of the admiral's daughter Jane, a blonde beauty born in 1807 whose portrait was relegated to the back staircase amid a faint aura of scandal. Questions as to why she was hidden were met with mutterings about her being "very wicked."[21] Pamela's curiosity was pricked further when she discovered that not only had Jane written an intimate personal diary, but her parents had burned all but the first and last twenty pages.

Persistent digging by Pamela revealed that Jane was a sexual adventurer who at twenty had abandoned her impotent older husband, triggering a rare aristocratic divorce. She left him with her infant son, conceived through an affair, and bolted to Paris to resume her liaison with an Austrian prince as well as with the French novelist Honoré de Balzac. The prince would not marry her, despite the pair going on to have two daughters, as he was from a Catholic dynasty and she a

Protestant. Jane moved on to the king of Bavaria, before taking up with an Albanian brigand chief bristling with pistols and unsheathed yataghan swords.

Finally, at fifty, the so-called "Scarlet Woman" fell in love with Sheikh Abdul Medjuel el Mezrab, twenty years her junior, when he protected her from marauders on a trek to the ruined Syrian city of Palmyra. After insisting he disband his harem, she married for the final time and thereafter lived a life of sexual passion in a wind-blasted Bedouin tent in the desert, humbly washing her young Arab nobleman's feet and milking his camels. Riding barefoot out to tribal skirmishes at the head of Abdul's horsemen, she dressed in traditional robes and face veil with only her Digby blue eyes visible. Jane died in Damascus in 1881 at the age of seventy-four, an absent mother to a brood of children by multiple lovers and inspiration for several breathless novels.[22]

Somehow Pamela laid her hands on one of these books and—without a word on the subject from her parents—learned about the thrilling subject of sex. When she bled for the first time, Pamela was alarmed as she had not been warned about periods and was thereafter banned from riding or swimming for five days every month. Her consolation was that she was now a real woman and, inspired by Jane, dreamed of escapades overseas. Deprived of other indications of the male form, she galloped up to the Cerne Abbas giant, an ancient fertility symbol that loomed over the village in the nearby hills. Jumping over its twelve-meter tumescent phallus carved out of the chalk she exclaimed with a giggle, "God, it's big!" Looking back down toward Minterne, Pamela vowed that, like Jane, she would live life to the full: "When I am old enough, I will leave this place and never return."

2

After a relentless campaign of begging and guile the Digbys conceded defeat and agreed to allow fifteen-year-old Pamela to attend boarding school. Pansy chose Downham School, a private establishment for girls in Hertfordshire, and decided to send Sheila too, in part to keep an eye on her willful sister. On their way the sisters spent a night in London, where Pamela saw her first play, stayed in her first hotel and in the morning traveled to Downham in her first school bus, where she mingled for the first time with girls of her own age. She quickly discovered most were more worldly and that it was easier to make friends with the teachers, who within a year made her a prefect. Pamela was accustomed to ruling over her siblings and read the riot act to less model students who were not always grateful. Even Pamela considered herself "a terrible bore."[1]

As Pansy's daughter she was hardwired to gloss over hurt or hardship, and Pamela claimed she had been "very happy" at Downham, making friends for life such as Clarissa Churchill, Winston's niece. A cool enigmatic presence even then, Clarissa's recollection varied. "She was fat and freckly with red hair and mad about horses," she said. "We used to bully her."[2] Pamela's tendency to flush bright pink egged on her taunters and she depended heavily on Sheila who was "very supportive of me when we were in school."

After eighteen months of narrow and undemanding teaching, Pamela's maths remained rudimentary and her spelling atrocious. She left in the summer of 1936 with nothing but a diploma in domestic science (otherwise known as cooking and sewing), meaning university was out of the question. Few women took degrees in any case but even if nothing much was expected of her, Pamela felt deprived of a "good education" and was determined to find other ways to take stock of the world. Her parents, though, were chiefly concerned with enhancing her worth as a potential wife. That autumn they sent her to learn French with a family in Paris, but although occasionally permitted to venture to the Sorbonne or the Louvre to attend classes on history of art, Pamela remained on a tight leash. Buying a *jus de raisin* in a café on the Champs-Élysées was a rare treat. "It's just grape juice but to me it's still more exciting than champagne."[3]

In early 1937 she moved on to Munich for further "finishing" with Countess von Harrach, whose Austro-German family had been prominent nobles in the Hapsburg empire. After leading such a cosseted life, Pamela's arrival at seventeen in the city of the headquarters of the National Socialist party dramatically exposed her to humanity's darkest side. Hitler already exerted a fevered grip over Germany and the previous year had dispatched troops to reoccupy the Rhineland in violation of the peace treaties signed at the end of the First World War. Britain and France had failed to react to the Führer's aggression—many in the English upper classes were pro-Hitler as a bulwark against Russian Bolshevism—but his appetite for conquest was clear. As was the growing persecution of Jews. And yet droves of aristocratic girls like Pamela were sent to be immersed in Bavarian culture, which was considered more polished and disciplined than that of France.

Pansy was a rarity in her class for having Jewish blood from an eighteenth-century forebear, Moses Levy. When Pansy railed against Nazi brutality while visiting Pamela, Countess von Harrach rebuked her in case someone overheard, and instructed Pamela to look away if she saw Jewish properties being smashed up or even people being attacked. Rather than the Nazi perpetrators, it was Jane Digby who attracted the countess's condemnation as "one of the most wicked Englishwomen who ever came to Germany."[4] Apparently fearing that Pamela might emulate Jane's behavior, she arranged for her to be heavily chaperoned. The countess retired for the evening at nine, however, and assumed her English charge did the same. Pamela grabbed her chance to discover what night-time Munich had to offer.

Other British aristocrats focused on the fun. Pamela was unusual in wanting to make sense of the violence she witnessed, already demonstrating a curiosity absent in most of her peers, male or female. Kenny's experiences in the Great War had made him a committed pacifist and Pamela knew that he and Pansy wanted to believe that peace would prevail. They shuddered at the rise of fascism but were horrified by fellow Conservative Winston Churchill and his bellicose pronouncements to a disbelieving Britain on the scale of the threat. The prospect of another war had become almost a taboo subject for them. Yet Pamela found it impossible to spend time in Munich that spring without a nagging sense of dread. SS troops goosestepped past her in the streets and Germans greeted each other with "Heil Hitler!" and a raised-arm salute. Millions were being recruited into a new army of the Third Reich and dissent was brutally crushed, using the swastika as a rallying symbol of national pride. Curious to know more about the figure who inspired such fanatical support, Pamela sought out Unity Mitford, whose family she knew from home. Unity was an intimate of the Führer and soon after Pamela was invited to take tea with him one Friday afternoon in the Englischer Garten.

Pamela spotted two "very good-looking" officers in Hitler's entourage as she entered the spring finery of the park, but the Führer was a disappointment and did not "make any big impression, except that I knew he was not our friend . . . He seemed made of tinfoil as later caricatures made out and he was sort of nervous."[5] In person, Hitler was only marginally taller than her five foot six and less threatening than his rabid speeches on the radio. Beyond him extending a welcome to Germany, her accounts of that day were short on detail and skeptics have surmised that the encounter sprang from her imagination. Pamela related that she had come away baffled by how a man so lacking in charisma exercised such an implacable hold.[6] However unsatisfactory, the meeting marked the start of Pamela's lifelong mission of self-education about politics and power.

In the autumn of 1937, Kenny was asked to judge a horse show at the Royal Winter Fair in Toronto and he and Pansy decided to take their eldest daughter with them to keep her in their sights. After several days at sea, the trio docked in New York and made their way to the Fifth Avenue home of their friends William and Elsie Woodward. One of the last grandes dames of New York, Elsie enraptured Pamela with her hostessing at her six-story mansion, which was staffed by the same sort of retinue of butlers, footmen and maids as at Minterne, but seemed much more fun because of the constant buzz of visitors. Even more exciting was that Elsie treated Pamela as a "grown-up," taking her to a former speakeasy and to glitzy Manhattan parties.

Pamela's joy was bridled by Pansy's caution. Decades later Pamela remained indignant about her embarrassing wardrobe. "Here we were, living in an enormous house with thirty-six servants," she would say, "and there was never any money to spend on clothes."[7] Pansy forbade her from wearing black and Pamela endured teasing from young Manhattanites about her "little girl" frocks of pale chiffon. "You were kept very young until you came out," she railed.[8] "God, it was awful!"[9]

Even so, New York offered Pamela tantalizing glimpses of different lives. Particularly thrilling was a radical docu-musical produced by the International Ladies' Garments Workers' Union called *Pins & Needles*, her first exposure to a non-Tory worldview. And on her first visit to a nightclub, she threw herself into the African American-inspired new dance craze called the Big Apple. City life was eye-opening but Pansy and Kenny were standing by her side like sentries. Even more than their clothes, Pamela envied her American contemporaries their freedom from parental control. The merest prospect of adventure, though, always made Pamela look radiant.

After a week, the Digbys traveled up to Toronto and took a suite at the Ritz Hotel before accepting an invitation to go hunting with local notables. One of them was handsome George McCullagh, a self-made newspaper baron also of little formal schooling but with an obsessive drive to win life's trophies. At thirty-two, he had risen from delivery boy to owner of Canada's prestigious *Globe and Mail*. McCullagh was married with two children but Pamela knew that Canada's "wonder boy" was hooked when he ran a photograph of her in his paper over the caption "Graceful English rider thrills Toronto Hunt." "He flirted with me which obviously flattered me at seventeen," Pamela recalled, especially as he also appeared to be interested in what she said. To a newspaper man with political ambitions, her tales of Munich life surrounded by Nazis added to her allure. For Pamela, it was ecstasy for her observations to be taken seriously by such a prominent man, especially when she hardly dared broach them at home.

McCullagh made his next move, inviting her to ride out at his farm, but a Canadian friend warned Kenny of McCullagh's reputation with women and so Pamela was forbidden from going. This merely spurred her on and she sneaked out of the Ritz to meet up with her admirer but was found out by her parents, who were understandably angry.[10] Pamela denied anything untoward happened but thereafter she was never again the ingénue. McCullagh continued his pursuit by filling her hotel room with bowers of orchids and tulips but even Pamela later agreed it had been "lucky" that the Digbys were about to leave for New York and thence for home. Her "flirtation came to an end," but the jaunt to North America had been "quite a revelation."[11]

3

The campaign to get Pamela safely married off started in earnest on the Digbys' return to Britain, helped by a spread about their American trip in *Tatler*.[1] It was useful projection for a country girl about to enter the upper-class marriage market known as the Season. Pamela was allowed to practice in the Little Season, a round of hunt balls leading up to Christmas 1937. Pansy also took her up to Scotland to see her sister Eva for further instruction. Lady Rosebery had not only landed an earl (descended from the Rothschilds) for herself but her eldest daughter (Pamela's cousin Lavinia) had married a duke. That said, Lavinia's choice—the Duke of Norfolk—had got her staunchly Protestant family "riled up" as he was England's most senior lay Catholic.[2]

On one visit to her aunt, Pamela befriended Popsy Winn, the daughter of Lady Baillie, the Anglo-American owner of Leeds Castle in Kent. Both were about to "come out" and were rehearsing their curtseys for when they would be presented at court. Popsy was so enamored of Pamela that she brought her to meet her mother, an introduction that was to change Pamela's life. Lady Baillie—Pamela was soon addressing her as Olive—presided over a weekend salon at the castle combining high politics with Hollywood, and a weekday one at her London townhouse on Grosvenor Square, a few steps from the new American Embassy. Olive took a shine to the Digby girl who, since her flirtation with George McCullagh, shared her fascination with power (and how it could be used for good as well as evil) and powerful men. The daughter of a wealthy American mother (a Whitney) and an English lord, Olive took up what her fellow American Elsie Woodward had started in opening Pamela's eyes to the world. Brutally, Pamela dropped Popsy in favor of Olive.

Pamela enjoyed another lucky break when Kenny's outside bet on a horse came spectacularly good at the Grand National. With some of his £6,025 in winnings,[3] he bought his daughter her first car, a much-loved little Jaguar, and rented a house in London for her Season, on Carlos Place, close to Lady Baillie's. Also nearby was the London home of Sarah Norton, another debutante and the goddaughter of Lord Mountbatten (who asked Sarah to find a nice girl for his nephew Prince Philip of Greece).

Not even Hitler subjugating Austria into an *Anschluss* with Germany in March 1938 was sufficient to halt the preparations for Pamela's coming out. Neville Chamberlain's government remained wedded to appeasement and life in London carried on much as normal. A few weeks later queues of limousines containing mamas, their daughters and a mass of white feathers and diamonds were inching up the Mall to Buckingham Palace. The ceremonial route was lined with waving onlookers eager for a glimpse of the next generation of ladies, countesses and duchesses. On arrival, Pamela and Pansy stepped out onto a red carpet to be ushered by liveried footmen to the ballroom, where stately women in tiaras were seated next to daughters dressed in virginal white evening dress.

At the end of the room, the king and queen sat enthroned on a crimson dais under huge crystal chandeliers, the lights reflecting off the mirrored doors all around. After what seemed an interminable wait, it was Pamela's turn to be presented. She curtseyed low and the king kissed her hand before she executed the difficult backward walk without looking around or falling over her train. The moment marked the beginning of her Season. At last she would be permitted to converse with men—if they were from the right families, of course.

To that end there would be an exhausting round of balls every night from Monday to Thursday, starting at 10 p.m. and finishing at 4 a.m., with the occasional dinner in the country on Fridays. Fears of war might be mounting but the principal concern at these events was filling a dance card with the names of eligible young bachelors. Competition to bag the most favored in wealth or rank was cutthroat, with the mamas constantly raising the pressure.

Pamela had twelve weeks to hook a husband, knowing that if she failed a new cohort (including Sheila) would come out the following year and she would be "old stock." "It's bad enough to be put up for auction," one debutante of that era conceded, "but to be put up for auction and find no takers . . ."[4] Neither shy nor silent like many of her fellow debutantes, Pamela did not conform to the required "balance of coquetry and innocence,"[5] nor to the fashion for tiny waists—some of the most fashionable dresses measured just seventeen inches around the middle. Pamela's Canadian triumph was not to be repeated and she became one of those girls absconding to the powder room, or reduced to filling her dance card with fake names. Deborah Mitford, who came out the same year, described her as "rather fat, fast and the butt of many teases."[6] Some men seem to have taken pleasure in her humiliation. At one particularly dog-eat-dog evening, the future Earl of Derby jibed at her rounded physique with "I see the chestnut mare is in foal again" loud enough to ensure she heard as she walked by.[7] She cared deeply about the put-downs; her only defense was pretending that she did not.

Pamela again felt like an outsider because of her wardrobe. Contemporaries who lived a cosmopolitan life in London had closets stuffed with sequinned ballgowns (sequins were her impossible dream) costing £20 each. "When you lack confidence, clothes make a great difference," she recalled.⁸ "I felt a country bumpkin. It scared me because I could not compete." Pamela's budget was £8, which bought her an unflattering frock unlikely to bag a duke. She claimed to have "suffered terribly" but would brook no pity.⁹ "Pamela Digby smiling as happily as ever," wrote a society diarist, unaware of her private tears.¹⁰ "She was a red-headed bouncing little thing," Nancy Mitford observed acidly, "regarded as a joke."¹¹

Part of the problem was that Pamela could not feign interest in men her own age, who seemed childlike in comparison to McCullagh. Their crass attempts at conversation revolved around how foreigners and foreign lands were "bloody." Seemingly oblivious to the growing menace from Germany, they ridiculed the idea that any woman might be interested in—let alone know about—serious matters. They neither worked nor expected to, relying on (in some cases fast-dwindling) family fortunes. Pansy was unmoved by Pamela's craving for something more sophisticated. Her generation believed it important for young women to "retain the dowdiness of the countryside" lest they be viewed as "unpresentably fast."¹² Pamela was banned from wearing lipstick, especially in fashionable shades of plum, and eyeliner was also taboo (although she discovered the trick of running her finger along the grates of fireplaces to smudge the soot around her eyes). It did not help that her tormentor Clarissa Churchill—described by Deborah Mitford as "more than a whiff of Garbo in a dress by Maggy Rouff of Paris"¹³—was vogueishly svelte. Pamela took to slipping away to the dimly lit Four Hundred Club on Leicester Square, the night-spot favored by less judgmental members of London's upper classes. As long as she returned before the national anthem was played at the end of the ball, her absence might not be noticed.

Even Clarissa was eclipsed by an American newcomer—Kathleen Kennedy, whose father, Joseph, the new ambassador, had shipped his large family over from Boston. She too had a dazzling wardrobe of outfits and combined this with a friendly demeanor. "Not strictly a beauty," was Deborah's view, but Kathleen's fresh-faced effervescence had made her "by far the most popular of all."[14] She made the English girls look muted; her relaxed sense of fun—kicking off her shoes even in polite society—shocked some but greatly endeared her to others. She teased but avoided the abrasiveness of her brothers and persuaded the reserved English to come out of their shells. The Kennedys' great wealth (even if made rather than inherited) freed her of the obligation to land a rich husband; her insouciance ensured she was pursued by some of the most eligible of all. "The British upper classes loved the way she played up to her Americanness," one biographer has explained.[15] As the weeks passed without a single decent proposal Pamela struggled to contain feelings of envy, confessing later to having acted like "a snob."[16] Kathleen—widely known as Kick—also looked down on her, once telling her brother Jack that Pamela was a "fat, stupid little butter ball."[17]

The Season's swankiest party was held in Kick's honor at Prince's Gate, her father's fifty-two room official residence in South Kensington. Three hundred guests entered the white stucco mansion opposite Hyde Park via a walkway bordered by lupines. The ambassador understood the power of theatrics and abundance. He had stocked his cellars with two thousand bottles of champagne and spent hundreds on clothing his family in couture. Kick and her mother, Rose, greeted everyone in the ballroom before the dancing began to the songs of Cole Porter and Noël Coward, finishing with a rousing rendition of Bob Hope's hit "Thanks for the Memory."[18] By contrast, Pamela was reduced to trying to enliven the small and staid dinner parties her parents held for her at Carlos Place with games of sardines, a form of hide and seek involving squeezing into tiny spaces with other players. "There was quite a lot of ooh-la-la behind the curtains," Sarah Norton recalled.[19] Some of the less confident young men found it all a little overpowering.

It was only at the end of the Season that Pamela enjoyed any real success. Hugh Fraser, a dashing young man, fell for her so deeply that he started to make plans for them to elope, but at the last moment she had second thoughts about his committed Catholicism and painfully called it off. Having seen the reaction to her cousin Lavinia's marriage, she feared making both families (who were probably unaware of their relationship) deeply unhappy. Clarissa Churchill, a fellow Catholic in whom Hugh had confided, thought "that was the moment the real and future Pamela showed herself. She combined a canny eye for chances with a genuinely warm heart." Clarissa noted with remorse that despite her cruelty at Downham, Pamela had never borne a grudge and had been "consistently kind and thoughtful."[20] The Season ended. Carlos Place was closed up. The Digbys returned to Minterne. Pamela had failed her first great test.

4

Although rare for a woman to take the wheel, Pamela was frequently seen beetling along the Dorset lanes trailed by clouds of white dust. Her Jaguar was her independence and she used it to escape, even if Pansy insisted she take a maid as chaperone. Pamela headed for Sarah Norton's or Olive Baillie's Mayfair residences—both establishments bustling with the sort of urbane people she craved. Weekends in London, inhaling conversation about politics and the arts, were so much more exciting than the hunting and shooting chatter at home.

In late August, she ventured north for a race meeting at York, where an older, richer crowd were gambling with high stakes. Eager to share the thrill, Pamela placed £50 (when her monthly allowance was £10) on a horse "they all said was going to win."[1] It was agony when she found herself having to visit an unimpressed Kenny in his study to ask him to cover her losses. Her folly left her no funds to run her car so she "decided to go abroad, to get the hell out"[2] but it seems baffling that her parents were willing to let their eighteen-year-old daughter go, as if in denial of the dangers. An increasingly rabid Hitler was threatening all-out war unless Czechoslovakia surrendered the Sudetenland region to his control. After whipping up a patriotic fervor by falsely accusing Prague of atrocities against the Sudeten population of ethnic Germans, the Führer was massing his troops along the border. France, Britain and the Soviet Union had all signed obligations to protect Czechoslovakia against aggression, and with

Hitler poised to invade, war seemed imminent. Civilians were digging trenches in Hyde Park. Millions of gas masks were being distributed. Bomb shelters were being built and hundreds of thousands were volunteering for the armed forces.

Then, on September 15, 1938, prime minister Neville Chamberlain boarded a plane for the first time in his life to meet Hitler at Berchtesgaden. Over the next couple of weeks, negotiations continued and in a meeting at Munich at the end of the month, the Sudetenland was handed to Hitler against the wishes of the powerless Czechs and without a shot being fired. Chamberlain believed the sacrifice of what he dismissed as a "faraway land" would satisfy the Führer's lust for an even greater German fatherland and he returned to a hero's welcome in Britain, promising he had secured "peace for our time." His greatest critic, Winston Churchill, was widely ridiculed when he declared, "You were given the choice between war and dishonour. You chose dishonour and you will have war." Churchill's views on Hitler polarized the country but the Digbys were united in wanting to believe that Chamberlain was right and that peace was now assured.

Pamela arrived in Paris some time afterward where she found the discomfort of her run-down accommodation a small price for her freedom. Pamela could at last socialize as she wished and in the nightclubs of Montmartre entered a world of dazzling continental hedonism. One new friend was Rosamond, daughter of Daisy Fellowes, the heiress to the Singer sewing machine fortune who had once stripped naked on a chaise longue in a failed effort to seduce Winston Churchill. Around Pamela's nineteenth birthday in March 1939, Rosamond—whom she considered "very chic and marvellously rich"[3]—invited her to the family villa at Cap Martin in the South of France. They were joined by Gogo, daughter of the celebrated fashion designer Elsa Schiaparelli, who gave all three girls shocking pink evening stoles.

Pamela's red hair and milky skin—unusual sights on the Riviera—were admired and she was finally spoiled for male attention. "I flirted like crazy but I didn't know how," she recalled, claiming it was all very innocent. Her friends judged her a little obvious, even writing a ditty that began: "There was a young lady called Pam; who was continuously being the ham."[4] Not that Pamela cared what they thought, simply exulting in the fact that she was considered attractive. This was "really living" at last.[5] She found the men equally intoxicating, especially Grand Duke Dimitri Pavlovich of Russia, a forty-seven-year-old cousin of Tsar Nicholas II and Prince Philip of Greece, whom she thought "the most beautiful man . . . all the girls were mad about him." It was a triumph that it was Pamela out of the friends whom he invited to lunch—the first time she had a meal alone with a man. The fact that he had had an affair with Coco Chanel and been involved in the plot to murder Rasputin added to the thrill.

The bliss came to an abrupt halt after only a few days. Far from pacifying Hitler, the Munich Agreement had fed the beast. German troops were marching on from the Sudetenland into the heart of Czechoslovakia and it was clear that Poland was next in Hitler's sights. A humiliated Chamberlain warned that if Germany attacked Poland, Britain and France must come to her aid. Pamela was hastily "shoved" onto a packed overnight train back to Paris, having to stand all the way, her privilege suddenly counting for nothing.

Back in Britain, Pamela's romantic life once again hit the buffers. Kenny had high hopes of an engagement to Rowley Baring, the future Earl of Cromer, but not even the prospect of becoming a countess made him marriage material in Pamela's mind: parental keenness on such a dependable fellow was the kiss of death. Several other men showed interest—she had lost weight and gained confidence since her adventures in France—but they all seemed to be tame re-creations of her father. Kenny and Pansy tolerated ever more young people descending on Minterne to assist in Pamela's search. Even Kick Kennedy made the trek down to Dorset. The two women had started to become close. This more assured Pamela knew from her childhood that jealousy was a sin and appreciated Kick's insight into world events as, like her brothers, she had been expected to be able to discuss politics from an early age. In return, Pamela was supportive to her American friend who was, behind the sparkling smile, not quite the untroubled woman she had once been. Her great love, Billy, the Marquess of Hartington, who was in line to become the next Duke of Devonshire and take over the magnificent stately home of Chatsworth, hailed from a notably anti-Catholic family while the Kennedys (especially Kick's mother, Rose) were unbending followers of the Roman faith. Both knew there was trouble in store.

The sheen had also worn off her father, Joe, now at the center of a swirl of allegations about his sexual conduct. The way he "ducked into his private office in the embassy" with some unsuspecting young woman and "then reappeared shortly afterward with a smile on his face" was deemed reprehensible.[6] Kick never mentioned it, but her friends back home had for years viewed Joe Kennedy as a predator. As they had matured into young women, he had become insistent on kissing them goodnight on the lips, touching them gratuitously or parading in front of them in just a towel.[7] Some suggested he had tried to go further. Fewer and fewer took up Kick's invitations to come to stay. They feared that if they complained, they would be ignored, or never believed. Or worse still, blamed.

As Kick's occasional guest in London, Pamela found her own name linked to the ambassador. Although on good terms with the rest of the family, especially twenty-one-year-old Jack, she became reticent about Kick's father, later remarking to a friend that Joe Kennedy's eyes had an icy look when he had done "something truly unconscionable."[8] The friend, British diplomat Sir John Russell, had reason to believe that Pamela would know, as did others of that prewar London milieu. There were reports that Kennedy had sneaked into her bed one night and tried to force himself on her. The rumors went on for years and eventually, to Pamela's horror, would spectacularly surface in print.

Many believed that Kennedy had, at the very least, overstepped the mark. And Jack enjoyed telling stories of how his father had once tried to get into bed with one of his sister's friends, whispering as he began removing his robe, "This is something you'll always remember." Jack thereafter told female visitors, "Be sure to lock the bedroom door. The ambassador has a tendency to prowl late at night."[9] Kennedy men treated it as a joke.

Joe Kennedy's misconduct would probably have been overlooked had his willful blindness to Hitler's brutality not become intolerable. He had been secretly meeting German officials, including the Führer's minister of economics, to President Roosevelt's fury. Now that Hitler had made a mockery of appeasement, opinion was shifting on both sides of the Atlantic. Kennedy was increasingly isolated and there were calls in Congress for his resignation. For now at least, he remained in post, but his family were beginning to pay the social cost.

Pressure was mounting for Pamela to find a husband before it was too late, and the eligible young men went to war. The new Season had begun and it was Sheila's turn to be presented at court but Pamela was determined to bypass another mortifying round of debutante balls. Happily, Lady Baillie had spotted how the nineteen-year-old Pamela was becoming remarkably politically engaged and that older men found her exciting company. She flattered them (and indeed Olive herself) and was eager to learn the arts of the political hostess. Week by week at Lady Baillie's salon, Pamela received an education that would shape the rest of her life: how to make useful connections, gather interesting groups and revive flagging conversations; how to pay attention to the tiniest details of menus, seating plans and accommodation, and bring in expert help such as the Parisian interior designer Stéphane Boudin. Pamela was usually the youngest present as she was favored over Olive's own daughters, a privilege that did not endear her to them.

It was not just Lady Baillie's opulent entertaining that drew guests, but its setting. Rising as if by magic above a stillwater lake, Leeds Castle is one of the most romantic in the world. Visitors crossed a stone bridge from one island to another to enter a kingly medieval building known as the Gloriette. Here, Pamela befriended Hollywood legends such as Jimmy Stewart, Clark Gable and Douglas Fairbanks Jr. (who found her "engaging, intelligent, charming and nice"[10]), who had been invited to lure in big political names with their silver screen glamour.

There was, however, one prominent figure who was not permitted to cross the threshold: Winston Churchill's son Randolph. Olive's was one of many fashionable households who considered him intolerable. His unsubtle pursuit of sex angered her, especially his own habit of slipping into the bedrooms of unaccompanied strangers at weekend house parties to try his luck. When his friend Lady Mary Dunn suggested, "You must get a lot of rebuffs," Randolph had replied with a guffaw: "I do . . . but I get a lot of fucking too."[11] Endowed with good looks and entitlement, he managed to seduce a string of older women, until they tired of his drunken brawls. Everyone still remembered the fortieth birthday party for the society beauty Lady Diana Cooper in Venice back in the sultry summer of 1932. The most glamorous gathering for years had been ruined when one of Randolph's infamous volleys of insults sparked a melee of fists and broken bottles. Wherever Randolph went, scandal ensued. Churchill senior, through most of the 1930s out of government and out of favor, had become only too aware of his son's failings, writing him a series of furious letters including one protesting that "Your idle & lazy life is very offensive to me. You appear to be leading a perfectly useless existence."[12] Yet he had been an overindulgent father, pouring out double brandies for the adolescent Randolph and encouraging him in the absurd notion that as he shared a birthday with Pitt the Younger he too was destined to become prime minister by the age of twenty-five.

Growing up, Randolph had met virtually everyone of any importance at his father's men-only dinners and had been allowed to expound his own half-baked views—at length—in their company. Given every advantage of education and connections, he gambled money he didn't have (requiring constant bailing out by his cash-strapped parents) and was obnoxious to waiters. Winston deplored the way his son gave "nothing in return"[13] for his privilege but ostentatiously favored him over his three sisters as his male heir. Randolph was widely and viscerally disliked save by a few souls who succumbed to a charm that was elusive but on occasion powerful.

Lacking his father's warmth and his mother Clementine's judgment, the bumptious Randolph continued to act as if a parliamentary career was his birthright. When the Conservatives refused to adopt him as a candidate, he stood as an independent on two occasions, splitting the Tory vote and handing the seats to Labour. The uproar hurt his parents deeply. Raised voices and slammed doors were all too frequent at Chartwell, the Churchills' country house, and Clementine had begun to dislike her son. In return, Randolph held women, including his mother, in low esteem.

Lady Baillie was not willing to tolerate the way he sought to exclude women from taking part in public life. His thinking had barely changed since Eton, when he wrote an essay entitled "Women and Their Place in the World," a work he had considered worthy of a leather binding. The "better a woman speaks," it declared, "the more embarrassing I find it."[14]

Pamela was entranced by the way Lady Baillie's great wealth insulated her from such prejudice and allowed her to speak and live as she pleased. She kept an entourage of male admirers that included David

Margesson, the Conservative chief whip, and thirty-seven-year-old MP Geoffrey Lloyd, in full view of her surprisingly compliant husband, Sir Adrian Baillie, another member of Parliament. Pamela was unsure "whether she slept with one of them or all of them."[15] Not the sort to be invited to Leeds Castle weekends, the Digbys were nervous about their daughter's exposure to such louche-living politicians but were preoccupied with Sheila's debut, which was also not a success. "My parents were absolutely right" to have reservations, Pamela reflected. The Leeds Castle set were not perhaps the "most desirable" company for a young woman but they made her feel thrillingly alive.[16]

She relished the intellectual cut-and-thrust, the drama and the very high stakes of the men's discussions of the crisis in Europe and events in the House of Commons—and, to her delight, was encouraged to sit in. Flattered by Pamela's starry-eyed interest, Margesson was one of several senior politicians to take the trouble to induct her in the low cunning of high politics. He fascinated her with "black book" gossip about MPs: who was gay (then illegal), who had a mistress, who was drowning in drink and who was misguided or past it. Pansy fretted that her daughter was leading a frivolous life, but the truth was she was taking a master class in the exercise of power in a democracy, in an environment where news was phoned in by the hour. Describing Margesson and other Leeds Castle politicians such as Anthony Eden as her new "guardians," Pamela began to trade the occasional snippet of information of her own. Perhaps she even mentioned her meeting with Hitler, which would certainly have commanded attention. Despite the seriousness of the times, however, she never forgot to be fun. After dinner, a performance by Lady Baillie's favorite tenor Richard Tauber or dancing on the gleaming ebony floor also helped to lift the mood.

When not at Leeds Castle, Pamela stayed with Sarah Norton. "We thought she was frightfully sophisticated," related Sarah, although "she didn't have money."[17] Pamela was getting herself into deep water with gambling debts—apparently having forgotten the lesson she had learned at York racecourse the previous year. One night she lost so heavily at poker she experienced that sickening feeling of overreach all over again. Having exhausted her father's patience, she resorted to crying "all night until the debt was forgiven."[18] Her skill at cards rapidly improved but it was clear she needed a supplementary source of income.

In the Gloriette one weekend, she discovered one of England's richest men. Known as Fulkie, the darkly handsome 7th Earl of Warwick had been the first British aristocrat to star in a Hollywood movie and was rumored to have had affairs with Marlene Dietrich and Greta Garbo. Sparks flew between them, and Pamela sent him her bills to pay. When Fulkie ignored war's long shadow to make his annual jaunt to watch the horse racing near Paris that July, Pamela secretly went with him. For the sake of appearances Fulkie put her up at the Plaza Athénée while he booked into the Ritz but they were spotted canoodling at a nightclub. After Fulkie boasted in ungentlemanly fashion that he had bedded Pamela the first night and kicked her out on the second,[19] word got back to Lady Baillie, who was furious that a nineteen-year-old risked harming her reputation in such a way. "Use your head!" Olive roared. Yet Pamela found it all "terribly exciting" and in a flourish worthy of Jane Digby told friends that she "never minded people getting upset" at what she was doing. "If I really wanted to do it, it seemed alright to me."[20] In any case, she insisted, "nothing much happened."

Fair or not, Pamela's status was set: if not wild, she was certainly considered fast. There were now half a dozen men circling. She registered the power of the female form and flexed it with tight skirts and the seductive way she walked in high heels. Yet she also fervently wanted to be taken seriously, to be involved in important matters, to be intellectually stimulated. Men had the money and opportunities but ultimately, for her, "there was no alternative" to marriage.[21] She was not a fool. She would go further than most of her female contemporaries but not "cross the Rubicon" in the debs' language of the day. In any case, there were no reliable contraceptives and pregnancy out of wedlock would be disastrous. Not for the last time, Pamela's reputation was not quite the reality. But if the rumors were not to impact on her future as a wife she had to make her move.

As the evenings began to cool at the end of August, war loomed and she thought she would have to marry one of those callow English lords after all. On September 1, when Germany invaded Poland, Ambassador Kennedy rang up President Roosevelt and told him "it was the end of the world, the end of everything."[22] Two days later, Pamela was staying with Lady Baillie in Grosvenor Square when at 11:15 a.m., in his "pewter-grey" voice, Chamberlain declared war on Germany.[23]

5

At teatime a few days later, Pamela was looking around an apartment in Victoria belonging to Lady Mary Dunn when the telephone rang. David Margesson had obligingly pulled strings to land Pamela a job as a junior French translator at the Foreign Office on £6 a week, saving her from the summons back to Dorset to serve as a private under her mother's command in the women's auxiliary branch of the army. And now Pamela was taking over the flat for £2 10s a week as Mary was moving to the safety of the country. Mary gestured to Pamela to pick up the receiver. She knew exactly who would be on the line.[1]

Mary was fond of Pamela but she was of a jealous disposition even if she was herself serially unfaithful. Pamela had recently informed her that she had dined with her husband, Sir Philip Dunn, twice while she had been away on a trip to America. It is likely that it was no more than that—Pamela volunteered the information and was close to Philip's sister Sheila. Maybe it was down to his sardonic wit that Philip told Mary that he had slept with Pamela as a sort of provocative joke.[2] Or perhaps he was simply lashing out at his philandering wife. Pamela insisted that attractive men like Philip "did not make passes" at unmarried nineteen-year-olds.[3] Either way, Mary had decided to wreak her revenge. Now she had worked out how.

That morning, Mary had been leaving the Ritz through the revolving doors just as Randolph was arriving. He barged the doors around again to join her on the pavement outside, wanting to invite her to dinner as he was determined not to be on his own when his regiment, the 4th Queen's Own Hussars, might be sent to war at any moment. So far he had had no takers and Mary also fobbed him off, having instantly alighted on a better idea. "I've got a red-headed tart up my sleeve," she explained to a chum. "She will do for Randolph."

When Pamela picked up the phone, a male voice declared "This is Randolph Churchill." "Do you want to speak to Mary?" she replied. "No. I want to speak to you." "But you don't know me." "Mary Dunn said I could invite you out to dinner," he announced, adding as an afterthought, "What do you look like?" Pamela replied, "Red-headed and rather fat, but Mummy says puppy fat disappears." After furious nodding from Mary, Pamela agreed that Randolph could pick her up at seven but afterward she quizzed her friend as to why she had set her up with this strange man. "He's a bit too fat, but very amusing," Mary replied with a smile. "You'll have a very good time!"[4] Randolph first took her for drinks with Lady Diana Cooper and his cousin Edward Stanley, who considered Pamela a "luscious little piece" and tried to entice her to dine with him instead.[5] Pamela stuck with Randolph, excited to be going out with someone whose famous father was now back in government as First Lord of the Admiralty (not one of the great offices of state but in charge of the Royal Navy so significant nonetheless).

Pamela had spent recent evenings in the Four Hundred Club full of foreboding. Hardly a shot had been fired but dwelling on the carnage of the First World War made her male friends talk gloomily about what was to come. Some were asking the head waiter to discard their half-drunk bottle of whisky, saying, "Take this, I won't be coming again—I'm going out to get killed." It was a relief that Randolph had said they were to dine at Quaglino's, a bright and buzzy restaurant in St. James's.

Randolph's voice boomed across the tables to people he knew, only occasionally turning to Pamela to declare her "divine." Having plenty of opportunity to observe her twenty-eight-year-old date, Pamela took in his fleshy good looks. His gray eyes were busy, his blond hair brushed back from a high forehead, his speech witty and informed. Most attractive was his "absolute certitude" in himself and the future. The war would be bloody, he explained to a captive audience, but he was certain of victory in the end. It was marvelous to be out with somebody Pamela admitted she "didn't give a damn about," and especially one irrepressibly optimistic.[6] Over coffee, Randolph finally looked at her intently and came to the point. He did not love her, of course, but she looked healthy enough to bear his child. His father, who had a zealous belief in the Churchill male line, expected him to sire a son before he left for war. So, in haste, would she become his wife? His proposal had all the romance of a business transaction. In a sense, that was what it was. Caught by surprise and beguiled by the chance to marry into a political family, Pamela agreed.

The next morning, Ed Stanley called her up to warn, "He's a very, very bad man and you shouldn't go out with people like that." "But he's one of your best friends," she protested. "Yes, he is one of *my* best friends—but he shouldn't be one of *yours*." More determined than ever, she saw Randolph again the following evening. This time he deserted her to talk to the editor of *The Times* at a neighboring table. "He took absolutely no notice of me," she complained. "I was really rather annoyed."[7]

Then Randolph just disappeared and Pamela began to think the idea might be "idiotic" after all. Rather than going to Pansy for advice, that weekend she consulted Lady Baillie and David Margesson, who chorused their opposition to the notorious drunk and troublemaker. Word was that that week alone Randolph had asked nine women to marry him—including three on a single night—but Pamela was the only one to say yes. Desperate not to lose face, she argued that if Randolph proved as bad as all that she would simply "get rid" of him.[8] She dreaded telling her parents, however, not least as their views of Winston had hardly changed for all that his warnings about Hitler had come true. By Monday, Pamela was wobbling and Margesson reminded her that it was not too late to back out. Finally, to her friends' great relief, she did.

Within minutes Randolph swung into action. On the rare occasions he chose to be, there were few people more magnetic—he was knowledgeable, eloquent and could be surprisingly thoughtful. After five days of being wooed with gifts and attention, Pamela rejected the gloom-mongers and decided that they were "back on track" and officially engaged.[9] The couple drove down to Kent to meet Randolph's parents but Chartwell was not the grand country seat Pamela was expecting. The house was dark and its many levels and awkward spaces only slightly improved by expensive alterations. There were five reception rooms and nineteen bedrooms (including the servants' quarters) but no grand baronial hall or ancestral picture gallery as at Minterne. Rather snobbishly, Pamela considered it "tiny" and "suburban."[10]

More to her liking was Winston, who hurried from his painting studio to greet his son's new fiancée. She found this rotund man with pink face, sloping shoulders and pronounced lisp "adorable" and not the warmonger she had imagined from her parents' disapproval. Pamela discovered that "he knew more about my family than I did" and one of his first questions was startling: "Are you Catholic?" Randolph reassured his father she was nothing of the sort and that her wayward Gunpowder Plot ancestor had met his comeuppance. Winston was evidently thrilled about the wedding, welcoming the "reconnecting link" between the Churchills and the Digbys.[11] His own first love, he told them, had also been a Pamela (Pamela Plowden, later Countess of Lytton) and he had a thing for redheads. When Clementine joined them, Pamela noticed how Randolph had inherited his mother's large, intelligent eyes and fine bone structure, if not her cool nature. Clementine made sure Pamela wanted for nothing and yet kept any enthusiasm for the forthcoming nuptials extremely well hidden.

The next day the betrothed couple motored down eerily quiet roads to Minterne, where the Digbys took Pamela aside to inform her she was "impossible" for rushing ahead with such an unsuitable match.[12] Randolph had neither title nor financial means, and then there was his drinking. Kenny was teetotal—his vice was a box of chocolates delivered weekly from Fortnum & Mason—and Pansy indulged only in an occasional sherry. No doubt they counted the number of times Randolph's glass had been refilled that evening with mounting horror. "Everybody," Pamela discovered, was "against us getting married except Winston," who declared that all you needed for matrimonial success was "champagne, cigars and a double bed!"[13]

Kenny dealt with the sorry turn of events by escaping to Scotland on a shooting trip, leaving Pansy to try to talk Pamela into delaying the wedding to give her time to come to her senses. Clementine harbored her own doubts about such a "rash and unconsidered" marriage but felt it would be pointless to intervene as headstrong young people would simply elope.[14] In truth, she was astonished that Pamela, who she thought "a real honey pot," had accepted Randolph.[15] A clearly tenacious character, at least she had a chance of bearing what Clementine knew was to come. The engagement was announced two weeks after they had first met, with the wedding to take place ten days later. Nancy Mitford supposed it was Pamela's failure to attract other offers that had obliged her to "fly to the altar" in such haste.[16]

Despite bowing to the inevitable, Pansy excused herself from taking care of the wedding arrangements on the grounds that she had an "Important War job."[17] This left an overburdened Clementine to cope while also supporting Winston in dealing with the first mass casualties of the war, including the sinking of a passenger liner by a U-boat. No one seemed happy—least of all the betrothed. Ed Stanley was horrified by the palpable tension when they spent the Saturday before the wedding with him at his friend Maud Russell's home in Hampshire. Randolph did not even pretend that he was in love, loudly proclaiming the marriage to be Hitler's "fault." He was, he said in front of a frowning Pamela, marrying simply to ensure the chain of Churchill men. Puzzled by the whole tawdry business, Maud Russell, a distinguished patron of the arts, found Pamela "pretty in a common way," with a "silly manner" that was probably down to nerves. Only when she took the trouble to talk to her did Russell realize she was "not silly at all."[18] Another guest, the painter Rex Whistler, also took to Pamela and gave a sketch of her to Randolph as a wedding present.

Randolph preferred the striking Cecil Beaton portrait over the mantelpiece of his flat at Westminster Gardens, a few minutes' walk from the Houses of Parliament. A huge watercolor of a serene beauty with white hair and wide blue eyes, it dominated the room. On her first visit, Pamela exclaimed: "Ah, that is your mother!" The likeness was uncanny but she was soon put right. The woman was Mona Harrison Williams, his much-married older lover in Venice that notorious summer of 1932, who had long since moved out of his reach. Randolph's cousin Clementine Mitford attributed his continued infatuation with her to his "hankering for the unobtainable" as well as an Oedipus complex betrayed by the fact every woman he fell for looked like his mother.[19]

As if another woman's face in her fiancé's home was not sufficiently uncomfortable for Pamela, what Randolph told her about his relationship with his mother was deeply troubling. He constantly vied with Clementine for Winston's love and believed that her jealousy had made her hate him. Having come from what Pamela considered a normal family, she thought Randolph's account "exaggerated and ridiculous" but he claimed that "the first time she came down to take me out at prep school she slapped me on the face in front of all the other boys."[20] Some who had known him all his life believed that Randolph had indeed been deprived of maternal love, as Clementine had tried to discipline her insolent child in the absence of sustained effort by Winston. When Clementine once reprimanded her son for his pursuit of another older woman he had shot back: "I need her. She's maternal and you're not."[21] Randolph was in search of unconditional love—the sort he assumed a mother would normally give—but from a woman who would ask for virtually nothing in return. The result was an inferno of arrogance and crushing insecurity, charm and insufferable rudeness. No wonder he had been turned down so often, yet Pamela saw a clever and well-connected future husband whose worlds of politics and London society would be opened to her. A career of her own was out of reach but here was a man she could counsel on his. In her eyes, for all his boorishness, Randolph represented a permanent escape from Dorset life to the national stage and that was a prize she was prepared to pay for. She also could not conceive of how to pull out now without losing face.

6

Pamela eschewed a traditional white dress and veil in favor of a wedding outfit she thought denoted her independence. Laid out on the bed at Mary Dunn's apartment on the morning of Wednesday, October 4, 1939, was a petrol-blue knee-length dress with a fox fur jacket, and a beret with a jaunty feather. Her auburn locks neatly curled, Pamela made up her face in vivid colors she knew would displease her mother. Finally, she picked up a bouquet of pink and white lilies and climbed into the waiting car. The drive to St. John's Church in Westminster took her past pillar boxes dressed in yellow bands designed to turn red in the event of chemical attack. Sandbags were piled up outside office buildings and barrage balloons loomed in the cloudy skies above. There was no mistaking this was a war wedding, down to the gas mask she was obliged to bring with her. Randolph, his best man and her father were in uniform, as were several other guests.

Despite Clementine's attempts to keep the ceremony private, crowds pushed forward with excitement as Pamela climbed the steps under the white pediment of the church. The vicar, who kept his gas mask in a crimson clerical satchel, began the service and shortly Winston, always given to tears, started to cry. His youngest daughter, seventeen-year-old Mary, fuming about wearing a cast-off fur coat of her mother's for the "chief family excitement of the season,"[1] sat beside him in the front pew, sizing up her new sister-in-law. Far from the sophisticated impression Pamela had hoped for, Mary decided she was just a "fairly dowdy country girl with freckles."[2]

When the newlyweds emerged, Randolph's fellow officers created a guard of honor with their ceremonial swords. Ducking to protect her quill, Pamela linked arms with her new husband before the congregation of sixty adjourned to Admiralty House. It spoke of Winston's isolation in a Chamberlain-led government still largely composed of appeasers that no one from the Cabinet attended his son's wedding. Undeterred, Clementine served champagne with a stand-up lunch followed by ice cream.

Kenny smiled dutifully but had withheld part of Pamela's £5,000 dowry citing "uncertainty of war" (but privately blaming uncertainty over his new son-in-law). Pansy managed to look mildly pleased in striped dress and pearls. Pamela looked ecstatic. None of them had any idea of a drama unfolding elsewhere in the room. Randolph's best man, Seymour Berry, had sent Pamela a diamond and sapphire brooch as a wedding present that morning, only to spot it on Mary's dress. Realizing she must have opened the parcel believing it to be for her, Berry alerted Randolph, who grabbed the pin off his sister, leaving her disappointed and upset. Berry later bought her another present to make amends for the mix-up, but Pamela felt Mary never forgave her for the humiliation.

To Pamela's mind the wedding was her "first freedom."[3] Even so, when the couple drove to Belton House, a romantic seventeenth-century stately home in Lincolnshire, for their honeymoon, she was nervous about the first night. To her surprise, Randolph set about not so much making love to his new wife as educating her. For hour after hour he read out long extracts of Hilaire Belloc and Gibbon's six-volume *Decline and Fall of the Roman Empire*. To ensure she was paying attention, between bouts of snoring or farting, he barked, "What was the last sentence?" "Can you imagine!" Pamela related afterward. "Hilaire Belloc was fine, but Gibbon was too much."[4] Her opinions or desires—and indeed the delights of Belton—were not of interest. Randolph was molding her into his ideal version of Pamela Churchill—well-read but obedient, elegant yet dependent, in awe of her husband's brilliance and willing to endure his behavior, however appalling. Lovemaking—when it finally happened—was less about connecting than conquering. Intimacy was anathema to him—perhaps in part because of his experience as a nine-year-old child at boarding school, when a master had lured him into his bedroom and made him "manipulate his organ." It was difficult to believe Randolph when he dismissed this event as unimportant, claiming he was "in awe" of the man and that he realized it was wrong only when "the housemaid came in without knocking to deliver his laundry."[5]

Pamela was excited when, soon after the wedding, the couple were invited to Cherkley Court, the mock-French Surrey mansion of Lord Beaverbrook, who owned newspapers including the *Evening Standard*, where Randolph had worked before the war. Beaverbrook was a rapacious, Machiavellian buccaneer loathed by Clementine Churchill as a malign influence over Winston, although Diana Cooper celebrated him as a "strange attractive gnome with an odour of genius about him."[6] Randolph bristled at Pamela's immediate bond with their sixty-year-old host, who was everything she had hoped for from her new life. Since meeting George McCullagh, she had been intrigued by how press barons were increasingly shaping politics. Beaverbrook (also Canadian by birth) was a master of the art. In return, the owner of the largest-circulation newspaper in the world (the *Daily Express*), was captivated by how the fun and flattering new Mrs. Churchill had learned from her tutors at Leeds Castle. Randolph fumed as Pamela held her own in the discussion of current events and assuaged his discomfort with Beaverbrook's wine and by belittling what she said. When she protested, he told her to shut up. Later that night, Randolph accused her of showing off and of falling under "Beaverbrook's spell."[7] As many wives have done in similar circumstances, Pamela decided she must rein herself in to please her "brilliant" husband.[8] The naïve young woman who had married in haste was already beginning to repent.

As the weeks passed, the expected catastrophe of total war did not happen. In a "numbing continuation of anxiety and boredom," Cecil Beaton complained of "undramatic weeks of waiting that were perhaps the dreariest of all our lives."[9] Each day was defined by shortages, restrictions and the hated blackout, but so far not by the feared hail of bombs. Despite Winston's efforts, there had been huge losses of merchant shipping out in the Atlantic but Hitler's main attention was still to the east, where he was dividing up Poland with Stalin. No one knew how long this "phoney war" would last, or how to keep warm in the coldest winter for a century. A thick fog enveloped London, heightening the sense of ennui.

Randolph's regiment was still not dispatched overseas as many others had been. He returned to his regimental headquarters at Beverley, a sleepy market town in East Yorkshire. Pamela found them a modest semi-detached house nearby for £3 a week—a step up from the caravan she had been assigned for Randolph's brief first posting at Tidworth on the edge of Salisbury Plain. In Yorkshire, the gossip among the sergeants' wives was that "We have nothing to worry about as long as Mr. Churchill's son is in the regiment—none of our husbands will be sent abroad."[10] This infuriated Randolph, whose flaws did not include physical cowardice, just as patience was not one of his virtues. He demanded his father intervene, but this time Winston held firm and advised his son to accept his situation "with good grace."[11] Although she approved of Winton's refusal to seek special treatment for his son—and believed that Randolph's problems in large part lay in having previously been spoiled by his father[12]—Pamela was the chief casualty. Randolph vented his frustration by ramping up his drinking and his humiliation of her.

One evening at the house of Lord Kemsley, owner of the *Sunday Times*, Randolph angrily branded his host a "quisling" for continuing to support appeasement. Pamela thought the accusation justified but was mortified at his loss of control.[13] She watched her husband with fading pride and mounting horror—even if his insults were considered "original."[14] At home, the raging became worse. Randolph kicked furniture, punched walls and spewed torrents of verbal abuse. When sober—and when what he called the "black fog"[15] had lifted—Randolph might apologize and promise to reform. For a moment, he could be charming, even sweet. Alcohol more and more bewitched him, though, and prevented him from performing in bed. She found her new life "very unsettling and unhappy."[16]

When she next saw Sarah Norton, Pamela admitted that her marriage was in trouble. Every time she tried to tame Randolph's behavior he accused her of exercising "feminine tyranny" like his mother.[17] Yet she dreaded his absences—which were frequent—almost as much as his presence. For then Pamela's only company was his "odious" little white dog and his even more disagreeable maid who reminded her of the sinister Mrs. Danvers in Daphne du Maurier's latest novel, *Rebecca*. Randolph's servant also taunted her mistress by unfavorably comparing her to her predecessor, pointing to publicity posters of a vampish American actress called Claire Luce and telling Pamela, "Oh, she stayed for breakfast." And indeed Luce's visits were so frequent and blatant whenever Pamela was away that Randolph's senior officers ordered him to discontinue them as a matter of respect for his wife. No believer in male monogamy, Randolph could see no reason to—rules were for others, not for him.

The reason for his sporadic unexplained absences (including the one just after they met) now became clear. Luce had been sleeping with Randolph for years—and signed erotic photographs of herself for him—but she was not his only illicit lover. If he was capable of love, it was not for Pamela but for Laura Charteris, an "adventurous, dark-eyed, piquant-faced" woman whom he obsessively pursued.[18] She had rejected his proposals (even when her own marriages foundered) but occasionally allowed him into her bed.[19] Pamela's old fears of being fat and frumpy came back to haunt her. Unable to pour out her heart to the many who had advised her against Randolph, Pamela reserved her "absolute fury" for "this terrible maid . . . She hated me and I hated her."[20]

Yet when Pamela had the opportunity to support her husband, she grasped it. For weeks Randolph had been ribbed by his fellow officers about his bulging waistline. His exercise regime, as he loved to brag, was of the indoor variety of drinking and gambling but he claimed to be tougher than them all. Unimpressed, the officers wagered £50 that he could not walk to York and back—nearly a hundred miles by road—in twenty-four hours. He took the challenge to heart and Pamela's sympathy was aroused, knowing too well the sting of mockery. She helped him train every evening for three weeks, put him on an energy-boosting diet and rubbed his feet with methylated spirits to harden the soles. Losing the bet was out of the question. To forgo the money was unthinkable—Randolph confessed he had an urgent need to pay off a debt.

He set off at three in the morning and kept up a good pace on the way to York. The return journey was more challenging. Pamela drove behind him with her headlights on, tooting the horn if Randolph slowed to under the required four miles an hour. Trying to stay awake and warm in an unheated car, she jumped out to help Randolph take off his boots when his blisters became too painful and padded his socks with cotton wool. Freezing rain lashed down and in the last hour the escapade became a "desperate struggle." To their credit, the couple arrived back at camp with twenty minutes to spare. Randolph expected praise and £50. He met "derisive laughter" and a refusal to pay. The ultimate indignity came from his commanders, who put him on fatigue duties—menial tasks such as digging holes—as punishment for leaving his post.²¹ It was yet more proof that her husband was not the glittering figure she had hoped but rather an object of disdain for subordinates and commanders alike.

Inconsolable, Randolph barely thanked his wife. He craved devotion like a drug but, as his cousin Anita Leslie explained, "when he got it he abused the giver."²² Unlike Claire Luce or Laura Charteris, Pamela had agreed to be his wife and always to be there for him—and this he presumed but could not forgive. The fact that Laura had a husband and Claire was uninterested in marrying was key: Randolph had a "poacher's eye."²³

To add to Pamela's woes, the bills kept flooding in, including one for a £100 Cartier bracelet that Randolph had bought not for her but in his continued pursuit of Mona Harrison Williams. Even if they had received the £50 winnings, the money "wouldn't have paid off even a tenth" of what they owed.²⁴ Randolph had his lieutenant's pay and Beaverbrook had generously agreed to go on paying him £750 a year, half of his old salary at the *Evening Standard*, even though he no longer worked for him. Yet Randolph continued to spend as if he had a mighty fortune like many of his friends. Women were supposed to let men deal with finances but an anxious Pamela found final demands for booze, shirts, shoes and his gentlemen's club, White's. Randolph dipped deep into her dowry to pay the most vociferous claimants but the invoices kept coming. And yet when they dined in restaurants—often with a very affluent crowd—Randolph insisted on picking up the tab. Pamela thought it "ridiculous because they could afford it while he couldn't."²⁵ It was as if he was trying to buy friendship.

Pamela considered returning to Minterne but rejected the idea as humiliating. Instead, she spent more time with her in-laws at Admiralty House, where she was enthusiastically made welcome. Clementine was an elusive character. Even her youngest—and favorite—daughter Mary considered her gifted and beautiful mother more of a "deity" than a parent. Yet Clementine's defenses melted with her perfectly behaved daughter-in-law, who also became "immensely fond" of her and began to call her Mama. Soon they were sharing confidences about the challenges of marrying Churchill men. They agreed that they expected "their women to understand them totally" while not spending "much if any time" trying to understand their women.[26]

Clementine had surrendered her life to her husband's career and well-being. She had taken care of him personally—shoring him up and running an immaculate household—and politically (counseling, chiding, tempering and encouraging). It had been an exhausting choice—once compared to hitching herself to a hurricane—but rewarding because of her unflinching belief in Winston's destiny to lead his country. Clementine loved her husband, for all his bombast and bluster, and he was humble in his devotion to her. Pamela could see how Randolph had inherited exaggerated versions of his father's faults but few of his redeeming qualities. Clementine advised her to pack her bags and go away for a few days without a word to teach Randolph a lesson. The mother-son relationship had always been fraught and now she took Pamela's side against her own child. "Randolph is treating *our* [author's italics] Pamela very badly," she informed Winston.[27]

Pamela also set out to enchant her father-in-law, pealing with laughter at his wit, cutting his cigar, playing him at her childhood game of bezique. Her choice of a gold fountain pen for Winston's sixty-fifth birthday on November 30 went down particularly well and he signed his wartime papers with it. She made easy company compared to his daughters, who had his affection but not necessarily his favor. Nervy Diana did not share his love of politics, and having already been through one harrowing marriage could not offer the amusing company he craved. His beloved Sarah, known within the family as Mule for her stubborn ways, suffered from internal demons that prevented her from becoming the straightforward confidante he wished for and that she would so have liked to have been. Mary was still young and rather gauche, and as Pamela already knew, quick to take offense. By contrast, Pamela was immersed in world events, undemanding, attractive and full of verve, and adored Winston without reservation. It did not go down well with his daughters that she began to address Winston as Papa, or that she was taken into the heart of his world.

Randolph also began to feel uneasy about Pamela's popularity with his parents, whom he knew to be disenchanted with him. He found himself more and more excluded from Winston's presence even as Pamela was drawn deeper into it. Those who knew how hard it was to get close to Winston—one likening it to a game of snakes and ladders[28]—were awestruck by how quickly Pamela joined his innermost circle. Yet she had failed in one key respect. Each month she hoped for a sign. Winston began to ask, "Are you having a child?," and when she replied, "No, I'm afraid I'm not," he remarked that it was "very disappointing." Clementine and Pansy had each conceived their first child within a month of marriage. It was now a matter of urgency that she got on with producing the Churchill son and heir. Her future depended on it.

7

By the new year, rumors about Pamela's marriage were flying around like Randolph's infamous tirades. "Some of us thought that it was not going to last," recalled the Labour politician Michael Foot, an unlikely friend of Randolph's who considered him a "rampaging male chauvinist."[1] Like many men of the time, Randolph expected his wife to bend to his will and Pamela realized her marriage was doomed unless she took a more submissive role. Admitting failure months after going against family and friends to take his hand was inconceivable. She grew noticeably quieter on public outings and refrained from complaining about Randolph's drinking and absences. She cooed, soothed, flattered and fawned. Shortly afterward she got pregnant. Naturally it would be a boy. Her place at the heart of the Churchill world was surely guaranteed.

Pamela was excited about informing Papa and Mama that she was with child, rather more so than her own family. Randolph had recently rowed with his exasperated parents over his debts but happily he was with his regiment, and Pamela visited them in the early spring alone. Her sense of fun always lifted Churchill's mood and Clementine led a reluctant Mary away after lunch to leave him with Pamela while he finished his glass of port (a privilege normally reserved for men). Winston continued to rage at Randolph's conduct, so Pamela waited for the right moment before finally venturing her news. Winston's fury evaporated and "his eyes lit up with great joy." He poured himself another glass of port before rushing off to tell Clementine, who was also "very sweet."[2]

Pamela gave up her unhappy life in Yorkshire to move in with the Churchills at Admiralty House, where she was thrust into the cockpit of dissent over the conduct of the war. Prime Minister Chamberlain, secretly suffering from terminal bowel cancer, continued to equivocate, even now believing it preferable to sue for peace. In stark contrast, Winston's Admiralty was hell-bent on engaging the enemy. Pamela cheered him on and, now privy to events as they happened, was thrilled when Winston ordered the Royal Navy to attack a German tanker, the *Altmark*, even though it was located in technically neutral Norwegian waters. HMS *Cossack* rescued the three hundred Allied prisoners on board (whose vessels had been sunk by a German battleship) and killed eight German sailors. Winston's belligerence provided a much-needed morale boost to a tense and fearful Britain but commanded little support in Cabinet or indeed his own social circles. So the devotion of his daughter-in-law did not go unappreciated. Pamela believed in Winston "more than any god" and he—a man vampiric in his hunger for the love and energy of others—rewarded her fealty by dispatching her to Leith in Scotland to greet the crew of the *Cossack* when they sailed into port. In what was her first public duty as his representative, Pamela amply repaid her father-in-law's confidence. Only nineteen, dressed to the nines and determined to make her mark, she reported back to Papa on her "thrilling" day in the way she knew would appeal to his swashbuckling tastes. The *Cossack* sailors had "enjoyed their hand-to-hand fight tremendously," she informed him, and "many of the Germans had jumped through the port holes out of fright." She had found it comforting to know that "we can be ferocious."[3]

A week later the navy sank a U-boat south of Shetland with a barrage of depth charges and torpedoes. Pamela took a seat in the House of Commons gallery to watch Papa report to MPs on his latest triumph, reporting back to Randolph that the Commons had "fairly vibrated with approval."⁴ The parliamentary spectacle had been marred, however, by waves of nausea. As her pregnancy progressed, she risked Randolph's disapproval by accepting Lord Beaverbrook's offer of a chauffeur-driven car. Max had observed Pamela's leverage over Winston (not least as the mother-to-be of the Churchill heir) and wanted to position himself as her indispensable godfather. To placate Randolph, Beaverbrook restored his *Evening Standard* salary to the full rate.

Randolph marked Pamela's twentieth birthday in March 1940 with a "tiny" gift, noting that the unspecified item was "washable," and yet their letters suggest this was a brief golden period in their marriage. Soon afterward Pamela cabled to thank "darling Randy" for "SIX MONTHS OF SUCH LOVELY HAPPINESS."⁵ But just as the war took a grisly turn in April with Hitler invading Denmark and launching a massive attack on Norway, so did her health deteriorate. Morning sickness developed into uncontrolled vomiting—a condition known as hyperemesis gravidarum. She was admitted to a Harley Street clinic, writing to Randolph to tell him of her "Hellish time."⁶ She yearned for her husband to comfort her but it seems he did not respond. It became clear her husband shared with his father an impatience with ill health in others. The worse her condition, the less attentive Randolph became. "At night I just lie awake," she pleaded in vain, "longing for your arms around me." One morning Pamela woke to find herself bleeding heavily and doctors warned her not to move, to try to prevent a miscarriage. "Don't worry darling," she wrote to Randolph while lying on her back. "I'm keeping dead still."

The fighting in Norway dominated Admiralty House around the clock on her return but Clementine somehow found the time to be "angelic" to her daughter-in-law, who thought her tender care "so different" from her mother's dislike of weakness. The real prospect of losing his child prompted Randolph finally to make contact but Pamela now knew to play down her troubles—including when she vomited up blood, as "it was only from my throat." "The only man I love, loves me," she wrote to him, and she was even "glad" to suffer as it was all for "baby dumpling."

Now that the relative quiet of the "phoney war" was at an end Pamela kept abreast of events however bad she felt. Clementine and a stream of distinguished visitors briefed her on the Norway campaign, which saw British land forces engage with the German army for the first time in seven months of war. Pamela began to fret that Randolph's regiment might be dispatched to what was fast turning into a bloody fiasco, for which Winston was at least in part responsible. The singular leadership he had brought to bear in sea battles was less suited to this new, more complex theater in which careful coordination and planning mattered more than bulldog daring. The Churchill household was rigid with fear that failure would bring Winston down in the same fashion as the bungled and bloody attempt to seize the Gallipoli Peninsula in the First World War. "There is great tension here," Pamela informed Randolph. "The thunder clouds have gathered, but the rain has not started to fall."[7]

Better news came with reports of the navy having sunk a dozen German ships off the coast of Norway but Pamela was instructed that for security reasons she must keep even victories to herself until they were officially announced. When Randolph found out she had deliberately withheld news from him, he exploded with jealous rage at her privileged access to the secrets of war. She tried to soothe his pride by insisting her circumspection had been "agony" but he continued to fume.[8] The fact was that Clementine considered Randolph dangerously unreliable and lived in daily fear of him embarrassing his father, but had no such concerns about Pamela's discretion, despite her youth. Consequently, as her sickness receded Pamela was admitted to a tiny circle of people referred to as "padlock" and given an almost sacred trust by being permitted to sit in on highly sensitive discussions.[9] She could be relied upon to know almost instinctively when to be silent and was fully aware that it was "better to be dull than dangerous."[10] Randolph had always expected to be the one to be privileged by his father as confidant supreme. In his youth, he had been treated as a grown-up in preparation for the role, but now in his late twenties he was handled like a "wayward and untrustworthy child."[11]

The fighting in Norway went from bad to worse. Eleven Royal Navy ships were sunk and British and French forces driven into a humiliating retreat despite outnumbering the invaders. In Parliament, a gray-faced Chamberlain was condemned by both sides of the House in a stormy debate on whether the government was fit to run the war. One of his own backbenchers rose to his feet and, echoing the words of Oliver Cromwell to the Long Parliament of 1653, roared at the prime minister: "In the name of God, GO!" A perilous sense of drift became deeper still on the morning of May 10 when, as Winston had feared, German tanks rolled into the Netherlands and Belgium in an "avalanche of fire and steel."[12] Invasion of Britain could now be a matter of weeks or even days away. By 11 o'clock a weakening Chamberlain had reluctantly decided to step down. That afternoon, the king summoned Winston to Buckingham Palace to become prime minister.

Randolph raced back to London to ensure that it was he who accompanied his father into Downing Street the next morning. Unusually, he stayed with Pamela for several days as Winston took up the reins and Britain shifted to maximum alert. Pamela was in the House of Commons on May 13 to witness Winston inform the British people—and Berlin—that appeasement was over. "You ask what is our aim?" he declared in his first appearance as prime minister. "I can answer in one word—victory. Victory at all costs!" Pamela's heart soared with pride. "I firmly believe that if Winston had not become PM things might have gone very differently," she later reflected. "Winston was decisive, uncompromising and full of fight."[13] Taking up residence with the Churchills in Downing Street "coloured" her "whole life."[14] "Nobody," she mused, "ever had the chance to see politics as much from the inside as I did."[15]

Winston appointed Max Beaverbrook Minister of Air Production, giving Pamela another political inroad. And it was not just Conservative politicians whom she mixed with but, for the first time, figures of the left. The following week, Pamela was at Max's London home, Stornoway House, with the Labour leader Clement Attlee, a member of Winston's coalition government, and his deputy Arthur Greenwood. (The support of both men was crucial as Winston could not rely on the full backing of his own party.) Everyone was waiting for news and emotions were high when Max was urgently called to Downing Street.[16] He returned with confirmation that Hitler's Panzer Corps was now storming through France.

A fortnight later, Pamela was on a rare trip out of London with Randolph when they heard that Winston had ordered the evacuation of 340,000 Allied troops from the beaches of Dunkirk in northern France, where they had been trapped by the remorseless German advance. They wrote to offer him their encouragement at this "grim moment"—and to thank him for once again bailing out Randolph for unpaid bills.[17] The weather was perfection—a golden sun beating down on the late spring splendor of peonies and poppies—but the nervous tension almost intolerable. German tanks were patrolling the streets of Paris and Nazi troops were marching down the Champs-Élysées. After just six weeks of fighting, France, Britain's only major ally, capitulated. Thousands of German bombers and fighter planes started to mass along the Channel for Hitler's next move. On June 18, Winston leveled with the British people that the "whole fury and might of the enemy must very soon be turned on us."

Britain went into an overdrive of preparation. Iron railings were melted down to make weapons, place-names were painted over on roads and stations, concrete fortifications were built in the fields of southern England and a Home Guard was set up, attracting more than a million volunteers and donations of old hunting guns and opera glasses. Winston gravely informed Pamela over Sunday lunch that in the event of a Nazi invasion he counted on her to go down fighting and take at least one "dead German" with her. Pamela, whose bump was now pronounced, protested she had neither a gun nor the training to use it. Winston sternly retorted, "But you can always use a carving knife!"[18]

Outside the family, he could be sterner still, barking at his officials, humiliating those he disliked or did not rate. Pamela witnessed how Winston's temper betrayed the unbearable pressures of the post he had craved all his life. She also saw how "Mama" skillfully tackled Winston for what she described as his "rough, sarcastic and overbearing manner." Clementine urged him to show "kindness and, if possible, Olympian calm" in order to coax the best out of his staff in extreme conditions and prompted him to remember the importance of moments of fun and color even in war.[19] Pamela observed the strength of Clementine's influence. There was a quiet power in being a great man's counsel and constraint. Sadly, Randolph had made it clear that he had no need nor desire for her to play the same role for him. He was unfathomably lonely and yet was repelled by the notion of truly sharing his life.

Pamela's parents-in-law welcomed her help, however. In early July, the Free French leader General Charles de Gaulle was coming to Downing Street for what was expected to be a tense lunch. Thirteen hundred French sailors had paid with their lives when Winston ordered the navy to open fire on the French fleet anchored at Oran in North Africa, to prevent it from falling into German hands. Pamela, who had been privy to the agonizing before the attack, was enlisted to try to keep the meal as cordial as possible. But when Clementine told the general that she hoped the remaining French fleet would support the British in their continued fight against the Nazis, de Gaulle rose to his full six foot five to reply that it would give him more satisfaction to turn their guns on the British. Known for her "electrical storms," as Clementine's daughters dubbed her outbursts, she did not hold back in reprimanding de Gaulle for his hostility toward an ally and host. Tensions mounted still further when Winston intervened to upbraid his wife. If it was all rich meat for a twenty-year-old, this was just one occasion when Pamela's calm but calculated presence appears to have been indispensable. From then on, she was regularly deployed to charm the future French president into supporting the British position, although even she on occasion found him "difficult." Later, de Gaulle would acknowledge her efforts by sending her "respectful homage" and giving her child a cherished book, one of the few personal possessions he had managed to smuggle out of France.

The constant demands on Clementine's time—including helping Winston with his illustrious speeches—were exhausting for a woman whose health (and temper) had always been delicate. Now she had found a solution. Pamela had proved herself as an ideal substitute when she was too busy or tired. Over time Pamela increasingly stood in for Clementine as hostess and became a trusted participant in gatherings of historic importance. Her dinner companions included foreign leaders, Winston's chief of staff General Hastings "Pug" Ismay, other generals, airmen and admirals, but also senior ministers such as Max Beaverbrook, Anthony Eden (now Foreign Secretary again) and Labour's Ernest Bevin (Minister of Labour). Sitting by their side, she became familiar with virtually every aspect of the war, becoming better briefed than almost anyone apart from Winston himself. These dinner companions in turn came to see Pamela as a power in her own right, having earned the ultimate accolade in British political life—the confidence of the prime minister. She had something else too. During the darkest days of war, her red hair, bright blue eyes and translucent skin made an impact on anyone who crossed the threshold of Downing Street. "The auburn alluring Pam Churchill," the society diarist Chips Channon called her,[20] later hailing her as the "Crown Princess of England."[21] The acclaim was exquisite, heady and, it would transpire, of strategic importance.

Pamela's rising star only made Randolph more obnoxious. One weekend, he accompanied her to Chequers, the prime minister's official country residence, and offended almost everyone, including his father. Winston's appalled new private secretary, Jock Colville, found Randolph "noisy, self-assertive, whining" and "one of the most objectionable people" he had ever met.[22] If the prime minister loved his son—confessing that weekend that he "would not be able to carry on" if he were killed in the war—it was also clear he liked him less and less.[23]

There was relief when Randolph returned to his regiment in Yorkshire, but in early August he was back in Downing Street on leave. After dinner the seven months pregnant Pamela retired to her bedroom and Randolph set off for the Savoy to meet a friend, the American journalist Red Knickerbocker. The two men boozed through the night, then Randolph drove back to Downing Street at six in the morning, witnessed by Winston's security chief, before stumbling up to Pamela's room in the eaves where he fell into bed fully dressed. Around 7:30 a maid knocked on the door and presented Pamela with a summons from Clementine. Pamela found her mother-in-law in bed, eating breakfast on a tray wearing white gloves, a tell-tale sign familiar to all Churchills that she was angry. "Darling, where was Randolph last night?" Clementine demanded. Sensing disaster, Pamela burst into tears. Clementine revealed that Randolph had left secret military maps in his unlocked car, where any passer-by could have taken them. Such a security breach could become a "terrible scandal" and might even finish Winston as prime minister.[24] A miserable Pamela went to wake Randolph, informing him that his mother wanted him out of the house at once.

Apparently contrite, he made a show of promising to stop drinking.

Instead of reforming, however, Randolph just made more trouble. Intent on presenting himself as an intimate of his father, Randolph informed Claire Luce of Winston's contempt for Joe Kennedy over his vocal support for appeasement, information Luce immediately relayed to the U.S. ambassador. When word of Kennedy's fury reached Downing Street, there were fears that Randolph might have irreparably damaged relations with Washington at a time when American support was vital for Britain's very survival. The crisis was of course down to his own failings—and this was far from the last occasion Randolph was to pose a serious threat to the war effort—but he chose to blame Pamela, accusing her of taking his parents' side against him. He decided this gave him license to sleep with whoever would have him. The uniformed son of a prime minister in wartime was spoiled for choice.

When the Battle of Britain began on July 10, Winston shared his fears with Pamela that invasion on a "terrific scale" was imminent. German bombers were laying waste to airfields in southern England while Hurricanes and Spitfires jousted with Messerschmitts for control of the cloudless skies above. Every conversation revolved around the latest figures on enemy planes shot down and RAF planes lost. The Luftwaffe were soon sending over hundreds of aircraft a day, stretching the RAF to its limit. On August 20, Winston acknowledged the nation's debt to the heroic young pilots fighting against seemingly impossible odds, informing Parliament that "never in the field of human conflict has so much been owed by so many to so few."

Fuming at still not seeing action himself, Randolph received unexpected good news with an invitation to become the MP for Preston in the north of England, following the death of the incumbent. He had tried and failed to be elected three times—his personality and right-wing politics not finding the favor he had expected. Now under a wartime political truce, he would take the seat uncontested. Pamela wrote from Chequers that she was "so happy about Preston my darling & so proud of you."²⁵ Now, at last, she would be able to play her role in great affairs through her husband, as Clementine had managed for so long. "What fun we are going to have with Politics in the future," she cooed. But if she hoped that this fresh start would transform Randolph as a character as well as her own life, the omens were not encouraging. Critics put his selection down to nepotism, a painful truth that fueled his ample sense of grievance.

Aware of Randolph's resentment at her closeness to his parents, for the sake of her marriage Pamela decided she needed a home away from her beloved Downing Street. Brendan Bracken, one of Winston's closest aides, found her a former rectory to the north of London, at Ickleford in Hertfordshire, that would soon be available for an astonishingly low rent. She told Randolph how much she was longing for it: "Just you and me there together, all to ourselves . . . Please write me a note that you love me."²⁶ He did not answer.

From teatime on Saturday, September 7, and for fifty-six nights thereafter, London was shaken, flattened and burned by the fury of the Blitz. At first the bombs rained down on the terraced houses of the East End near the docks, then they came steadily farther west toward Downing Street. As she entered the final stages of pregnancy, Pamela was kept awake by the sirens for five hours at a stretch while knowing that her top-floor bedroom was particularly vulnerable to blasts. Churches, schools, shops, pubs, stations, theaters, Centre Court at Wimbledon, London Zoo—even hospitals tending casualties in half-lit rooms—were hit. Thousands died; many more were made homeless. The Blitz became a twentieth-century vision of hell.

A temporary shelter was hastily created in the wine cellar under 10 Downing Street, a seventeenth-century building rickety even in peacetime. There were only two bedrooms, but Clementine bagged one for herself. Pamela shared the other with her father-in-law, taking the lower bunk bed as, now heavily pregnant with "baby dumpling," she felt too unwieldy to climb to the higher one. Joking that she had "one Churchill on top of me and one inside me," she struggled with the narrow mattress despite retiring exhausted after dinner every night at around 9 p.m. She dropped off until 1 or 1:30 in the morning, when Winston would enter the room and pull himself up to the top bunk. It turned out that his snoring was little quieter than the sirens, so that marked the end of her night's sleep.

There was something else keeping her awake. Mary, wife of Winston's cousin John Spencer-Churchill, the Duke of Marlborough, had given birth to her second son in July and had decided to call him Winston. In Pamela's mind this was a disaster. Her own unborn baby was to be the prime minister's third grandchild—Diana already had two children—but the first with the all-important Churchill surname. With her marriage so fragile, Pamela craved the additional security of being the mother of the only child bearing the prime minister's name. Pamela's sobs enlisted Winston's sympathy. He agreed to press the duchess to change her plans for her son and, unwilling to upset the war leader, Mary duly switched to Charles. No one seems to have contemplated that Pamela was not carrying a boy.

Pamela knew her presence in London to be a comfort to Papa, but the scale of the bombing was horrifying and she obsessively kept tabs on the numbers of dead and injured. The nights and days were etched with fatigue; the attacks were relentless. Feeling "useless" in her condition, she eventually departed for Chequers; photographs of her in the gardens there show a heavily pregnant woman with an impossibly youthful face and eyes like pools of fear. A few days later, she wrote to Randolph: "I think this bombing of London so terrible. How brave the English people are."[27]

The Churchills' gathering at Chequers in mid-September for Mary's eighteenth birthday was inevitably overshadowed by the Battle of Britain reaching its climax. President Roosevelt had notified Winston of intelligence suggesting Hitler planned to invade in seven days and the Germans were expected to throw all they had at taking aerial control to clear the way. Winston asked Pamela to accompany him and Clementine on a visit to Uxbridge in west London, the command center of the RAF's Fighter Squadron, to witness the death-fight that could well decide the country's fate. On hot, cloudless September 15, the trio descended fifty feet below ground to the operations room. Taking their seats on a darkened balcony overlooking a huge map of England and the Channel, they were transfixed by the young raid-plotters tracking German planes as they stormed over the coastline in huge herringbone formations. On the other side of the room, a wall of red bulbs lit up one by one to indicate each RAF squadron as it took to the air. "Very frightened," Pamela watched as the last light came on. She knew that meant there were no more squadrons in reserve to intercept any further waves of Luftwaffe bombers and their fighter escorts. As the young RAF pilots battled thousands of feet above them, the fight for freedom was indeed in the hands of the famous Few. After what seemed like hours, they were informed that the depleted ranks of enemy planes were at last turning for home. Breaking his silence in the car back to Chequers, Pamela heard Winston say: "There are times when it is equally good to live or to die."[28] It was not until later that evening that they were informed that they had witnessed the critical victory against Hitler's plans of achieving air superiority ahead of an invasion. It was now certain that Britain would fight on, but also that the struggle would be lengthy.

Redolent of wood smoke and antiquarian books, Chequers came to life at weekends but otherwise Pamela found it gloomy. The grand old house also did not provide the seclusion she had expected—the thud of anti-aircraft guns and roar of aircraft were reminders of the closeness of war. Nor was it unknown to the Luftwaffe. In 1937, Hitler's foreign minister Joachim von Ribbentrop, then ambassador to Britain, had visited it at the invitation of former prime minister Stanley Baldwin. Furthermore, its half-mile entry road intersected a U-shaped drive of pale-colored gravel that lit up white by moonlight. From ten thousand feet, it was almost as if an arrow pointed to the house—a navigation gift at a time when pilots depended on landmarks to direct their bombs.

That Winston was a key target was also clear. One time, shell splinters had crashed through the Downing Street windows and embedded themselves in the walls. On another occasion, a bomb narrowly missed but killed four people nearby, shattered remaining windows (which were fixed up with brown paper) and tore doors off their hinges. Thereafter there was no heating or hot water. Clementine urgently called on the army to grass over the Chequers driveway but as yet there were only a few aging sandbags around the house and no bombproof chamber to retreat to. "I wish you were here to hold on to," Pamela wrote to Randolph, apparently believing it was army duties keeping him away. "If only this war would end & we could always be together."

Pamela's pregnancy dragged on past her due date into October. Tired of waiting, she dressed her new white Pekinese puppy in baby clothes and sent it down the corridor to Clementine, who thought the joke hilarious. She in turn rushed to see Winston, saying "Look— look what a surprise I've got for you!" Winston merely wanted to know: "Is it a boy?" His response made clearer than ever the pressure on Pamela to produce a son.[29] Apologetic for being overdue, she fretted that she was being "a nuisance to everybody" and out of the loop, so she pumped Clementine for political updates and informed Randolph that she had "managed to worm out of her the exciting news that N. C. [Neville Chamberlain] has at last resigned" from the War Cabinet. On their wedding anniversary on October 4, she wrote that she was "so proud" of being his wife and that "other people are just nuisances." She excused herself from official dinners—the "whole Navy seem to be here this weekend"—as she did not "feel decent enough to be looked on." She did not forget, however, to remind him to reply to letters of congratulations for becoming an MP.[30]

On October 6 Luftwaffe bombs hit London's sewage works, releasing an appalling stench across the capital, but Pamela insisted on coming two days later to watch Randolph take his seat in the House of Commons. As she was now a week overdue, the doctors insisted she bring a canister of laughing gas (a mix of oxygen and nitrous oxide) with her into the gallery, in case she went into labor. Nothing happened but the following evening, after supper back at Chequers—bathed dangerously in bright moonlight—the pains finally began. A navy nurse was summoned to the principal bedroom where Pamela lay among the pillows in a huge four-poster bed draped in lace. As contractions came faster and deeper she called out for Randolph. Downstairs, Clementine and her staff were urgently trying to track him down. Few answered their calls because another major raid was underway in London, with one bomb penetrating the dome of St. Paul's Cathedral to crash into the high altar. At Chequers, Pamela labored on and on, sucking in the laughing gas with each surge of pain. As she pushed with all her might, she could hear the approaching roar of enemy aircraft and soon they were flying overhead as she lay helpless and panting.

Next came the "swishing crescendo" of a huge device rattling the windows, pouring in choking gray dust and shaking the very bones of the house.[31] The breath seemed to be drawn from her lungs by the shock, but the explosion "neatly heralded" the birth. At 4:40 on the morning of October 10, Pamela's baby entered the world with only the unflappable nurse in attendance.[32] The night sky was still alive with enemy bombers but Pamela wrested the laughing gas mask from her mouth and repeated the same question half a dozen times. "Is it a boy? Is it a boy?"

8

"I've told you six times already," the nurse exclaimed impatiently. "Yes, it's a boy!" The new mother had fulfilled her duty. Randolph had failed in his. While his wife was in the throes of childbirth and in fear for her life, he had been in the arms of Diana Tauber, wife of Lady Baillie's favorite tenor, and did not arrive at Chequers until well after the event. Winston, however, could hardly have been keener to set eyes on his namesake. Leaning over to kiss the new Winston Spencer Churchill, he exclaimed with moistening eyes, "Poor kitten, what a terrible world to be born into!"[1]

Chequers filled with friends and family to view the new arrival, who cried noisily in a pram "open for inspection."[2] The Germans probably "don't think I'd be so foolish as to come here," Winston surmised at lunch. "I stand to lose a lot, three generations at one swoop."[3] Clearly, it was not worth taking the risk. Workmen were filling the giant craters where the bombs had landed and soon they would finally grass over the drive. Plans were also afoot to move the prime minister and his entourage to a better-concealed stately home (Ditchley Park, forty miles to the northwest in Oxfordshire) whenever the moon was high.

Fatherhood had had no obvious softening effect on Randolph. "He talks of world domination as the greatest ideal," Jock Colville noted in his diary with a shudder, "and says he admires the Germans for desiring it."[4] Spared that particular incident, Pamela was determined there would be "no more living in other people's houses" and typically did not care to reverse a decision once made. To help with the costs of the move to Ickleford, the Digbys offered spare furniture from Minterne and £200 toward the decorating of her new home, while Clementine picked up the £164 bill for the curtains. But still the demands flooded in and shortly after giving birth Pamela went to Winston (not for the first time) to plead for help. He agreed to settle the couple's debts but on condition that no more would accumulate. "Yes," Pamela assured him, "this is the end."[5] Randolph was now making good money, drawing an MP's salary of £600 a year on top of his *Evening Standard* income plus his army pay. And yet when Pamela was shopping in Harrods soon afterward, the assistant refused to put her purchases on account. Humiliated, she confessed her predicament to Clementine, who was "wonderfully kind . . . but very nervous also."[6] At this point onlookers were torn between admiring Pamela's determination to make her marriage work and despairing at the pointlessness of aiming to improve her self-destructive husband. If war, marriage, a seat in Parliament, a marital home and fatherhood were not going to, then what would?

Randolph resumed his place at the bar at White's, racking up another huge tab. It was here that he heard that Lieutenant-Colonel Robert Laycock was recruiting for a new commando unit to serve in the Middle East. Many of Randolph's drinking pals, including Evelyn Waugh, had already signed up and so—believing he might finally see action in their company—he stomped into the office of his commanding officer to ask for a transfer. He was so shocked to be told that his fellow officers could hardly wait for him to leave that he burst into tears. "That was one of his endearing traits," his cousin Anita Leslie generously observed. "His honest childlike desire to be loved and his amazement when he discovered he wasn't."[7] After Randolph left, the 4th Hussars were sent to Crete, only for many of them to be wiped out. Pamela knew that Randolph was now hated even more—the wives believing that it was because he had left that their husbands had been sent to their deaths.

Randolph joined No. 8 Commando at their training camp at the Scottish coastal resort of Largs just as Pamela took up residence in Ickleford. At Pamela's invitation, Randolph's sister Diana and her two children also moved into the fifteen-room house to help with the running costs, as Randolph had refused to increase his wife's £8 weekly allowance.[8] Even so, Pamela was skipping meals—essentials such as butter, eggs and bread were soaring in price as well as being rationed—and retired shivering to bed at 6:30 in the evening to avoid lighting the gas fire. Nor was she immune from the bombing even here, thirty miles from London—occasionally an explosion would wake the baby—and she placed buckets of water and of sand at the ready in case they were hit by an incendiary. Fortunately, her parents dispatched her old nanny from Dorset, enabling Pamela to organize meals for evacuated children and run a canteen for three hundred workers from nearby factories.

Despite the challenges, there was a satisfaction in receiving visitors to show off her son in her own house with its elegant white paneling. Friends such as the Soviet ambassador Ivan Maisky and his wife—who had awakened a lifelong interest in Russia—found her "awfully proud" of young Winston but complained about what Maisky called the "Churchill commune's" discomfort and cold.[9] The ambassador, a committed anglophile, thought Pamela "on edge" in Randolph's company but when alone she glowed. She had lost even more weight since giving birth and her jutting cheekbones made her eyes look like enormous jewels.

When the queen's favorite photographer, Cecil Beaton, came to take pictures of her with her baby she was thrilled with the results. As was Winston's close ally Duff Cooper, Minister of Information (and Lady Diana Cooper's husband), who recognized their powerful emotional impact. He was soon negotiating for a collection of portraits of mother and son to be acquired by *Life* in a ploy to try to win over American public opinion. Beaton himself had been entranced by his subject, finding her "triumphant . . . with Raeburnesque red curls."[10] On another photoshoot at Downing Street, he drew a charming portrait of her, the gouache strokes on blue paper glorying in her red-gold hair. It did not go unnoticed that it was Pamela rather than her housemate Diana—a blood Churchill—who had been chosen to represent the best of Britain. Or that wherever Pamela went, important people flocked to pay court. Diana hated the whole set-up. "My mother wasn't happy," her daughter Celia Sandys confirms. "They were very different people."[11]

Baby Winston was just three weeks old when Pamela traveled up to Largs to see Randolph with his fellow commando officers, men of entitlement and military ineptitude with names such as Bobbity, Bones and Fruity who were referred to by the professional soldiers serving under them as "scum."[12] One troop leader was unable to read a compass; another failed to turn up to a night-time exercise because he could not make out his watch in the dark.[13] Pamela could scarcely contain her horror at their incompetence and Randolph set out to humiliate his wife in return. He abandoned her every night, ostentatiously picked his nose in public and urinated in front of a group of women, proclaiming, "I'm a member of Parliament!"[14] His fellow officers were more welcoming, including Waugh, who was in awe of Pamela's "great superiority of knowledge" about world events.[15] Randolph was meanwhile busy rowing with the management of Largs's Marine Hotel over his bill. In three weeks, he had spent £54—£2 more than the annual rent on Ickleford.

Pamela remained the dutiful wife, toward the end of November attending Randolph's maiden speech in the Commons. Yet their growing mutual dislike overshadowed the baby's christening on December 1 at the parish church of Saints Peter and Paul, perched dramatically on a Chiltern hilltop near Chequers. The heavy gray cloud matched the somber mood. Bombing of Britain's cities continued, claiming around a thousand lives a week. Downing Street had been largely evacuated and the Churchills had moved into safer quarters known as the Annexe, around the corner by St. James's Park. Privately Winston thought the imminent threat of invasion had receded but shipping losses in the Atlantic were colossal, making widespread starvation a real risk. Most of all, the prime minister could see no clear way to victory without drawing the United States into the fight, a prospect, given the continued opposition of large swathes of U.S. public opinion, apparently as remote as ever. Many Americans thought it another European war unworthy of American blood or dollars and the so-called Special Relationship did not yet exist. Ambassador Kennedy, nicknamed "Jittery Joe" for departing London as soon as the bombs started falling, had further stirred up emotions by claiming that democracy was "finished in England."[16]

Battered and bruised, Britain was clinging on but running out of cash for weapons to keep up the fight. Far from donating them, America charged top rate and Britain could not pay for half of what it had ordered, let alone what it needed; it was effectively bankrupt. Winston had spent days working on probably the most important letter of his life, setting out the desperation of Britain's plight to Roosevelt and pleading for more help in what he hoped was their joint aim of defeating Nazi tyranny. From her vantage point, Pamela knew that the U.S. must be wooed into the war if Britain was to survive much longer. She racked her brains for how she could help her father-in-law make it happen.

In January 1941, No. 8 Commando was ordered to Egypt to fight the Afrika Korps commanded by the much-feared General Rommel, known as the Desert Fox. It would be "terrible" to be parted, Randolph solemnly informed Pamela before setting sail on HMS *Glenroy* with enough luggage for a "film star's honeymoon,"[17] but with her living "very economically" and he with nowhere to spend money on board ship they would be able to pay off some of their debts. Pamela's hopes that finally seeing action would be the making of her husband did little to quell her growing doubts about her marriage or her fear that she was pregnant again. Meanwhile, a single raid on December 30 had destroyed large tracts of London's financial heartlands, eight Wren churches and several publishers' repositories containing five million books. Poland, Denmark, Norway, Belgium, the Netherlands and France had fallen to Nazi rule. Churchill's oratory could sustain Britain for only so long.

Roosevelt had studied Winston's letter sitting in a deckchair on the USS *Tuscaloosa*, as the warship cruised the turquoise waters of the Caribbean. Publicly he repeated that America would remain neutral but as London was being hammered by Hitler's bombers, Roosevelt felt the sense of urgency. He sat down for a "fireside chat" on the radio to inform the American people that despite being on the other side of the Atlantic they could not "escape danger by crawling into bed and pulling the covers over our heads," as "if Britain should go down, all of us ... would be living at the point of a gun." America, he said, had to become "the great arsenal of Democracy." Winston was cheered but worried about how long it would take for Congress to endorse the president's offer of help, or exactly what it entailed. Whatever it was, it was far short of America starting to fight.

The news that Roosevelt was to send a personal envoy to London to report back on the war was therefore of incalculable importance. The president was wary of Winston as a man and leader. Joe Kennedy had told him the prime minister was "always sucking on a whiskey bottle."[18] Roosevelt himself suspected he was "probably the best man that England had," but did he have more to him than rhetoric? Harry Hopkins—once described as FDR's "combination of Machiavelli, Svengali and Rasputin"[19]—was due to arrive on January 9 to find out, and the Churchills switched into a frenzy of preparations. Cancer had left Hopkins with only half a stomach and a scratchy disposition and so every comfort would be provided, from the most digestible meals possible in wartime to warm, downy beds. Background inquiries had revealed that Hopkins had the ear of the president and lived down the hall from him in the White House. His impressions of Britain would likely be decisive for America's next step. Alarmingly, however, Hopkins harbored fervent Angloskeptic views, suspected that Churchill wanted American help only to save the empire and was instinctively an isolationist. He would need considerable persuasion that Britain was a worthy cause. But another trait that the Churchills discovered was that Hopkins, a poor boy from Sioux City, Iowa, combined a Democrat's social concern with a weakness for glamorous high-born women.

Clementine set to work. By the time Hopkins arrived for a private lunch with Winston in the Downing Street basement, one of the few usable parts of the building, it had been dressed with flowers, chintz curtains and French neoclassical paintings. Especially prominent, however, was Cecil Beaton's most winsome photograph of Pamela with her baby. As Hopkins entered the room he could not fail to notice it, and over a preprandial glass of sherry he complimented Winston on his daughter-in-law's "delicious" beauty.

That weekend an excited Hopkins would meet Pamela in person in the old-world splendor of Ditchley. Clementine had noticed Pamela's power over older men (including her own husband) through a rare cocktail of flattering attention, smoldering sex appeal and an impressive grasp of geopolitics. In a carefully choreographed move, the twenty-year-old was deployed to weave her spell over forty-nine-year-old Hopkins. Washington's ultimate insider observed how Pamela shone as the "apple of Churchill's eye"; everyone else noticed how she swiftly became the "apple of Harry Hopkins's eye too."[20]

Later that month the Churchills hoped Pamela would have the same effect on America at large when Beaton's photographs graced the cover of *Life*. Recent issues had featured Katharine Hepburn and a range of starlets in evening gowns and bathing suits but Pamela's portrait with her baby, captioned "Pretty Mother," was a huge national hit. Its "symbolical loveliness," a reader's letter gushed, was "the most beautiful you have ever printed."[21] Inside, there were more full-page pictures of her, including a particularly sexy one in the pillared room at Downing Street. Her striped dress with lace collar showed off her shapely figure perfectly—a look that Beaton had also captured in his drawing. The Churchill offspring were relegated to a gallery of small images on later pages, looking on as this exquisite creature soaked up the limelight. The exposure had made her a celebrity at home and in the U.S., and considerably boosted Britain's place in the hearts of Americans. Pamela had been unleashed as the Churchills' most willing and committed secret weapon—but this was just the start.

Randolph was to be on board ship for a month, going the long way around to Egypt via the Cape of Good Hope to minimize the risk of attack. Back in a snow-blasted Britain, Pamela remained silent about where he was for security reasons and in turn rarely heard from him. Randolph was soon at his drunken worst, sunbathing while his men trained relentlessly, prompting ugly rumors that they were plotting to knife him once the unit went into action.[22] After dinner he joined boozy all-night sessions of poker and roulette where the stakes were rarely less than £50 a go. By the time the *Glenroy* reached Suez he was £3,000 down (£119,000 today).[23] "Poor Pamela will have to go to work," observed Waugh in a letter to his wife, Laura.[24] Randolph sent a telegram to Pamela which she referred to as the "bombshell," followed by a letter asking her to settle his debts "in the best way possible," suggesting an absurd repayment schedule of £5 or £10 a month to each of the creditors on an attached list. "Anyway, I leave it up to you," he concluded, walking away from his mess, "but please don't tell my mother and father."[25]

Incensed at his recklessness, Pamela was at "breaking point."[26] She had provided a son and heir, run a household on a comparative shoestring and stood by her husband. It was not only the impossibility of paying off the debts or that she knew her marriage was over; it was not just that she had hitched herself to a drunken, offensive adulterer; or that she had been raised to rely on a husband rather than herself: worst of all was that she now knew for sure that she was with child again. She could sell her wedding presents, including her diamond earrings and a couple of bracelets, but that would be nowhere near enough to pay off the debts and support another baby. Nor could she ask her own parents as they did not have the cash and her available dowry had long since gone. Pamela recognized that Randolph needed help that she was not equipped to give. "I was always up against the drinking," she said about deciding to give up on her marriage, and "I simply couldn't cope."[27]

In floods of tears, she weaved her Jaguar through the bomb-scarred streets of London to the offices of the Ministry of Aircraft Production, where Max Beaverbrook was expecting her. Swearing him to secrecy—a sure way to grab the Beaver's attention—Pamela poured out her troubles and asked him to advance two years of Randolph's salary. The seasoned old player saw an opportunity and after a long pause said he would not pay a penny. Pamela was stunned; she had not countenanced the idea of him refusing. It seemed a "little thing to ask,"[28] especially as she had made Beaverbrook young Winston's godfather. Beaverbrook was enjoying toying with a beautiful woman in distress. Eventually he screwed up his face and said, "If you want me to give you a cheque for £3,000 I will do it for you," but as a present and on condition that nothing would go to Randolph. The idea "smelled of danger" as "Max had to have control of the people around him." "I can't do that," Pamela replied.[29] Yet what were her options? After a few moments she changed her mind and accepted the money and the consequences. She would let out Ickleford and take up Beaverbrook's offer to lodge Winston and his nanny at Cherkley so she would be free to work. The work was unspecified but having observed her exceptional hold over important men such as Harry Hopkins and indeed Churchill himself, Beaverbrook calculated that Pamela's spirit of adventure offered exceptional potential for her country and for him. She could lead an independent life but there would be strings attached.

"That was the first realisation that I was totally on my own," Pamela later recalled, "and the future of my son and [me] . . . was entirely dependent on me."[30] That afternoon she returned to Ickleford, wondering what the future might hold but knowing that she would have to play a canny game well beyond her years. Beaverbrook invested in tight-fitting evening frocks, high heels and natty tailored suits to help her in her new role in Britain's desperate struggle to survive. Pamela was conscious of her female powers but neither she nor Beaverbrook could possibly have known how they would turn out to be of such historic importance or how far she would go. Fate intervened once more when she miscarried a few days later.

Pamela did not dwell on her loss—she almost certainly felt relief—and showed a ready business acumen in subletting Ickleford to a Church of England children's home for £3 a week, rendering her a nice £2 profit. She moved into the five-star Dorchester Hotel to share a "bilious-coloured" top-floor room with Clarissa Churchill for £6 10s a week—a comparatively low rate because of the heightened risk of blasts and incendiaries and the deafening roar of gunfire. The Australian prime minister, Robert Menzies, soon invited them to drag their mattresses into the relative safety of the windowless hallway of his ground-floor suite. The lower stories were otherwise occupied by the rich and powerful of London, enticed by the idea that the Dorch's modern steel-reinforced concrete construction would save them from all but direct hits. At the beginning of a raid, Pamela and Clarissa often headed for the art deco foyer to join a galaxy of Cabinet ministers, actresses, prostitutes and "clench-jawed" brigadiers drinking champagne to the accompaniment of a band. Cecil Beaton likened the scene to "a transatlantic crossing in a luxury liner, with all the horrors of enforced jocularity and expensive squalor."[31] When a device fell particularly close one night and the whole building wobbled, a notable gossip columnist threw himself on the floor and everyone looked on at his lack of sangfroid with embarrassment.[32] Pamela continued to dine most nights with the Churchills, although she tried to avoid the "tricky" matter of explaining why she had "suddenly upped, separated myself from my baby and wanted a job in London."[33] As yet they had no idea of her deal with Beaverbrook—or the debt bombshell—and she was relieved to be able to tell them the Minister of Supply had offered her a clerical job on £12 a week.

Pamela was thrilled with this life. "It was a terrible war," she said, "but if you were the right age, the right time and in the right place, it was spectacular."[34] She was happily shot of her husband, her baby and her parents—the three constraints on her freedom. She was admired and respected, and the war had liberated women to lead lives never possible before. Randolph needed someone selfless like Clementine but Pamela knew herself to be cut from different cloth and neither was motherhood her true calling. She decided to take advantage of Randolph's absence to try her hand at politics, traveling up to his constituency to meet voters, even if only as his proxy. The opportunities for more excitement seemed almost limitless and she "wanted to get out and do things."[35] "I was young and headstrong and had no ideas of just being an old-fashioned wife." Striding down the Dorch's plush carpeted landing one spring day in 1941, she found herself thinking: "Here I am, twenty years old, totally free, wondering who will walk into my life."[36]

9

As the heroic bastion of Nazi resistance, London became the sexiest city in the world. It was a "Garden of Eden for women," confirmed the *Time-Life* correspondent Mary Welsh, "a serpent dangling" from every lamp post offering "warm if temporary affections."[1] Another observer spoke of how sex hung in the city air like fog.[2] Fear and *carpe diem* kept inhibitions at bay and sex outside marriage lost its long-standing taboo. While Randolph was besieged by flies two thousand miles away in a sweltering army camp in Egypt, Pamela was free to embark on the "most exciting time" of her life.[3]

Yet the danger was constant and real—even on her trips to see young Winston at Cherkley. Once, on the train returning from Leatherhead to London's Waterloo station, she was bombed twice within an hour. "I was shoved under the seat and somebody fell on top of me [and] all the glass came in."[4] And while the wounded were removed from the carriages another bomb crashed into nearby houses. Such near misses became part of the fabric of life but intensified its every moment. Some of Pamela's friends were among the dozens killed at the Café de Paris off Piccadilly Circus, previously considered safe as it was in a basement. The bombs fell down a ventilation shaft, decapitating the bandleader Snakehips Johnson in mid-song. In the East End, where Pamela regularly volunteered, forty children were buried under rubble when their school was hit, leaving her violently shaking with horror.[5] And yet the carnage intensified the appetite for partying. No one wanted to confront their fears alone. If there was sometimes little to eat, there was plenty of booze to steady nerves and music to drown out the noise. Pamela loathed the dreary routine of her ostensible job at the Ministry of Supply (and quickly gave it up) but lived for the evenings when there were multiple invitations to drinks, dinner or dancing. There was one particular event, though, when patriotic duty called.

Averell Harriman had arrived from America to take charge of the $42 billion ($600 billion today) Lend-Lease military aid program, which Harry Hopkins had encouraged Roosevelt to implement on his return from his much-extended trip to Britain.* So beguiled had Hopkins been by Winston, Clementine and Pamela—and the pluck and glamour of the country they embodied—that many in Washington thought him bewitched by some Churchillian spell. America must urgently do all it could to help Britain, he informed the president, through renting out vital hardware in return for assets rather than cash. When Congress agreed to Lend-Lease in March 1941, it did not amount to a declaration of war on Germany but in effect represented the end of American neutrality and a lifeline to the Brits. Harriman, a dark-haired lothario of vast wealth, was chosen as Roosevelt's special representative to run the program from London. Once again, the Churchills had to "bust a gut" to convert a key American to the British cause and to ensure that he delivered the planes, ships, weapons, food and medicines most urgently needed. Pamela was well aware that virtually no one at this point was more crucial to Britain's survival.

Hopkins instructed Harriman that Pamela was more plugged in than "anyone in England," and was a figure he must cultivate immediately on reaching London.[6] Sure enough, it was only a few days before Harriman first met her at Chequers one Friday night in late March.

---

* In May 2022 President Biden brought in an aid program for Ukraine based on America's 1941 arrangement for Britain.

He spent most of the evening in conversation with Winston, while Pamela assessed the newcomer. Before her was a sexed-up vision of athletic American manhood who looked younger than his forty-nine years, the antithesis of the increasingly blotchy and bloated Randolph. He was the best-looking man she had ever seen and another pivotal American to recruit to her fan club. This time she planned a different approach to that deployed with sallow-faced Hopkins, who was "a dear . . . [but] not a pinup."[7] She knew what to do and was willing to do it—above all, for Winston and her country.

Her chance came a fortnight later, when invited to a dinner of salmon and early season strawberries at the Dorchester in honor of Adele Astaire, sister of the dancer Fred Astaire and wife of Lord Charles Cavendish. (The Dorchester was largely unaffected by rationing as long as its clientele were able to pay.) Harriman, fresh from the barbers, was in high spirits, having just had Roosevelt sign off his first Lend-Lease consignment of cheese, eggs and evaporated milk. It was a surprise to no one that Pamela, shimmering in a skin-tight shoulderless gold lamé dress bought specially for the occasion by Beaverbrook, secured the chair next to him in the private room on the eighth floor. The seating plan had also been engineered by Max, who knew the power of Harriman and the urgent need to find a way to influence him.[8] By the time dessert was served, all was going to plan. Pamela was well into what friends came to call her "mating dance."

The hard-nosed son of a renowned robber baron who founded the Union Pacific Railroad and set detectives on Butch Cassidy and the Sundance Kid, Harriman was expected by Anglophobes in Washington to be more resistant than Hopkins to a Churchill charm offensive. Yet his aloof demeanor and polo-playing lifestyle belied Harriman's insecurities. As a boy he had had to overcome a stammer and was fearful of his disciplinarian father and more recently the scorn of his razor-tongued second wife, Marie. He had grown up dreading being alone but struggling with humor and was known as the ultimate wallflower even at his own parties. For many years he had suffered remorse for not fighting in the First World War and profiting from it through his shipping interests. His fervor for money-making had since waned and he was desperate to atone for his past. In fact, he had badgered Roosevelt so hard to be put to good use in this new global conflict that he had made himself ill with bleeding ulcers. Roosevelt had never been inclined to bring Harriman into his inner circle but recognized that he might make a good envoy to London, where his patrician manner would fit well with the ruling elite.

Roosevelt's emissaries were "looked over very carefully" by the Churchills, Pamela explained. "Who they were; why they were; what they were."[9] A "special welcome" was duly tailored to Harriman's character, starting with a flattering guard of honor and a biplane to whisk him Hollywood-style to see Winston at Chequers. "I was very excited, feeling like a country boy plopped right into the centre of the war," Harriman admitted (although his idea of rural living involved his family's 100,000 square foot mansion at Arden in upstate New York, with forty bedrooms, private power plant and three lakes). Driven by an iron will to win, Harriman had never really done fun. Some thought him boring, others a plodder. Now, in the next stage of his "special welcome," an astonishingly sexy young aristocrat, with glowing milky skin, magnificent curves and the allure of her Churchill status had eyes only for him. Averell, as she already called him, could scarcely resist the way she leaned forward to capture his every word, stroked his forearm with her fingertips and laughed deliciously at his attempted repartee, her tongue pointed erotically behind her teeth. They talked about the war, Churchill, Beaverbrook and Hopkins, and also the feeling in Washington. Averell was astounded at her perception and knowledge but also her curiosity about Roosevelt's thinking. When the bombing started an hour after sunset the party turned out the lights and pulled back the blackout curtains to watch the silhouettes of hundreds of enemy planes against the searchlights patterning the night sky.

Then the planes turned directly toward them, bearing in closer and closer. This was, as Pamela observed, a "very fortuitous" raid.[10] As they watched Selfridges department store succumbing to fire, Averell invited her to his palatial lower floor suite "so we can talk easier."[11] Clarissa looked in vain for Pamela in the lobby. As the bombs whined and crashed, Averell was peeling off that gorgeous golden dress. While the building quivered from the worst raid in London to date and shrapnel rattled down onto the streets, Pamela lay naked in the arms of the man who might be able to bring the horror to an end. Averell was intoxicated by the whole glorious adventure. Sex had never been so thrilling—as Averell remarked later, "there was nothing like a Blitz to get something going."[12] This was a strategic alliance of the highest order that could be vital to helping Winston in saving the country. But it amounted to much more than the act of seduction. Pamela finally had a vocation. Her true war work had begun.[13]

Not long after dawn, Pamela and Averell rose to inspect the damage. Hand in hand, they crunched their way across glass-strewn streets and past raging fires, seeking solace from the shock in each other. The area surrounding the hotel had borne the brunt of the attack, in which more than 450 tons of bombs had blasted the heart of London over nine hours. The Dorchester had suffered a few smashed windows but the shirtmakers' shops of Jermyn Street were wrecked and a vicar had been killed on the steps of his church while beckoning people in to take shelter. Tall townhouses had had their façades ripped clean off, a pair of curtains flapping at an absent window or a stair carpet stranded without stairs. A few cars passed by, the look on their drivers' faces hinting that they had dead bodies on the back seat. Miners drafted in from Wales picked delicately through the rubble, trying to find anyone alive. Scattered across the wreckage were a variety of personal belongings—a bra, a sock, a twisted lampshade. The pair headed toward Downing Street in the spring sunshine to see that Winston's old Admiralty buildings had also been hit, the smell of cordite and rising dust hitting the back of their throats and wetting their eyes. As they crossed Horse Guards Parade they were spotted by Jock Colville hurrying to work. The news spread like wildfire.

Max was one of the first to hear and was ecstatic. Harriman had been in the country three weeks and already he was "compromised." Not only was he supping at Churchill's table, but he was sleeping with his daughter-in-law. From now on, Averell and Pamela took care not to be seen in public, but they were frequently together at Chequers, Cherkley, Ditchley and Stornoway House. Fortunately, Pamela's flirtatious manner with practically every powerful man provided cover for the obvious attraction between them. The secrecy combined with the nightly raids electrified the relationship. As Pamela realized, "in wartime you get straight to the core of people."[14] She immediately started to make the most of her conquest, going far beyond the traditional female role originally envisaged by Beaverbrook. Well versed in what Winston needed to know, she made a mental note (writing things down was too dangerous) and initially passed on to Max (effectively her control officer), then quite soon directly to Papa, anything she gleaned about what the Americans were thinking.

Mutual suspicion at a personal and national level—exacerbated by the rifts of colonial history—meant that there were few free-flowing channels of communication between Washington and London. Yet now Pamela was in a prime position to pick up snippets of high-level American conversation, throw-away comments, stories of Washington politicking, fragments of intelligence and any statistics she could glean. She was also deft at sifting information in the other direction to boost Britain's case for more aid. Beaverbrook "launched her and taught her how to be a catalyst on a hot tin roof," observed Tex McCrary, an American journalist who watched her expertly trawling for useful data. As he put it, "she was inhaling."[15] By virtue of her wits, beauty, name and social expertise she had positioned herself as a vital go-between with Britain's most strategic allies.

"It was very important—these Americans," Pamela pointed out. "As long as they weren't in the war, it was very precarious."[16] Her position was precarious too. She could not let on to Harriman—however close they became—exactly what she was doing. Indeed, she remained keen to keep discussion of her role under wraps until after her death.[17] Subtlety and discretion were key—as was presenting her case artfully. With her help Harriman was translating Britain's most urgent needs into action, persuading his president, for instance, to authorize American ports to repair British warships when the dockyards at home were either bomb-damaged or overrun. Jock Colville marveled at how swiftly Harriman was recruited as a key member of Churchill's circle and a champion of Britain. By ensuring the British received the deliveries they needed when they needed them, Harriman "deserved the golden opinions he won."[18]

There was more. America would remain uncommitted to the fighting until Japan's attack on the U.S. naval base at Pearl Harbor eight months later. In the meantime, the Anglo-American relationship remained fragile and untrusting. Questions kept coming from Washington: was Churchill a drunken has-been as his critics suggested? Could Britain really hold out? Was America wasting money on a hopeless cause? Winston's—and even Hopkins's—assurances carried only so much weight. But now Harriman too was categorical that American aid was being put to good use. He became so zealous in his devotion to the struggle—working from the Harriman Mission at 3 Grosvenor Square—that when he made a brief trip home he also found friends regarding him as "unduly pro-British."[19] Pamela was handling information of huge global significance that could affect millions of lives. Her pillow talk was reaching the ears of leaders and influencing high-level policy on both sides of the Atlantic. Within weeks of Randolph's departure and reaching rock bottom, she had her own astonishing career. No paper qualifications needed.

10

Winston and Clementine Churchill's childhoods had instilled in both of them a worldly approach to sex. They were devoted to each other—Winston did not share other leaders' rampant libidos—but both were born to promiscuous mothers who had broken with the social norms of their day. American-born Jennie Jerome Churchill reputedly sported a small tattoo and bedded some two hundred men, while Clementine's equally energetic mother, Lady Blanche, ran up to ten lovers at a time. Now sex would help to lure Averell into the family and ultimately, it was hoped, help bring America into the war.

Far from trying to stop Pamela's affair with Averell, the Churchills contrived to thrust them together: the national emergency took precedence over all else, including the ruins of their son's marriage. Clementine regularly invited them both to weekends at Chequers or Ditchley, where Winston showed them Alexander Korda's new film *That Hamilton Woman*, about England's most famous mistress, watching it himself twenty times, tears rolling down his cheeks at Lady Emma's luckless end. A few doubt that the Churchills were abreast of the full nature of Pamela's erotic adventures although there were several reports of Averell's nocturnal sorties down the Chequers landing and Pamela herself said they "knew perfectly well."[1] "It was fine with them," she insisted. "They understood how difficult Randolph was."[2] Winston "loved his family deeply," explained one of his private secretaries, Anthony Montague Browne, but "they came second to his purposes."³

The calamitous conditions of 1941 meant that almost any consolidation of Britain's ties to America—up to and including seduction—could be considered an act of patriotism. If Pamela sleeping with the most powerful American in Britain was the best and perhaps only way of prizing out closely guarded thinking on the American side, then so be it. Just as her intimate conversations were a particularly effective means of transmitting Britain's urgent needs to continue the fight. Pamela was not the only Churchill woman to seduce an important American. Having split from her husband, Vic Oliver, Sarah was conducting a discreet affair with the married new U.S. ambassador, Gil Winant, who bore an uncanny resemblance to Abraham Lincoln. Yet Sarah was tortured by self-doubt and, unlike Pamela, was not emotionally equipped to act as the ultimate backchannel between the British high command and the pinnacle of American power. Winant, a devoted supporter of Britain, did not in any case have the same clout in Washington as the man the Churchills referred to as "our Averell." Pamela targeted her attentions well.

An excited Averell told his daughter Kathleen that it was "a unique privilege" to be at the nexus of the fight against tyranny,⁴ and thereafter Pamela relayed to Max that Kathleen was now desperate to come over to London. Pamela's access to her lover was of immense national importance and Max calculated that Kathleen's presence would provide vital cover for her father's affair. He therefore secretly arranged for her to be offered a job with Hearst's International News Service in London and even to pay her salary.⁵ Kathleen arrived in May with a caseload of prized rarities, notably silk stockings, Guerlain lipsticks and Stim-u-dent toothpicks, missing by days an even worse bombing raid than the one of mid-April. More than fourteen hundred had died in a single night and St. John's Church in Smith Square, where Pamela had married Randolph, was reduced rather symbolically to an empty husk. Kathy, an outdoorsy type with aristocratic bearing, knew of Pamela from her *Life* cover and was entranced by her in person as "one of the wisest young girls I've ever met."[6] Pamela had not, of course, benefited from the rigorous education that Kathy had enjoyed at her private boarding school in Virginia but the American soon discovered that she nevertheless knew "everything about everything, political and otherwise."[7]

Pamela strategically befriended the new arrival by organizing visits to a hospital caring for children traumatized by the raids, as well as throwing a party in her honor at the Dorchester. It was a well-honed Churchill formula of exposing important American visitors to the horrors of war but also flattering them with glittering entertainment. As the Churchills had hoped, Kathy was soon writing angry letters to friends and family, railing against Americans who still believed they should "do business with Hitler."[8]

Kathy in turn introduced Pamela to top American correspondents, including Ed Murrow and Charles Collingwood of CBS and Bill Walton of *Time-Life* (who had begged to be introduced to the prime minister's daughter-in-law after hearing she was the most beautiful redhead in London). The reporters gathered at the Dorchester or the Savoy in search of diversion—and information. Pamela was gratified by the respect she was paid by the "boys," impressed as they were by her aura of sex and proximity to power. No doubt she drip-fed them selected tidbits supportive of the British position. Such company was a far cry from her disastrous Season of 1938 but Pamela still felt the derision of her young compatriots. Her supposed friend Sarah Norton noted in her diary that Pamela "irritates me so much. One day I'll hit her."[9] The young men could also scarcely contain their jealousy at her new circumstances, one snorting with contempt that he had "heard she attended all cabinet meetings."[10] Pamela kept a dignified silence but developed a "weakness" for her more appreciative American crowd and conducted flirtatious friendships with practically all of them.

When Averell and Kathy moved into a three-bedroom suite at the Dorchester, Pamela came too. What was going on was clear to many and extremely obvious to Kathy, accustomed as she was to her handsome father's success with women. An old schoolfriend of hers, now a reporter on the *New York Post*, was once sent to interview Averell and had exclaimed afterward to Kathy: "For God's sake, tell your father . . . to wear a gas mask so I can concentrate on what he is saying."[11] Kathy did not raise the subject with Pamela, though, until one Friday when the two women were driving to the country. Finally, she blurted out that she was "not a total fool" and that she had chosen to stay on in London specifically to provide her father with an "alibi."[12]

Averell, whose family was one of the richest in America, was called a "cheap old bastard" by his wife, Marie, but changed the parsimonious habits of a lifetime to pay Pamela's expenses and provide a generous allowance. Max was also expressing gratitude in monetary fashion, particularly now that his newly acquired role as Minister of Supply meant he was dependent on Averell's help with Lend-Lease. "Beaverbrook was using Pam," explained the reporter Tex McCrary, as the bait to lure Harriman to Cherkley, where he could be "worked on."[13] Harriman was only too delighted to be lured. He was sleeping with Pamela, treated as Churchill family and hobnobbing with Winston's most influential political ally. Pamela understood her worth, brutally describing Averell as "a hick from America" who "knew nothing" about negotiating his way around the corridors of power in Britain. "Averell would never have had this close relationship with Winston and Max without me."[14] Her relationship with him was transactional but also hot-blooded. Power was an aphrodisiac for them both and Pamela was more than repaying her debt to Max by providing him with access and a stream of information. "Beaverbrook was a gossip-monger," observed McCrary, "and Pamela was his bird-dog."[15]

Randolph was too consumed with his desire to see action to take an interest in what was happening at home. As no one trusted him in battle he had been transferred out of the Commandos to Cairo, a staging point for the British Empire, as a desk-bound intelligence staff officer. He decided this entitled him to drive around the officially neutral city in a car with a flag fluttering on the bonnet, a privilege normally reserved for full colonels. The Randolph effect was instant. Senior officers turned purple at his insolence and habit of invoking his father's name. Moving into the stained-glass splendor of Shepheard's Hotel, Randolph took up a perch at the American Bar. The soothing tinkle of ice in gin was interrupted only by his outbursts over the notorious slowness of the service. Meanwhile, fashionable women presided over luncheons (unlike in most of London, there was a cornucopia of food) and drinks parties. And when Randolph tired of smart society there were beautiful prostitutes, whom he openly paraded at Madame Badia's *boîte*.

Randolph embarked on an energetic pursuit of Maud Marriott, known as Momo, the wife of a colonel in the Scots Guards and daughter of an American financier. Fourteen years older than Randolph and again resembling Clementine, with dramatic dark eyebrows and huge gray-green eyes, Momo fitted the mold of mother-substitute precisely. She enjoyed Randolph's ardor (and the sensitive information he shared with her) if not his physical attentions, referring to him as the "problem child." He took no pains to disguise this relationship or any other. Indeed, he was still writing rambling emotional letters to Laura Charteris back in Britain and sent her stockings and a red velvet dress. Although he claimed to Pamela that he was slogging away day and night, it was a marvel he got any work done at all.

Randolph's favorite fleshpot was the Mohammed Ali Club—"a very swagger affair," he wrote to Pamela, "to which all the rich Pashas belong"[16]—but which was thick with spies. Edward Stanley once accompanied him but was so appalled by Randolph's loose tongue during a tantrum at a member of the club's staff, he lodged an official complaint.[17] Yet again, arrogance and liquor had got the better of

Randolph and his bandying-around of military secrets caused apoplexy among the security chiefs for whom he was supposed to be working. Word of his disgrace reached Pamela, whose reaction veered from shame to disgust. She heard nothing to persuade her that her marriage was worth saving. When Mary Churchill was wavering over a proposal, Pamela worried that her young sister-in-law was in danger of repeating her own mistake. She rushed over to Chequers to warn Mary off. "Don't marry someone because <u>they</u> want to marry <u>you</u>—but because YOU want to marry them," she pleaded. Mary thought Pamela's intervention patronizing, even if she did eventually see sense and turned her unsuitable suitor down.[18]

Fears of imminent invasion had faded since the Battle of Britain and more shipping was getting through thanks to American patrols in the western Atlantic (likely due to Hopkins's influence). Winston was now a hero for many across Europe as their last hope of salvation from Nazi terror. Yet it had been a humiliating spring. After Dunkirk, the Brits prided themselves on their skills at evacuation but the forced exit from Crete in May, after an airborne German invasion had overwhelmed Allied forces there, had been chaotic and costly. Winston conceived of the idea of sending Averell to Egypt to report on how American supplies could strengthen the British position. Incredibly, he arranged for Randolph to act as Averell's military aide on the trip—reasoning that this would embed the American as his personal representative as well as Roosevelt's—but he must have known the risks. Averell left for Cairo from Cherkley, where he had spent the weekend with Pamela, swimming in Max's heated pool. In his luggage was a letter from Winston to his son that was an exercise in discretion, including a wholesome reference to Pamela making friends with Kathy and planning to share a country cottage with her.[19]

Averell had thrown himself into every aspect of the British war effort, from food to fuel to how the first deliveries of American aircraft were faring in battle (the P-40 fighter turned out to be "no goddam good"[20]). Now, with Randolph at his side, he was to spend a month inspecting British bases across North Africa. During their tour Randolph was delighted by how Averell appeared not only to be fully captive to the Churchill position but, as hoped, saw himself as working as much for Winston as for Roosevelt.[21] Ignorant of his relationship with Pamela and flattered by the attentions of such an important Washington figure, Randolph gushed to his father that Averell had become his "favourite American."[22]

Randolph decided to honor this great ally by chartering a dhow, a beautiful Arab sailing boat with blood-red and white sails, to cruise the Nile by moonlight. A handsome gesture was inevitably marred by Randolph's drinking and gloating about his fling with Momo. Averell hid his distaste, allowing himself to talk only briefly of Pamela's beauty and intelligence. Still unsuspecting, a few days later Randolph gave Averell a letter to take back to Pamela in which he described the American as "absolutely charming" and having spoken "delightfully" about her. "I fear I have a serious rival!"[23] he concluded, but only in jest.

Pamela was content for her husband to remain in Cairo for as long as possible, although the thought of Averell being with him had been unsettling. She and Kathy spent several weekends in the cottage Averell had rented for them in the hills south of London at Beare Green in Surrey, lounging with the young pilots in the local pub and watching with sinking hearts as they left for another mission knowing that some would not return. Over time, the women discovered their differences. Pamela's confidence had grown from the low base of her failed Season just three years earlier but inherited wealth had imbued Kathleen with self-belief from birth (even a Roosevelt daughter, Anna, was struck by her being "so damn self-assured"[24]. Kathy peppered her language with expletives while Pamela had been raised to consider swearing unladylike—although she quickly adopted the salty Americanism "goddam." Pamela went out of her way to avoid conflict, but her new friend relished it. When she wrote a withering piece in *Newsweek* about Adele Astaire, her target screamed at her across a Soho restaurant, calling her a "bitch to end all bitches." Kathy was amused by the reaction, which enraged Adele even more.[25] Kathy was disliked by some of her colleagues for her abrasive comments[26] but knew better than to attack a Churchill in public, even if she was beginning to resent Pamela's sexual success. "These English women may not have my silk stockings," she wrote coyly in her Hearst column, "but they have something else, something I'd like to catch hold of."[27]

As Diana Churchill had discovered, it was not easy to live with another woman who was constantly the center of attention. Kathy thought that all the flattering photographs Pamela had taken of her by Cecil Beaton indicated she must have "a narcissist's complex—not quite—but she sure does fancy herself." She had no idea, of course, that their purpose had almost entirely been for pro-British propaganda. It was not just Kathy who resented Pamela's ascendance. Lady Baillie was "a terribly frustrated bitch," Kathy wrote in her diary, "to be so jealous of someone else having Ave's attentions."[28]

Randolph's connections outranked his recklessness and in September he was promoted to major, becoming director of propaganda at the British Army's General Headquarters in Cairo. Pamela sent him a wifely message of congratulations to which he replied, "Darling, I am so glad that you are hearing good accounts of my work." He finally thought to send Pamela parcels of goodies readily available in the Egyptian capital, such as honey, sugar, jam and sweets. Having barely seen his son since birth, he dispatched some bananas to young Winston, but they arrived hard and green. The little boy was forced to eat them—fresh fruit being such a rarity—and as a result was put off bananas and, for a time, his father.[29] Evelyn Waugh wrote to Randolph from London to sound a note of warning. "I have seen Pamela—her kitten eyes full of innocent fun," he said, "showing exemplary patience with the Americans."[30] Randolph ignored it.

Operation Seduction USA was reaping dividends. Hopkins and Harriman were apparently successfully annexed to the British cause. To most Americans, however, the war thousands of miles away seemed an irrelevance. There was lingering resentment at the 117,000 American troops lost in the First World War (half to combat, the rest to Spanish flu) and millions of German or Italian heritage still felt bound to their mother countries on the other side of the fighting. Irish Americans felt conflicted or hostile to Britain because of its domination of the old country for centuries (Ireland itself remained neutral). America's own hard-fought independence seemed comparatively recent, and many felt keenly what they considered to be rank British condescension. A fierce anti-colonialist, Roosevelt pulled back from the edge of confrontation time and again, refusing to commit American troops to combat. There was much talk of Britain commanding the moral imperative but there was no declaration of war. Britain fought on with unpredictable Russia, since Hitler's invasion in June 1941 the only major ally. The country could survive a little longer but without the might of America it would not win. Finally, after much lobbying by Britain's champions, Roosevelt invited Winston to a secret conference in Placentia Bay, Newfoundland, on August 9. Winston sailed through tempestuous seas with Hopkins at his side, nursing hopes of a breakthrough. Averell was also to join them, to help Winston press Roosevelt for more support. Afterward, Averell wrote to Pamela and Kathy, telling them that the "historic meeting of the great men" had taken place. "It is to be seen whether the seeds sown will bloom."[31] In the end, Winston returned largely empty-handed other than a wordy declaration of aims—known as the Atlantic Charter—for a war that America was still refusing to join.

Pamela did not go to Newfoundland and never met Roosevelt—and yet they knew a lot about each other. Largely paralyzed below the waist from polio, the president still had a roving eye for beautiful women and relished saucy gossip. His cigarette aloft in a long holder at the corner of his mouth, FDR got a "big kick" when Hopkins informed him about Pamela's affair with Averell. Jealous of Winston's mythical status as war leader, he was tickled by the idea of his emissary in London "bedding his ally/rival's daughter-in-law" and eager to know more. Powerful men often recognized something of themselves in Pamela, which was part of her growing legend. Despite being a world apart in education and experience, she and the president were seducers and manipulators—understanding others' weaknesses and strengths, and how to leverage them. Roosevelt of course operated through special envoys backed by the supremacy of the United States; Pamela relied on her wits and sexual allure.[32] Yet she did her homework on her targets exceptionally well, including him. When FDR sent her a signed photograph of himself, she informed him she had placed it next to one of her father-in-law, and that young Winston addressed both portraits as "Grandpapa."[33] Whether true or not, she delighted the American president with the notion that he had imposed himself further into Churchill family life. Roosevelt also called himself a juggler "who did not let his left hand know what the right was doing."[34] Pamela was learning how to work on several different figures at once in different ways, but remain in charge. Others lowered their guard; just like the president, she did not.

One hundred and twelve days after the Placentia Bay meeting, on the somber Sunday of December 7, 1941, the Churchills' inner circle gathered for dinner at Chequers. Pamela, Averell and Kathy were present, as was the security chief "Tommy" Thompson and Ambassador Winant. Depressed that even now America was stalling, Clementine had taken to her bed. Winston held his head in his hands and barely spoke but around nine o'clock his valet Sawyers brought in a radio and switched on the BBC news. There was a lot of static that night but toward the end of the bulletin there was a sudden interruption for an announcement. Everyone stood up, uncertain how to react. They had just been able to make out that there had been an attack on the United States, but where? "Did they say Pearl River?" asked a wide-eyed Thompson. "No," Averell shouted out, "I think it was Pearl Harbor!" The not knowing was unbearable but a secretary rushed in with signals confirming that the Japanese had bombed Pearl Harbor and much of the American fleet based there was damaged or sunk. Once understood, the room erupted. It was possibly the most significant moment of the war and sent out shock waves of possibility. Pamela watched the spectacle of Winston dancing a "jig" in his silk dragon-print dressing gown while Averell stood by the fireplace looking serious but equally relieved. The prime minister hurried out to place an urgent call to Roosevelt, who talked of all "being in the same boat now." The carnage was horrifying but it meant that America was finally in the fight. After months and years of waiting and hoping, "the inevitable had finally arrived," Harriman recalled. "We all knew the grim future that it held, but at least there was a future now."[35] Like the prime minister, who had battled tirelessly for this moment, that night Pamela slept the sleep of the saved. The Americans were coming with all their might and the "war would be won."[36]

11

Pamela's life had become a performance. In January 1942, *Tatler* was discreetly summoned to an airfield to photograph her throwing her arms around Randolph's neck when he came home on leave for the first time in a year. She hastily booked a separate room at the Dorchester and Averell hotfooted it to America, cabling Randolph to pretend he was "bitterly disappointed" to miss him.[1] Pamela thought she could keep up appearances this way for the ten days Randolph was expected to stay. Unfortunately, Winston's political difficulties, including an upcoming vote of confidence in the House of Commons, persuaded Randolph to delay his departure. In constant fear that he would get wind of her "special operation," Pamela dutifully went to watch her husband in the parliamentary debate but was left "squirming" with embarrassment at his extreme rhetoric against Winston's critics. The fact was, it was understandable that MPs were dismayed that America's entry into the war had done little to stem the flow of bad news. Two great battleships had been lost and Rommel had pushed back British forces in the African desert. Winston won the confidence vote, but detractors noted how he lost battle after battle. Most humiliating of all was February's surrender of thirty thousand troops to the Japanese in Singapore which the prime minister—still weakened by a suspected heart attack on a trip to Washington—described as the largest capitulation in the nation's history. Morale was at its lowest since the outbreak of war.

It was surreal when Pamela and Randolph spent one of his first weekends home with Max at Cherkley, only for Averell to join them, even sauntering into their bedroom for breakfast on the Sunday morning. The young woman whose every emotion had once been betrayed by furious blushing was now able to conduct herself with cool detachment, while Averell had always been notoriously cold-blooded. Randolph, oblivious to others, sensed nothing. His reunion with Pamela had, however, descended into increasingly violent acrimony. Stung by criticism from friend and foe alike that he had never seen action from his cushy desk in Cairo, Randolph reverted to his usual coping mechanism of drinking and rowing. His arrogance had already infuriated his constituency association in Preston, which Pamela had nurtured through her twice-monthly visits. The couple argued about money (although he avoided asking where hers was coming from); the way he still kept her awake all night by reading aloud; his continued hostility to his mother; and his fury at Pamela leading an independent life, leaving young Winston at Cherkley with his nanny. "I want you," he yelled, to "be with my son." When Pamela pointed out that the child was also hers, he exploded: "No, *my* son. I'm a Churchill!"[2]

Randolph expected blind obedience—or, as Pamela confided to Kathy, the pasha-level attentions he enjoyed in Egypt[3]—but she would no longer countenance obliging a husband who preferred a "bachelor's life."[4] The Churchills sympathized, telling Randolph to be kinder to his wife, who was "a great treasure and blessing to us all."[5] Indeed, so delighted were they with her devotion to the national interest that they had started paying her a tax-free sum of £500 a year—and would do so for the rest of their lives.

Winston's and Clementine's interventions only made matters worse—Randolph was incensed that while he was posted thousands of miles away his parents favored Pamela's company and were giving her money. And yet, far from ingratiating himself, he continued to enrage them with attacks on the conduct of the war. Mary wrote in her diary that although Randolph claimed to love their father, "he never seems not to say or do something because of any harm it might do to Papa."[6] As ten days' leave stretched into several weeks, family arguments became more "savage, more personal and difficult to contain."[7] Discreet moves were made to dispatch Randolph back to Cairo but secret cables show that he was not wanted there either. One, from the Minister of State in the Egyptian capital on March 7, stated: "No (repeat no) suitable job immediately available. Advise you to keep him."[8]

Despite Pamela's gift for covering up troubles with a playful smile, it was becoming impossible to keep up her pretence and she no longer held back about her loathing for Randolph,[9] confessing she had "no intention of sticking" to him.[10] She even perhaps hoped he would be killed.[11] Kenny Digby rushed up to London, where he retreated into the bedroom at the Dorchester with his daughter for a whispered conference on what was now a full-scale family crisis while an "exuberant and vociferous" Randolph caroused with Evelyn Waugh outside the door. She "hates him so much that she can't sit in a room with him," Waugh noted, and when her father left, she avoided the men to pace "up & down the minute hall." Her fury at Randolph made her look "very pretty & full of mischief."[12]

Whatever her own feelings, Pamela could not countenance the thought of placing more of an emotional burden on Winston by suing for divorce immediately, and it was possibly Clementine who intervened at this point to avoid further trouble. Another secret cable was transmitted to Cairo, formally instructing the Minister of State to issue "definite orders" for Randolph to return at once—whether he rejoined his old regiment, the commandos or the propaganda office was "immaterial."[13] He just had to be got away from his wife.

Randolph finally left on March 26, at which point Pamela threw discretion to the wind and moved with the Harrimans into an apartment on Grosvenor Square. Sarah Norton was just one to consider Pamela "very stupid and naughty" by "living with a man who had a wife in America, whom he had no intention of divorcing."[14] It was now that Winston mentioned that he knew there was talk about what she was up to. After what was clearly a gentle warning about the need for discretion even when engaged in the national interest, he muttered about the "triviality" of such gossip "in the midst of the mighty concerns of war" before dropping the subject for good.[15] Word had indeed got out about the affair—if not what lay behind it—and Pamela was blamed rather than Averell. When the Duchess of Devonshire invited him to Lismore Castle in Northern Ireland, she refused to allow him to bring her along.[16]

Now that America was officially at war, thousands of often wealthy Americans vied with each other in search of the ultimate adventure of living in London and to be inspired by Churchill's defiance. Their money, status and confidence did not always endear them to the locals, who started to grumble about the Yanks being "overpaid, oversexed and over here." So many congregated around Grosvenor Square—now known as Little America—that Pamela believed herself the only British woman living there. She was accused of becoming Americanized, having begun to tell the time American fashion—such as a "quarter of one"—and "writing someone" rather than "to" them. Averell was no longer the only American she was sleeping with. Of the multitude of attractive Americans in town, she as the fabled Pamela Churchill could take her pick. There was strategic purpose in her selection—each one was a man with clout in the war effort and soon she had developed an astonishing collection of bedfellows. Nonetheless, when Averell fell seriously ill with paratyphoid Pamela devoted herself to nursing him. He never forgot her tenderness or the way she tracked down oranges and lemons from American forces' supplies and enlisted the chef at Claridge's to make him a special nutritious soup. Never had the all-powerful but lonely American known such care.

Randolph's return to Cairo was essential but mercifully brief. To his fellow officers' relief, he soon left to join the Special Air Service with some of his friends from the now-disbanded No. 8 Commando, finally to operate behind enemy lines. Even Clementine was surprised at the depth of Pamela's indifference to him putting himself in such danger. "She feels all is for the best," Clementine informed Winston.[17] In May 1942, Randolph played a minor role in an SAS raid on Benghazi, deep in enemy territory in Libya, with the aim of blowing up two ships. The mission was a failure, but he sent home accounts of holding out in a house and emerging with Tommy guns and handfuls of grenades. This derring-do thrilled his father, and in her friendliest letter for a year Pamela told Randolph that Winston was "terribly proud."[18]

After the Benghazi raid, the car Randolph was traveling in collided with an army truck and he was left with crushed vertebrae, requiring him to be placed in an iron brace. News that Randolph was to be invalided home in July created a kerfuffle in London and a "rapid shift around" of sleeping arrangements.[19] Pamela moved into a temporary abode on Park Lane loaned for the emergency by Sarah Churchill (who was privy to the affair), who in turn took her place at the Harriman flat in Grosvenor Square.

His much-longed-for taste of action—however cursory—had not improved Randolph in the flesh. As soon as Pamela set eyes on her husband—his huge gut straining his army belt and his skin covered in boils—she had to turn away. Pamela "can no longer bear the sight of Randolph," reported a friend.[20] His hopes of a hero's welcome and a compliant wife also met the harsh reality of hearing himself described as "Mr. Pam."[21] Pamela was being feted both by Americans and by Winston (he often summoned her to his side at crucial moments) while the bloviating Randolph felt unfairly deprived of his right to be made a minister like his brother-in-law Duncan Sandys, who was Financial Secretary to the War Office. Randolph deluded himself, ignoring how his conduct rendered any such appointment impossible.

At White's he found the talk even less to his taste. Pamela's affair with Averell was evidently common knowledge and he a renowned cuckold. It is difficult to overestimate the rage he felt at Pamela humiliating him with a man he admired. Stoked by alcohol and grievance, he stormed back to his wife. Rumors soon circulated that he had vented his fury on her physically[22]—even intimates of the Churchill family talked of hearing about Randolph's "beastliness." Pamela never publicly mentioned any assault—although she did describe her husband as "rough and cruel,"[23] as well as "unbalanced and horrible"[24]—but then she was of a generation for whom admitting to a violent marriage cast shame on the wife. What is clear is that there was now a well-established pattern to Randolph's behavior.

Nor did Randolph's eruption end there. He rampaged around to his parents' quarters at the Annexe and in volcanic mood accused them of condoning Pamela's adultery with Averell under their roof and sacrificing his feelings for what they deemed the national interest.[25] "Not only did these events destroy my parents' marriage," young Winston reflected later, but they had a "devastating" impact on Randolph's relationship with his father for the rest of his life.[26] Most disturbing of all was when he threatened to put the entire Anglo-American alliance at risk by going public with the affair. He wanted, Pamela later wrote, to take revenge by causing "harm to people in high places."[27] So "violent" did the row become that Clementine, fearful that Winston might have a seizure, had Randolph removed and instructed her staff that she was never again to be left alone with her son.[28] The stakes for the conduct of the war could scarcely have been higher.

Randolph's threats wreaked untold damage on Winston's already low morale and physical strength. Beaverbrook was summoned to try to limit the political fallout.[29] The scale of the crisis frightened Pamela and she took his advice to try to mollify Randolph. She brought young Winston to live with her in her own apartment on the top floor of 49 Grosvenor Square, where the lease was in Max's name even if Averell paid the £652 annual rent plus a yearly allowance of £3,000 via Beaverbrook's account at the Royal Bank of Canada. (Between both men, all the debts had been settled, leaving her free to enjoy the money for herself.) Averell also gave her a car and a highly prized petrol ration card.

When Pamela remonstrated with Randolph over the damage he was causing and pointed to his own infidelities, he walked out, telling her the marriage was a failure and that he would not be back. Even now, she went through the motions of trying for a reconciliation for the sake of her father-in-law. She failed. Plucking up courage, she went to see Winston in the Cabinet Room to tell him she and Randolph planned to divorce, although nothing would be done until the end of the war. Winston replied that he recognized the marriage was "not any good for you both, so I don't want that for you. You have my permission."[30]

The rift between parents and son reverberated throughout the family. Clementine took Pamela's side but while Mary was "furious with Randolph for causing such mayhem and misery" she also claimed that all three sisters were "indignant" at Pamela's adultery.[31] While this may have been a wishful interpretation—given Sarah's helpfulness in lending her flat to Pamela—the rows brought dark family undercurrents to the surface. Mary felt "bitter" at the way that Randolph had always been favored in the past simply because he was a man[32] and that it was Pamela who now enjoyed an elevated status with Winston that seemed to supersede her gender. Sarah also wished that her father was as "crazy" about her as he was his daughter-in-law. This was a family where the briefest display of Winston's godlike benediction was treasured like moondust. "My love & admiration of Papa is almost a religion to me," Mary admitted. "I sometimes feel I cannot hold the emotions I have for him."[33] Watching Pamela blossom into not only a political player at Winston's side but also a figure of impossible glamour had left Mary "miserable," a "clod" dismayed by her dull wardrobe and unkempt hands.[34] Eventually, she confided that because her father loved Pamela so much, she felt an "unworthy but very real stab of jealousy."[35] She tried insisting to her parents that they should not "make out she's a poor pathetic little lily . . . maltreated by Randolph." Spam—as Mary came to call her—had "many gracious & civilised qualities" and was a supreme operator but she was unable to "shed many tears over the breakup."[36] Randolph had wanted a son; Pamela "glitter & fun and a new milieu—both have got what they wanted & now there is an end."[37]

Marie Harriman, who had once caught the eye of Al Capone, chewed gum, danced the Charleston and, as only a wealthy woman can, enjoyed a "merry irreverence for money."[38] Never one to be intimidated by her husband's rather forbidding character, she liked to barrack Averell for being "such a stuffed shirt!" If anything, he was a little afraid of her. An authority on Impressionist and post-Impressionist art, she owned the Marie Harriman Gallery on East 57th Street in New York and on their honeymoon in Paris in 1930 she had Averell buy Van Gogh's *White Roses*. Eyesight problems had prevented her from accompanying her husband to London. Not that she was lonely back home. She kept company with a bandleader called Eddy Duchin, the "Cocktail Casanova," the widower of her best friend who had died in childbirth in 1937. She had even brought Eddy's baby son Peter, who called her "Ma," to live with her at Arden alongside her own two children by her first marriage. "I don't think Averell probably ever minded about Marie having an affair," Pamela speculated. "How could he?"[39]

Mouche—the Harrimans' resident nanny—was dragooned into

action to send Kathy dresses, stockings and makeup. Soon she was dispatching similar parcels to Pamela from a list entitled "Pam's Wants." Marie became suspicious but was content to ignore what was going on in London while appearances were maintained. After Randolph found out, pointed innuendos began to appear in the American press, leading Marie to fire off a cable to her husband: "KEEP YOUR AFFAIRS CLEAN AND OUT OF THE PAPERS OR YOU WILL BE FACING THE MOST COSTLY DIVORCE IN THE HISTORY OF THE REPUBLIC."[40] Averell vowed to end it with Pamela but his good intentions gave way to his passion. Harry Hopkins became alarmed, fearing damaging stories blaming the president's envoy for breaking up the marriage of the son of the prime minister.[41] Averell was offered high-level jobs in Washington—with even the role of Secretary of State dangled as a possibility—to lure him away from temptation. Yet the man whose unmitigated ambition had literally made him ill in the past turned down such prizes to stay with Pamela.

Finally, Averell was given no choice. The president summoned him to Washington to inform him he was to go immediately to Moscow—fifteen hundred miles from London—as American ambassador to the Soviet Union. Unable to face the intense emotions of the moment—and fearing his own weakness—Averell wrote to Kathy to ask her to break off the affair for him. "Help Pam straighten herself out—poor child," he told her. He then instructed Kathy to burn the note or keep it locked away.[42] Dreading a devastating scandal, she kept it secreted in a jewelry box for the rest of her life.

12

Pamela's magnetic power was too much for Averell. When he returned to London he snatched the chance to see her again and she was by his side as he and Kathy were driven to their flight to Moscow on the "dark day" of October 13, 1943. Started as a strategic alliance, their liaison had grown to be much more, but Averell had paid a heavy price. He was being dispatched to a capital where he would never enjoy the romance, access and sense of personal importance that had thrilled him in London. Building a relationship with Stalin—while obviously crucial to the chances of victory—promised to be arduous and dour even with Kathy as company. Afterward, Pamela returned home for a "quiet cry" and to prepare the Harriman apartment as Colonel Jock Whitney would be moving in a few days later.[1] Jock, a high-ranking intelligence officer attached to the Office of Strategic Services (the American counterpart to Churchill's Special Operations Executive), had briefly been a lover the previous year when he had arrived in London three months after marrying his second wife, Betsey Cushing. Soon he would be again. It was extremely convenient that he was close to key OSS figures such as Allen Dulles (who would go on to head the CIA). Within twenty-four hours she was chatting over lunch with Jock and arranging his supplies of champagne. Pamela was not "very sad" for very long.[2] She had work to do.

The affair was never serious, but Jock had become a genuine friend as well as another key American asset. Behind the super-confident façade, he was a shy man who found Pamela a nonjudgmental listener. Combining a warm heart with a huge bank balance, Jock was already paying her a stipend (on top of Averell's allowance) but he also sought to protect her from Randolph. She had heard little of her husband since he had made a half-hearted attempt at a rapprochement in May, but Jock warned that he was back in town and had already drunk the White's bar dry. Soon afterward, a message arrived that Randolph had gone to her flat to visit young Winston and, not trusting him to behave, she left Jock and dashed back. Winston senior had been rhapsodizing to Randolph about Pamela's mothering skills—perhaps in an attempt to defuse tensions—relating that she took "infinite pains" with her son.[3] Randolph remained unconvinced. By the time she burst into the apartment he was interrogating the three-year-old, who had not seen his father for so long he had no idea who he was. Randolph jibed Pamela for not having taught Winston to read and bristled when the boy responded to an instruction with the Americanism, "OK, Butch," demanding he say "Yes, Father" in a cut-glass English accent instead. Before leaving, Randolph announced that he would return the next day. He never came or bothered to phone for another month. When he did reappear, he took the poor child to an interminable lunch at the Ritz.

Winston and the accoutrements of nursery life were rarely in evidence at the flat, though he would sometimes be allowed to greet Pamela's guests before bed. Almost entirely raised in the company of adults, the boy was precocious. Even Max confessed to have been shocked when his godson asked if he would have a cocktail with him. Most evenings since taking up residence with her son at 49 Grosvenor Square—or the Attic, as she called the cozy top-floor apartment with its peach-colored walls, posies of flowers and dormer windows—Pamela gathered small groups of useful Americans and only occasionally an infatuated Brit whom she considered of less strategic value. She had started these soirées before Averell left but now ramped them up to almost every night of the week to glean as much intelligence as possible. Handpicked guests included an array of generals such as George Marshall, Dwight Eisenhower and Ira Eaker, top-flight diplomats and officials over from Washington's State Department and the Department of War plus media moguls (including her old Canadian admirer George McCullagh of the *Globe and Mail*). "There isn't one I'm not on the most intimate terms with!"[4] she liked to boast. Yet discretion was rigidly maintained. No one could count on getting lucky.

If tempers frayed, she skillfully intervened to smooth and soothe, never allowing herself to be moody or to utter a word of complaint. Pamela was usually the only woman—these were men, with wives or girlfriends several thousand miles away, who felt the pressures of war without female support. Why would she invite competition for their favors? And, most of all, their information? One exception—Janet, a high school English teacher married to Ed Murrow—endured an uncomfortable evening, noting that "Unless you were important in some way, you weren't very welcome."[5] She did not come again. The important male guests treasured the five-course dinners of oysters, salmon, beef, chocolate and whisky. Some of the British felt uncomfortable at such largesse: food was elsewhere so scarce that a woman seen throwing breadcrumbs to the swans on the Serpentine had been arrested for waste.[6] The relentlessness of four years of war had reduced many to unwashed exhaustion in drab rationed clothing. Yet here was Pamela, her skin and hair glowing and table overflowing. The food her butler served largely came in special consignments from the U.S. Air Force; the couture was provided by Max or Averell.

Eyes sparkling, she laughed appreciatively at her guests' wit, the bawdier the better, and squeezed the hand of the man of the moment in an affectionate, conspiratorial manner. In such a seductive yet understated setting, the conversation around the candlelit table was relaxed and—this being the point of it all—extremely forthcoming.

Edwina Mountbatten's salon on Chester Street might have been grander in style but was far less consequential. There was something slightly homely about Pamela's—the men joked and teased almost as if family—but the intent could not be more serious. At just twenty-three, she was handling the complex and sometimes conflicting emotions, fears and ambitions of some of the most powerful men in the Free World and helping to shore up the Anglo-American alliance. When the sirens began and the nearby Hyde Park guns signaled the approach of enemy aircraft, newly arrived Americans shook with fright, yet Pamela continued talking "casually and cheerfully" even as the bombing reached a crescendo and shrapnel pelted the Attic roof.[7] After coffee a call would sometimes come in to her number—Mayfair 5975—from Downing Street and she would say, "I have to go. He's calling me now." An armored car would then whisk her off to the prime minister (through the raids if necessary) and over a late-night game of bezique she would pass on everything she had gleaned on American political thinking and military priorities.[8] Only a handful of people knew the exhausting service she was performing night after night; outside her gilded world it looked like she was just living the high life while others suffered.

In many ways, Averell had left at an opportune time. The war was entering a new stage and other powerful Americans needed to be wooed to British thinking. The dinners were one technique, but an individual approach was also required. First up was Ed Murrow, whose nightly broadcasts to millions of American homes famously began with the words "This is London." Feted by Roosevelt and courted by Winston, he had arguably done more than any to wean American opinion off isolationism. Now there were new tensions across the Atlantic, not least over the question of whether America should focus its might on the Pacific or on the European theater. Pamela had known the driven but rather shy Murrow for a couple of years, but always in a crowd. To enlist his further support, she had persuaded Brendan Bracken, Winston's influential new Minister of Information, to offer Ed the job of editor in chief of the BBC but he had turned it down.[9] It was time to take a different tack.

At thirty-five, Ed looked like a younger Averell, if a little rougher-hewn. (Pamela's favorites were of a type—masculine, dark-haired, tall, not a blond pretty boy among them.) The similarities mostly ended there. Having paid his way through college by washing dishes, Ed scarcely disguised his contempt for the older man born to wealth. Prone to mood swings, he was charismatic but cultivated an aura of mystique. He fueled himself with gallons of coffee and constant cigarettes—when making love, he let the ash drop on the pillow—and some said his finger was never far from the self-destruct button. Success had elevated him to a glamorous household name able to buy pinstripe suits from Savile Row, if not to escape the discomfort felt by someone of humble birth hobnobbing at the Connaught Hotel or stately homes. Although a fan of Winston's wartime leadership, his politics were to the left and he was a stern critic of privilege and flummery. Yet when Pamela, daughter of a lord and member by marriage of a ducal dynasty, turned her big sapphire eyes on him, Ed was powerless to resist. Pamela "sort of cried" on Ed's shoulder about Averell leaving.[10] Soon she was in his bed.

She offered him personal proximity to the summit of power. He provided her with another vital American alliance. Ed was "full of complexes"; he had worn hand-me-down clothes as a child in Polecat Creek, North Carolina, while his father worked as a locomotive driver. "He was conscious that everything he had, and had done," she said, "was through his own making."[11] Such an upbringing had left him with more than a ferocious work ethic. Via the King James Bible, his Quaker mother had instilled in her son not only a felicity with the richness and rhythm of language but a niggling sense of guilt. Ed fell fast and deep for Pamela, but his conscience was not going to leave him in peace.

Ed encouraged her to question the tenets of the Conservative Party and class-bound notions of fairness that had hitherto defined her worldview. "You're spoiled," he told her, "and you don't understand what real life is"[12]—a failing he tried to overcome by taking her to eat in pubs "like normal people." Pamela's politics shifted. Never again would she accept that things had to stay the same. Ed's "extremely liberal" views on equality—as she called them—had a "big influence" and she took a greater interest than ever in Roosevelt's Democratic administration. She also learned how, back in 1930, Ed had helped remove a bar on black delegates attending National Student Federation of America conventions, awakening an early interest in racial justice. She watched him extend the same courtesies to postmen as he did to potentates, in contrast to Averell whose manner verged on "feudal." "If it hadn't been for the war," she reflected, "I would never have seen a whole other side of life."[13] She listened to Ed talking of Marcus Aurelius, Roman emperor and Stoic philosopher who believed in a simplicity of living and in approaching life "not as though one had a thousand years but as if each day was the last." Far from resenting this didacticism, she was excited by it. "He was totally different from anybody I'd ever met."[14]

By early 1944 they were discussing his divorce so that they could marry. For all his class-warrior credentials Ed was in a hurry to go places; she thought her skills and connections could help him get there quicker. Sensible Janet, with her homespun looks and calm practicality, sensed what was happening but was at a loss as to how to fight back against such a siren. "There was an aura about [Pamela] because of Churchill," a friend remembered.[15] Many years later Charles Collingwood, another CBS war correspondent, explained that the Pamela effect went far beyond her eminence, however. She had "the most beautiful of the famous English complexions . . . Absolutely strawberries and cream. Figure magnificent . . . Ed was knocked off his feet by this absolutely glorious . . . young woman."[16] Janet hoped it was a passing infatuation but there were signs it was not. Pamela lifted the spirits of a natural melancholic and Ed afforded Pamela—not his wife—the honor of sitting beside him in the studio as he broadcast to the American nation. It cannot be said that she took pains to conceal her triumph or to mitigate Janet's humiliation. But then neither did Ed.

Of course, the affair delighted the Churchills and Max (who invited them to weekend together at Cherkley). Both Pamela and her new lover were in the business of explaining Britain to America. Carefully selected information no doubt found its way into Murrow's radio broadcasts. As the Churchills had hoped, his genius for bringing the "Nazi menace across the ocean and into the homes of Americans" helped to muster U.S. public opinion behind Roosevelt's decision to privilege the war against Hitler over the fight against the Japanese.[17] Similarly, Ed began to broadcast on the BBC, explaining American politics and peculiarities to a British audience. Pamela was also now promoting the U.S. viewpoint—to the extent that Max even accused her of turning "anti-British." She was outraged, although she conceded that she had become "very American."[18] It was surely true that her loyalties were increasingly blurred.

Ed may have bowled over Pamela in a way that no one had before but he had one major flaw. It was not his lack of wealth—Pamela was sufficiently enthralled by his fame to overlook this—but his habit of flying into a rage at the mere thought of her seeing another man. And she was running a whole network of them. When Jock Whitney left London early in 1944, Pamela picked up with the unshowy thirty-nine-year-old wunderkind Major General Fred Anderson, commander of the American bombing forces coming into their own in the lead-up to D-Day. The liaison, described by Bill Walton as "solid politics," yielded yet more strategic gold. Pamela used her position to help deal with a potentially serious Anglo-American dispute on tactics ahead of the Normandy landings. Anderson heavily favored daylight precision bombing to minimize civilian casualties while the RAF promoted night-time area bombing as safer for air crews. "Winston used Pamela to plant [British] ideas on the American generals," explained Walton, now one of her closest friends. And then Winston, knowing she was sleeping with Anderson, would quiz her on their reaction.[19]

Max also wanted access to this new conduit of information, and invited Pamela to Cherkley with Anderson on numerous occasions. After a huge explosion on one visit seemed to lift the house off the ground, she wrote in the visitors' book: "bomb fell at 4:40 a.m." Underneath, the lovestruck Anderson wrote "ditto."[20] Her simultaneous dalliance with Britain's funny and ruthless Chief of the Air Staff Charles "Peter" Portal can hardly be coincidental. Pamela denied sleeping with Portal, but his wife, Joan, was certain she had, and "despaired" of how her husband was behaving while she was away in the country.[21] The top airmen from both sides of the Atlantic were in thrall to Pamela, the ultimate go-between.

Competition for her favors was intense. When she booked into the London Clinic in November 1943 to have her tonsils removed, her bedside resembled a high-level convention of the Anglo-American alliance. Dozens of well-wishers came bearing gifts including "a million" flowers, honey, books, eggs, pears and grapes. Anderson arrived (with ice cream, an impossible luxury, but then the U.S. Air Force had a reputation for glamour) and so did Ed—fortunately at different times. Admiral Harold Stark, commander of American naval forces in Europe, sent the "sweetest note" and General Ira Eaker, commander of American Army Air Forces in Britain, "sort of looked after me."[22] Only Randolph failed to turn up, claiming to be "too busy."[23]

Being confined to a hospital bed for a few days—and even a minor hemorrhage—did not keep Pamela from her work. She quizzed her visitors for information and kept a close eye on the news, including Winston's latest Cabinet reshuffle, her blood-spotted bedsheets covered with the morning papers. In sickness as in health, the circus rarely stopped. Young Winston could barely conceive of having his mother to himself. When the raids picked up again, he was moved out to a country cottage with his new nanny, Bobbie, and when Pamela came to visit after her operation, his first question was "Who have you brought with you?" He refused to believe her when she said, on this occasion, no one.[24] While she had been in the clinic, he had gone to spend a day with his father but he had been terrified and it had not been a success. That night, the little boy woke up sobbing, "You went and left me."

Eager to help Pamela in her work, in early 1944 Winston and Clementine offered to have him stay with them at Chequers. There was by now so little winter fuel, however, that even the prime minister's residence was icy. Clarissa Churchill, who was convalescing there after having her appendix removed, slept in her fur coat. Young Winston developed bronchitis and Pamela came down from London wearing green sequins in her hair to perform what Clarissa cynically called her "mother-act."[25] The boy was delighted to have her attention and pleaded with her to go for a walk in the woods with him on his tricycle. Chatting away, Pamela noticed how living with his grandparents—even in the thick of preparations for D-Day—was bringing him out of his shell. His grandfather even made time to stage exciting train crashes for him on his model railway. To have his mother with him too would be perfection. As they were returning to the house, they met an empty car arriving and young Winston turned to Pamela with glee: "Perhaps that has come to take the generals off and then you can have tea with me." Alas, as soon as they came through the door, Jock Colville scurried over to Pamela to announce she was needed by the prime minister. The boy had his tea alone. Hours later she was released to put him to bed and read him a story, but she fretted: "Poor lamb . . . I do hope I am not neglecting him."[26]

Pamela had no such qualms about Ed, who struggled to contain his jealousy. In March 1944 when Pamela was ill again, he climbed the six floors to the Attic to deliver her two Hershey bars because the lift did not respond. At the top he found out why. An aide to Anderson was holding open the doors to deliver Pamela a carton of prime steaks. Ed exploded, pretending to be exercised about American-bought meat being diverted in this way but in fact he could not bear that he had been outclassed by a rival. In the ensuing row, they agreed to part company. The separation did not last but the memory of Ed's rage did. There was a controlling side to him that began to chafe.

During the war years, Pamela disappeared on several occasions because she was unwell. Most of her absences are explained by illness but not all. It would have been disastrous to have an illegitimate child, but birth control was either basic, such as rudimentary condoms, likely to cause infection—early forms of the diaphragm—or the unreliable coitus interruptus. Abortion was illegal but common because of the huge number of unwanted pregnancies during the sexual frenzy of wartime. The possibility of conceiving was a constant danger of which Pamela would have been all too aware as an occupational hazard, one that had to be dealt with if necessary.

"As you know I don't like women,"[27] Pamela had once told Averell, but there were exceptions if they had something serious to say. One evening she invited to dinner Betty Gibbs from the embassy in Washington who Pamela believed was the first woman to be given diplomatic rank. She also responded to other professional women who had succeeded in male fields, such as the American war reporters Mary

Welsh and Martha Gellhorn. Another exception was Kick Kennedy, who had left London in 1939 but by summer 1943 was back to work for the Red Cross—and to see her old beau, Billy Hartington. Kick was astonished by the transformation in Pamela, now judging her to be the "glamour girl of London"[28] and a power in the land rather than the stupid, fat butterball of the 1938 Season. Pamela decided in turn that she would not judge Kick—considered the nicest of the Kennedys—by her father's evident faults.[29] After five years of waiting, in May 1944 Kick defied her mother to marry Billy. Pamela admired her pluck and comforted her when her brother Joe Jr. was killed in action. The two women became closer still when, after just four months of marriage, Billy was shot dead by a sniper in Belgium.

No one had been surprised to hear of Pamela's break-up with Randolph; more unexpected was her continued closeness to her parents-in-law. Randolph was convinced Pamela must have mesmerized his father and raged that she was enjoying the perks of being his daughter-in-law while having failed to be a "satisfactory wife."[30] Both Winston and Clementine had become dependent on Pamela. Within hours of Averell leaving for Moscow, Clementine phoned her up to commiserate on his departure, saying she knew how "very sad" Pamela must be. Without mentioning Randolph, she asked Pamela to help with forthcoming official duties including visiting the king and a service at Westminster Abbey.

Pamela played a key role at many pivotal moments. It was she who was called in to support Winston at Chequers on the exceptionally tense Friday night of the Allied landings in Sicily in July 1943. They marked the first major engagement of U.S. troops in Europe, a precursor of D-Day and a test of Allied unity as the mission had initially met strong reluctance from the Americans. Now it was going ahead—Pamela had no doubt helped the prime minister win over Washington—but early reports were hardly auspicious. The first paratroopers were supposed to land at midnight but strong winds were delaying the operation. Pamela thought it best to bring out the cards for bezique, and the distracted prime minister was soon losing heavily while one report after another told of bad weather blowing aircraft off course and high seas making amphibious landings treacherous. Papa talked gloomily of the responsibility he bore for the lives of the thousands of young men involved. It was often over cards that he was his most candid, but the fears of a blood-soaked failure made him a tetchy companion needing skillful handling. Finally, at four in the morning a secretary rushed into the room announcing: "The winds have died down. The landings are taking place."[31]

It soon became clear that the Allies would successfully take Sicily—victory was declared by August 17—but the divide between British and American views became ever wider. Winston wanted to drive on up the Italian mainland to force Italy out of the war altogether but Washington preferred to divert resources to the future Operation Overlord landings in Normandy. Pamela would have her work cut out in projecting Winston's views now that Uncle Sam had taken the driving seat. Yet when American commanders came to Britain—thus entering Pamela's orbit—they usually became more amenable. When asked years later whether there were tensions with General George C. Marshall, Chief of Staff of the U.S. Army, over the timing and location of the Second Front, she thought not. He had come to London "quite often" and not only "got on very well with the PM" but had of course been a much-favored visitor at the Attic.[32] She had found him "charming."[33] An Anglo-American compromise was found, and D-Day postponed until the British were broadly ready and willing.

Another recruit to Pamela's stable in 1944 was Bill Paley, Ed's womanizing boss at CBS who was now working as deputy chief of the

Psychological Warfare Division under General Eisenhower. The brief relationship, although warm to a point, was business-like. She did not love him; she respected him but feared his ruthlessness. "Very few people really impress Pamela," Richard Holbrooke, one of her closest political allies, remarked later. "She said she thinks Bill Paley is the toughest man she knows."[34] Duty called, however, and Pamela did her homework. Paley was a Jew who had spent his life trying to penetrate the American establishment—she noted how he embroidered tales to make himself sound more interesting[35]—but was barred by the elite WASP (White Anglo-Saxon Protestant) country clubs back home. He had a thirst for acceptance and access to power; Pamela needed information and to extend her American influence, so she summoned him to the Attic. "Pamela's parties were very, very good," Paley said, besotted with his aristocratic new friend. "She was extraordinary in the way she took care of her men." Pamela sourced his liquor and his cars and showered him with invitations to the fanciest salons. "Anything you need or want, please call me," she told him.[36] Enthralled and grateful, he too became a passionate defender of the British cause through his radio empire, and thereafter also helped to bankroll her lifestyle.

Pamela denied the affair—although Paley's wife, Dorothy, knew all about it—perhaps to avoid further problems with Lady Mary Dunn, who had long been in love with him. When Lady Mary encountered them at Claridge's she noted Pamela's "very proprietary" manner. She was "filled with jealousy," not least at the way Pamela was looking "exquisite," and she came away feeling "sour as a bit of old rhubarb."[37] Paley, for his part, enjoyed teasing his lovers for years by confessing he had slept with Pamela.

What is remarkable is that she not only avoided scandal but remained friendly with these men for the rest of their lives, their shared experience of the horrors of war forging an unspoken but unbreakable tie. Ed talked about the Blitz as being "something no one should go through"[38] but Pamela's men recognized her courage in sticking it out and loved her for it (incensing their wives back in the safety of America because they could not compete). Her lovers might express hurt or disappointment—such as Jock Whitney complaining when he left London "you might have written me a line"—but she won them around.

Pamela believed her confidence to sleep around in traditional male fashion stemmed from the fact that she was accustomed to being alone. Most women then depended on men and after Randolph she no longer would. She was in love with Averell but never thought she would spend her life with him. "There was really no sense of faithfulness involved. I was totally free," she said, to sleep with whomever she deemed necessary and she did not worry about other people's feelings, believing "the only person who would get hurt . . . is myself."[39] As for the wives at home—well it was wartime and they were distant figures she had never met apart from Janet Murrow, whom she did not rate.

Jealousy was unavoidable—except, it seems, for Pamela. For her, total war suspended ordinary rules. It was her job to keep all the plates spinning and she could not afford to be sentimental. "I see many people . . . but I have the satisfaction of not looking forward to one date more than another," she once said like a true professional.[40] Pamela was juggling many and competing relationships with powerful older men, but she called the shots.

Pamela was hell-bent on even more adventure but Clementine quickly stamped on her idea of training to become one of the women flying planes from factories to airfields. Her daredevil driving style and poor head for figures made it distinctly unwise and anyway, her special talents were needed elsewhere. Brendan Bracken had come up with another means of spreading her intelligence net. Since autumn 1943 Pamela had been running the new Churchill Club at Ashburnham House, close to the Palace of Westminster, for American servicemen in search of a cultured evening's entertainment. The club offered lectures and concerts, and Pamela pulled in every star she knew—and soon she knew many—from poets T. S. Eliot and Cecil Day Lewis to the actors Clark Gable (star of *Gone With the Wind* and now flying combat missions for the U.S. Army Corps), David Niven (who was training British commandos), and Jimmy Stewart (copilot of American bombers). They all dropped in and sometimes came back to the Attic for drinks or dinner. No one turned down an invitation from Pam Churchill. So many made their way up the fine staircase to the club rooms on the first floor that General Eisenhower found himself having to help out in the kitchen.[41] Even new rounds of bombing did little to keep people away. At one particularly "noisy" evening in October 1943 a six-inch piece of shell came crashing through the window. It was bad form not to keep calm and carry on.

However enticing the cultural program, there was no doubt who was the main attraction. One American correspondent compared her to "honey drawing flies . . . Every man in London was attracted by her."[42] Elie Abel, a GI who later wrote a book with Averell, confirmed that the "main sport was just gazing on Pamela."[43] She laughed with the men and patted them on the arm. Her come-hither style and tight-tight skirts made her appear available even when she was not. For the right men at the right time, though, she was. She found out their thinking, their fears and sometimes their next moves even before they did. As Walton put it: "The information you could pick up there! The room would be filled with generals, captains and majors, all of whom were mad for Pamela."[44] "A lot of people were . . . in love with me," she conceded, but her chief motive was patriotic and she did not "give the time" to those who were not useful to her.[45]

Pamela's strategic sex life is now recognized by scholars of diplomacy and war as "politically significant."[46] She is considered a master of the game, one that muted the distinctions between loyalty to Washington and to London, creating a supreme and (relatively) integrated war machine. We will never know exactly what she told to whom. We will never know how those crucial transatlantic personal connections—so easily underrated—would have developed without her special brand of contact. It is understood, however, that this young woman of little education, once denounced by her contemporaries as fat, frumpy and stupid, knew exactly what she was working for. She decided what information to extract, whether to pass it on or withhold it and also how to spin it, all in the pursuit of eventual Allied victory. By using her name, her personality, her sexuality and her smarts, she helped to weave, sustain and elevate a web of political, military and emotional ties between America and Britain that many today call the Special Relationship. One that began between the sheets of the Dorchester Hotel. In the process, she arguably became the most influential courtesan in history.

13

Early on the morning of Tuesday, June 6, 1944, the phone rang persistently in Pamela's apartment. Groggy from her late-night duties, she picked up the receiver to hear Fred Anderson tell her to turn on her radio before he hastily hung up. An hour later the BBC reported that Allied troops were landing on the beaches of Normandy. After five years of war, months of frantic activity, weeks of her menfolk disappearing without word, hours of Allied planes filling the skies, this—finally—was D-Day. The most important day of the war and yet also, she thought then, the loneliest of her life.[1] She did not dare bother friends embroiled in the greatest seaborne invasion in history. More than seven thousand boats, eleven thousand planes and the first wave of 150,000 men had been dispatched; everyone was busy and she no longer had a major role to play. Ed was anchoring a marathon edition of CBS news, informing America that "here in London the steadiness of the civilian populace is one of the most remarkable things I've ever seen."[2]

However remarkable London was, it would never be the same. "Even if there are still many battles to come," Pamela thought as she dressed, "it was the beginning of the end."[3] The poor, battered city was no longer the command center of the war and as Churchill's power was fading—in favor of the Americans—so was her own. Even her dinners had come to an end, her guests too preoccupied to attend. She felt crushed by the emptiness ahead. Pamela spent the morning sitting by the phone, for the first time feeling an outsider.

The "boys"—her favorite war correspondents—were away competing to file the first reports back from the beaches. While rumors abounded, details were sketchy. Eventually, one or two were able to send word but Pamela thought they sounded "too optimistic."[4] Bill Walton (practically the only close male friend who made no physical or emotional demands on her) had not made contact since parachuting into France with the American 82nd Airborne Division. She knew he had been nervous, and Anderson confirmed that he was likely to be enduring a "sticky time" as the 82nd was meeting ferocious opposition (and would indeed see thirty-three days of bloody combat). Frantic to know if he was still alive, she asked the prime minister's office to find out. Even at such an hour a request from Pamela received high priority. Urgent inquiries discovered that Bill had dropped into a pear tree, a bemused American general having tracked him down and asking if he was with British intelligence as Downing Street itself had asked after his welfare.[5] Word was swiftly dispatched back to a relieved Pamela that Bill was unhurt. Other friends were not so fortunate.

Intimate with the long, tense months of preparations for Operation Overlord, Pamela agonized over the risks of failure. She had watched Winston ground down by the worry and exhaustion of it all, still working sixteen hours seven days a week and frequently summoning her for discussions over games of bezique. Her low regard for General Montgomery, commander in chief of Allied Ground Forces, did nothing to reassure her. Three days after D-Day she was still anxious, despite the prime minister's confident statement to the House of Commons, and over afternoon tea was trying to persuade her journalist friend Mary Welsh of "the stupidity of over-optimism about our chances in Normandy. The weather is terrible and we are having trouble landing supplies."⁶ Pamela railed against those (notably the American newspaper tycoon William Randolph Hearst) continuing to party—"I nearly vomited . . . but maybe I'm a prig." Hearst was too useful not to forgive, however, and in any case her fears (and disapproval) abated after a quiet dinner she gave in the Attic that Friday for Anderson and Winston's chief of staff, General "Pug" Ismay, an occasion she found "thrilling." Pug "was full of stories of the week" and she felt that she was again "right on the inside of the invasion."

She found out even more at the weekend at Chequers, which was so full of generals and politicians that young Winston had to surrender his room to share her bed, obliging Bobbie to sleep on the landing. Hearing that Montgomery had set up headquarters on French soil, Pamela started to accept that the liberation of Europe was "within reach."⁷ As usual at such moments, she was called in to play bezique with Winston. And then on her return to London to report back to Max.

The Allied invasion was progressing but the payback had been deadly. On June 13, a pilotless V-1 flying bomb had been launched from the French coast, landing an hour later in Mile End, east London, killing six. So terrifying was this futuristic new weapon that at first the government maintained a news blackout to avoid panic. However, when Pamela drew back the curtains to see another "black monster with a flaming tail" roar past her window, she knew from secret intelligence that it was in effect a huge jet-propelled bomb with wings.⁸ Shortly afterward, its engine stopped and three seconds later there was a dull, explosive thud. Soon V-1s were landing on a chastened city every half hour over eighty more days and nights until she thought she was "going mad."⁹ Word of the Nazis' latest "sheer damnable devilry"¹⁰—nicknamed doodlebugs or buzz bombs after the noise of their engines—inevitably spread as thousands were killed and a million buildings across Britain were damaged or destroyed. The very air smelled of death. Difficult to intercept and with no pilots to attack, Pamela feared that there was no practical reason for the onslaught to stop. It would be a fateful irony to succumb to what she called this "uncanny & sadistic" bombardment now that the Allies were back on European soil.[11] Many who had been resolute through all the dangers found they could not contend with the macabre idea of being killed by a "wholly mechanical enemy."[12] For the first time Pamela considered closing the Attic and sending her treasured possessions to Chequers, but she had no intention of leaving London altogether.

By Sunday, June 18, she had slept little more than four hours across the previous three nights but at 9:30 a.m. she reported for duty at the Churchill Club, where she was in sole charge of a packed house. At around eleven she heard the deafening buzzing that signified the approach of yet another bomb, while a hail of flak from anti-aircraft guns poured down on the club roof and through the windows. Just as the V-1 came overhead the engine cut out. As one they froze, in silence. They either had a couple of seconds to live or they would hear the bang signifying it had landed on some other poor souls nearby. The crash came, the building shook and they all breathed again, Ashburnham House having got away with a few more broken windows. Pamela dashed outside to find that the Guards' Chapel in Wellington Barracks, where her parents had married, had taken a direct hit. The morning service had been packed with British and American soldiers—many of them her friends—when a ton of explosives had gone off just as the choir began to sing the Eucharist. The concrete roof had come down, crushing 121 people to death.

Reeling from shock, Pamela turned down an invitation to accompany Clementine to Chequers as the raid raged on, feeling she was needed at the club. She remained on duty until after nine in the evening, when she received a summons from Papa, who had rushed back to London. The usual cast of secretaries and generals ran in and out of the Annexe, but an emotional Winston chose to dine alone with Pamela.

The following weekend, she was once again invited to Chequers but, hearing that Randolph was back in the country, she asked Max if she could stay at Cherkley. It proved a wise move. Randolph was in truculent mood, stirring an "uneasy mix of irritation and affection" in his father.[13] By dinner the black mist was shutting down any remaining inhibitions. Puce-faced, he branded his wife a "whore" and proceeded to list the names of her lovers as he yelled at his parents and sister Sarah, and a number of speechless generals. The marines stationed outside the door could hear every word as, roiling with bitterness and self-loathing, he focused his wrath on his parents for encouraging her. Sarah—the family peacemaker—remonstrated with Randolph for upsetting their father but, calling her a bitch, he swiveled around and struck her in the face. As Sarah recoiled, Winston turned a deathly white and Clementine feared he would have another heart attack. He ordered the marines to eject his still-ranting son and each man swore he would never see the other again. Randolph in a booze-fueled fury was not new but the bad feeling ran deeper than before. Word of the violent scene seeped out to the clubs of London. It was widely agreed that Winston had spoiled his son and now he was afraid of him.[14] Once again Pamela—although absent—was at the heart of the rift.

Desperate to ease the Churchills' distress, Pamela suggested an urgent meeting with Randolph in the hope of preventing another fracas. A few days later, she arrived late for lunch with him at the Dorchester, shaking from two narrow misses with doodlebugs in the space of an hour. Aware that Randolph was to leave the country at 4 p.m., she quickly downed two double brandies before opening as calmly as she could. Recounting that she had heard "many second & third hand tales" of what he had said, she insisted that if he had "any grievances" she would like to hear them direct from him. She would, she told him, remove "the child" to a new home in the country and would "not see too much" of his parents. In return, he was not to upset them or cause further embarrassment, until a divorce could finally be granted after the required three years of separation. Randolph appears to have been taken aback by this preemptive peace offering. Thanks to Pamela's skillful diplomacy, he agreed. The pair ended up having an "amiable" lunch.

In any case, many key Americans had left London for France and it was no longer necessary to see Winston as regularly as before. She also had to look to the future after the war, in which she needed to make a new life away from the Churchills. Pamela left the Dorch in high spirits, confident that "everything will go forward smoothly & there should be no more rows over me." Afterward she climbed into her bed to recover but was summoned by an anxious Winston for a briefing on the outcome of the lunch (which he had paid for). "He was sweeter & kinder than ever," she wrote to Averell in Moscow, and was clearly reluctant to be distanced from her, but she thought she had convinced him it was for the best. It would also "be good for little W to live a little less grandly and to see more of me."[15]

Winston and Clementine were more upset than Pamela had realized at the prospect of being separated from her and their grandson. She had become a mainstay in their political and personal lives, and Clementine—who felt that the "terrible scene" with Randolph had left a "permanent grief and darkness"—questioned the necessity of such a dramatic break. Randolph scrawled a hostile note making it "very plain" that his parents' feelings were of no interest. "I am not asking papa to agree to anything," he wrote when Clementine pleaded. "He knows my views. I know his. They are clearly irreconcilable."[16] Soon after, an overwrought Pamela was diagnosed with scarlet fever and kept in quarantine for several weeks.

"I must say your pals are doing wonderfully," a recovering Pamela wrote to Averell in July about the American armies advancing through France. "God knows where they'll be by the time you get this." By late August their "pals" had rolled down from Normandy into Paris. Despite the threat from German snipers, the partying had already begun. Everyone who could flocked to the City of Light. Envious from afar, Pamela got her chance to cross the Channel in mid-September, seemingly in a plane sent for her by one of her tame generals. The Hôtel Ritz was rammed—particularly the Petit Bar on the rue de Cambon, which became a riot of reporters on expenses, well-heeled army men and film stars, including Marlene Dietrich ("very nice," Pamela thought, but "disappointing to look at"[17]) who was there to entertain the troops but also privately delighting two generals. In the mix were a number of local young women—with pubic hair dyed red, white and blue—who descended on American uniforms in the way they had only recently targeted Gestapo. Ernest Hemingway, a notorious magpie collector of other people's experiences, was buying martinis for anyone who would listen to his boasts of having killed numerous Germans with the Resistance. Recognizing the self-deluding macho type at once, Pamela did not join his crowd of credulous hangers-on.

The lights, black-market food and unmarred streets of Paris were dazzling, the city's beauty largely untouched by agreement with the Nazis. The future historian John Wheeler Bennett was astonished by the hotels gleaming "in guilty splendour." Across town, Ed was working flat out and had warned Pamela not to join the "stampede" to Paris as it was, in his words, "pretty grim." He felt a puritan contempt for the "well-fed but still empty-looking faces around the fashionable bars," noting that "the last four years seem to have changed them very little."[18] Pamela saw it differently. After so long at the epicenter of the war, she felt she had never enjoyed simply being young. Until recently

London had been the most exciting place on earth but "the exaltation of danger" had gone.[19] The Americans could afford to occupy the moral high ground. They would return to their booming cities at home; she had a gray, depleted London on its knees emotionally, physically and financially. Ed soon left Paris in disgust but Pamela stayed on. "I can see her there that September," Bill Walton recalled. "Perhaps the world looked open to her then. Paris was free. She might be able to leave London, the filth, the soot, the hunger" behind her as well as her "foolish, ambitious and terribly unlucky marriage."[20]

Pamela did return to London, though, not long after. She had a lecture program to organize for October at the Churchill Club and with her stars frequently rushing off to Paris it was a challenge to fix dates. She relished the intellectual challenge, selecting speakers on subjects such as the new notion of international war crimes trials. The audience "asked good questions—but I don't think any of us found the answers."[21] Her favorite generals only passed through London now but she made a point of accompanying so many of them to the airfields that the bemused officer in charge remarked, "Hello, you make them all don't you!"[22] The void they left prompted her to accommodate new suitors. "Tonight, I am entertaining Harry Luce," she told Averell, revealing the identity of her latest conquest. The last time she had dined with the owner of Time-Life magazines, he had sent her roses with a card inscribed: "What a wonderful audience you are."[23] Luce was never more than a brief fling, however, and was not going to provide the future she longed for. "It's almost a year since you left here," she wrote plaintively to Averell. "Wish you'd hurry up and come back." Her days at the club were numbered; the reason for its existence would soon disappear. And what purpose would she have then? "How about," she asked Averell, "you giving me a job?"

Within days another even more deadly rocket—the V-2—was slicing silently through the air at supersonic speed toward London. "There are days when a vivid imagination is a definite liability," Ed informed the American nation. "There is nothing pleasant in contemplating the possibility . . . that a ton of high explosive may come through the roof with absolutely no warning."[24] Despite her promises to stay away, Pamela took refuge in the underground bunker beneath the Annexe where the Churchills worked and slept during the worst bombardments. Yet for the first time she could not conceal her frustration with the direction of the war and by implication Winston himself. "Ten days ago they gave us to understand that it was all over," she complained, "and now it looks as if we are going to have [V-2s] right up until the time that Germany is beaten."[25] Progress was faltering (although the Soviet armies seemed almost unstoppable in the east). September's plan, formulated by Montgomery, for Allied paratroopers to break through German defenses in the Netherlands, ended in thousands of needless deaths. Operation Market Garden was halted at the Rhine and the strategic bridge at Arnhem was famously never captured.

Pamela struggled to resign herself to the prospect of another winter of fighting. Now most of her friends had left London she was again inevitably drawn further into Churchill life. She lunched with Sarah and weekended in Chequers. Clementine invited her to the family Christmas, but the invitation was hastily rescinded with "great regret." "I find our Christmas plans may cause friction," Winston told Pamela, "as some of the family are worried about the effect on Randolph." Clementine was equally saddened, writing: "What has happened is a grief to me . . . Your loving 'Mama'" (the first time she had added quotation marks to Mama).[26] Pamela discovered that Mary had softened her thinking toward her brother and had been vehemently against her joining the family party in case it made a reconciliation between Randolph and his father impossible. As ever Pamela seemed—or affected to be—unperturbed, telling Averell that it was "all very unimportant," but the only constants in her life for the last five years (Papa and Mama) were now to an extent cut off from her.[27] She still bore the Churchill name, and saw them from time to time, but her ties to them and Downing Street were inexorably weakening.

Pamela decided Ed was her best bet for a fulfilling future. He talked often of marriage, discussing his desire for a son as, after a decade together, Janet had yet to conceive. And yet, despite his promises, he would never quite commit to leaving his wife. Ramping up the pressure, Pamela left mementos from their meetings, such as a book of poems with her name in it in Ed's bag or a pair of her gloves in his pocket. "She was," Janet believed, "sending me a message."[28] Equally, when Ed visited Pamela's country cottage he warded off rivals by signing her visitors' book in capital letters. Tired of the humiliation—and the bombing—Janet departed for New York in September 1944, leaving the coast clear for Pamela but also triggering Ed's Quaker sense of guilt. He played the two women off against each other—promising Pamela he would seek a divorce while writing to his wife, "Let's renew the contract" with "an indefinite option."[29] Eventually, Ed returned to America, where he told Bill Paley that he had decided to end his marriage. Determined to talk him out of it, his boss admitted that he too adored Pamela's aristocratic heritage, was enchanted by her company, lauded her skills with men. She was, Paley exclaimed, the "greatest courtesan of the century"—and that meant she was all wrong for Ed![30]

Exhausted from his work and the emotional turmoil, Ed decided to take Janet to catch some winter sun on a Texas ranch. Now was the time that Pamela expected him to request a divorce, but according to Janet the subject was never mentioned.[31] By the time both Murrows came back to London in February 1945, she was finally pregnant. Thrilled by impending fatherhood, Ed broke it off with a distraught

Pamela but his resolve soon melted. "He was torn between a wife he loved," said a friend, "and a woman with whom he was wildly in love."[32]

Now her war work was over, Pamela found time to be a more hands-on mother, although her heart was not really in it. One of her benefactors bought a box at a children's show, and with Bobbie she took young Winston with two of Diana Sandys's children and a friend. "Never take four children to a theatre," she wrote to Averell after one of her charges nearly tumbled into the orchestra pit. "It was hell." In a further sign of trouble, Pamela sacked the nanny, prompting the boy to wake crying for Bobbie in the night, but Pamela was undeterred. "Bobbie was a real bitch," she wrote, "telling everyone, even strangers, that I neglected my child shamefully."[33] In fact, now she had more time Pamela felt a growing closeness to her son and when alone let him sleep in her bed. And as the bombing in London finally receded, she moved him back to the Attic, where he was looked after by her Scottish housekeeper Marion Martin (whose other role was agony aunt to Pamela's lovers). Mrs. Martin stayed on for thirty years and Pamela liked to talk of how the devoted woman had "brought up Winston"[34]—an observation perhaps more candid than she intended.

Pamela never gave up on Averell either. She wrote to him virtually every week. Averell undoubtedly missed the excitements she had brought him but was also plagued by remorse. He had kept her informed of his dealings with Stalin but now he started to write regularly to Marie, even suggesting that his wife join him in Moscow. War alone was no fun. His staff noticed he had become imperious since he left London, where he had seemed so happy.[35] Fearful she was losing Averell too, Pamela's letters became wistful about their times together in the English countryside. "What fun if we could go back to . . . the summertime & the ponies & the chopping of wood. I badly need a man here who can chop."

Stalin had chosen a location of maximum discomfort for a conference of the Big Three—Russia, America and Britain—in February 1945 in a bid to diminish Roosevelt (who was fading fast and would be dead within two months) and Churchill (whom he knew also to be ailing). On the shores of the Crimean Peninsula, Yalta was daunting to reach and the accommodation full of bugs, of both bed and clandestine varieties. Nevertheless, Pamela envied Sarah Churchill, Kathy Harriman and Anna Roosevelt for accompanying their fathers. All three women were playing roles at a historic summit on finishing the war and starting the peace.

Winston might have left Pamela behind—now that the family bust-up had pushed her out of his inner circle—but she remained extremely well briefed. Even two thousand miles away in London, she did not require a listening device to feel she was almost in the room when the Allies discussed what was effectively—and hugely controversially—the division of Europe between the Soviets and the West. Several protagonists, including Fred Anderson, Kathy and Peter Portal, kept her informed through a flurry of uncensored letters couriered back by well-placed friends. Each gave accounts of disputes, compromises and fears of leaving Churchill on his own with Stalin late at night, in case the Soviet leader started flattering him and he "gave away the store."[36]

It was clear to Pamela—as much as anyone, because of her multiple informants across different camps—that America's focus was now on the growling Soviet bear rather than the tired old British lion. If the atom bomb being developed in Los Alamos did not bring an end to the war in the Pacific then Russian military support would be needed to finish the job. And so for now, British fears of the bloodthirsty Soviet occupation of Eastern Europe—the Red Army was already committing vast atrocities in Poland—were largely ignored. "At this point everyone's crossing their fingers & hoping for the best," Kathy Harriman told her friend from what was a forlorn spot, surrounded by bombed-out villages and ravaged countryside.[37] There was no one else to write to other than Pamela, who might understand the brutality she and her father had witnessed in Russia and the fears (shared by Averell but downplayed by Roosevelt) of the threat Stalin's expansionist regime posed for the future. And only Pamela would appreciate her pride in her father when she wrote, "Ave's in there pitching as you can well imagine & reports so far are very favorable."[38]

By contrast, Peter Portal, lacing his thirty-page letter with "I love you so much" and "I simply must see you very soon after I get back," had no intention of praising his rival.[39] "I am sorry to tell you," the RAF chief wrote, "that the general opinion among our people here is that Averell is not having great success with the Russians . . . He certainly looks older than when I last saw him."

In the end, the three great allies of the Second World War put on a show of unity in a joint communiqué on striving for peace in which everyone "in all the lands may live out their lives in freedom from fear and want." In reality, Yalta marked the "inevitable clash" of the conflicting visions that the two sides brought into the war: Anglo-American idealism, articulated in the Atlantic Charter, of fighting for freedom and self-determination, versus Stalin's stark ambition to create a chain of client states along the Soviet Union's western border. Wiser heads began to view Russia not as a tricky yet essential partner but a power fundamentally opposed to the West. Pamela was steeped in Churchill's distrust of Stalin, who had replaced Hitler as his chief obsession. And indeed within a few months the tensions and recriminations of Yalta would escalate until the hot war fought by the three-way alliance was replaced by the Cold War that rendered it apart.[40] Averell had characteristically given his all and now he wanted out of Moscow. Looking to the future meant difficult decisions on what to do about Marie and Pamela.

. . .

The end of the war "scares me," Pamela wrote to Averell. "I am afraid of not knowing what to do with life in peacetime."[41] Everything had been "motivated by a common purpose of winning the war" but at the age of twenty-five, about to be divorced, with nowhere to go and nothing to do, she found herself on her own. It began to dawn on her how astonishing the past few years had been. For now she was engrossed in the forthcoming election, the first of her adult life, and knew almost all of the key players on both sides of the political divide. During the war she "met and admired a lot of the socialists"[42] who—having helped run the government in the wartime coalition—were no longer holding back on attacking Winston and the Conservatives. And having ventured outside her gilded circles, she now sympathized with many of Labour's policies, particularly on welfare.[43] She had also astutely observed that Winston's support was ebbing across the country at large. "Labour are quite strong & seem to think they have a chance," she reported to Averell.[44]

Pamela tried to keep busy at the Churchill Club but she was lonely. She found out Averell had returned to America only via a news item on the radio. "I miss you so much, please come here," she pleaded in vain.[45] The sense of loss pervaded the VE Day celebrations on May 8. Pamela watched the jubilant crowds from her window but, like many women who feared their lives were about to contract, could not dispel feelings of foreboding. Though not even the Blitz had prepared Pamela for what she saw in June. Offering to help set up entertainment for British airmen across Europe, Pamela was flown at low level across the Allied mass-bombing targets of Bremen, Hamburg and Essen. From her place in the cockpit, it was an apocalyptic vision that drove her thinking for the rest of her life. "I only wish every man, woman & child in England could see what I've seen," she told Averell. "We were 28 ½ mins flying over Hamburg & during all that time there was nothing but rubble for as far as I could see—it was like a city that has been dead a thousand years."[46] Later she saw at ground level the monumental problems of occupying Germany, including the handling of millions of displaced persons. In August came the shocking news of the American atom bombs dropped on Japan, killing up to a hundred thousand instantly and many more in the months and years to come. For the first time in her life Pamela felt a "desire" to tell the world about the insanity of conflict but also the moral costs of victory. She even toyed with an offer to write for *Newsweek*.[47] Her desperation to win one war had turned into a lifelong compulsion to help prevent another.

The thought of *doing* was more enticing than reporting, however. After years of operating close to the center of power, she could scarcely imagine not taking an active part in reconstructing the world, a postwar task described by future U.S. Secretary of State Dean Acheson as only "a bit less formidable than that described in the first chapter of Genesis."[48] Having enjoyed working in Randolph's constituency, she dabbled with the idea of standing as an MP. One problem was that she was unsure she was still a Tory and yet could not countenance the disloyalty of standing for Labour against a party led by Winston.[49] An even greater hurdle was that it was still rare for a woman to enter Parliament, particularly one as young as Pamela. And crucially she had witnessed how unelected advisers with the ear of the prime minister—such as Beaverbrook, Bracken or indeed Pamela herself—had far more access than all but the most senior MPs.

On July 26 the election results came through. Labour had won with a majority of 146 seats. "There has been a landslide to the left," Pamela wrote to Averell. "*The Times* today summed it up best: 'Gratitude belongs to history & not to politics.'"[50] Reflecting how her own allegiances had changed, she welcomed the result even as she regretted the personal hurt to Winston. Yet now it was all over, how could her life ever be as exciting or meaningful again? At Churchill's side as he had waged a world war, she had tasted the thrill of power. Now it had seeped away and she would spend the rest of her life in its pursuit. Not only had Winston become a once great has-been but a depleted Britain had also been toppled. Once its empire had dominated the world but the effort of surviving two world wars had relegated it to a secondary league in fear of its future. From now on, there would be just two superpowers: Russia and America. One frightened her; the other represented everything she desired.

ACT TWO
Peace

14

Casey Murrow was born in London on November 6, 1945, and Pamela was bombarded with newspaper pictures of a delighted father cradling his baby son. Soon afterward Ed returned to New York to negotiate a new role at CBS, leaving Pamela feeling as if she was being abandoned in the London rubble. "Life here frankly is not much fun," she wrote to Averell. "Had a letter from Jock tonight and New York life sounded so gay & festive."[1]

A month later, Pamela's uncontested divorce came through on the grounds that Randolph had deserted her for more than three years. In a letter to Pansy, Churchill blamed the split on the war, adding that "everything must be centred upon the well-being & happiness of the Boy."[2] Pamela, though, had other priorities. She dispatched five-year-old Winston to spend Christmas at Minterne with her parents, whom he barely knew, and boarded a plane to join Ed at the Ambassador Hotel in New York. Janet was a helpless bystander in the battle for her marriage, reading of Pamela's divorce and her arrival in America while nursing her newborn in London.

Pamela delighted in the Christmas lights down the length of Park Avenue, the vivid colors and healthy faces. Ed was equally thrilled to see Pamela and formally asked her to marry him. He had been promoted to vice-president of news and his fame and talents would surely take him further still, perhaps even into politics. Such prospects electrified Pamela and together they went house-hunting on the Upper East Side.³ Ed was besotted and she thought she was too.

Ed flew back to London to inform Janet but exploded with rage when he heard that Pamela had taken up an invitation from Kick to the Kennedys' ocean-front compound in Palm Beach, Florida. What for her was the chance of a sun-drenched holiday putting war, winter and rationing behind her was for him equivalent to "visiting Hermann Göring," Hitler's deputy in Nazi Germany. Ed could never forgive Joe Kennedy's anti-British attitude nor reconcile himself with Pamela's willingness to overlook it. And he knew nothing of Kennedy's other failings—while Pamela herself seems to have been so keen to go she overlooked them. Enjoying the airy modern rooms of the Kennedy home, she was perturbed by why Ed wanted "to go spoil it all for me by making me feel as if I shouldn't be there."⁴

The Kennedy matriarch, Rose, disapproved of divorce and sex outside marriage (believing in the strictest Catholic teachings that birth control was a sin and sex only for procreation and forbidden during pregnancy, menstruation and old age). Yet she was another older woman who took to Pamela, perhaps because of a shared experience of marrying into a male-dominated dynasty. Pamela was enthralled by her immersion into American politics, Rose lending her a stack of current affairs magazines so she could keep track of the quick-fire Kennedy conversations at the dinner table. And especially Jack's plans to run for Congress in Massachusetts using his family's fame and fortune in the fight for Boston's working-class votes. How could he position himself as, effectively, a millionaire for the masses? Would his disarming smile, youthful sense of promise, war record and public-spiritedness suffice? Pamela noted the tight Kennedy discipline invested in winning, whether in sport, business or politics. The family was a study in perpetual action but there were strict rules, such as never arriving even a minute late to the table. Witnessing the potency of the Kennedy name prompted Pamela to take stock of her own. The

Churchill brand yielded a mixed reception at home, where Winston had been rejected by the electorate, but in America it turned out to be pure gold.

Not normally known for her generosity, Rose was so impressed by Pamela's assimilation into American life that she bought her a wardrobe suitable for the Florida heat.[5] Staying in the shade to avoid sunburn, Pamela's pale skin and elegant new frocks caught the eye of the American diary column by Cholly Knickerbocker, which listed her among the "Best Sundressed Women in Palm Beach."[6] Pamela resisted when Max cabled from Fleet Street, asking her to make a "swift return" to work for him on the *Evening Standard*.[7] He had even arranged for the rent to be paid on the Attic for another three years, but she decided that her life was to be in America with Ed, whatever his flaws. What did Britain offer a woman with little of her own money, no qualifications and, now that Winston was out of Downing Street, no links to power? There had also been hurtful comments that she had enjoyed the war "high on the hog." People could not possibly understand or even know what she had done—and given the sensitivities involved she could never tell them. She had served Britain in every way she knew, but in the process had fallen for America and Americans. Ed had promised to be back in three weeks with the divorce under way and she could not know that, thousands of miles away in a bombed-out London, he was soaking himself in booze and battling with his Quaker's qualms. After a fortnight he cabled, saying "Casey wins. God bless you and forgive me."

Pamela "collapsed" at receiving the news. "He'd been so definite," she said, "that Janet would never stand in his way."[8] He had never been "so in love" with anyone in his life, Ed told a friend, "but it wasn't meant to be."[9] After the initial shock, Pamela recognized that the relationship had probably always been doomed. "What he had to do for his conscience—and God knows he had a conscience—he had to do. He wouldn't have been happy otherwise."[10] Yet Ed wanted it all, persistently calling her, and it was Pamela who eventually demanded a clean break. "I just had to survive," she explained.[11] The Murrows packed up in London and, in his farewell broadcast, Ed thanked his wartime hosts for "tea, hospitality and . . . inspiration." Leaving much of his heart with the British people, and one above all, he could barely contain his emotions when he gave his final salute: "You were living a life," he declared, "not an apology."[12]

Many thought Pamela had had a lucky escape. Averell had warned her off Ed and even Betsey Whitney chipped in that the last thing that Pamela needed after Randolph was another self-absorbed journalist. In her heart she knew that marrying Ed would not have been "very sensible"—he was too controlling and insecure—but she kept his letters locked away for the rest of her life.[13] Pamela returned alone to the Ambassador Hotel, where she subsisted on allowances from Jock, Bill Paley, Averell, her parents, the Churchills—and Randolph, when he met his alimony obligations such as the school fees for young Winston. Pamela was a well-kept woman but the Ambassador was pricey and so was living in New York. She confided that she was running out of money to Kathy, who generously offered her *Newsweek* salary to tide her over.[14] Pamela gratefully accepted, but what she needed was a rich new man.

She became a frequent sight on the zebra-skinned banquettes of the El Morocco nightclub, where gossip columnists spotted her dancing with Stanley Mortimer, the ex-husband of Betsey Whitney's sister Babe. It came to nothing—Pamela introduced him to Kathy and they married eighteen months later. Still, both Babe (in search of a new spouse) and Betsey (who wanted to keep hers) saw the younger Pamela as a threat. One night the Harrimans also came to El Morocco and spotted Pamela a few feet away. Averell sat motionless, his face blank, pretending not to see or hear. Marie rose to her feet, whipped off her dark glasses and targeted an "exaggerated stare" at her onetime rival.¹⁵ If the subject of Averell's London romance ever arose, Marie treated it as though he had gone through a "period of temporary insanity."¹⁶

Beaverbrook repeated his invitation for Pamela to become a full-time journalist, hoping to cash in on her society contacts. With no other options, Pamela returned to Britain and started work on the Londoner's Diary gossip column at the *Evening Standard* on £15 a week—half Randolph's prewar rate, although as the paper's political editor Charles Wintour noted, she put in a "very short day."¹⁷ In truth, Pamela felt uncomfortable reporting on her friends and she again toyed with the idea of entering politics. David Margesson and Max talked her out of it. They could not conceive of her standing for any party but the Conservatives, and only one Tory woman had been elected in 1945 compared to twenty-one for Labour, out of a total of 640 MPs.¹⁸ Almost all the successful female candidates were also much older.

It was now—after a long and painful silence—that Pamela heard from Averell. He had been appointed to London as ambassador and was moving back to Britain. Within days she was moving back into his bed. Kathy could no longer provide cover, of course, and the liberal attitudes of wartime had hardened. They revived their full-throttled affair, but Averell was keen to avoid damaging his career with scandal and had asked Marie to join him in London from September for appearances' sake.

Just before Marie was due to arrive, Pamela wrote an article for the *Standard* sympathizing with a once famous beauty who had been cruelly abandoned by her lovers. Beaverbrook erupted at the none too subtle cry for help¹⁹ and ordered Pamela to "get the hell out of town" before Marie read the piece, presenting her with a one-way ticket to New York. He saw too plainly the dangers to his own position of a scandal involving his newspaper and the American ambassador. Just as she was leaving, though, President Truman summoned Averell back to Washington to become Secretary of Commerce. It was, finally, the cabinet position Averell had craved, and the last time he saw Pamela was to inform her he was immediately and permanently shutting her out of his life. He would, he declared coldly, allow nothing to come in the way of his political destiny.

If Pamela felt fury at the way Randolph, Ed and Averell had treated her, she admitted she bottled it up "for years." She suffered a major loss of confidence but was unwilling to admit to Pansy that she had "made a mess of things."[20] She could not bear the thought of her mother urging her to "give up the giddy life" and to "live quietly in the country" like her.[21]

Pamela arrived in the Big Apple by ship two days after Averell landed by plane. Again Max instantly "shoved" her out of the way,[22] this time to Montego Bay in Jamaica. Pamela fumed but was ordered to stay put in the Caribbean while Averell settled into his new job. In an act of rebellion Pamela used her exile to file not Max's preferred social flimflam but a serious piece on the squalor of a government hospital in what was then a British colony. When she was eventually allowed to return to New York, she veered off track again with an exclusive profile of Belgian statesman Paul-Henri Spaak, a friend from her Downing Street years and now the first president of the United Nations General Assembly. The failings of empire and the UN's future were not what Max wanted to read from his top society writer. Pamela and Max parted company. Her life as a journalist was over.

Pamela had not seen five-year-old Winston for months, despite him suffering chronic bouts of ill health. He had led an itinerant life since the war, passed from one set of grandparents to another. Now Pamela was back, Winston lived with her in the Attic from where her butler, Sam Hudson, took him to school near Sloane Square on the number 74 bus. Hudson was a rare male constant in the boy's life, obligingly playing football with him in Hyde Park. His dapper appearance contrasted with Randolph's nicotine-stained fingers and mercurial rudeness. Young Winston learned to identify the triggers of his father's explosions—"any hint of dilatoriness, inefficiency or surliness by a waiter, taxi driver, or especially, any employee of British Railways"[23]—and to brace himself for episodes he found "traumatic in the extreme."[24] A typical day out started with being dumped in the lobby of White's while Randolph filed copy to a newspaper or drank. Eventually Father would take him to lunch at a starchy table in the Ritz Hotel grill room, where Winston sat in mortal dread of any delay in the service. Losing his parliamentary seat and failing to cloak himself in military glory had intensified Randolph's bitterness.

Britain, meanwhile, was paying a high price for its triumph over Hitler. "The taste of victory was exhilarating," wrote one commentator, "but the taste of almost everything else was absent."[25] Food was indeed scarce, prices were high and many streets were still left pitted with bombsites. "Seldom if ever," Ed reported on a trip to London, "has a war ended leaving the victors with such a sense of uncertainty and fear."[26] In the winter of 1946 to 1947 the weather piled on the misery. Mary Churchill married Christopher Soames in February 1947 during the worst blizzard for sixty years, and thanks to a miners' strike the reception took place in a frosty ballroom by candlelight.

It was hard for Pamela to resist an invitation from Diana and Duff Cooper, now British ambassador to France, to stay at the official residence in Paris. Here Diana, a woman of icy blonde beauty, became her latest matriarchal figure and mentor. Pamela made an instant impact on *le gratin*, or top layer, of Parisian society, emerging from the war years in eye-popping finery. Christian Dior's New Look focused on ultra-feminine full skirts with pinched waists and soft, sloping shoulders—an extravagance in fabric and corsetry unthinkable in London—but Pamela represented something even more glamorous. She was an almost mythical creature, an aristocrat bearing the Churchill name at a time when Winston was coming to Paris to receive the Médaille Militaire in front of crowds chanting "Vive Churchill! Vive l'Angleterre!" Inhaling the adulation, she began to scheme as to how she could make Paris her permanent home and somehow trade on her own Churchillian pedigree.

15

While she dreamed of Paris, there was only one woman of Pamela's acquaintance who was almost as absorbed as she was in politics back home. To live at the heart of Westminster, Kick Kennedy bought an eighteenth-century townhouse in Smith Square and was toying with standing for Parliament, in the footsteps of her compatriot Nancy Astor, who had become the first woman to take a seat in the House of Commons back in 1919. A shared search for purpose in a postwar world where opportunities for women were once again shrinking brought Kick and Pamela even closer together.

Pamela also appreciated that her friend was, unlike so many other women, neither jealous nor disapproving. It no doubt helped that Kick was secretly sleeping with the married Earl (Peter) Fitzwilliam and Pamela was happy to provide cover on glamorous jaunts such as to the Grand Prix de Paris at Longchamp racecourse. This was the carefree life of luxury Pamela might have enjoyed at nineteen, had it not been for the demands and dangers of war, and nothing was going to stop her now. Pamela realized that, even while she sought serious new fulfillment, it was no longer "a sin" to enjoy herself.[1]

Pamela felt a sense of exciting possibilities as she cheered a 33-to-1 outsider across the finish line at Longchamp. The winning chestnut colt belonged to Prince Aly Khan, who was in ecstatic mood that night when Pamela attended his summer ball in the Bois de Boulogne. Flowers and balloons in the prince's racing colors of hot pink and green bedecked the tables, pink champagne flowed and guests danced to two live orchestras. A notorious seducer, Aly was the son and presumed heir of Aga Khan III, who claimed descent from the Prophet Muhammed and was regarded as a living deity to fifteen million Nizaris (the largest branch of Ismaili Shia Islam).

Thirty-six-year-old Aly locked eyes with Pamela and moved through the crowd to ask her to dance.[2] As they swayed to the music, he pulled her tight against him, tracing languid circles on the small of her back with his hand.[3] There was something electric about the way he focused on her response. By the time she left the ball, carrying goodie bags of scent and Hermès scarves, she had experienced a physical ecstasy she had never known. When Pamela excitedly told Kick she had accepted Aly's invitation to dinner the following week, her friend exclaimed: "You can't do it, Pam!" Aly was too blatant, too casual, a speed-freak and thrill-seeker. Kick's fears were no doubt heightened by the endemic racism of the day as for all his wealth and success in bedding high-born women, as a man of color Aly was far from universally accepted. Even seven years later, Nancy Mitford, for one, was still referring to him as "Jungle Jim."[4]

Kick's opposition made Pamela more determined and she replied: "Why can't I? I think he's very attractive." Pamela did not want him as a husband—Aly was "never a pivotal point in my life," she said, "just a very exciting friend"—but she was after adventure, and if she could ruffle feathers by breaking a taboo like Jane Digby that was a bonus. He whisked her off on his private plane to dine in another country (an unheard-of idea at the time) or down to Château de l'Horizon, his whitewashed villa on the French Riviera with clifftop pool and a chute descending straight into the waters of the Golfe-Juan. Pamela found his astonishing sexual drive "fun and kind of dangerous."[5] Aly could survive on three hours' sleep but after one momentous session, Pamela dozed off in the Mediterranean sun and required hospital treatment for third-degree sun burns.

Randolph had been mechanistic, Ed smoked throughout and Averell was a "wham bam thank you ma'am!"[6] man unfamiliar with foreplay or experiment, but Aly was an expert lover who put Pamela's satisfaction first. As a teenager he had been sent to a doctor in Cairo for six weeks to learn the ancient Arabian art of Ismák, including how to hold back his sexual climax through muscle control to ensure the satisfaction of his partner. Dipping his fingers in rosewater apparently also helped him keep an erection for hours, one friend claiming he "liked the effect it had on women," enjoying getting "them out of control while he remained . . . the master of the situation."[7] Aly taught Pamela sexual techniques, including keeping an ice bucket next to the bed so that when pleasuring a man she could pop ice cubes in her mouth to prolong his ecstasy.[8] Another was called the Egyptian wave and involved flexing her own intimate muscles during intercourse to stunning effect.[9] She already understood the erotic effect of enthusiasm.

The Riviera was now waking up from the war, a sunny catwalk of dreams for playboys, film stars and moguls from across the Free World. Perfection in women was presumed. Pamela spent mornings in the beauticians before presiding over buffet luncheons for ten or more people, but she merely picked at her food, changed her outfit three times a day and touched up her hair and makeup hourly. If Aly was around, there would be dancing under the umbrella pines until four in the morning or drives along the Corniche in one of his Bentleys or Lagondas, him dressed in crumpled linen jacket and silk cravat. Pamela helped restore the modernist villa from the damage inflicted by its Nazi occupiers, creating the first real home of Aly's life. Her informal touches (inspired in part by the Kennedy home in Florida) such as huge sofas in beige linen, rich rugs on tiled floors, shelves of books, abundant flowers and colorful Impressionist artworks were widely admired at a time when most grand Riviera villas bordered on frumpy. Pamela marshaled Aly's staff, ensuring the maids were attired in black with spotless white lace aprons and sending the bills to the Aga Khan. Fortunately, unlike most of Aly's other women, he valued Pamela and her stabilizing presence in his son's life. He even hoped she would become the permanent chatelaine at L'Horizon. Pamela was wiser now and knew that such a limited role would never satisfy her. Aly was not interested in politics nor extending his life much beyond the pursuit of pleasure.

By 1948 France seemed like paradise to a war-weary Brit like Pamela. Thanks in part to the huge aid granted by the Marshall Plan (an unprecedented American-funded European recovery program) the French economy was thriving, and its industrial base had in any case emerged from the war relatively unscathed. By contrast, Britain was exhausted and no longer had the resources to fulfill its obligations overseas. It was the end of Pax Britannica (the British Empire acting as global police officer) but would Washington step into the void?

Senators and congressmen flocked to Europe to see the revival in France—and the sad decline of the old mother country—for themselves. One of them was thirty-year-old Jack Kennedy, now ensconced as a congressman, who came over in autumn 1947 to look into how widespread economic struggles were boosting support for the communist cause. First, he planned to stay three weeks with Kick at Lismore Castle in Ireland, which had been in Billy's family since 1754. Pamela was pleased to be invited along and no doubt took the opportunity to quiz Jack on how he had won his seat through a focus on workers' postwar concerns such as housing and the minimum wage. She vigorously agreed with him on the need for military strength against the threat of the Soviet Union (which he had publicly described as a "moral and physical crisis"). There was a pragmatism and optimism in Democratic Party ideas that Pamela also found more appealing than either Labour or the Conservatives at home.

Entering Congress was only the first step for Jack, and one morning he approached her "rather quietly, rather apologetically" to ask if she would come with him on a private expedition to find the "original" Kennedys.[10] When the others went to play golf Pamela and Jack set off in Kick's gleaming new station wagon. They weaved their way through sunlit fields of the southeastern corner of Ireland to a little town called New Ross. We will never be sure why two notorious seducers took six hours to cover the thirty miles to their destination on the banks of the River Barrow. Jack certainly had a penchant for women who had slept with powerful men—his future wife, Jackie Bouvier, once saying that he could not be in the "same room with a woman with a past without getting an erection."[11] That said, Jack's boyish looks and lack of genuine interest in women beyond the excitement of the pursuit—in his book, "sex was something to *have done, not to be doing*"[12]—would not have impressed Pamela, who disliked one-night stands. Nevertheless she found power compelling, and Jack already exuded it.

Jack asked Pamela not to tell his sister about their day as they pulled up outside a little white house with chickens and geese patrolling the front yard. "A tough-looking woman came out surrounded by a mass of kids, looking just like all the Kennedys," Pamela later recounted.[13] Jack said he was from America, looking for Irish relations, and after discussions over cups of tea inside the cottage he concluded—with, according to Pamela, rather more confidence than the family—that they were indeed third cousins. Their hosts were more certain that Pamela must be Jack's wife. When she denied it, they retorted "Ah, soon to be, no doubt!" By the time they left, after taking the children for a drive around the village to squeals of excitement, their hosts were smitten with them both. The journey back was quicker but by the time Jack and Pamela drove into the castle grounds, Kick was angry and suspicious as to why they were late for dinner. Jack soothed his sister, and in any case the day had been worth it: Pamela had helped Jack establish vital "green vote" credentials that would come to define him as the ultimate American politician and make him a hero on the Emerald Isle.[14]

Soon afterward they both returned to London, where a worryingly skeletal Jack booked into Claridge's and within hours found himself slipping in and out of consciousness. When he managed to call Pamela, she urgently summoned her doctor, Sir Daniel Davis, who rushed Jack to the London Clinic. There he was diagnosed with Addison's disease, a potentially fatal failure of the adrenal glands. Pamela was due to take young Winston to Château de L'Horizon and so she asked Mrs. Martin to bring Jack home-cooked soup every day in the hospital (a kindness he recognized years later by inviting her to his inauguration). The first to know, and one of a tiny circle who would ever know in his lifetime, Pamela kept the diagnosis secret for fear of derailing Jack's career. The Kennedys informed the papers he was suffering from a relapse of wartime malaria, but Jack knew who had saved him to fight another day.

Pamela understood how to keep secrets—including Kick's infatuation with the famously daredevil Peter Fitzwilliam. In May 1948, though, Kick had finally returned to America to inform her mother of her intention to become Peter's wife. Even the servants cowering in another room were shocked by the ferocity of Rose's reaction. If Kick married Peter, Rose screamed, she would be disowned by the Catholic Church for marrying a divorcé. And, most brutally, she would be dead to her.[15] Back in London, Kick poured out her woes to Pamela over lunch and pleaded with her to join her and Peter on a chartered plane almost identical to Aly's for a trip to L'Horizon. Pamela wavered—but she had already made plans to follow them down in a couple of days and never liked changing her mind. She drove with them to the old London airport at Croydon to wave them off, Kick looking chic in a navy suit and clutching her rosary beads. Once they reached Paris, Peter thought it would be fun to stop for lunch, brushing aside the pilot's warnings of a brewing thunderstorm in the Rhône Valley. The couple returned late to find the pilot furious that they would now be flying through the worst of the weather. They took off into calm skies before entering the tempest just north of the Ardèche. For twenty minutes, they were tossed around by violent winds until a wing sheared off and the plane shot out of the clouds into a mountain.

Kick's father was the only family member to attend her funeral, a high requiem mass at the Catholic church on Farm Street in Mayfair. Rose refused to come.[16] Her coffin was taken to Chatsworth, where she was buried under a headstone with the words "Joy she gave, Joy she found." Consumed by grief, Pamela feared she would never find another female friend who did not think her an "oddball."[17]

At Kick's funeral, Pamela encountered Randolph for the first time in a while. Luck had not smiled on him since they parted. His journalistic career was not flourishing, and neither was his health. He lashed out at virtually anyone but reserved his most odious insults for women, and several had slapped him in public. After years of distressing rows with Randolph, in old age Winston had turned to Mary's husband, the solid and respectful Christopher Soames, as confidant and support. Randolph began to fear he would lose all the privilege he had once presumed—even the family seat at Chartwell—to his brother-in-law. Without the sponsorship of his father, Randolph was also struggling to reenter politics, so he decided to make overtures to the person best equipped to help him: his ex-wife.

Randolph did not bother with romance or regret but set out to exploit Pamela's insecurities with a callous ruthlessness. All her American friends had "deserted" her, he told her, and she faced a lonely future. If only she would "live a normal life as an English person" she would be happy. He admitted to "some terrible mistakes" but accused her of behaving just as badly. They should reconsider for the sake of young Winston, he argued, but for Pamela there was also the prospect of being able to help Randolph's political career.[18] Bereft of other options, she agreed to a trial weekend at Evelyn Waugh's manor house at Stinchcombe in Gloucestershire. Randolph drove in his typical lunatic style, made worse by several drinks, talking at her without once giving her the chance to speak. When she stepped out of the car with relief, Waugh was agog at her Riviera attire in the setting of an English country village—"heels nine inches high like something in *London Life* & trailing yellow skirts." Later he asked incredulously, "Are you reconciled?" "No," she replied bluntly. "Just a little trip."[19] The moment women conceded an inch, Randolph treated them with contempt. By the morning, Pamela was able to tell him that the "little trip" was over and she would never again be his wife.[20] She longed for respect and he would not give it.

Within three months, Randolph had married June Osborne, a contemporary of Pamela's at Downham School. During their brief courtship she had threatened to commit suicide and accused him of indecent assault. Waugh observed that she must "be possessed of magnificent courage" to go on to marry Randolph,[21] and indeed it is difficult to imagine why she did. An emotionally fragile woman, she gave birth to a daughter, Arabella, the following year but by then the marriage was falling apart. On one occasion, Randolph reduced a restaurant in Sloane Square to appalled silence by shouting at June that she was "a paltry little middle-class bitch."[22] In private, the pattern repeated itself when the verbal assaults turned physically violent. June's terror only made him worse. Pamela knew herself lucky to have escaped but that still left her adrift.

16

Prince Jean-Louis de Faucigny-Lucinge, descendant of King Louis IX of France and patron of Salvador Dalí, was tired of babysitting seven-year-old Winston in the absence of his mother. A week after Kick's death, Pamela had taken the boy out of his London school and flown down in Aly's plane to the prince's house at Cap d'Ail. Shortly afterward she had gone on alone to L'Horizon, where she intended to spend most of the summer of 1948, hosting Aly's friends and the stream of women he took to bed. Aly and Pamela were lovers and close friends but not exclusive, and she was free to use L'Horizon almost as she wished. Meanwhile, it was not clear, least of all to the slight and sickly Winston, when she would come back to fetch him.[1] The prince's son, Guy, was of a similar age and presumably Pamela had assumed the arrangement would work for everyone but patience was wearing thin. "No one knew whether she had forgotten," recalled Rosamée de Brantes, Guy's cousin, who was also at the house, "or whether it just suited her."[2] Pamela *was* aware that the correct and courteous Jean-Louis (a widower she had met at Diana Cooper's Paris parties) was scandalized by her staying away, but "life was moving too fast to worry about it."[3]

One lunchtime at L'Horizon, the sound of a motor boat approaching could be heard over the roar of cicadas. Pamela walked down to the jetty to see two impeccably groomed Italians. One introduced himself as Prince Raimondo Lanza from Palermo, but it was the "wonderful" one with a profile like a Roman emperor who caught her eye. His name was Gianni Agnelli—or "Jonny," as Pamela pronounced it—and he was heir to Fiat, Italy's largest and most powerful corporation. She explained that Aly was not there—at her suggestion he had taken his latest amour, the Hollywood great Rita Hayworth, on a trip to Spain—but Gianni was not bothered. He was captivated by this voluptuous redhead with sapphire eyes and the sexiest walk he had ever seen, who was a Churchill to boot. For an Italian who had fought against the Allies in the Second World War, to meet the Great Victor's renowned former daughter-in-law was mesmeric. Pamela was wary of a man she would only recently have considered an enemy, but Gianni seemed "nice and fun" and so she accepted his invitation to a gala that Friday at Monte Carlo.

A year Pamela's junior, Gianni was the first younger man she thought worthy, but when he asked her if she would sail with him down the Italian coast to Capri she refused. She was dining that night with the Duke and Duchess of Windsor: the former Edward VIII and Wallis Simpson had taken a villa nearby and had befriended her as one of the Riviera's must-have guests. He would wait for her and leave at midnight, he replied. The thought was beguiling but her concerns real. She, a Churchill, would be going off to a formerly fascist country with a man whose grandfather had vastly enriched himself as a close associate of Mussolini and a supplier of trucks and tanks to the Italian and German armies. True, Gianni had switched sides toward the end of the war when it became clear the fascists had lost but she hardly knew him and also did not speak Italian. It was then that a telegram arrived from Randolph to say he was on his way from England to see her. That made up her mind. She sent word to Prince Jean-Louis to keep "the child" for another week, afterward explaining her flightiness with "well ... I'd never been to Italy."[4] Randolph arrived to find his ex-wife gone and Winston parked with the prince. Pamela was determined not to worry about Randolph's inevitable rage—she had endured it for too long.

Thick clouds were blotting out the stars as she boarded Gianni's twelve-meter yacht, but he ignored the weather warnings and Pamela already knew better than to display fear. Soon the boat was sawing through huge waves and a glass of water on a shelf above her bed smashed down onto her head, cutting her forehead. There was blood all over the cabin, and at first light they sailed into Portofino, from where Gianni took her to a hospital in Turin. While she waited afterward for her stitches to be removed Randolph was calling anyone he knew in Italy to bellow down the phone "Where is she? Is she out whoring? Why has she abandoned my son?"[5]

Frightened he would pursue her to Turin, Pamela sent word that she was still in the hospital and unable to receive visitors whereas in reality she was soon cruising through calmer waters down to Capri, where she and Gianni stayed at a pastel-painted villa rented by his friend Count Rudi Crespi. They arrived late at night, and when Rudi came into the room the following morning with coffee, Gianni threw open the shutters and told him, "I want you to meet Pam. I'm crazy about her." She walked in, naked, and came over to Rudi, who noted the milkiness of her skin. She shook his hand, sat on the bed and "demurely" crossed her legs. An astonished Rudi told friends she was the first natural redhead he had ever seen.[6]

For all his playboy lifestyle, Gianni returned to his Fiat desk in Turin early every Monday morning, even if the Allies obliged him to let a professor of banking take the helm. He knew that he urgently needed to win powerful backers—and decouple the Fiat and Agnelli names from fascism—to keep the company within family control and save it from ruin. Fiat's factories had been virtually destroyed by Allied bombing and without immediate large-scale American help the company would be unlikely to survive the turbulent postwar years. From his childhood of moneyed splendor in a Turin mansion,

Gianni had been raised to believe "what is good for Fiat is good for Italy"[7]—indeed, the company accounted for nearly 5 percent of the country's entire economic output and employed one in thirty of its workers. His ultimate goal was therefore to embody power and continuity when national governments were typically weak and short-lived, and to drive the ruins of Italy's postwar economy toward success and prosperity. The Agnellis were accustomed to direct links to Italian prime ministers of all political colors. Now, though, Gianni urgently needed an entrée to world leaders and to learn to operate at their level at a time when the Allies were weighing up whether Fiat should be confiscated from his family permanently. Pamela was sexy and fun but she offered something other women could not: connections at the highest political and military levels in Britain and, even more importantly, America. For a onetime Axis officer with soaring ambition for himself and his country, there could hardly be anyone more useful for cleansing himself and his company of the past and securing a viable future.

Gianni set out to win Pamela over with excitement. He recognized in her a kindred fear of boredom after the intense effort and heroism of the years of fighting for survival. "An entire generation suffered from a kind of post-traumatic stress disorder," observed a distinguished British contemporary of Pamela's. "It was not a specific mental disorder" as with veterans of combat but "the skittishness that comes from living with the fear of sudden death."[8] Family tragedy—his father had been decapitated in an air crash when Gianni was fourteen and his mother died in a car accident a decade later—had also given Gianni a fatalistic love for thrills. A Friday night might be enlivened by taking a helicopter swooping over the magnificent white edifice of the Grand-Hôtel at Cap Ferrat and out to sea, jumping into the water and swimming back to the rocky shoreline. Or he would drive Pamela at grand prix speed through the narrow Turin streets. Police would flag them down—but often just to ogle Gianni's metallic-green Ferrari with red leather interior. As his granddaughter Ginevra Elkann put it, "when he was around, the pace of life changed."⁹

Gianni's fast friends included other playboy princes on the Côte d'Azur such as film star Errol Flynn and Greek shipping magnate Aristotle Onassis. "We partied like crazy people," Gianni admitted,¹⁰ in cocaine-fueled carousing sessions known as *les nuits blanches*. Aircraft, boats, servants, skiing, fast cars and palatial villas were taken for granted, as was meeting any member he liked of the family football team Juventus. There was something of *The Great Gatsby* about it all. One woman supplanted another, and when his sister Susanna once told him she was in love, he had been shocked, "How is that possible? I thought only servants fell in love."¹¹ Gianni may have considered himself resistant to love but within weeks Pamela's usefulness meant she became central to his life in the way that no other woman had. The benefits went two ways—the effect on her lifestyle, wardrobe and jewelry collection was startling.

On October 1, 1948, Diana Cooper was traveling first class on the sleeper from Rome to Paris, and when the train stopped at Turin, a uniformed butler boarded with luxurious luggage, sheets and towels monogrammed with the Agnelli crest, a soft plaid rug and even a small bunch of flowers. The flurry was followed by "no less than Spam Churchill in the radiance of her success and beauty" and filling the compartment with "expensive scent." Before the train pulled out, she could hear Pamela and Gianni whispering "anguished farewells": "Spam's back curved over the window in coquettish kissing so longs, wagging its tail under the darkest sleekest of baby mink coats." As she finally turned to greet Diana, the giant gems at Pamela's ears "socked" her jaw leaving dark marks on her skin. One of her fingers was also black under the weight of her ring.¹²

Parading such baubles in Paris, Turin or on the Riviera was one thing, but Pamela knew better than to wear them in London. When she visited the Churchills, she placed the jewels in her handbag, not least because she knew they frowned upon her fraternizing with a man they called "that Italian car mechanic." And yet when Winston senior saw her he forgave her, as his secretary Jane Portal (Peter Portal's niece) remembers: "I went up to Churchill's bedroom one morning with the papers and there was this beautiful girl curled up on the end of his bed, making him chuckle and making him happy."[13]

Many have divided Pamela's life into parts according to her men, but it is not that simple. While she was falling for Gianni she still fervently hoped to find a meaningful role of her own. And Pamela had an uncanny knack of being in the right place at the right time. She rejected Turin in favor of Paris, which "for ten years after the war" was the "hub of everything."[14] That meant, in particular, the international institutions charged with reconstructing Europe and building a new postwar world order—efforts that she continued to yearn to be part of.

First, though, Pamela needed somewhere to live. Through the Coopers' parties at the British Embassy, she had met Paul-Louis Weiller, the enormously wealthy cofounder of Air France whose Jewish heritage had seen him stripped of his French citizenship by the Vichy government in 1940. Since the war ended, he had extended extraordinary generosity to high-ranking Allied figures, perhaps hoping to buy himself the security brutally denied him before. Pamela was included in his largesse when he gave her the use of an "adorable" house on rue Delabordère in the wealthy suburb of Neuilly. By the time the Duke and Duchess of Windsor moved to their mansion close by, she was part of their regular social circle, attending Christian Dior's funeral a few years later arm in arm with Wallis. She dined at their house twice a month, occasions she found a "great showcase of perfection." Never included in royal circles in London, she thought of the duke as "my King" and was fond of Wallis, who taught her how to run a household to regal standards. "Now and again" the Windsors would deign to dine at Pamela's.

In postwar Britain—when extramarital sex had once again become taboo for women—there had been a growing society reaction against Pamela's wartime erotic escapades. Their strategic purpose was of course unknown, and she was widely dismissed as a "scarlet woman"—her fling with Aly Khan merely increasing the disapproval in the snobbiest salons. By contrast, "When she came to Paris she was a star," said jet-setter John Galliher. All the "attractive people" wanted to know this young and glamorous Churchill.[15] Pamela's social network became so extensive she divided it into three sections reflecting facets of her life.

First, her café society friends—led by the Windsors and multimillionaires Charlie de Bestegui and Arturo Lopez-Willshaw—offered opulent parties, super-yachts, world-class art collections and eye-catching *ménages à trois*. Her second circle of friends, the intellectuals, assisted with her unceasing quest to educate herself. The playwright and novelist Irwin Shaw, whom she knew from the Churchill Club in London, stepped in to help with the mission she tagged "Trying to Learn about Art" (she could not countenance being less knowledgeable than Marie Harriman). Belying her reputation as a gold digger (a charge she accepted as "fair game" as it was true that a lot of people she knew were "very, very rich"[16]), Pamela had a fling with the distinctly unwealthy novelist Maurice Druon.*

The designer Georges Geoffrey coached her in eighteenth-century French decor (she preferred the leaner lines of Louis XVI to the fussiness of Louis XV) by touring the back rooms of the antiquaries on

---

* Druon seems to have been greatly inspired by the liaison, publishing a novel called *The Film of Memory* (made into a movie starring Liza Minelli) about a great courtesan. She "seldom missed a famous man within her reach without bequeathing a memory," Druon wrote about his heroine. "Her lover was glory and her bed a pantheon."

the Rive Gauche. Christian Dior loved to see her wear his clothes and gave many to her, either for free or at knock-down prices. "All my life I've been told from my mother down, I couldn't wear red as I had red hair," she recounted. "Christian said, 'You have got to wear red. I'll show you which kinds.'"[17]

And perhaps contrary to her own expectations, Pamela collected several female friends in this group. "She liked other women and was a good gossip," remembers Stella de Rosnay, whose father Sir Gladwyn Jebb had taken over from Duff Cooper as British ambassador. "It's not at all true she only spoke to men."[18] Diana Cooper had introduced Pamela to Duff's Parisian mistress, the literary *saloniste* Louise de Vilmorin. Pamela thought Louise one of the "most seductive women I've ever met"[19] but there seems to have been little competition between them. Louise sent her hand-drawn cards with gushing declarations of affection. The fondness was real but so was the calculation. Pamela knew many prominent Parisians were seen as "rather suspect" for having "survived with the enemy," and while there was "never a suggestion" Louise had collaborated[20] she was undoubtedly grateful for the cachet of being friends with a Churchill. Pamela enjoyed the power this gave her but held back from becoming too close.

Pamela's third and favorite circle were her diplomatic crowd, who helped keep her plugged into high-level politics on both sides of the Atlantic. She bartered Churchill stories for up-to-the-minute insights into Washington's thinking on America's part in the postwar world order from figures such as Cy Sulzberger (of the newspaper dynasty that owned the *New York Times*). One evening, Sulzberger wrote excitedly in his diary that Pamela had told him that Winston had promised his family in 1940 that he would resign as PM the day the war ended. When the time came, he had of course gone back on his word. "Unfortunately, said P, even the slightest taste of power corrupts."[21] Sulzberger thought Pamela "nice, beautiful and kind" and his Greek wife, Marina, was her closest female friend in the diplomatic set but

Pamela could not help trying to extract information wherever she could. A junior official at the American Embassy—where she attended parties thrown by Ambassador David Bruce and his wife, Evangeline—was astonished at her attentions while she pressed him for information. "She doesn't interest me sexually," he told his wife, "but she makes one feel so wonderful, like a king."[22]

What preoccupied her most of all was the growing threat of a new world war. In Fulton, Missouri, on March 5, 1946, Churchill had publicly voiced alarm—which she had frequently heard him express in private—about the Iron Curtain descending from Stettin in the Baltic to Trieste in the Adriatic, behind which the peoples of Eastern Europe were subjugated to Soviet control. In a speech that articulated much of Pamela's own thinking and which she frequently cited, he coined the term Special Relationship to describe the emotional as well as geopolitical ties between Britain and America. Centered on cooperation in nuclear weapons development and intelligence sharing but deepened by "fraternal association"—Pamela might have called it something else—Churchill hailed it as the best (and perhaps only) way to resist Soviet expansion and the growing threat to the West. Thereafter it became clear that the Cold War was evolving into a psychological contest for hearts and minds (communism vs. capitalism) as well as an all-out military rivalry.

The prospect of conflict drew uncomfortably close in 1948 in one of the first major crises of the Cold War when the Soviets blockaded land access to the sectors of Berlin occupied by Britain, France and America in a bid to bring the entire city under their control. The Allies united to mount a spectacular airlift of more than two million tons of fuel and food for the stranded inhabitants. Moscow finally lifted the blockade in May 1949 but also unexpectedly tested its first atomic bomb. The world now had two nuclear superpowers hostile to each other and running an arms race. As a response to this increasingly frightening world, America and its Western European allies created the North Atlantic Treaty Organization (NATO) against their common foe.

NATO helped consolidate Paris's position when in 1952 it set up its headquarters at the Palais de Chaillot. Several of Pamela's wartime male friends took senior roles but women were rarely employed outside the typing pool and there were no openings for her. Paris also became home to the new European Coal and Steel Community (the precursor of the European Union) and the European headquarters of the Marshall Plan. The Plan's new special representative in Paris was Averell Harriman—and there was no way he was going to give Pamela a job. Inevitably, though, they bumped into each other. Stiff with the sense of his own importance, Averell remonstrated with her for "ruining her life" by running around with good-for-nothing playboys. Never taking kindly to sanctimony, she replied "Oh, they're good for something," and, twisting the knife, added, "Or should I say good *at* something."[23]

They did not speak again for fifteen years but Averell's rebuke stung Pamela precisely because in her late twenties she longed for a serious purpose but was constantly denied it, despite all her experience and connections. She could only listen and watch but not do. "In some ways she would have liked to have been a man," recalls Mary Churchill's daughter Emma Soames, "because she had a good brain and women then couldn't do what they wanted."[24] How to get around that problem became her ultimate aim.

Pamela was rarely at peace with herself over her relationship with young Winston. When they were together they were affectionate but the countervailing force—her desire for an important role outside the home—was perhaps stronger. As Pamela discovered along with many other women, the freedoms hard won during the war collided in peacetime with renewed pressures to conform and the idealization of the role of wife and mother. There were plenty of bad mothers but they escaped censure if they obeyed the norms. Pamela did not. Winston was passed from pillar to post, Jane Portal more than once finding herself putting the boy to bed at Chartwell in the absence of anyone else. Jane was struck by how the young Winston seemed resigned to being left behind by his mother but treasured his dressing gown decorated with the Agnelli crest. "He was an adorable little boy," she says, "but I remember feeling sorry for him."[25]

Susan Mary Patten, the socialite wife of an American diplomat, once had to pick Winston up from a Paris railway station because his mother was stuck with Gianni in Turin when snow grounded all flights. Patten claimed that that was "how she brought up young Winston. She would dump him with friends and neighbours" while she went off in search of a husband.[26] Pamela was "enraged" by only one aspect of Patten's account: "I wasn't ever looking for a husband," she insisted, at a time when it was inconceivable that single women would think about anything else.[27] "Everyone takes the same tack, that people didn't want to marry me. Nobody's ever thought I didn't want to marry."

Pamela's lack of interest in children was also considered weirdly unfeminine when maternity was rated as the ultimate in female fulfillment. The birthrate across the West was soaring—in America, women having six children were hailed as heroines—leading to a decade-long baby boom. Pamela loved her son but he was not her whole world and she did not want another child. "My mother was not maternal," was how the adult Winston saw it. He made the best of what was on offer. When Pamela treated him almost as a diminutive friend he obliged. "From the age of eight or nine, if she didn't have a male escort I was expected to be there in my navy blue suit, white silk shirt and smart tie."[28]

In January 1949 Pamela moved eight-year-old Winston to a boarding school in the Swiss mountains called Le Rosey, one of the most expensive in Europe, believing it would help his chronic asthma and eczema. The Le Rosey boys spent spring and summer terms in a château on Lac Léman near Lausanne, where it seems that Aly Khan (whose sons also attended "*l'école des rois*") provided her with an apartment. The lifestyle was certainly regal—boys dressed for dinner served by Swiss waitresses, while maids cleaned their rooms, did their laundry and polished their shoes. Perhaps it was Pamela's recognition of her own maternal failings that made her want the princeling treatment for her son. It was not all an easy life, however. The winter months were spent higher up at Gstaad, where the boys wore Ray-Ban Aviators for cutthroat ski races. Non-sporty types did not thrive; young Winston, who was the smallest boy in the school, suffered from severe homesickness but had to adapt fast.

Randolph objected to the boy being educated overseas. There was a flurry of legal letters[29] suggesting he might sue for full custody and Pamela enlisted the support of her former parents-in-law, pointing out that their grandson's health had improved. Randolph backed down but was bitter that his parents had again taken Pamela's side. He recruited an external ally—a man Pamela called the "beast."[30] Field Marshal Montgomery, often aggressive toward independent-minded women, disapproved of Pamela as much as she disliked him. While skiing in Gstaad early in 1951 he visited Le Rosey to take young Winston out to tea and wrote a stinging letter to Winston senior, informing him that his grandson was attending a school that was unsuitable and snobbish. If the boy was left there much longer, he reported, wishing to fashion the youngster in his own hardboiled image, "he might deteriorate both in character and what is less important, his work."[31] To Randolph's glee, Montgomery prompted a family hoo-ha about this "foreign" education and Pamela reluctantly agreed to send her son to school in England.

After a Berkshire prep school, young Winston started at Eton in January 1954, where he donned the school's famous top hat and tails but failed to fit in. It did not help that he had been living abroad and had acquired a slight French accent. Senior boys took it in turns to flog him for his chief crime of being called Winston Churchill—not least because his grandfather was prime minister again. As he wrote later, "the great thing about an English public-school education is one can go out into the world confident that life can contain few greater discomforts, humiliations or terrors."[32]

After one of Pamela's visits to Eton, senior boy Jacob Rothschild barked, "Who was that girl you were with yesterday?" Winston denied he had been with any "girl." "Oh! Yes," he countered, "I saw you with a very beautiful redhead!" Winston protested that he had been out with his mother, "but he refused to believe me!"[33] Pamela made his life still harder when she came to see him in a Mercedes—a German car, then unthinkable for most British patriots. As they drove away together, he burst into tears and wailed, "Why can't you be like other people's parents?"[34]

17

Pamela had no intention of being like other mothers. She finally dropped her concerns about the past and agreed to make Gianni and Fiat her new political project. By 1949 she had moved into Château de la Garoupe overlooking Cap d'Antibes—which he rented every summer for four months—giving her more time and space to work on her plans for him. In an era when women needed an "attachment to get ahead," explained Baroness Hélène de Ludinghausen of Yves Saint Laurent couture, "she seemed to attach better than anyone."[1]

First, a faultless La Garoupe became the envy of Gianni's friends. By the time he arrived, clutter had been cleared, candles lit, cushions plumped and Pamela and the staff dressed in immaculate evening attire. Gianni was emerging as a fashion icon, setting the trend for moccasins without socks, an expensive watch outside his shirt cuff and an untipped Chesterfield between his lips. Pamela worked on the other aspects of his life. Above all, she tutored him to rise above car production, which in truth was never his forte, to become a statesman in all but name, admired by the likes of future Secretary of State Henry Kissinger.[2] Princess Galitzine, an Agnelli family friend, noted that pre-Pam Gianni had had "quite a few rough edges." Pamela "civilised" him—encouraging him to become more polished and courteous—and shaped the international force he became. "She taught him a lot."[3]

Pamela steered Gianni away from anyone whose own wartime reputation might detract from her project (including the Windsors, who were near neighbors) and toward those politically advantageous to Fiat. When Gianni was away she feasted on gossip with Noël Coward.[4] When he was around, she drew in a more serious crowd and, through her, Gianni made important connections, including Bill Paley and Franklin Roosevelt Jr. (who became Fiat's distributor on the U.S. East Coast), and she almost certainly sparked his friendship with Jack Kennedy. She even pulled off the unlikely feat of getting him together with Winston Churchill at a dinner she organized at the Château de Madrid restaurant above Beaulieu, enlisting the Hollywood legend Greta Garbo to put the old man in a "very good mood."[5]

Gianni "wanted to transcend his Italian ways and background as he saw them as limiting," explains a member of the Roosevelt family. "His desire was to be part of the global scene. Pamela was his *passe partout* [access to the highest levels]." She was able to drill him in the political arts she had gleaned in Downing Street, identifying who held power, how the levers of power work and how to flatter world leaders and win them around, all in the cause of creating optimum conditions for Fiat and Italy. Pamela was never involved in the business itself. But she knew exactly who Gianni needed to see and what to say at a time when America looked on with rising alarm as Italian communists organized general strikes and food riots in the streets in a bid to sow chaos and ultimately seize power.[6] Gianni was able to forge tighter ties with Washington—including the newly founded CIA, where Pamela had connections through Jock Whitney and others—by presenting his company as a bulwark against the so-called Red Menace in Italy. Fiat's reconstruction was duly kick-started with soft loans from the Marshall Plan. Later, the CIA helped fend off communist-inspired strikes to ensure production of the new Fiat 500, its first mass-market model and a huge part of its postwar success. As Gianni afterward admitted, without America deciding to back him, "it all could easily have been taken away" with grave consequences for his country.[7] Gianni had a "huge responsibility to Italy," explained Frank Vreeland, a CIA officer in the American Embassy in Rome, and devoted his life to "make Fiat strong" to "strengthen the entire economy of Italy."[8] Fiat would indeed go on to lead Italy's revival and in time Gianni came to operate on an "equal footing with world leaders" and to be seen across the world as an "uncrowned king."[9]

Gianni repaid Pamela's help with a swanky apartment in Paris, a butler, a blue custom-built Bentley Cresta,[10] a chauffeur and accounts with top couturiers. After one brief visit, her befuddled father exclaimed, "How clever my daughter is to manage such a wonderful life on her tiny allowance!" Gianni also doted on young Winston, who came to stay at La Garoupe for a fortnight in the summer under the care of Mrs. Martin. There were often other children, creating something of a family atmosphere, and Mrs. M took them swimming on the sandy side of the rocky promontory. In the mornings, Winston liked to take his mother and Gianni their orange juice in bed. One time, when Pamela was about to sail off alone with her lover, Pamela told the sobbing child he must stay behind but Gianni said the trip was off unless Winston came too.

Her attachment to Gianni did not stop other men trying their luck. At the start of the summer holidays in 1949, eight-year-old Winston went to Paris for a rare few days on his own with his mother when Ernest Hemingway invited them to lunch at the Ritz. Afterward Hemingway led them down to the bar where he had held court after the liberation, walking past a glass display case containing a Swiss army knife with ivory handle. Winston pestered Pamela to buy it for him, but she was firm in her refusal. When they reached the bar, Hemingway claimed he needed to make an urgent call and returned a few minutes later brandishing the knife and giving it to Winston. If he meant to impress Pamela he only succeeded in enraging her. "I never really liked him," she said, "he was a troublemaker,"[11] but Hemingway, whose sexual hang-ups were notorious, had an unrequited crush on her. He wrote what she described as a "pornographic" verse called "Black-Ass Poem After Talking to Pamela Churchill"—one that through a series of rhetorical questions appears to explore the agony and anger of rejection. Perhaps the most revealing lines are: "Who, knowing treasure, does not fear, / When he has seen it close and near?"[12]

Pamela's four-hundred-square-meter residence at 4 avenue de New York occupied the piano nobile of a handsome building, with floor to ceiling windows looking over to the Eiffel Tower. Truman Capote, style fiend (and later author of *Breakfast at Tiffany's*) declared it one of the most beautiful in Paris.[13] Invitations to her champagne salons on Sunday evenings became highly sought after. She tried to match Gianni's aristocratic credentials (his mother had been a blue-blooded Bourbon del Monte) by filling her new home with antique porcelain decorated with ostriches—a proud declaration of her Digby heritage even if her parents rarely featured in her life. Pamela and Gianni were widely accepted as a couple—and she was now fluent in Italian—yet he never stayed overnight at the apartment and she sensed that he was holding himself back. Her suspicions were confirmed when Suni, her favorite of his sisters, warned her that he could "never marry somebody who isn't a Catholic."[14] If Pamela had not seriously contemplated marriage before, this apparent obstacle spurred her on. Her sister Jacquetta was converting in order to marry a Scottish Catholic. These were different times: why should she not do the same?

The Digbys and the Churchills opposed the whole idea—but not on the grounds of religion. Pansy and Kenny knew their opinion held little sway but Pamela also chose to dismiss old Winston's warnings that marrying a former enemy could not make her happy.[15] She took instruction from Father Christie at the fashionable Catholic church on Farm Street in London (where Kick's funeral had taken place) and sought advice on annulling her first marriage so that she would no longer be considered a divorcée. While Pamela's conversion was straightforward, the annulment was complex. Lady Baillie and David Margesson were dragooned into submitting depositions to the ecclesiastical courts that they had warned her against marrying Randolph and that she had done so only because it was wartime, imagining that if it did not work out she could divorce. The words "I could get a divorce" were pivotal, Pamela explained, as they showed in "the eyes of the church that I didn't believe in what I was doing."[16] The legal arguments dragged on at the Vatican long after she entered the Catholic faith. By then, Pamela's relationship with Gianni had changed.

His thrill-seeking life was never for the faint-hearted but Pamela's tolerance waned when, just past her thirtieth birthday, she became pregnant. Having a baby out of wedlock was not even considered—and without the annulment she was not yet free to marry Gianni. She did what many women did at the time, despite Rome considering abortion a mortal sin. Terminations were illegal in Britain, Italy and France, so she traveled with Gianni to Switzerland. He shed a few tears as he dropped her off at the clinic in Lausanne but chose not to wait, unwilling to confront the consequences of his own actions. He had begun to sleep with other women, but it was galling that he had leaped into bed with a model while Pamela was on the operating table and while she was nauseous after the procedure told her the details of the encounter.[17] Gianni could apparently give her anything—except fidelity.

Afterward, Gianni seemed more distant. Pamela hoped to provoke a reaction by having her own affair with the scion of a wealthy Greek shipping family, André Embiricos, but Gianni was unmoved. Or rather, it emboldened him to set out to seduce whomever he wanted, apparently without remorse. Gianni's decision to trade in renting La Garoupe for buying the even more lavish Villa Léopolda on the western flank of Cap Ferrat did not prevent a further cooling in their relationship. Pamela was still intent on transforming La Léopolda, once owned by the King of the Belgians, into a palace fit for the "king" of Fiat—bringing in the designer Stéphane Boudin, who had worked for both the Duchess of Windsor and Lady Baillie, to refresh the interiors and an English landscape gardener to improve the grounds. When she had finished, La Léopolda, with its enfilade of gilded reception rooms and majestic terrace looking out to sea, was acknowledged as the most spectacular estate on the Riviera, and for a while the most valuable house in the world. No luxury was spared—or needed to be as Gianni enjoyed an annual allowance said to have been more than $1 million (over $12 million today).

If Gianni was grateful to Pamela for her efforts, his increasingly wild partying suggested otherwise. "Gianni was perpetually high on cocaine," says an Agnelli family friend, citing rumors that his septum had to be rebuilt in platinum. True or not, Gianni had lost much of his sweetness and restraint. "Please accept again my apologies for the most unfortunate and embarrassing incident of last night," his fellow playboy Aristotle Onassis wrote to her after another raucous evening.[18] Word of Gianni's madcap lifestyle had reached the Churchills—and privately Pamela shared their alarm that he might encourage her son to do something foolhardy. Her fears were realized on a skiing trip to St. Moritz when Gianni took the boy to watch the Cresta Run. Hurtling head-first down the ice on a toboggan going eighty miles an hour was catnip to Gianni and he decided to have a try, leaving Winston with little choice but to follow suit. The first Pamela knew of it was when, from her vantage point halfway down the mountain, she saw a second, smaller figure fly past and guessed, to her fury, what had happened.

Winston was consequently sent to spend most of the summer of 1952 with his father and stepmother in Bognor Regis and his Digby grandparents in Ireland. When it was Pamela's turn, she avoided the South of France and took a house lent by Aly at Deauville. Pamela sat with Winston and his school friend on a windswept Normandy beach, her mind fixed on what Gianni was up to in her absence.

Winston returned to England in mid-August laden with a huge fillet of French beef for his Churchill grandparents—a gesture that was much appreciated as meat was still hard to come by.[19] Pamela dashed down to La Léopolda to be informed that Gianni was in Turin. Feeling tired while dining out with friends, she left earlier than expected, arriving back at the house just after midnight. Wanting to soak in the moonlit view before bed, she walked out onto the terrace, then let out a piercing scream when she encountered a couple entwined on one of her oversized white sofas. It was Gianni with Anne-Marie, the twenty-one-year-old daughter of their friend the Comte d'Estainville. "Pam was very upset, naturally, and she flew at the girl," said Eddie Digby, recounting his sister's unusual loss of composure. "Gianni tried to prevent her and got his face slapped. There was a hell of a row."[20] Pamela was enraged at their joint duplicity—she had been friendly with Anne-Marie—but most of all at being confronted with Gianni's lack of respect when she had devoted her life to his advance. Gulping for air between her sobs, she yelled at them to get out. "Gianni and I were staring like idiots," says Anne-Marie, while Pamela acted "like a tornado."[21]

Gianni offered to take Anne-Marie back to her parents while Pamela looked at the empty champagne bottles and consoled herself that young Winston had not witnessed the scene.[22] After they had driven off, she took a sleeping pill to blot it all out. It was 3 a.m. when the phone rang by her bed and she was informed that Gianni had crashed at high speed into a butchers' truck on the Corniche, near the Cap Roux tunnel. Anne-Marie had suffered only scratches and had been picked up by friends of Gianni's, who washed her cuts with gin and took her home. The three butchers were also thankfully not seriously hurt and were quickly "taken care of" to avoid a lawsuit. It was Gianni who had borne the brunt of the impact, and it was not clear whether he would survive.

Pamela rushed to the hospital in Nice where Gianni had been taken after being cut from the wreckage. He was unconscious, the doctors informing her that amputating his crushed right leg might be the only way of saving him and so he was already being prepared for theater. Knowing Gianni would never forgive her for allowing them to proceed, she blurted out that he had taken cocaine—she had seen the evidence on his bedside table—so the surgeon was obliged to abandon all but minor surgery under local anesthetic. For the next few months she stayed by his hospital bedside, Father Christie writing to her that "Providence operates to make us into the type of person he wants us to be."[23]

Finally, Gianni was discharged to Villa Agnelli near Lucca, where his three sisters insisted on taking charge. Steely individually, collectively formidable, they set about using their brother's convalescence to reclaim him from Pamela, whom they thought a gold digger and "too bossy." "They went to war against her," Marina Branca, a friend of the family, recalled.[24] "They erected a barrier around themselves," agrees Gill Ross, a British former au pair for one of the sisters. No one from a different background was ever "good enough."[25] Fearful that Pamela's devotion would result in a formal marriage proposal, they argued the crash would never have happened without her undignified scene. Gianni was equally critical, claiming that an Italian woman would have maintained a decorous silence. "I don't like people who display their feelings, who scream and squeak," he said. "It doesn't look nice."[26] His younger brother Giorgio, who had been badly affected by their mother's untimely death, even tried to shoot Pamela through her bedroom door. He missed but shook her up even more. The crash and its aftermath also forced Pamela to acknowledge that Gianni would never change, and to consider how much she wanted a future in which "starlets would be popping out of every wardrobe."[27]

In February 1953, Pamela's annulment came through—around the time Gianni made a substantial contribution to the Catholic

Church—but far from paving the way for them finally to marry, it presaged the end. "Everything I'd done . . . was Gianni," she recalled. "I'd never really thought what would happen afterwards." She had not inherited great wealth and nor as a woman could she earn it but returning in defeat to England was surely too great a humiliation. "What in life," she thought, "is ever fair?" Seeking solace in one of Turin's old churches, she sat alone under the vaulted ceiling and sobbed.

The Agnelli sisters had meanwhile set their sights on an exquisite young aristocrat with a swan-like neck said to be the longest in Europe, who hailed from the ideal Italian bloodline to produce the next Fiat heir. Seven years younger than Pamela, Princess Marella Caracciolo di Castagneto had been in love with Gianni for years and was also apparently not the sort to fly into jealous rages. The sisters invited her to Villa Agnelli, where Pamela believed they "stuffed" her into Gianni's bed.[28]

Gianni knew the sacrifices he would demand of any future wife (even if he was actually reluctant to commit to anyone) and that Pamela could not make them. "If I marry an Italian, she will never leave me," he told her. "If I marry you, you will." She knew he was right and it was she who decided it was better not to marry at all.[29] She packed her bags to get out on her own terms. Pamela could not have been more helpful to Gianni but perhaps she had overstepped the mark in such a conservative society as Italy, where strong-minded women were seen as unattractive. "When people want something very much, they always think it's going to be possible," she thought, but now she knew it could never be.[30] Gianni was an Italian man of the 1950s and did not want a marriage in which his wife wished to operate as his equal. Knowing what he was about to lose, though, Gianni sat in silent tears as they journeyed north together, the car windows flecked with sleet. When they reached the French border checkpoint high on an Alpine pass, he stepped out to walk to another car driven by a chauffeur. Pamela watched in the rear-view mirror as the love of her life limped away through the snow. As he was driven back to Turin, she returned to Paris alone.

In October 1953 Gianni came to see Pamela at the Paris apartment—which he had transferred to her name—looking deeply troubled. It was far from the first time he had sought her counsel on political issues over the past few months. This time it was on a personal matter. Marella was pregnant and would not, as he put it, "do anything about it." Marry her! Pamela told him. He was adamant he did not want to, but Pamela was insistent. She could see Marella was perfect for him in a way that she never could be, and that of course she would keep the child. A month later, Marella and Gianni became husband and wife at Osthoffen Castle near Strasbourg. And yet Ghislaine Graziani, widow of Gianni's great friend Benno, talks of how Gianni's relationship with Pamela was enduring and "never just an affair."[31] Gianni had already started the habit of phoning her at seven every morning, as he did for the rest of her life. "Jonny and I," Pamela herself observed, "never broke up but we parted."[32]

18

Pamela switched seamlessly from answering the phone with the Italian "pronto" to the French greeting "*Ici Pam*."[1] It signaled even before Gianni married Marella that her relationship was over and she would be after another. She had kept the apartment, the Bentley and other "alimony" from Gianni, but when Pamela sashayed through town wearing couture and a determined smile, the wives and mistresses of the rich men of Paris took a collective deep breath. Even Nancy Mitford was on red alert over her sometime lover Gaston Palewski, a dapper Gaullist politician of Polish heritage. "Pam Churchill is after the Polish Beau Brummel," she wrote in high dudgeon to Evelyn Waugh. "He is puzzled, but not displeased."[2]

Approaching her mid-thirties, Pamela set about her mission with military precision, involving large beauty cases of expensive potions, Porthault silk pillowcases (said to prevent wrinkles), lie-ins until noon and fasting on nothing but water and lemon juice. Exercise hardly featured in her itinerary but on his way to the Duchess of Windsor, Paris's most sought-after hairdresser, Alexandre, visited every day to rinse her locks in chamomile to enhance color and shine. Vendeuses from Dior and Balenciaga dropped by to fit her for dresses, pinning the fabric to flatter her size four figure. "She had very nice legs," said one from Dior, "good shoulders . . . and beautiful breasts, probably the best I ever saw in my life . . . The bad thing was her waist."[3] Pamela played up her *décolletage* and had a maid cinch in her middle for the

1950s hourglass silhouette. She seemed astonishingly glamorous to her teenage niece Celia Sandys. "It was an incredible transformation," she says of Pamela's years in Paris. She became "charismatic, captivating."[4]

A single daytime outfit cost 3,000 francs, an evening one three times that. She needed dozens to compete in a social milieu even more vicious than New York, where the female blood sport was judging another woman's hem a centimeter too long or too short. "It was not a very attractive period," recalls Stella de Rosnay. "It was very judgemental of women."[5] At the end of each season Pamela donated her dresses to friends: a white Dior scattered with diamonds went to Marina Sulzberger. A full-time maid, Ernestine, looked after Pamela's wardrobe and three more maids and a butler kept the elaborate apartment pristine (Pamela did not subscribe to mid-century minimalism). She could not, however, sustain this level of expenditure for long. "I needed a lover," she said, but not for love.[6] Out of necessity, she forsook political ambitions to reinvent herself as a full-time *grande horizontale*.

Élie de Rothschild was a member of a haughty Parisian clique that dismissed Pamela as a voracious man hunter, but he met her at a dinner party when his wife was out of town and was bowled over. "She was a handsome woman" but it was Pamela's manner, her friend the fashion designer Oleg Cassini thought, that was her "aphrodisiac." She became "the last of the great geisha girls. She looked deep into your eyes when she spoke to you," with a "hypnotic gaze" and "you felt empowered, bewitched."[7] Élie instantly appreciated what a trophy she would be to add to his châteaux, racehorses, yachts, art and vineyards. "I wanted to go to bed with her," he informed a friend, "and I did."[8] She had Élie hooked but to reel him in, Pamela bought a cigarette box from Cartier, had it engraved on the inside with a note about having enjoyed the most exciting night of her life, and sent it around to him.[9] Unaware that this was her custom, Élie felt he could lord it over even

Pamela's illustrious roster of lovers. And as he referred to her in the boorish terms that amused him: "Once it is washed, it is like new."[10]

A bony-looking man of thirty-six dressed in Savile Row suits and with a trim mustache, Élie had, under parental pressure, married *in absentia* while in a prisoner-of-war camp. His wife, Liliane, had gone to great pains to ensure he had enough food and had patiently waited for him. Yet on his release at the end of the war he had ungallantly made it clear that he wished he had been allowed to choose someone else. Later, when she found out about the affair, there were outpourings of sympathy for Liliane—a plain but amusing woman—and scorn for Pamela. "It was unpardonable," Stella de Rosnay explains, "to be Élie's mistress."[11] Few thought to blame Élie.

Pamela tried to justify herself by arguing (correctly) that "if it hadn't been me, it would have been somebody else."[12] It was, however, a strategic mistake, as many in Paris society deplored her ruthlessness. Influential figures such as Evangeline Bruce ostentatiously took Liliane's side against the transgressor she referred to as "that woman." Diana Cooper thought "courtesanship" was doing Pamela "harm," even if she had bagged an enviable collection of diamonds. "I'm fond of Pam (I find everybody says this before the lashing)," she observed. "She's a girl who is affectionate and likes to help people but . . . she is pitiless about Élie's wife. Can't understand how she can act so naggingly & selfishly."[13]

Worst of all was when the Queen Mother visited the City of Light in 1956 and Pamela was one of hundreds who expected to be invited to an evening reception at the British ambassador's palatial residence. Cynthia Jebb, the socially cutthroat wife of the British ambassador, reputedly declared that she would not have "that red-headed tart in my house," let alone have her mingle with royalty. Stella de Rosnay questions whether her mother used those exact words but remembers that the Foreign Office instructed the Jebbs to keep Pamela off the guest list: "She wasn't *très bien vue* because of her reputation. It was all so ridiculous and snobby."[14] Many of Pamela's lovers were welcomed without further thought.

Cynthia organized a low-key lunch for those deemed unsuitable for the royal event—"first and foremost," she wrote in her diary, "Pam Churchill."[15] Pamela declined the second-string invitation but knew she had no chance when the young Queen Elizabeth came to Paris on a state visit the following year. The snub rankled for the rest of her life, and she was determined that one day she would get even. Pamela began to draw parallels between her ostracism and that of her ancestor Jane Digby, one of the subjects of a 1954 bestseller, *The Wilder Shores of Love*. Such attention made Pamela "very proud of Jane." "I adore her," she said, but England "treated her so badly."[16]

Pamela's relationship with Élie was devoid of the physical and emotional magnetism that had enthralled her with Gianni. Pamela missed feeling "adored" but Élie's attentions were "very flattering to me at a time when I needed to be flattered."[17] He also bought her time while she reviewed her future but she did not intend to rush things. "There was none of this clock ticking," she said. "I'd had a child. I'd been married once."[18] She avoided being seen with Élie in public but after putting in a short morning at the family bank he would hurry to her apartment. Everyone knew, even the Duke of Windsor, who in July 1954 sat next to a female Rothschild at a wedding and asked her, "Can you tell me which Rothschild is having an affair with Pamela Churchill?" To which Liliane stood up in fury and replied, "Sir, that's my husband."[19]

Élie's generosity was nowhere near the Gianni league. True, when Pamela found what he agreed was a particularly desirable Louis XVI piece in a Rive Gauche gallery, she sent the bill to him. Occasionally, he would give a small parure of diamonds or emeralds. Mostly, though, he insisted on a limited budget. She could buy herself paintings if they cost less than fifty francs. Yet Pamela ran her apartment to Rothschild standards she had learned from her aunt Eva, the Countess of Rosebery (white-gloved butler, Sèvres dinner plates, monogrammed linens). She chuckled at Élie's attempts at humor, however coarse, and instructed herself in *terroir* and grape varieties so that she could converse about the family vineyard, Château Lafite. If he disliked a dress, she changed it and as he could not abide women making any noise during sex, she kept quiet as required. When young Winston was staying, she bribed him to stay out until a specified time.[20]

Élie did not require political guidance or his homes improved. Yet gradually he found himself wanting Pamela in his life permanently. He had been scarred by his experiences during the war, particularly being forced to wear the yellow star. Where others saw arrogance, Pamela recognized a man in need of confidence and knew how to give it to him. She became "very fond of Élie because he had so many hang-ups." Privately, she was excoriating about Liliane, saying that she pitied Élie for being married to a woman who, contrary to her public image, undermined her husband and who let him down by resembling, in Pamela's uncharitable view, "an old toad."[21] Liliane was not going to give up without a fight. She spied on Pamela's apartment, left her abusive notes and shunted Pamela's Bentley with her Mini.[22] An exasperated Élie told his wife he intended to marry his mistress but she refused to let him go.

Marella Agnelli had spent the first months of her pregnancy lying on sofas and reading French poetry. Unsympathetic to her condition—Pamela said that no one would dream of discussing women's issues with such a "very Italian man"—Gianni vented his growing resentment at his "sloppy" wife. Most wounding were his constant comparisons with Pamela. Gianni's sisters had expected calm acceptance from Marella. Yet when he cavorted with starlets at the Grand Hotel at Cap Ferrat—with stories of a bare-breasted Anita Ekberg chasing another of Gianni's conquests down one of the corridors—she exploded with destructive rage. On one occasion, Gianni burst into Pamela's room in a Monte Carlo hotel at five in the morning while his distraught wife was at La Léopolda overdosing on paracetamol.[23] Gianni fled to Pamela whenever he could, which hardly helped.

Pamela felt lonely, though, and in the absence of anyone else obliged the teenage Winston to traipse after her on summer trips to the Riviera. When Élie was around, he made no effort at all with the boy, who heartily disliked him. Gianni tried to cheer Winston up with a gift of a Chris-Craft mahogany powerboat and Max Beaverbrook gave him his own television. Yet such generosity could not compensate Winston for what he really wanted—a normal family life. Pamela was hardly sympathetic. "He never thinks of others but always himself," she complained to Randolph, "and the moment things aren't the way he wants them he sulks and is odious."[24] Foxed by conflicting emotions of anger and guilt, Pamela also resorted to giving money and pulling strings for Winston rather than paying him attention. Ultimately, her sense of maternal failure would almost destroy her.

It did not help that she felt out of sorts. When the Greek shipping mogul Stavros Niarchos invited her onto his yacht cruising around the Greek islands Pamela did not let on that she was suffering from chronic stomach pains but Diana Cooper noticed that Pamela's "torso" was "a bit on the spread."[25] Pamela's *mode de vie* was also increasingly unsettling. When with Gianni she had stayed in a chalet for her winter holidays at St. Moritz. Now she took a suite at the Palace Hotel—other guests included the ubiquitous Onassis and Niarchos—but there was no way she could pay the eye-watering prices and Élie would not. She juggled a troupe of wealthy lovers, one of whom she hoped would pick up her bill. Sex was her sport; she disliked skiing (skis were heavy and broken legs frequent) and her days were spent in beauty parlors preparing for her evening parade. Over the years Pamela told friends such as screenwriter Peter Viertel that "the bed part is less important than all the rest" but he was rightly skeptical. "She must have had a big physical message to hold those men."[26] Once asked who were the exciting conquests of those years, Pamela's voice dipped low: "Many, many, many . . ." She knew this hardly created a "family ambiance"[27] for young Winston and left him an hour away at Klosters under the care of a local Swiss woman.[28] Decades later, she found it impossible to "excuse" her conduct.[29]

She would not give up on Élie but was on the search for another option. Occasionally, she took up Onassis's invitations to cruise on his yacht, the *Christina O*, said to be the most luxurious (but tasteless) boat on the Riviera. With the raspy voice of a sixty-a-day smoker and dressed in shirts drenched in eau de cologne, Ari exuded power but Pamela thought him ugly, and vehemently denied his claims they were lovers. She preferred both Niarchos and his yacht, the *Créole*, a three-masted schooner with sails of white silk and walls hung with Renoirs, Cézannes and Van Goghs. When Pamela slept with him, he showered her with diamonds and furs, and settled her hotel bills, but sometimes all the self-conscious luxury palled, and he was not the answer. In September 1954 the travel writer Patrick Leigh Fermor spotted Pamela on the Greek island of Hydra, where the *Créole* was docked. She was "the focus of all eyes on the quay in pink shorts, gilt sandals and a-clank with gems" yet she was obviously unhappy. It was "a pretty good hell" on board, she confided to him, with "heavy" male "banter" over "sumptuous but straggling meals at all hours."[30] Niarchos also had a disturbing temper, once storming out of her Paris apartment simply because he did not care for the fashionable sole aux noix de coco she had asked her cook to prepare for him.

When she turned thirty-five in March 1955, she began to despair. That July, she sought answers in a popular new fad by commissioning a sixteen-page personal horoscope.[31] Pamela's stars apparently described her as someone with a "never-ending internal dream" who was "trying different paths with a passion." Although her men were "at the centre of her existence," she should not consider remarrying before she was forty-one and, the astrologist warned, 1971 would be a particularly challenging year. Although "expert" at the art of living and "charity to others," her health was only average and she might not be able to have another child. She kept the horoscope with her papers for the rest of her life, amazed at how accurate it proved to be.

Cruising on the *Créole* again that summer, Pamela was joined on board by Charles Wrightsman, an American oil millionaire and friend of Jack Kennedy. Her stomach pains were now so severe she could no longer hide them and Charles badgered her to have a checkup. Such an idea was a novel one in Europe—where medicine was largely focused on infectious diseases such as tuberculosis—but as she was planning a trip to America she agreed to consult a doctor in New York. After forty-eight hours of tests and a biopsy she left on the day before Thanksgiving to stay with the Whitneys, feeling increasingly concerned. On Monday morning she called the hospital to be told that she needed to come in for an urgent exploratory operation. After she came around, she was frightened to find a priest at her bedside and to be informed that surgeons had "found something." Apparently without obtaining her consent, they had conducted a hysterectomy. "We've taken away the baby-carriage," her doctor informed her, "but left you the play pen."[32] Details of the actual diagnosis are unclear—it seems that the American hospital suspected that she had cervical cancer, then the number-one killer of women, with a recent rash of famous victims such as Eva Perón, the First Lady of Argentina. (Some doctors blamed the cell changes caused by the spermicides many used for birth control.[33]) But her British physicians later deemed the hysterectomy unnecessary.

Hearing that Pamela was understandably distraught and knowing of her onetime passion for Ed Murrow, Clementine Churchill asked him to visit.[34] There was only one person, though, who Pamela felt was her own and she cabled Randolph to permit young Winston to join her in New York. When Randolph suggested Winston delay leaving until after Christmas, Pamela sent a telegram from her hospital bed: "AM SO LONELY AND ALONE WOULD MAKE ALL DIFFERENCE IF WINSTON COULD ARRIVE DECEMBER 20TH PLEASE REPEAT PLEASE CABLE YOUR AGREEMENT LOVE PAMELA."[35] When Winston arrived after a sixteen-hour flight, the doctors informed him that their actions had almost certainly saved his mother's life[36]—but they also had consequences, including the early onset of menopause.

Jock Whitney pressured Betsey to take in Pamela and Winston for Christmas at their estate near Manhasset on Long Island and after New Year at their plantation house in Georgia, with its magnificent avenue of magnolias dripping in Spanish moss. Pamela was waited on hand and foot while Winston went quail hunting and was served picnic lunches by uniformed staff. It was an old-school world sumptuously cushioned from social changes all around, including the release that month of Elvis Presley's huge hit "Heartbreak Hotel." Presley's multiracial influences and sexually provocative style heralded a pivot in popular music and society at large. Pamela sniffed the winds of change but could not see her way to a satisfying future for herself.

Trained since birth not to malinger, Pamela was soon seen at fashionable events back in Paris, most memorably Marie-Laure de Noailles's costume ball, which she attended as an ethereal Titania, the fairy queen in *A Midsummer Night's Dream.* Amid the excitement, no one noticed that she was still not her normal self. The fact was she continued to feel "lousy." Six months later she was in such agony she canceled a summer holiday in the South of France to return to New York for an operation to correct a defect in her intestine. Afterward, she was free of pain for the first time in years. "I feel reborn," she told Max,[37] and she also had a new plan.

Pamela believed that Randolph never struck their son but his violence against his wife, June, rose to new levels during the Christmas of 1955, when the boy was with his mother in America. When old Winston came to stay for New Year, June blamed her black eye on walking into a door but Randolph confessed to his appalled father that he was the "bruiser" and Diana Cooper knew of at least three occasions when Randolph had beaten June, leaving her "piebald" with "bruises from [his] fist & boots." June became so frightened that she would lock herself in the bathroom—even when Winston was in the house—but Randolph would tear the door off its hinges.[38] Eventually, the Churchills tried once again to shut their son out of their lives; at one point, Clementine hardly spoke to him for two years. He was so short of money he went on an American quiz show, *The $64,000 Question*, certain he would scoop the prize but crashing out in the second round. By November 1956, June had filed for divorce, Winston patting her on the hand, repeatedly saying he was "so sorry."[39] Randolph's sisters Diana and Sarah were also drinking heavily, with a trail of broken marriages behind them. It was as if the next generation of Churchills—bar the redoubtable Mary—were floundering in the shadow of the Great Man. Finally feeling physically fit, Pamela decided she must prove she could succeed where Churchill's son and onetime anointed successor was evidently failing.

19

Pamela's convalescence had rekindled thoughts of making America her home. Washington, DC, was acquiring a new cachet. The provincial town of the 1940s had become the political capital of the world with thriving universities, galleries and museums, and a social scene to match. America's economy was booming, its military might was unrivaled and it was growing in confidence as the leader of the West. There were opportunities galore and the visa section of the American Embassy in Paris was thronged with young people hoping to emigrate to the buoyant New World. The tides of power and prestige were shifting—if only Pamela could follow them.

Ed Murrow needed no encouragement to pick up their old friendship even if relations were now "more warm than hot."[1] He helped Pamela renew old contacts and make new ones in America, where he was hailed as the scourge of McCarthyism. Flying across the Atlantic was speeding up and she decided to visit more often. Pamela's interest in affairs of state, however, marked her out as an "oddball" in America at a time when the (largely male) editors of women's magazines presumed that their readers were uninterested in "broad public issues."[2] Yet she peppered her well-placed American friends, both Republican and Democrat, with demands for political news, keeping a close eye on the dazzling career of Jack Kennedy (now a senator and married to Jackie Bouvier) who gave her a copy of his bestselling book *Profiles in Courage* inscribed "To Pam with the very best wishes of her old friend."³ She also caught up with the Republican president, Ike Eisenhower, who entered the White House in 1952 and won again in 1956, when he rewarded Pamela's great friend and his major donor, Jock Whitney, by appointing him ambassador to Britain. She welcomed Eisenhower's pro-British instincts, even if he did not share Churchill's focus on the Special Relationship above all others, and liked to hark back to the times when she had talked war strategy with him. And yet now such a memory seemed almost embarrassing—1950s women absorbed by politics or foreign affairs were widely pitied.

Many believed Pamela's interest must stem purely from the fact she was again on the hunt for a rich husband. If she was, then it was less about the money or indeed the husband than, as Oleg Cassini observed, the "vehicle" they offered to her ultimate goal. As a single woman in her mid-thirties her sole route into politics in Washington, just as in Europe, was as mistress or wife. "Politically involved men interested her," Cassini confirmed, but as "a way of gathering power."⁴

Marietta Tree, an American socialite Pamela knew from London during the war, offered a rare female role model. She had managed to engage in Democratic politics via a long-standing affair with presidential hopeful Adlai Stevenson. Overall, the tide of female expectation was going the other way, reflected by the movies in Hollywood. The cerebral, androgynous actresses of the 1940s—Marlene Dietrich, Greta Garbo and Katharine Hepburn—were being supplanted by breathless blondes such as Marilyn Monroe and Brigitte Bardot.

Pamela had followed Averell's career from afar. After an abortive run for president in 1952, he had finally won an election (if only narrowly) two years later to become governor of New York. Marie had not been helpful, having warned she would "jump off a bridge"⁵ if he ran for office and resenting the need to rise before noon to host official morning teas.⁶ A leaden speaker who lacked the "common touch," his tenure as governor lasted only one term. In 1956, Averell tried and failed again to secure the presidential nomination. Thereafter, with a group of similarly minded colleagues called the Six Wise Men, he returned his attention to America's world leadership role, which had become bogged down by careless spats with Allied countries, especially France.

America's power was nevertheless growing as Britain's waned. The process accelerated after the Suez fiasco in 1956, when Pamela's old friend Anthony Eden, now prime minister, launched the ill-judged Anglo-French invasion of Egypt to try to wrest back control of the newly nationalized Suez Canal (a vital oil supply route). The invaders had to retreat under massive political pressure from Washington—the new superpower in effect humiliating the old. It was not just a question of American military and diplomatic supremacy, a severe testing of the Special Relationship or a painful British retreat from imperial nostalgia. French prestige had also been dented and the national mood was downbeat. Susan Mary Patten noted in her diaries that even the Paris art market was "deadish" and energy had migrated westward to New York, where there was so much new money to spend.[7] And when Charles de Gaulle returned from the political wilderness in 1958 he heralded an unwelcome new puritanical age in France. As a pillar of moral rectitude, Madame de Gaulle would apparently be "made physically sick" if she so much as encountered a divorced person.[8] After a decade in Paris, Pamela felt she had exhausted its possibilities.

Pamela's renewed interest in the U.S. encouraged Americans with the grandest social aspirations to flock to her Paris apartment. Fine French furniture was all the rage in New York and Pamela's collection was almost as admired as she was. Dining at Pamela's offered a combination of delicious food, her sexy laugh and lashings of a velvety liqueur de poire. She saw a lot of Jock Whitney, especially after he became ambassador to Britain in 1957 and even more so the following year when he bought the *Herald Tribune* newspaper and its operation in Paris. The Paleys also made the "pilgrimage"—although while Bill paid court to the great seductress, Babe (now married to him as she had hoped) secretly fumed with jealousy. Babe was even more disgruntled when her sister Betsey sent Pamela to stay at the Paley home on a trip to America in 1958. Babe went through the motions, including arranging an outing to the theater, but needed an extra man for Pamela to create a foursome. She asked her best friend, Slim Hayward, just leaving for one of her frequent trips to Europe, if she could borrow her Broadway producer husband, Leland. Assuming her husband (who had to work for a living) was unlikely to interest a notorious fortune hunter, Slim replied, "No problem."[9]

Pamela had already met Leland several years before, on a Hollywood producer's yacht, but she did not remember. He had not forgotten her. Everyone on board had been "dressed for cruising" but she had wafted around deck in nothing at all bar a set of twinkling diamonds. Perhaps she had simply not bothered with a moderately wealthy man at a time when her eyes were only for her Italian princeling. With his silver crew cut and craggy face, Leland was not classically handsome, but many women (including his former amour Katharine Hepburn) found his boyish smile "adorable." He had previously worked as an agent for the biggest stars in Los Angeles but his white flannel trousers and yachting shoes lent him an East Coast vibe that appealed to Pamela. As soon as he gave her to understand he was "semi-split" from Slim, she found him "absolutely fascinating."[10] Every other word was "goddam" or "sonofabitch" but his enthusiasm was contagious and even at fifty-six there was a magnetic sexual appeal to him. He in turn was besotted with this woman eighteen years his junior with a legendary past who gave him the full hypnotic treatment. Leland asked Pamela out a couple of days later when he bemoaned that Slim had tired of the theater, was a serial adulterer who preferred hanging out with Ernest Hemingway and resented the fact that he did not have more money.

Leland had been going through a fallow period in his career and Slim had discovered that "beneath the surface enamel" was a "fragile man and his failures were beginning to wear on him."[11] His constant dramas had left her feeling like an "underpaid nanny"[12] and she had sought relief in trips to Europe and a series of affairs, including with Frank Sinatra. "Slim was married three times," said the novelist Leonora Hornblow, who had introduced her to Leland, "and never learned to be a wife."[13] What Leland wanted was a companion and partner. Pamela saw the chance for her ticket to America.

By the time Slim and her traveling companion, Hollywood star Lauren Bacall, had traveled on to Paris, Pamela had returned home and developed a plan of astonishing guile. Immediately on their arrival at the Hôtel Ritz, the concierge handed Slim a message from Pamela inviting them to supper. Slim and Lauren (known to friends as Betty) purred through the cold November evening to avenue de New York in Pamela's Bentley, to be ushered up to her softly lit apartment. The conversation over soufflé was, according to Slim, "extremely pointed" toward exploring her marriage. When Pamela asked outright whether Slim was happy with Leland, she naïvely replied, "Well, no marriage is perfect . . ." before the butler entered to announce a cable call from America and Pamela excused herself. Betty and Slim huddled to speculate which "big shot" it might be as transatlantic calls were still hugely expensive. Neither had even an inkling that the caller was Leland.[14]

When she returned to the table, Pamela seemed to know that Leland was arriving the next day and revealed that she had already organized a dinner party for the Haywards the following night. Slim still suspected nothing when she returned to the apartment with her husband twenty-four hours later, to find that Pamela had booked tickets for a play she thought Leland would find "amusing." Pamela sat next to Leland at dinner and again at the theater, and later took the group of twenty to a nightclub where she danced with . . . Leland. Slim wondered who was paying for it all but it did not occur to her what Pamela might be up to. The Haywards left the next morning for Munich to negotiate with Baroness Maria von Trapp for the rights to *The Sound of Music*. In the afterglow of clinching the deal, Slim forgot all about Pamela but Leland, the impulsive romantic, was entranced. Over the next few months he flew to Paris a dozen times on the flimsiest of pretexts.

Pamela was so excited by her "fast and furious" romance she consulted Ed Murrow about her new beau, to be told he was "marvellous."[15] But he also warned her of the consequences if the relationship were to become serious. As a theater producer Leland relied on Bill and Jock as investors. If Pamela moved in on Leland, Babe and Betsey had the means to make life difficult, socially and financially. Pamela was genuinely shocked but as Celia Sandys notes, "You can't make that much of a splash in the world without making enemies."[16]

Pamela hesitated. What should she do about Élie? Would he ever be free to marry her as he frequently promised? Did she want that anyway? Leland pledged he would divorce Slim but she had heard that before from Ed. Her "heart was with Leland" and her head with America but opting for him would be a gamble that she might well lose. On the other hand, did she want to be alone now that her possible brush with cancer had made her confront her own mortality? Was there also a recognition that it would be easier to sustain her Churchill connection in America, not least because Winston was himself half American? Leland would surely meet the great man's approval as, rather than being a European from a compromised country, he had contributed to winning the war by training British and American pilots. Since parting from Gianni she had seen the Churchills more often again, to the delight of both sides. (She had even been invited to Downing Street on the historic day in April 1955 when Winston had gone to Buckingham Palace to resign.[17]) On the other hand, Leland had warned her about the "horrors" of dealing with his troubled children's problems. She had not met them but how bad could they be? At least young Winston was now an adult, studying at the University of Lausanne for six months before going on to Christ Church, Oxford. Finally, at nearly forty, she felt her lotus-eating years were over and would she get a better offer? "Leland swept me off my feet," she recalled, and she sensed that she could make a difference to his work even if it was not political. "There was something very vulnerable about [him] that attracted me enormously."[18]

Pamela informed Élie that after five years of patience on her part she was leaving him for a future in America as Leland's wife. Élie pleaded with her to stay but became embroiled in "a big, big, big drama" with his family. The hurdle was once again religion—Élie had maintained his faith throughout his incarceration by the Nazis and the notion of divorcing a Jewish woman to marry a divorced Catholic convert was hardly popular. After a council of war, the Rothschilds informed Élie: "If you divorce, you're out."[19] Élie later told a friend that Pamela was the only one he had ever loved but his family had closed ranks against her.[20] When Pamela called for her cook one day, she found he had been let go.

After that, Pamela gave herself a fortnight to leave Paris for good. Élie was downcast but helped her sell her apartment for the hefty sum of $500,000.[21] Her courtesan life had been lucrative—she was now an independently wealthy woman with cash, jewels, frocks, an enviable collection of furniture and artworks and her own London apartment. On June 1, 1959, Cholly Knickerbocker reported the imminent arrival in New York of the "famous international siren."[22] Or as Leonora Hornblow put it, "here into their midst comes the vixen."[23] Pamela moved into a New York hotel and formally accepted Leland's proposal but soon questioned the wisdom of her haste when he delayed asking Slim for a divorce. "You just have to make up your mind," she mused, "and let the chips fall where they may."[24] She had no real idea, however, what she was letting herself in for.

20

It was a moment of peril that required nerves of steel. Leland had neither mentioned divorce to Slim nor canceled a "second honeymoon" she had planned in Europe. Finally, a week before they were due to depart, Leland deployed the hoary old excuse of "something has come up at work" and persuaded Slim to travel to Madrid on her own. Once the coast was clear, Pamela marked out her territory. She dined out alone with Leland in fashionable restaurants, spent weekends at the Haywards' house next to the Paleys' on Long Island and weekdays at rehearsals of *The Sound of Music*. She also briefed her tame gossip, Cecil Beaton, who she knew would pass word on to Truman Capote. "Your item about Leland and... the notorious... Pam C <u>stunned</u> me," replied Capote, who instantly relayed the news across New York.[1]

Pamela sent for young Winston to meet Leland and to her relief after his dislike of Élie, they hit it off, finding common interest in photography and, later, flying. Winston so enjoyed Leland's "open manner and dry humour" he asked to stay for the whole summer but detected "consternation" in his mother's voice at the idea of a prolonged visit.[2] She agreed but only if Winston busied himself with a job rather than getting in her way. She was helping raise funds for Jack Kennedy's campaign for the Democratic candidacy in the 1960 presidential election and she asked him to give Winston a job in his Washington office. But Randolph vetoed the plan in what Winston described as the "bluntest telegram" he ever received from his father, thundering that "since 1776 revolting colonists have resented us limeys interfering in their affairs."[3]

Pamela urged Winston to ignore his father but he did not dare and so she asked Jock to fix him up at the *Wall Street Journal* instead. Pamela only had to ask for many doors to open but if Randolph was jealous of her connections, Leland recognized the dangers. When Jock arranged for the eighteen-year-old Winston to cover a presidential press conference at the White House (normally the preserve of star correspondents), Leland was adamant he should not go. "Do you think you, as a cub reporter, would be sent down to Washington to do that unless you were who you are?" he roared. Pamela saw Leland's good sense. "It was very good for Winston," she realized later. "He didn't go."[4]

Winston was most excited about the chance to spend time in America with his mother, thrilled that their own relationship appeared to be blossoming now that Leland had made her "so happy." More enticing still for an only child who had no memory of his parents being together was the prospect of joining a family. He even suggested dropping out of Oxford to live in New York, bringing the ever-faithful Mrs. Martin with him. "She has, like me, few friends," he pleaded.[5]

Alas for Winston, it was not to be. He remained at Oxford, although he was determined to have a voice in his mother's new life. She was now with a man of limited means and she needed to let her French servants go. "Darling Mummy" would not in any case be required to dress to the exacting standards expected by *le gratin* in Paris.[6] Leland's extravagance during their courtship had suggested he was far wealthier than he was and Pamela carried on spending as she had always done, even though her own pockets were of course nowhere as deep as those of a Rothschild, Niarchos or Agnelli. She soothed Winston's worries with a gift of a brand-new Jaguar and Gianni added a white Fiat 600 for his use in the U.S.

As someone who understood Pamela better than most, Clementine was thrilled about Leland as she had been worried that Pamela had, despite her outward gaiety, been lonely. "I have often wished," Clementine told her, "that you would find a man you could truly and deeply love & that you would marry him."[7] Young Winston's delight at the prospect of joining the Hayward family had not, however, been universally shared. While Slim was in Spain, Leland invited his twenty-two-year-old eldest daughter to dine at Le Pavillon in New York, instructing her not to wear "too much of that crappy eyeshadow."[8] Over his third Wild Turkey bourbon, Leland declared he had met a wonderful woman he was going to marry. "But you're already married," Brooke pointed out, having like all three Hayward children become fond of their stepmother, Slim. His intended was "the greatest courtesan in the world!"[9] he retorted with pride. Brooke came to realize that her father "loved the idea that he and all these very rich, powerful and talented men were sharing her. It energised him. He was part of a club. The Pamela Club." To top it all, Pamela was related to Winston Churchill, "who had won the war."[10]

By the time Brooke, a part-time model, was to meet Pamela a couple of days later, she had built up a vision of a redheaded temptress. When thirty-nine-year-old Pamela opened the door of her hotel suite, Brooke judged her "matronly" and her Dior dress badly fitting. Pamela was nervous, and if she thought a diamond and sapphire brooch would win favor with her prospective daughter-in-law, it backfired. Brooke considered the gift excessive and almost certainly a cast-off. She remained unimpressed over dinner, discovering that Pamela knew next to nothing about the stage, the Hayward family's first love.[11] Brooke did have to admit that Pamela was a fast learner, though. Within weeks she could quote the gross earnings of every theater box office in New York.

Two weeks later Leland flew to Europe to talk to Slim. "For your own protection, for your own dignity, don't marry her!" she yelled at Leland after he finally requested a divorce. "Nobody *marries* Pam Churchill!" It was all too late, however. Slim realized that Pamela had employed "stealth" and a "genius for long-range planning" while she had been complacent. She understood what Slim had never grasped: Leland "liked being taken care of."[12]

When Slim returned to America in September, Leland denied that Pamela had already played hostess at the house in Manhasset but the evidence was plain. Pamela had even placed red stickers on furniture and paintings she wanted Leland to claim in the divorce.[13] Slim had been outmaneuvered but as an old friend observed, she was no "pushover" and refused to grant a divorce.[14] Drawing on the dark media arts she had learned from Beaverbrook, Pamela fought back by briefing the newspapers that she would be married by November. New York society was agog and swiftly divided into warring camps, with Babe Paley heading up the pro-Slim contingent vowing "undying enmity to that bitch." Pamela hit back at accusations of being a homewrecker, saying "I can't help it if someone doesn't want their husband and someone else . . . decides they do."[15]

Meanwhile, she moved into an apartment at the Carlyle Hotel, which she fixed up with her best French furniture and scented candles imported from Rigaud in Paris. The overall effect was of a European boudoir, a haven for Leland who craved luxury and quickly moved in. Determined to forget about her political dreams, she threw herself into Leland's work, accompanying him to New Haven where *The Sound of Music* was due to open for its pre-Broadway tryout. Here she helped smooth out friction between the lyricist Oscar Hammerstein, whom she found sweet and gentle, and the "big ego" composer Richard Rodgers.[16] Creative tensions were constant but so was the focus on the bottom line. Unused to the sharp end of commerce, Pamela exclaimed that she thought she had joined "an artistic family but all anybody ever does is talk about money!"[17]

Leland was a workaholic who drove himself to the point of

exhaustion and beyond, and was delighted at Pamela's determination to get involved, thereby proving she was different from Slim. Even her English accent was a prize—although she updated her hairstyle into a more practical American look and swapped long European baths for quick New World showers—and she moved easily in theatrical circles, knowing many figures from their stints in London in the war. The touring life was not, however, the pampered existence she was used to. The woman who had once reigned over the Riviera found herself in a motel bedroom at midnight, cooking chicken hash for the cast on an electric frying pan, having first sliced up the meat in her bathroom basin. No longer needing her Paris couture, she lent one of her gowns to Liza Minnelli to play a princess in a proposed musical remake of *Roman Holiday*.[18]

Such sacrifices did not deter Pamela from marrying Leland, nor did warnings from a series of concerned friends who informed her of a medical condition that caused him internal hemorrhaging when under severe strain. He was also addicted to sleeping pills, suffered from extreme allergies and a phobia of snakes, smoked heavily, drank too much bourbon and would eat only white foods, such as creamed chicken, mashed potatoes and vanilla ice cream. Then there was his family. His first wife had been institutionalized after a severe breakdown. His second wife, Margaret Sullavan, once a magnetic Hollywood actress, had become a depressive recluse. The three children she had with Leland were beautiful and talented but he had starved them of his time and fobbed them off with cash, encouraging them, according to their own mother, to "correlate *money* and *love*."[19]

His youngest child, Billy, had ended up as a suicide risk and Leland had had him detained at a mental health clinic in Kansas after he had set fires around the house.[20] Bridget, two years Billy's senior, had been treated for depression at a psychiatric facility in Massachusetts. Appearing to have improved, she had been released to live in New York but was a habitual shoplifter prone to silent rages. Only

Brooke seemed comparatively stable but in her teenage years she too had been a tearaway, described by her high school as "reckless, wanton" and responsible for ruining the health of at least two teachers.[21]

The cost of the clinics was crippling Leland, loading on the pressure to come up with ever more Broadway hits.[22] His spending instincts remained uncurbed, however, and he kept quiet about his financial problems but fretted out loud about burdening Pamela with his children as well as his health. At the time, she did not worry unduly but then, as she put it later, "ignorance is bliss."[23] Pamela reflected on her breakups with Ed and Gianni, how she had been cast out by Averell for the sake of his career and shunned by the Rothschilds. Coming up to her fortieth birthday, the truth was that she had few other options. "I'm going to marry him," she told the fashion editor Diana Vreeland. "I've had everything in my life, but I've never really had a husband."[24]

21

Pamela did not backtrack but New Year's Day 1960 tested her resolve to the limit. Margaret Sullavan, whose psychological battles had taken a darker turn, died from an overdose of barbiturates. Full of remorse that the breakdown of their marriage had contributed to her demise, Leland was inconsolable and Pamela feared he might be about to have another episode of bleeding. The tragedy also pitched her against Leland's children for the first but by no means the last time. When Leland dispatched Pamela in his limousine to inform his eldest daughter of her mother's death, an enraged Brooke appeared to blame her for the fact that her father had not come in person.[1] Later, Pamela was making arrangements for the funeral when she took a call from a store, asking her to authorize a new suit for Billy to be charged to the Hayward account. According to Brooke, Pamela declined.[2] Whatever her motives—a fear of uncontrolled spending, distrust of a young man with a past or resentment of the trouble he caused his father—her relationship with Brooke and Billy was set on a downward spiral.

Spring came and Slim was not budging on the divorce. Pamela and Leland had been living together for almost a year and he worried that she would tire of waiting and return to Paris. Leland offered Slim virtually everything he had, including the house on Long Island (which she accepted) and his share of the royalties from *The Sound of Music*, which she declined believing it a dud.[3] Finally, Leland insisted they install themselves in Las Vegas where after six weeks of residency he could secure a quickie divorce. For Pamela the prospect of finally "getting out was euphoria"[4] but nothing could have prepared her for Las Vegas life. It was not so much the industrial-scale gambling—she enjoyed playing the machines after the hotel bellboys told her which ones were not fixed. It was more the food—huge helpings of red meat and fries served at ungodly hours, such as dinner at six. "God, how awful! I mean, it really was!"[5] Word of her neon-lit sojourn in the Nevada desert was received with astonishment in England, although Nancy Mitford merely described the whole saga as "infinitely dreary."[6]

On May 4, 1960, the divorce and settlement with Slim finally in the bag, Pamela and Leland flew to Carson City, Nevada, to be married in a hastily arranged ceremony presided over by the mayor. On hearing the news, Winston and Clementine Churchill cabled "so happy for you darling Pamela," sending their love.[7] Pamela's Catholicism had proved long-lasting—she liked its order and discipline—and now she insisted that she and Leland marry again in a Roman Catholic church. Leland, who was not religious, was first obliged to get an annulment of his first marriage. Over the next year, Pamela used her connections to push it through. The Kennedys—particularly Joe, who (perhaps out of guilt) pulled strings on Pamela's behalf[8]—were helpful in persuading the Church to support her. The second ceremony was duly held under the soaring roof of St. Gregory the Great at Harrison in New York State.

Pamela's victory over her rivals was complete. Leland's campaign of self-destruction as he frantically searched for his next hit was another matter. His waking hours were spent on up to four phones at once in his office on Madison Avenue, scripts piled high all around him, or at the corner table at the Colony Club, pouring himself shot after shot from his personal bottle of Wild Turkey. Pamela constantly feared another life-threatening bleed, and once they had moved into a lavish new apartment at 1020 Fifth Avenue, bought for $220,000 of the proceeds from her Paris residence,[9] she insisted he give up the club and come home for lunch. Pamela had installed her collection of museum-quality French pieces and paintings to stunning effect. The vast sunken living room overlooked the tiled roofs of the Metropolitan Museum of Art, a view almost Parisian in charm. Most prominent of all, however, were the cherished mementos of her golden era—her Winston Churchill books with their personal inscriptions to her.

Four servants and a chauffeur ran the household to the exacting standards Pamela had grown to expect during her years with Gianni and Élie. Such European elegance was written up in magazines, tributes that Leland greatly enjoyed. Pamela's master stroke, though, was to spoil him personally. She knelt down to remove his shoes the moment he came through the door and brought in a masseuse to relax him. When he made calls, she would listen in on an extension, taking notes to discuss afterward. His bedside table was stacked with books or magazines she thought might interest him, marked up with what she hoped were helpful comments about theater takings, film reviews or ideas for new plots. Evening engagements with friends—up to and including Jack and Jackie Kennedy, whom they saw frequently—would be canceled if he was tired and supper ordered on a tray. She even affected interest in his beloved baseball.[10] Perhaps even the great Madame de Pompadour herself—renowned mistress of King Louis XV of France—would have been impressed at the way Pamela placed Leland and his work at the center of her universe. Yet such devotion to her husband's career was hardly recompense for the lack of her own and she began to feel trapped. As Leland's health improved, so hers deteriorated. This was a time when social pressures on women to hide their intelligence behind a wall of fluff had led many housewives to gulp down tranquilizers like "cough drops." The feminist writer Betty Friedan talked of millions of wives suffering from a "nameless aching dissatisfaction."[11]

Not long after their marriage, on October 17, 1960, at the age of twenty-one, Bridget locked herself in her apartment and took her own life. Leland retreated to an armchair to drink bourbon and cry. Just as with Margaret's death, it was as if Pamela's impeccable composure was all that could stop him falling apart. What happened next is open to dispute. By Brooke's account, Pamela accompanied her to Bridget's apartment to choose clothes for her burial and found two pearl necklaces that had belonged to their mother. Brooke admits to being "notoriously lackadaisical" with her belongings and claims Pamela suggested they would be "much safer with her" at the Fifth Avenue apartment, where she had a ceiling-high safe with velvet-lined drawers for her huge collection of diamonds, pearls and emeralds.[12] Pamela had no such recollection. Either way, it seems likely that the pearls were eventually moved for safekeeping and certainly they were not there when Brooke wanted them back a decade later. Their disappearance would spark a conflict between the two women that would leave no one unscarred—like a real-life version of *The Eustace Diamonds* by Anthony Trollope. After Bridget's funeral, Billy remarked that suicide "seems to run in the family."[13] Five months into her second marriage, Pamela hardly dared think what might happen next.

22

With semi-regal pageantry, on January 20, 1961, Jack Kennedy was inaugurated as the first Catholic president of the United States. Handsome and romantic, in the new television age he resembled, as one observer remarked, a "prince of the blood."[1] Pamela was fascinated by how Jack's youth, wealth and vigor—and love of ceremony—had come to embody New World supremacy over weary old ex-colonial Britain. The carefully curated Kennedy aura reinforced his country's status as a superpower overseas but also offered a confident optimism for social justice at home. Meanwhile, Hollywood and the advertising agencies of Madison Avenue were translating politics into a commodity, selling this invigorating new president "like soap flakes."[2] This was also the time when ambitious junior officers of the Second World War Pamela had known in London were coming into power. She dared to hope that she too might play a part.

Not even the raging snowstorm that had paralyzed Washington the day before the swearing-in deterred the vast crowds. Pamela and Leland had been invited by the Kennedy family but surprisingly did not attend. It was almost certainly on the insistence of Leland—who never liked Washington—that they went instead to Palm Beach, for a holiday at the home of socialites Loel and Gloria Guinness.

There would be plenty more invitations to the White House—including a New Year's Eve reception in 1962 and a trip two days later to the Vanderbilt estate in Florida with both the Kennedys and the

Agnellis (to Pamela's delight Jack and Gianni bonded over a shared love of sailing). And Pamela remained friendly with Jackie, though they were "never close, but I don't think anybody was."[3]

It was not for lack of trying on Pamela's part. She wrote a heartfelt note when Jackie lost her newborn son Patrick in 1963, prompting a reply describing Pamela as an "angel."[4] When Jackie admired Pamela's flower displays, she sent her baskets for the arrangements in the White House. After Jackie remarked on her Rigaud scented candles, soon they too were in the official residence. When Jackie decided to rid the White House of ugly reproduction furniture, she called for donations of pieces appropriate for the executive mansion of a superpower, but also the counsel of Pamela's friend Bill Walton and her designer at La Léopolda, Stéphane Boudin.

It was tantalizing to be so close to power during the Kennedy administration yet frustrating that she was kept at arm's length. When Pamela was invited to Hickory Hill, Bobby Kennedy's house, one morning back in April 1961, it was not to discuss the breaking news of the failure of the Bay of Pigs invasion with JFK's attorney general but for young Winston to play tennis with Bobby's wife, Ethel. The woman who had shared comparable setbacks with Churchill during the war found that Bobby was sleeping upstairs after working through the night. Later she discovered him ("looking twelve years old") with a towel wrapped around his waist, comforting one of his sons whose goldfish had died.[5] Pamela noted how Kennedy men showed more consideration to their children than their wives—or women generally. They were "unabashed chauvinists," according to Kay Graham, who later rose to fame during Watergate as the formidable publisher of the *Washington Post*. They were not interested in the views of middle-aged women and made them feel "boring."[6]

It would surely not have been considered "feminine" for Pamela to quiz Bobby on why the American-backed operation in Cuba against Fidel Castro's pro-Soviet communist regime had ended in humiliating chaos. She had harbored a fervent belief in America's sacred leadership role since the war but what did the Bay of Pigs mean for American power and prestige? Four months later Jack Kennedy's mettle was tested again when the communist East German government walled off East Berlin to stem the river of refugees seeking freedom in the West. Pamela watched history unfolding and bitterly regretted still being out of the fray.

Jack and Jackie Kennedy were "enormously kind" to Pamela, though, even in adversity. When the Haywards came to Washington's National Theatre in September 1962 for the opening of Leland's controversial musical *Mr. President*, Pamela thought that perhaps only Jack's support could save them from his "biggest disaster" to date.[7] Many in Washington considered a "corny" production about a fictional president facing conflict with the Soviets crassly ill timed when in real life Moscow was busy siting missiles in Cuba, just ninety miles off the coast of Florida. Americans were even seeking out their nearest nuclear shelter and wondering whether it was safe to send their children to school. The composer Irving Berlin was "so scared" about the audience's reaction he told Pamela that he feared he was "going to be lynched." The White House called Pamela beforehand to confirm that the real president had some "dramas going on" but could spare time for either the first or second half. Which would she prefer? Cannily she replied that it would be better after the interval "because if he comes for the first thing and walks out, that'll be trouble."[8] Kennedy loyally did as she suggested, arriving to a helpful flurry of camera flashes with Jackie in floral silk trousers and cape.

Inspired like so many by Kennedy's inauguration call to "ask not what your country can do for you but what you can do for your country," Pamela believed she had much to offer her adopted homeland from her Downing Street experience. Kennedy was a devoted admirer of Churchill and in 1963 awarded him honorary American citizenship—accepted on his behalf by Randolph and young Winston—in a ceremony the president had personally worked on for months. It filled Pamela with pride and she relished how Jack was positioning himself in Churchill's footsteps as the personification of freedom.

It was a constant disappointment, however, that her president and friend was less interested in women's political skills than his hero, who had of course relied so heavily on Clementine and Pamela. Jack had no women in his Cabinet (unlike his predecessors Eisenhower and FDR) and fewer in senior posts than either Truman or Eisenhower. He did, however, set up the Presidential Commission on the Status of Women, chaired by Eleanor Roosevelt, which reflected a growing recognition of women's involvement outside the home. And the first tentative Equal Pay Act was passed in 1963, finally acknowledging that women should not work for pin money.[9]

Even so, at a time when there was no sustained, effective female access to the Oval Office, Pamela's genuine friendship with the president was widely envied, even while she craved a real job. It was only part consolation to be drawn into the political dinner party circuit of Georgetown. At one such evening in early 1963, attended by Diana Cooper, Pamela was seated near both Jack and Jackie, while the Secret Service ate chicken salad in a child's bedroom upstairs, having installed a special line to the White House in case, as Diana put it, "button 'War'" had to be pressed.[10] Such evenings—although informative—sometimes added to Pamela's frustration. So many of her wartime connections were key figures in Kennedy's Washington but few had operated at her level back then. Some were out of bounds, including Ed (whom Jack had appointed head of the United States Information Agency), as in a fit of jealous pique Leland had put an end to their purely platonic lunches. Jack considered Averell to be over the hill although after persistent lobbying he made him an Assistant Secretary of State, but Pamela could only glimpse him at a distance. And beyond galling for a woman who had once presided over conversations of global significance was having to follow the imported British upper-class custom of leaving the room after dinner with the other women while the men engaged in the meatiest discussions of affairs of state over whisky and cigars without her.

Pamela's detractors have poured doubt on whether she was really a Democrat in the 1960s. Yet it is clear that she was largely in agreement with Kennedy's New Frontier policies and especially his plans to widen the social safety net—an ambition she saw, perhaps improbably, as a modern version of her parents' patrician concern for the poor back in Dorset. Her papers also prove that she raised funds (seen as a permissible female activity) for Bobby in his 1964 run for the Senate, prompting a letter from him thanking her for her "support" and "very generous contribution."[11] Later she actively supported Bobby as he geared up for a presidential run in 1968—admiring the way he spoke passionately against racial injustice as well as the Vietnam War—and persuaded Leland to advise him on his television appearances (even though some believe her husband's interests, if party political at all, veered toward Republican).[12] She was trying to reenter politics in any way she could but Leland insisted he and showbusiness came first.

The touring theater life, though, began to pall. As did Leland's conspicuous lack of a major hit since *The Sound of Music*, although it helped that the film rights had been sold to Twentieth Century-Fox. For the first time, Pamela found herself the one with the money and she decided to spend some of the remainder of the proceeds from her Paris apartment on a country home as, she declared, "No Englishwoman can live in the city seven days a week."[13] She chose an exclusive area around Mount Kisco, a village with a faintly European feel in Westchester County, forty miles from Manhattan, and chanced upon the "most hideous modern house." What it did have was something of the remote privacy of Minterne, hidden away down a mile-long drive with views over Croton Lake. Pamela paid $90,000 for it a week later and the house was registered solely in her name, satisfying her desire for the country mansion being a girl had denied her. She set about making the gardens as much like Dorset as she could.

Leland's allergies and phobias were worse in the country but he was placated with a helicopter pad to allow him to hop swiftly back to the city if needed. Pamela renamed the house Haywire after Leland's cable address and wanted it to be a bold modernist statement. Her money, finally her choices. In defiance of Digby tradition she installed numerous contemporary bathrooms as well as shagpile carpets, one of America's first microwave ovens and early remote-control televisions. She also built a separate octagonal wing for the master suite with special closets for Leland's three hundred pairs of shoes and scores of wristwatches. "This big house is so arranged that the lovers should be unruffled by droppers in," noted a surprised Diana Cooper.[14] Brooke did once drop in, only to find her stepmother posing naked on the diving board. She rarely came again.

Still sensitive about her lack of education, Pamela had huge bookshelves built for thousands of leather-bound tomes (provided by her neighbor Bennett Cerf, cofounder of the publisher Random House) from the essays of Montaigne to Chaucer. Pamela pioneered the art of decoratively displaying the volumes to look casually intellectual—an arrangement that Diana sketched to copy at home—without it being quite clear how many she had actually read. The Haywards were popular hosts, putting on glittering formal dinners or all-American hot dog gatherings around the pool. Regular invitees included Frank Sinatra and Pamela's warm-hearted friend Kitty Carlisle Hart, star of the Marx Brothers' *A Night at the Opera* and widow of playwright Moss Hart. Guests were offered a glimpse of the pasha treatment Leland enjoyed, the exacting modernist interior designer Billy Baldwin finding an overnight stay "an experience you can hardly believe . . . There is the best reading light, the most marvellous sheets, the best breakfast . . . it is as if she had a genie to fulfil your every desire."[15]

Pamela brought in a political set when she could, such as for the fundraiser for Bobby Kennedy. Mostly, though, she invited a theatrical crowd to please Leland. Fortunately, she found certain actors "very unspoiled" and willing to be the nonjudgmental friends she craved. "If they like you," she found with relief, "they're not making it up."[16] Leland was wonderfully happy, surrounded by the creatives he adored and cosseted by a woman other men desired. The revelation that Leland referred to his wife as La Bouche spread like wildfire in the men's clubs of New York. "She has," he boasted, "the best mouth on either side of the Atlantic."[17] Peter Duchin, now a top society bandleader like his father, and who also came to live in Westchester County, noted how Pamela "seemed the perfect wife,"[18] but it was far from the perfect marriage.

Pamela insisted she was "perfectly happy" but over a lengthy summer visit, Diana Cooper detected worrying signs: "Pam a trifle too waif & stray—not a stick of makeup—hair not touched." Photographs taken by Leland also show her frown lines deepening by the year.[19] Diana was in no doubt that he was to blame and that the marriage was not as "serene" as people imagined. She was particularly disturbed by his possessiveness. It was "not the way to keep a wife" and Pamela was being exploited as nanny, nurse and protector. "I get worried," Diana wrote home to her son John Julius. "I feel she could do better." Most of all, Pamela seemed bored and lonely, Diana complaining that she "hounds me with affection."[20]

Pamela thought she could occupy her mind by opening a shop on East 57th Street part owned by her favorite designer Stéphane Boudin. Hoping to cash in on the popular "Pamela look" of candles, tasteful trinkets and flowers, she had kept "working girl hours," trilled the

New York Herald Tribune, "for the past nine months."[21] When it opened in October 1963, the store was part salon, part hobby and wholly uncommercial. Fevered publicity drew an early flurry of customers but it lasted less than four years and was not helped by celebrity clients like Ethel Kennedy being slow to settle bills running into thousands.[22] Rather than improving the Hayward finances, the enterprise drained them.

Pamela was keeping shop on November 22, 1963, when she heard on the radio about the fatal attack on Jack Kennedy in Dallas. Pamela's friend of twenty-five years had become the embodiment of the virile superpower that had entranced her for her entire life. And now he was slain by an assassin's bullet on a day that shook America more than any other since Pearl Harbor. "The bottom of everybody's life fell out. Our hopes. Our beliefs," she recalled. "I knew him well, but for everybody it was the same."[23] Yet it wasn't. He had been a loyal friend as well as a cherished path—however narrow—into the power salons of Washington. The president had been about to make a Cold War commitment in a speech that would present Americans as "watchmen on the walls of world freedom"—words that chimed with Pamela's great hopes for her adopted country—but tragedy had struck again. The celebrity philosopher Isaiah Berlin spoke for many when he said, "I feel less safe."[24] Asked whether Americans would laugh again the Democratic politician Pat Moynihan replied: "Yes, we will laugh again. But we will never be young again."[25] While Bill Walton draped black crepe at the windows of the White House for the arrival of the president's body, Pamela must have wondered whether America would ever believe in itself in the same way again.

Pamela introduced the newly divorced Brooke to several (in her view eligible) young men and was appalled when she homed in on someone who was, in the words of *New York* magazine, "the most unacceptable human being she could find."²⁶ The actor-director Dennis Hopper moved into Brooke's apartment and covered it in black oil paint embedded with cigarette butts.²⁷ Since his appearance with James Dean in *Rebel Without a Cause* in 1955, he had developed a particularly deranged brand of hell-raising. The Haywards tried to persuade Brooke not to marry him, Leland pleading with her even as he walked her down the aisle in August 1961 to change her mind. When she refused, he and Pamela left directly after the service, leaving Brooke's childhood friend Jane Fonda to offer her apartment for an impromptu wedding breakfast.²⁸ Nor were relations much better with Bill, who had joined the U.S. Army. Pamela twice pulled strings with old friends in the military over "some problems" with her stepson's conduct but he, like Brooke, was given the cold shoulder when he tried to come to stay.

There was always, by contrast, a lavish welcome for straitlaced Winston, including a twenty-first birthday party covered by the newspapers—usefully reminding their readers of Pamela's Churchill heritage when she made little use of the name in Leland's showbusiness circles. Leland rarely saw his own children but he made time to encourage Winston in his love of flying, paid for him to train as a pilot and celebrated again when Winston graduated from Oxford. It was not until Brooke finally divorced Hopper that Leland found anything encouraging to say to her, congratulating her on the "first smart move" she had made in six years. Pamela having been right about Hopper's unsuitability as a husband was not appreciated. She and young Winston had the devotion of the man whose favor eluded his offspring. Of the Brooke-Pamela war that ensued, a family friend remarked that "it was about who Daddy loved most."²⁹

Leland had a new project to throw all his energies into, finally one that appealed to Pamela, who got deeply involved. Based on the British original, *That Was the Week That Was* offered pioneering political satire presented by David Frost, who commuted over the Atlantic weekly. "It was a tour de force to do it every Friday," Pamela said, "and the more it got rave reviews the harder it was to keep it up to scratch."[30] During 1965 Gloria Steinem, a vocal and charismatic founder of the women's movement, was one of the show's writers. She and Pamela became friends and lunched together to, as Steinem put it, "trade stories of [their] respective worlds."[31] Even so, Pamela continued to claim she did "not like feminists." "I think they've done their own cause enormous harm," she would later say of the symbolic burning of bras.[32] And yet over time Steinem influenced her and explained how the women's movement, far from peddling man hating, could help her overcome her own thwarted ambition. It was the start of a long and winding journey but by the time Steinem set up the groundbreaking magazine *Ms.* in the early 1970s, Pamela was ready to come along.[33] "It meant so much to have your support and blessing," Steinem told her. "Your presence and kind words were symbols of women's new consciousness and unity."[34] Yet after Steinem suggested they "make a little political trouble together," Pamela was not comfortable and stepped back from the friendship, replying she was "sorry not to be of more use."[35] Though now in her mid-forties, she was not yet the political troublemaking sort.

Steinem and the Hayward children were a far cry from Pamela's normal city life, which revolved around a golden slice of Midtown—Leland's favorite haunts such as Le Pavillon and the Colony Club, but also the restaurant La Côte Basque. This was home to *flaneur*-in-chief Truman Capote—once a Slim-ite "unto death" but now switching his attentions to Pamela, whom he found "enormously entertaining."[36] He thought her complexion was as if "saturated with dewy English mists, something every dermatologist ought to bottle" and he likened her hair to a "winter sunset."[37] He included her in his collection of beautiful rich "ladies who lunch" whom he called the Swans of Fifth Avenue—women who were hostage to their obsession with physical and domestic perfection. They included Babe Paley, Gloria Guinness and, now she was often in New York, Marella Agnelli. Seemingly untouched by Steinem's campaign for female emancipation they spent days in beauty parlors, barely ate (they smoked through lunch with long, elegant cigarette holders) and had full-time maids just for ironing their curtains. New York hairdresser Kenneth Battelle looked after them all and singled out Pamela (who was also the poorest Swan) as the "sympathetic and generous-spirited" one who was "willing to listen . . . I got no sense of ego."[38]

The Swans lived lives of savage competitiveness but considered Capote their friend, someone to whom they could safely spill their secrets. "I think I've lived through every screw she ever had in her life," he revealed of his intimate conversations with Pamela. "Believe me, that's an Arabian Nights tale of a thousand and twelve!"[39] She was not the only Swan who naïvely imagined her life was off-limits for the stories that were Capote's stock in trade.[40] But perhaps she was the only one who wondered at the pointlessness of it all and still hankered for something substantive in her life even if it was not as activist for the women's movement. Pamela watched with fascination how Kay Graham, by now publisher of the *Washington Post* (taking over from her abusive husband after he shot himself), confounded her sexist critics to become one of a handful of serious female figures of national prominence. In November 1966 Capote held a Black & White Ball in Graham's honor in New York, inspired by the Ascot races scene in *My Fair Lady*, inviting only the "very rich, very talented or very beautiful"[41] to what the *Washington Post* described as a "social 'happening' of history-making proportions."[42] Guests were instructed to wear only black and white, and no jewels other than white diamonds.

Pamela spent the evening in the Plaza ballroom avoiding awkward encounters, including with Averell and Marie. Frank Sinatra and his wife, Mia Farrow, were present, Peter Duchin's band played and there were the Windsors, the Fondas, Andy Warhol, the Maharani of Jaipur, Lauren Bacall and Kennedys galore. Such success led Capote to believe he was socially invincible but "bitterness generated by years of sycophancy began to overtake him." Fueled by pills and booze, he started to publish spiteful "thinly veiled portraits of people . . . in whose drawing rooms he had starred so long."[43]

Pamela had sensed the warning signs and began to withdraw from Capote's orbit, but it would prove too late. She paid a heavy price in the short story "La Côte Basque 1965." Published in *Esquire* magazine some years later, the story centered on a lunch at La Côte Basque between Lady Ina Coolbirth, a heartless forty-ish femme fatale on the rebound from an affair with a Rothschild, and the supposedly naïve narrator. Lady Ina gossips about how the Duchess of Windsor never picked up the bill and how Prince Charles might "amount to something" as the only acceptable royal.[44]

Most telling of all was Lady Ina's account of how Joe Kennedy had taken sexual advantage of her as a young friend of one of his daughters. "The old bugger slipped into my bedroom," she says. "When I woke up he was already between the sheets with one hand over my mouth and the other all over the place." Afterward "he pretended nothing had happened [. . .] just the good old daddy of my schoolgirl chum." In the final, cruel twist Capote has her say with mercenary outrage: "He'd had me and I'd even pretended to enjoy it: there should have been some sentimental acknowledgement, a bauble, a cigarette box . . ."[45]

When the magazine hit the newsstands in 1975, most of Capote's old circle hit the roof. One woman portrayed as an attention-seeking "tramp" took a "truckload" of barbiturates and died. Lady Ina physically resembled Slim, who consulted lawyers about suing Capote, but his live-in lover made clear to her that the character was based on Pamela. Capote even has Lady Ina say she feels "safe" with her latest husband (presumably the highly dependent Leland) as "for the first time I felt I had a man I couldn't possibly lose."[46] When the story was later included in the book *Answered Prayers*, Capote informed his editors at Random House that Lady Ina was "not *based*" on Pamela—she "*is*" Pamela and insisted that he knew that an assault had taken place.[47] Truman was known to exaggerate in his stories but, according to his biographer Gerald Clarke, "most" of his accounts were at least based on truth.[48] As a Brit determined to battle her way up American society, Pamela vowed never to let down her guard in the same way again.

23

Pamela had been thrilled when Winston flew out to America in the spring of 1964 with his fiancée Minnie d'Erlanger and threw herself into the preparations for the wedding to take place in London in July. She bought the engagement ring, a valuable bracelet and several expensive dresses for Minnie, hosted a huge engagement party in New York and invited practically every famous name she knew to the big event. She even persuaded Gianni to lend La Gaiola, his private island in the Bay of Naples, for a suitably eye-catching honeymoon, prompting Minnie to tell Pamela that she was "the luckiest girl in the world to have the nicest possible mother-in-law."[1]

Pamela clearly hoped the wedding would reflect her generosity and social standing on both sides of the Atlantic, but her son soon disappointed her. Despite having been embarrassed by his father his entire life, Winston chose him as his best man. He did so even though the previous year he had been present at an excruciating evening on Onassis's yacht, sailing through the Strait of Messina, when Randolph had again branded Pamela a whore in a tirade at his increasingly frail father. Churchill's assistant, Anthony Montague Browne, described the attack, delivered with Etna erupting in the background, as "one of the most painful scenes" he had ever witnessed. His eighty-eight-year-old boss was so shaken, Montague Browne feared he was about to suffer a stroke.[2]

Pamela had by no means been a perfect mother, but she was

heartbroken at what she considered a definitive snub from her son. This was a point when she thought young Winston had decided to be a "guardian custodian" of his father's reputation, having bought into Randolph's claims that he had been unfairly persecuted by her. Choosing one parent's narrative over the other, he dismissed as untrue her accounts of him being terrified of his father as a child. Apparently, it had been "wonderful" to be made to wait interminably in the lobby at White's. A distressed Pamela thought that there was "a resentment somewhere in Winston" at the breakup of his family and that he had decided it was almost entirely her fault.[3] Pamela would spend the rest of her life trying to win back her son's favor.

Minnie was Catholic but young Winston had disliked his mother converting and had no intention of doing so himself, and so they married in South Kensington's register office. Old Winston and Clementine received a dozen guests afterward at their home in Hyde Park Gate, and the Pol Roger flowed. Pamela had hired the celebrated Canadian photographer Karsh to fly in specially but not even his artistry or her "white silk Balenciaga suit and black tulle turban of considerable attitude" could disguise the tension on her face as they gathered in the garden with Randolph.[4] Later there was a large, more public reception at the Hyde Park Hotel before the bride and groom flew off for their honeymoon. On their return, helped by a handsome check from his grandfather, Winston and Minnie bought Broadwater House, a white clapboard property on Chailey Common in Sussex. Pamela could have sold her London flat for much-needed cash but kept it on for Winston's use.

When Pamela received news that Churchill had suffered a massive stroke and slipped into a coma, she immediately flew to London to be near him (and was fortuitously in the country when Minnie gave birth prematurely to her first child). On her last visit, she had most unusually failed to raise his spirits—and at one point he had turned to her and said, "I have done my bit. I should be allowed to depart in peace."[5] On January 24, 1965, Churchill passed away (just a couple of days after Minnie's son Randolph was born). Pamela wished the old war leader could have seen the emotional outpourings from a country that had rejected him in 1945. Invited to the state funeral on January 30, Pamela was given a prominent position under the dome of St. Paul's Cathedral, raising the eyebrows of the permanently outraged. "Really the placement at St. Paul's!" exclaimed Nancy Mitford to a friend.[6] Mary Soames had been adamant, though, that Pamela would not be included in the family group for Churchill's private burial.

Pamela watched a stooped and ailing Randolph lend his arm to his mother as she walked into the cathedral where thousands waited in the congregation, including former president Ike Eisenhower, the most senior figure representing the United States. President Lyndon Johnson, who had taken office after JFK's assassination and just won his own mandate in the recent election, was ill with pneumonia and unable to come but sent the presidential plane to bring back Eisenhower and the rest of the American delegation. Eisenhower offered Pamela a ride home and she found herself seated next to Averell. Pamela had kept in touch with his daughter Kathy but this was the first time she and Averell had spoken since Paris in the early 1950s. The feeling on both sides was electric.

During the nine-hour flight across the Atlantic, they talked about young Winston's marriage, the birth of Pamela's first grandchild and her life with Leland. The conversation also turned to how, at the age of seventy-three, Averell was frustrated at his lack of electoral success. He had enforced the silence between them all these years but in the final moments before landing, he asked, "You are happy, aren't you?"[7] Her response is not recorded.

. . .

Three months later, Pamela lost another pillar of her wartime years when Ed Murrow succumbed to lung cancer at the age of fifty-seven. Thirteen hundred people attended the service on Madison Avenue, few of them knowing of Pamela's place in Ed's heart or the hopes she had once shared with him. His loss made her life seem even more stifling.

After Churchill's death, Pamela kept close to Clementine by lending her the London apartment before she could move into her own. She also thought it important to remain outwardly friendly with Randolph—whatever the provocation—for fear of further upsetting her son. Randolph was a "wonderful person," she told a journalist nearly two decades later. There was nobody she might enjoy more having lunch with once a week but "a little of him went a long way."[8] Randolph moved in many of the same circles as Pamela—the Kennedys, the Rothschilds, the Paleys—and they made allowances for his conduct as the son of their idol. They also sympathized with his sisters, especially Sarah, after humiliating pictures of her drunk and disorderly appeared in the press. On one occasion, after a tussle with the police, she even served a ten-day sentence in Holloway jail. After years of her own struggle with depression and alcohol, in October 1963 Diana took her own life.

The American chatterati speculated as to what had gone wrong. At one Washington dinner, Pamela's friend and Kennedy White House insider Arthur Schlesinger had asked the then president why his family had "turned out so well" and the Churchills "so badly." Jack had replied that although his father was a controversial and even brutal man, the Kennedy success was due to him. "He made his children feel that they were the most important things in the world," he recounted. "He held up standards for us, and he was very tough when we failed to meet those standards."[9] Pamela knew that it was far from that simple—although it was true Churchill had been foolishly indulgent of his only son when he was growing up. Unlike Jack or Bobby Kennedy, though, Randolph had had to contend with Great Man's Son syndrome and had been crushed by the Churchill name. As she had no burden of expectation, Pamela could see the potential the name might have for her.

Full of self-loathing and resentment at what he knew to be a spoiled and wasted existence, by the mid-1960s Randolph was sustaining himself on soup, whisky and a hundred cigarettes a day. Anita Leslie judged her cousin to have "destroyed everything of himself except his brain."[10] Randolph's disintegration spurred Pamela on: if he could no longer carry the Churchill flame as his father had once intended, then could she move in to take up the challenge?

24

In the decade of the Rolling Stones, the Summer of Love and mass protests against the Vietnam War, Leland's high-rolling musicals looked stale. It was instead his son who scored a phenomenal hit when he teamed up with Peter Fonda in 1969 to produce *Easy Rider*, hailed as a "portrait of counter-culture heroes raising their middle fingers to uptight middle-class hypocrisies."[1] Directed by Bill's former brother-in-law Dennis Hopper, the low-budget movie celebrated dope-smoking long-haired bikers and made Jack Nicholson a star. It also reaped a fortune at the box office and won Hopper an Oscar nomination. His success cruelly contrasted with Leland's failure to adapt.

Leland had again sought answers in Wild Turkey and by the mid-1960s had developed acute pancreatitis and suffered a minor stroke that left him with a limp. Pamela found herself in the role of carer as he went in and out of the hospital and switched his dependency from bourbon and cigarettes to morphine. Soon she was selling her most precious possessions—including, in 1969, the Fifth Avenue apartment—to pay his medical bills. She spent just a fraction of the $450,000 proceeds on a pied-à-terre in the Beekman Building on Park Avenue while Leland moved her jewels into a bank deposit box—she rarely had occasion to wear them. Pamela had little idea of the extent of the financial crisis overwhelming Leland but knew they needed cash fast. She plowed everything she had into the financial black hole. Next to go was her London flat and then almost all her Paris furniture in a fire sale—even a beautiful clock she had bought from Christian Dior's estate after his death in 1957.

Leland was secretly also selling off their possessions, most likely including some of the jewels. "I know what I'm doing and I'm doing it on purpose," he told a friend.[2] Another time, he admitted that he was interested only in having enough money until he died and after that Pamela would be on her own.[3] Meanwhile, Pamela was angry at those she thought had done little to help Leland's career when he needed it and kept them away from Haywire. To Brooke's eyes she was holding her father "prisoner." "Without her permission," she complained, "you couldn't even talk to him over the telephone."[4]

Peter Duchin was, however, welcomed for his youthful cheeriness and he observed that Pamela had become a "terrific nanny." After dinner, Leland would ask her to read out loud the juiciest extracts about Jane Digby from *The Wilder Shores of Love*. The first couple of times Peter was as enthralled as his host but he eventually became irritated with the obvious suggestion that Pamela had modeled herself on "Aunt Jane." He also tired of her "potted imitations" of Churchill, "whose name she could not seem to mention often enough."[5]

From time to time, Pamela seems to have sought respite from her duties as Leland's nurse and "nanny." At least once she was spotted dining with Averell at a remote spot not far from Haywire. "I saw them together in a restaurant, cosily entwined at a corner banquette," said a witness, "not particularly wanting to be seen."[6] No doubt to please her, Averell also began a correspondence with Winston as he sought to become a Conservative MP, reassuring him that his initial failure in 1967 was down to Labour working particularly hard to stop a Churchill from winning.[7] Averell kept quiet about his own views of Winston but others were not so reticent. When he finally became an MP for Stretford in Greater Manchester in 1970, some of his colleagues found him brash and uncomfortably hard right.

Shortly after midnight on June 5, 1968, Bobby Kennedy, campaigning for the presidency in Los Angeles, was shot multiple times by a lone gunman. He died the next day—just two months after the assassination of Martin Luther King Jr. had set America ablaze and five years after the death of his brother Jack. The country felt on a knife edge and Bobby's murder at the age of forty-two—after his attempts at racial reconciliation—dominated the news across the globe and once again shook Pamela's faith in her chosen homeland. Hours later, Randolph succumbed to heart failure in his sleep. "Poor Randolph Churchill died today," noted Cy Sulzberger in his diary, "as always, a footnote."[8]

Pamela was invited to Bobby's requiem mass at St. Patrick's Cathedral in New York and on the funeral train to Washington. Afterward Rose Kennedy made a point of thanking her for her "whole-hearted support" of her son's causes.[9] Pamela then flew to Britain for Randolph's funeral. Jackie Kennedy, one of those who succumbed to his charm, later wrote of Randolph's "incredible sweetness."[10] Pamela knew the truth about a man who had been abusive to her and his family and poisoned her relationship with her only child. But in the 1960s women did not speak out and so she kept silent.

25

On a Wednesday in February 1971, the phone rang as Leland was rushing out of the apartment to a preview of his new play, *The Trial of the Catonsville Nine*. He was swearing away as usual when, mid-sentence, he stopped talking; Pamela rushed into the bedroom to find him unconscious. At the hospital, it was confirmed that he had suffered another minor stroke and he reluctantly asked a group of friends, including the handsome oncologist Dr. William Cahan, to accompany Pamela to the opening night.

The *Catonsville Nine* was about nine Catholics who went on the run after destroying Vietnam draft papers. Although Pamela desperately wanted the fifteen-year-old war to end and felt the shock at the cost in young lives of such protracted defeat, she was unsure about the play. Leland, however, saw it as his last chance of relevance, speaking out about the quagmire of Vietnam, the subject then pervading all American life. At its peak half a million Americans had fought in the conflict and nearly seventeen thousand of them had died during 1968 alone. The psychological effects on the country (known as Vietnam Syndrome) prompted long-lasting revulsion at the idea of any future military excursions overseas.

Pamela's appearance at the theater with Dr. Cahan rekindled gossip that she was lining up her next husband. The whispering saddened Pamela, who was at least used to it, but maddened Dr. Cahan, whose already rocky marriage came under further strain.[1] Against his doctors' advice, Leland discharged himself two days later but was almost immediately readmitted after another, far more serious stroke. "Poor Mr. Hayward is dying," Pamela's friend Marina Sulzberger wrote in her diary. "Pam has not left his side . . . and is heroic."[2] Finally, she took Leland home, where on March 18 he took another turn for the worse. Pamela alerted Brooke to come immediately but she arrived at a darkened house ten minutes too late.

Pamela had known times of happiness with Leland, despite the challenges, and invested everything she had—emotionally and financially—in her marriage. "He loved me and I loved him," she said, his loss marking "the worst moment of my life."[3] Pamela's devotion did not go unnoticed in Hollywood. Betty Bacall, friend of Slim, client of Leland and now a fan of Pamela, wrote, "You were such a good wife, Pamela—and filled his life in a way it had not been filled before." Katharine Hepburn had seen how Pamela had "reassured and protected" him when "his whole framework and body was beginning to crumble." "I used to wonder what you were like," she wrote, "then we met and I fell in love with you too—warm, sweet creature."[4]

It was only when she tried to buy essentials that Pamela discovered Leland's raft of unpaid bills and that his bank accounts were either empty or frozen. Friends found Pamela distraught, with mascara-stained cheeks, her staff mostly gone, the fridge empty and without enough money to buy a dress for the funeral. (Fortunately, the socialite and philanthropist Brooke Astor stepped in to buy her one.) Pamela had plowed her own depleted funds into keeping Leland alive—retaining only the deeds to Haywire—and once again she was faced with paying off a husband's debts without the means to do so. Some suggest that Gianni stepped in to pick up the most pressing demands, but Jock Whitney's business adviser was blunt about Haywire. "You've got to sell this house," he told Pamela on the day of the funeral. "You can't afford it anymore." Unwilling to give up her home, she retorted with classic Pamela bravado: "How do you know? In three months' time, I may marry Niarchos or Onassis!"[5]

Three days after Leland died, her brother Eddie read out his will, which Pamela had not previously seen. He left her a half share of the Manhattan apartment—which she had in any case financed—and a half share of his mother's modest house in Van Nuys, California. The other half of the properties were to go to his children (as he had promised their mother) and there was no cash. Pamela went into performative mode when guests arrived for the funeral, taking Frank Sinatra and Jackie Kennedy (who had herself married Ari Onassis in 1968) for private viewings of the carnation-strewn coffin. That night, however, Brooke recounted that Pamela could contain herself no longer, railing at how Leland had left her "penniless."[6] How, after she had plowed in all she had, could so little be left?

Eventually, Bill and Brooke agreed to swap their interest in the Park Avenue apartment for Pamela's share in their grandmother's house in California.[7] It was when they came to Haywire to pick up the smaller items they wanted that, as so often in the madness of grief, relations descended into acrimony. "I saw everything disappear from my house," was Pamela's recollection. "An absolute fleet of locusts came down."[8] Bill remembered differently. He claimed that many of Leland's possessions were already missing, including his four best cameras, a valuable collection of cufflinks and most of his watches. Further rows broke out when Brooke and Bill accused Pamela of inflating the price of the books and photo albums they wanted to purchase from the estate—and so she gave them to the New York Public Library for a tax credit instead.

Wounded and besieged, Pamela did something she recognized was incendiary. At Leland's memorial service a month later, she had Winston rather than Leland's children read the lessons from Revelation and Corinthians. "Winston was deeply fond of Leland, who had filled a void in his life," she tried to explain—but Brooke and Bill felt bitterly that they had never had enough of him in life and now also in death.

Just before the service, Brooke had visited Pamela at Leland's office on Madison Avenue to ask for her mother's pearls. Pamela was evasive, although the suggestion was that Leland must have secretly sold them to keep going.[9] This seems probable given his comments to friends and the state of his finances—and indeed his estrangement from Brooke while she was married to Hopper. The explanation did not satisfy Brooke, however, and she urged her brother to launch a lawsuit against Pamela as an act of revenge.[10] Eleven years of marriage to Leland had stripped Pamela of her fortune—in the long run it would cost her much more.

Rather than selling Haywire, Pamela took out a $30,000 mortgage to keep her head above water.[11] And soon she began to receive Leland's share of the royalties from *The Sound of Music*. Yet these funds—and other relatively modest stipends—were a fraction of what she was used to or needed to run Haywire and she did not have a job—nor the obvious qualifications to get one—to top them up. Her instinct was to become a semi-recluse but she accepted an invitation from Frank Sinatra to Palm Springs. Slightly to her surprise, she found him "sweet" and that he "cared more about his friends than anybody."[12] Pamela was less enthused about his sprawling compound, which she thought "perfectly appalling."

At fifty-five, Frank was divorced again and facing a traumatic dip in his career as musical tastes had long since run away from macho crooners toward more sexually nuanced rock'n'roll figures like Mick Jagger. Pamela had "adored" the much-younger Mia Farrow when she had been married to Frank, but their marriage had become a battleground for wider changes in society—with Frank stranded in his belief in masculine supremacy, unable to tolerate competing with the success of his actress wife or her having ideas of her own. Farrow's androgynous figure also symbolized a new freedom from the corseted curves of Marilyn Monroe. Since their divorce three years previously, Sinatra had been lonely and, not for the first time, sightings of him with the far less threatening Pamela prompted talk. "There is speculation in California that Frank Sinatra is thinking of marrying again," wrote the *Sunday Express* on June 6, 1971, barely three months after Leland's death. "His bride to be? Pamela Hayward."

Pamela denied they were in a relationship although many, including Sinatra's biographer James Kaplan, believe he proposed.[13] Pamela, now set on her own more liberated future, was hardly going to hitch herself to another aging man on a self-destruct mission. However much she claimed to see the best in people, that was one relationship she would never get into.[14] The truth did not stop rumors of Pamela chasing Sinatra or that any rich husband was now at risk from the so-called "widow of opportunity."

Wounded by the speculation, Pamela flew economy to Britain to be with Winston and Minnie, thinking she would be "safe" with them. The trip was not a success. Winston and his family were "kind but they had their lives."[15] Minterne was not the same either, since her brother had hived off part of the house to convert into flats. She took up an offer from the Guinnesses to join them on their yacht in the South of France but again felt out of place—"you can't run away from sadness," she told a friend.[16] When Frank offered her a lift back to America on his plane, she took it but under the overcast summer skies back at Haywire, the gloom would not lift. Pamela had devoted herself to being a flawless wife. She had invested in Leland's life, interests and happiness. For her pains, she had been left with disappointment, debts and recriminations. And after a decade in America, she was further away from politics and power than ever.

ACT THREE
Power

26

Marie Harriman's death from a heart attack in September 1970 at the age of sixty-seven had hit Averell hard. After infidelities on both sides, his marriage had survived even if his career had been disappointing. He had held plenty of important jobs—including negotiating a treaty banning above-ground nuclear tests and leading the American delegation at the failed preliminary Paris peace talks on the Vietnam War—but successive presidents had never rated him as a close ally. Even now, he longed for one last key role. After burying Marie in the Harriman family plot at Arden, next to a space left for him, he went down to his Florida house at Hobe Sound in a deep depression. He rarely left the house and when he visited, Peter Duchin found him "so listless he could barely watch the evening news."[1]

By spring 1971, Averell had finally begun taking an interest in the world again and saw that Leland had recently died. Wondering how Pamela was faring he asked Bill Walton—their mutual wartime friend—where she was. Too late, the amused Walton told him, she had just left for Europe and would not be back for months. "Would she want to see me?" Averell inquired.[2]

Pamela's friends were worried about her. "I saw that Pamela was miserable," says her neighbor, the prominent journalist Lally Weymouth.[3] Her mother, Kay Graham, was holding a party in Washington and she urged Pamela to attend in her place. After much persuasion, Pamela agreed and Kay's secretary rubbed out Lally's name on the seating plan and wrote in Mrs. Hayward's instead. It became Washington folklore that Pamela had lobbied for the invitation as a ruse to meet Averell and that she also demanded a place near him at the table. As is so often, the rumors about Pamela were salacious enough for many not to worry whether they were true. Weymouth is adamant that Pamela played no part: "*I* engineered it . . . I just thought it would be fun."[4]

Pamela was mingling with the guests in Kay's Georgetown garden when Averell walked in, having no idea she was to be there. On seeing each other in the crowd, both immediately brightened and they spent the rest of the evening in animated conversation about the war. Those old days in London might by now have been receding in others' memories, but they had been the highlight of both their lives, the one time that they had truly felt important. "Do you remember when Max Beaverbrook did this . . ." or "When Stalin told you that . . ." energized them for hours. Who else still alive had been there at that time, known the characters involved and played a role in shaping history? When Liz Stevens, wife of the film director George, came to join them Averell snapped, "Why does she interrupt us? Can't she see we're talking together?"[5]

Within a few days he had visited Pamela at Haywire and a fortnight later she pulled up in a beige Cadillac outside his retreat at Sands Point on the north shore of Long Island, "looking glamorous and indomitable in her English country best." Averell shambled over to her in an ancient pair of seersucker shorts and Brooks Brothers jumper (he liked to wear weekend clothes until they were in shreds). Their embrace was "friendly but not too friendly," according to Peter Duchin, who with his wife, Cheray, was staying there at the time, before Averell showed Pamela to a guest bedroom.[6]

Later on the two couples went to dinner at a neighbor's house, where Pamela sparkled all evening. She was the "belle of the ball,"

Peter remembered, "solicitous of everybody, vibrant, filled with stories." Averell's hearing had been failing for some time but he now turned up his hearing aid so high it squeaked. The following evening Peter had an engagement with his band and returned to the house at one-thirty in the morning. Fancying a nightcap, he went out onto the screened porch where there was a bar and switched on the lamp, jumping at a loud shriek from behind him. Twirling around in surprise, he saw Pamela and Averell entwined on the sofa, her blouse unbuttoned and skirt around her waist. Averell's trousers were down at his ankles and lipstick was smeared across his face. "Jesus wept!" Averell bellowed as Pamela straightened her clothes and Peter fled.[7]

After exchanging excited whispers about "Ave's rejuvenation," Peter and Cheray were drifting off to sleep when there was a loud crash. Peter ran down the hallway, calling through Pamela's door, "Is everything all right?" "Just fine," Pamela replied. "The lamp fell over." In the morning, she came into their room in a sheer pink negligee to confess that the "ghastly sound" in the night had not been the lamp but Averell falling through the window. Intent on finishing what he had started, clad in silk pajamas and slippers, seventy-nine-year-old Averell had forgotten about the insect screen and although his ardor had been undiminished was now a "little bruised."[8]

Averell was delighted. Sex was a big part of his life but not of his marriage—he had complained that he and Marie were not matched sexually and she found him demanding and hasty. Since they had last been to bed together, Pamela had perfected her techniques and now Averell was, to his joy, the beneficiary. "I bet Ave hadn't experienced too many blowjobs in his life," remarked Peter, who used to discuss sex with Marie. "It was not an ordinary thing for people of that class and generation but Aly Khan had taught her all sorts of things."[9] "Averell wasn't bothered by her past," a friend observed later. "He had been part of it."

At another dinner in mid-September, Pamela leaned over to Arthur

Schlesinger to whisper, "It's the most incredibly romantic story. Imagine, after twenty-five years!"[10] Beaming with happiness, Averell announced to everyone at the table that they were to be married. Although often emotionally remote, Averell had always been a tactile man (and excellent hugger) and he and Pamela sat on the sofa holding hands. Barely six weeks after Kay's party, they formally announced their engagement and were snapped by the press at New York's City Hall picking up their marriage license. "Since we were both suddenly free and alone it just seemed the most natural thing in the world," Pamela proclaimed.[11] Gianni and Marella cabled their congratulations. Diana Cooper declared that after years of his maltreatment of Pamela, Averell was "fortunate" to have her.[12] Pamela tried to put a positive gloss on having been abandoned by him in the past, blaming it on his sense of duty, but privately it gnawed away at her that Marie had enjoyed Averell in his prime. She was determined to make the best of whatever time they had left.

Soon afterward, Averell proudly paraded Pamela to former presidents Harry Truman (in Missouri) and Lyndon Johnson (at his Texas ranch) on a grand tour of Democratic America. In the White House, President Nixon was so intrigued that he broke off from discussing the American balance of payments to ask his National Security Adviser Henry Kissinger for a full background briefing on Pamela, especially her years in Downing Street.[13] Across the Atlantic, Winston was dispatched to inform Clementine of the engagement, who exclaimed: "My, my, an old flame rekindled!"[14] Bill Walton, whose services as cupid had proved unnecessary, was astonished at Averell's renewed sexual energy, describing him as having become "quite a swinger."[15] Peter Duchin insisted that the "clincher" had been Pamela informing Averell, "I won't go with you to Washington unless I'm your wife."[16] In truth, Averell had needed no persuasion and was keen to marry before he turned eighty that November and "got too old."

On the morning of Monday, September 27, 1971, six months after Leland's death and a year after Marie's, Averell gave Pamela a passage from Psalm 16: "Thou wilt show me the path of life: in thy presence is fullness of joy; at thy right hand there are pleasures for evermore." A hundred guests had been invited for a cocktail party that evening but ninety minutes beforehand, the couple slipped out of Averell's Manhattan townhouse and drove eight blocks up Fifth Avenue to the Roman Catholic Church of St. Thomas More to be married. Winston could not make it but Pamela had shipped in Father Christie from London, the priest who had converted her, and three witnesses—Ethel Kennedy, Pamela's sister Sheila and Averell's daughter Kathy. That morning Ethel had sent the couple a note, "Oh happy day! I can't think of anyone I would rather see Ave marry—except me."[17] The bride's radiance lifted her face from the effect of years of strain. The groom looked jowly but rejuvenated and handsome. At least one reporter had been tipped off and was ready to ask Pamela as they came out of the church if she would always agree with Harriman's Democratic politics. His bride, wearing a plain white crepe dress and an enormous necklace of rubies, emeralds and pearls, dutifully replied: "Whatever he thinks, I'll go right along with it."

Back at the Harriman Beaux Arts mansion on 81st Street, the Duchins took their place among the guests assembling in the black and white marble hallway. Jock Whitney, Bill Paley and others from Pamela's New York circle joined them in climbing the red-carpeted stairs to the first-floor drawing room where the walls were covered with Marie's favorite art. Duchin thought it "spooky" that Pamela was welcoming everybody with Averell's arm around her when in his mind "it was still Ma's room . . . Her ghost was everywhere."[18] Only when Pamela trilled to a friend "We did it! We did it!" did Peter finally realize what had just happened, and that his beloved Ma had been replaced for good.

Despite famously lacking a sense of humor, Averell had chosen as his wedding gift a playful George Romney portrait entitled *Lady Hamilton as a Vestal*.* Lady Emma Hamilton's mane of chestnut locks had helped propel her into fame and fortune but she looks unhappy in the painting, as befits a woman whose life ended in destitution. Some thought the choice odd—but they were not to know that the painting reminded the couple of nights with Churchill watching Korda's Lady Hamilton movie. Pamela gave the man who had everything the application papers for her American citizenship—a necessary step for joining him in the political fray. In the space marked employment, she had coyly written "Housewife." Once she officially became an American, though, she had different plans.

---

* Vestal Virgins were priestesses in ancient Rome who took a thirty-year vow of chastity, whereas Emma Hamilton's lifestyle had been funded by lovers, most famously Admiral Lord Nelson.

Pamela was a precocious child who decided from an early age that it would be men who gave her what she wanted

Pamela at home in Dorset in 1937 with her parents, Lord and Lady Digby, and her youngest sister, Jacquetta. Pamela was already plotting her escape from the family's quiet country life

Jane Digby's legendary sexual adventures provided vivid inspiration to the young Pamela but were a source of embarrassment to her parents, who hid her portrait away on the back stairs to avoid further scandal

Pamela endured a disastrous first Season and was the butt of many cruel teases. She embarked on a surreptitious flit to Paris at the age of nineteen with the handsome 7th Earl of Warwick, a notorious playboy known as Fulkie, but her reputation with men was not yet the reality

Pamela became unusually close friends with the young Kennedys, particularly Kathleen and her brother Jack (on the right), seen with elder brother Joe arriving at the Houses of Parliament on 3 September 1939. When they first met, Kick dismissed Pamela as a 'fat, stupid little butterball' but both she and Jack dramatically changed their minds

Pamela married Randolph Churchill in October 1939, less than a month after they first met. She craved glitz and an entrée to politics; he wanted a son before he left for war. Disaster loomed

Churchill persuaded a heavily pregnant Pamela to take refuge from the Blitz in London at the prime ministerial country seat of Chequers, but she was left defenceless during yet another terrifying raid when German bombs fell right next to the house

Photographs of Pamela with her baby were used strategically during the war to win over American hearts and whip up support for Britain's fight against Nazi Germany. They launched her as Churchill's secret weapon in the Anglo-American alliance

Pamela's very special war work required a couture wardrobe such as this 1941 chocolate brown satin dinner dress with pin tucks and bejewelled clasps by top couturier Norman Hartnell. The sexier the dress the better for what she had to do for her country

Max Beaverbrook was a rapacious buccaneer and also, at least at first, Pamela's 'control officer'. She channelled vital war information to him and soon Churchill himself

Churchill and his wife Clementine depended on Pamela to operate Operation Seduction USA throughout the war but her place in their innermost circle caused ructions in the family. Here she is with Clementine, Sarah, Winston and Diana at Chartwell in 1945. At the back are Peregrine Churchill, Jack Churchill and Diana's husband Duncan Sandys

Pamela with two-year-old young Winston on their way to Lady Sarah Churchill's wedding. She loved her son but helping to win the war – and all that entailed – came first

Pamela targeted legendary CBS correspondent Ed Murrow who wielded great influence over his American audience. Even this hard-nosed reporter and stern critic of the rich was unable to resist her powers

Pamela became something of a fashion plate after the war, when the world was in thrall to Churchill's glamorous ex-daughter-in-law. Here she is posing in 1946 in black chiffon dinner pyjamas and a pink taffeta overskirt by Castillo. And yet she yearned for another serious role and a road back to politics

As Winston matured, Pamela came to enjoy his company. If she was, as a twentieth-century woman, to be continually denied a political career, she began to dream of her son rising to power in the footsteps of his grandfather

When she first set eyes on Averell Harriman in London in 1941, Pamela thought him the most beautiful man she had ever seen. Their sexual liaison had global significance but inherent dangers

Aly Khan taught her invaluable sexual techniques. Élie de Rothschild was just one of the beneficiaries of her prowess in bed. Here Aly and Élie are seen together at Chantilly in 1951

Gianni Agnelli with his wife Marella in 1977, accompanied by his close friend Benno Graziani. Benno knew all too well about Gianni's enduring feelings for Pamela

27

Now that Pamela had bagged herself a genuinely wealthy husband thanks to his huge holdings in the Union Pacific Railroad, there was no time to lose. Within days of the wedding, she embarked on what would become a huge transfer of wealth to Winston that changed his life and their relationship—but not in the way she had hoped.

She began by resettling on him the portion of her wartime dowry retained by her father, which turned out to have been wisely invested and bigger than she thought. Her next move involved Averell's money. For the past few months, Winston had frightened her with tales of flying a single-engine plane through storms between London and his Manchester constituency. Haunted by Kick Kennedy's death, she persuaded her lovestruck new husband to buy him a larger twin-engined Piper Seneca for $85,000. Winston was soon flying his family to holidays in Greece, also bankrolled by Pamela. "It was so kind and generous of you both to give me such a fantastic present," he wrote.[1] Even this largesse was trumped by a $1 million trust fund ($7.3 million today) and yet more to come. Later Winston was to claim that the money came from his mother's own resources and the sale of some furniture.[2] This hardly seems plausible given the scale of Pamela's financial wipeout after Leland's death. Furthermore, Winston wrote to Averell less than a month after the wedding to thank him for "what you plan to do for us and the children" and how it would "certainly make a big difference in our lives."[3]

Winston had already been generously funded by his mother's previous lovers and his own grandfather—he had inherited the foreign rights to Churchill's bestselling book *A History of the English-Speaking Peoples*. Yet he complained that he struggled to maintain the standard of living he had been brought up to expect on the salary of an MP, even when topped up by journalism and lecture fees. He and Minnie (who hailed from a wealthy family but had no real fortune of her own) were so grateful for Averell's generosity they later named their fourth child John Averell.

It was around this time that Averell's assistant asked him if he intended to stop paying the new Mrs. Harriman the monthly stipend she had received since the war. Averell was bored by account keeping and had not noticed the $20,000 or so slipping out every year and yet was also a man who fumed about others not turning off the lights. "Averell was as tight-fisted as any human ever born," notes a younger friend Frank Wisner, who braved "a very grubby neighborhood" to buy low-priced clarets for Pamela because she feared Averell would object to paying more.[4] Over time Pamela ensured that Averell loosened the Harriman purse strings—above all for Winston. Her privileging him over Leland's children had of course met with disaster but Pamela had a dangerous compulsion to go on trying to win her son's love with money.

Winston finally came over from London in October for a birthday dinner Pamela hosted for him and thirty-four guests. The following night she threw a wedding bash for five hundred at Averell's house at 3038 N Street NW in Georgetown. Senators, Supreme Court justices, TV anchors, ambassadors and columnists poured into the handsome Federalist townhouse leavened by a sprinkling of Pamela's theater friends. The new couple were bringing more glamour to Washington than anyone since the Camelot days of the Kennedys. "The old man was in love, maybe for the first time," his biographer Rudy Abramson observed. Where Marie had once "kidded and deflated" him, Pamela "petted and humoured and stoked the still-robust ego."[5] When she moved around the room, Averell stole admiring glances at her as if he could hardly believe his luck. Although newly forbidden from skiing by his doctors, he had taken up daily swimming to stay fit and attractive for her. Both would plunge nude into the N Street pool as it was not overlooked. Pamela "changed his life," recalled a friend. "He began to bloom like a rose."[6]

During what she called her "dreaming hours," Pamela allowed her imagination to soar as to how she could transform Averell's home into a political powerhouse fit for her new king. First in her sights was improving the layout of the smallish rooms on the ground floor. She had already discussed the possibilities with designer Billy Baldwin, who had flown down to Washington from New York. She envisaged widening doorways and pulling out mantelpieces, but Baldwin was concerned. "*You will not* make people think that you feel that Averell has been living in a dump," he warned her, "because he hasn't."[7] He urged her to respect the historic proportions of a residence built in 1805—exceptionally old by American standards. "This is not a beautiful London house!" he exclaimed. "But it's full of charm and you must behave."[8]

Pamela kept the structure, put her large collection of love letters and marriage proposals into a vault, and then erased every trace of Marie. She sent the Duchins all the photographs of them without even an explanatory note[9] and replaced the jumble of furniture with what remained of her Louis XVI pieces from Paris, velvet cushions embroidered with the Digby ostrich, and a multitude of flowers. Most importantly, and knowing the veneration it commanded in Washington, Pamela readopted the Churchill name and had her initials PCH stamped everywhere from matchbooks and stationery to towels and sheets, all under the Digby crest. The overall effect was "very Pam." No one could be left in doubt of her blue blood or political pedigree—or Averell's.

The hall became a gallery of Averell's political life, its walls lined with statement photographs of him with Churchill, FDR, Queen Elizabeth II and the Soviet leader Khrushchev. It pleased him even more when she instructed staff and guests to address him as Governor in recognition of his highest elected office. Arthur Schlesinger and Bill Walton began to speculate how much further he might have gone if Pamela had been at his side.

Upper-class couples rarely shared a bedroom and Averell made do with a single bed in a pared-down room half the size of hers. But Pamela did install a bed long enough for him after years of sleeping with his feet hanging over the end. She refused to occupy Marie's old bedroom nearby in favor of a suite at the other end of the house, with its own sitting room and open fire. In prime position, Pamela hung the Cecil Beaton portrait of herself as the sexy young woman Averell had met back in 1941. In the adjoining room Pamela installed a romantic George III four-poster bed bedecked in pale pink and green silks. An enraptured Averell joined her there most nights and every morning for breakfast. She enhanced every aspect of his life, from making his favorite cocktails to introducing him to cozy nights with supper on a tray watching political programs on TV, as well as the joy of chocolate. For her, the marriage was "the rounding of the circle," noted Kitty Carlisle Hart. It brought her "all she cared about: love, lovely things and the political arena."[10]

Much of Marie's art collection also made Pamela uncomfortable. She urged Averell to proceed with plans to give twenty-one paintings (including five Cézannes, a Picasso and a Seurat) to Washington's National Gallery in return for a substantial tax break. The works she wanted to keep were haunting, colorful or sexy—Picasso's beautiful *Mother and Child*, a Degas bronze called *Petite Danseuse de Quatorze Ans* and Renoir's flirtatious *Portrait of Mademoiselle Demarsy*. The greatest treasure was Van Gogh's *White Roses*, one of the most prized paintings still in private hands, which she hung over the drawing room mantelpiece.

Visitors who knew 3038 from before were astonished at how Pamela had made the house shimmer. Somehow it looked bigger, and certainly more splendid. It became a fitting monument to when Pamela and Averell were last together, a time that Averell considered his "heroic period"[11] and Pamela her most thrilling. Averell refused to accept his age as a barrier to more politics; Pamela was set on finding a way to advise and influence. Now that they were again an item, they both believed great things could be possible.

Word of this new Harriman redoubt rich with Churchillian ambition had reached the White House. American involvement in Vietnam was mercifully winding down but in October 1972 President Nixon was pondering his own political fortunes if the war came to an end before he secured a second term. "I don't want [the settlement] to come before the election," he told Kissinger. Nixon feared that otherwise he might "wind up like Churchill" in 1945, when the victor in war had met defeat at the ballot box. Nixon wanted to hear more about where Churchill had gone wrong and considered Pamela best placed to tell him, so he had his staff arrange a dinner for her with Averell and Winston. It was recognition that Pamela was bearer of the war hero's flame.[12]

Such lofty connections inevitably meant that wherever Pamela went, there was a chorus of critics. Not only was she seen as a British aristocrat with unparalleled reach operating on American soil but she had replaced Marie by beating the keenest local competition to nab one of the city's richest men. Pamela was aware that her rivals thought she had enjoyed more than her fair share of lucky breaks and that achieving her ambitions would not be easy or immediate. Washington remained, as one denizen put it, "a cauldron of biting nastiness,"[13] or as President Truman once correctly advised, "if you want a friend in DC get a dog." It was particularly tough for women. Pamela cast her eye over to Westminster, where her near-contemporaries such as Barbara Castle and Margaret Thatcher were aiming for high office, with some even being considered as potential future prime ministers. (Thatcher would indeed enter Downing Street after the landmark election of 1979.) In America in 1971, though, there were still only two female senators—both of whom had taken seats vacated by their husbands. Mostly, even for the most privileged and intelligent women, the only political role permitted was as hostesses. If that was all that was open to her, then Pamela was determined to use it to make her mark.

During Marie's time Averell had stinted on household spending. At their annual Thanksgiving weekend party at Arden, they had packed forty bedrooms with friends and served gallons of champagne. The house, though, was hideous and the food inedible, and the one manservant rushed off his feet. Guests staved off their hunger with heavy drinking before raiding the kitchen at night in search of scraps.[14] So Pamela brought in her own large team and Diana Vreeland was not the only friend to take "delight" in Pamela's new troupe of "very attractive" male servants.[15] Having worked for the new Mrs. Harriman was the highest recommendation and she was constantly fending off attempts to poach her staff by hiking their pay, but avoided Averell finding out by raiding the petty cash. For a rich man Averell had no real interest in displays of wealth; for one early birthday he proudly presented Pamela with a television aerial. The mistake was not repeated and he swiftly shifted gear, buying her emeralds from Russia. Pamela would show Averell sketches of a necklace, earrings or pins, and if he approved she ordered them. "She took great care of her jewellery," said a staff member, "she had a lot."[16]

Pamela also had Averell smarten up as befitting a statesman, ordering dozens of shirts (half with buttons, half with cufflinks) from

Jermyn Street and suits from Savile Row in London. If he balked at a bill she pouted and was almost always successful, but then almost always he loved the results. "She puts my favorite flower by my bed every morning," he told Peter Duchin in a tone of awe. "Your favorite flower?" asked Peter. "I don't know what it is," Averell replied, "but she puts it by my bed."[17]

Celia Sandys was one of many visitors struck by the standard of housekeeping, which had risen to greater perfection even than at Haywire. The phones were answered after a single ring and the sheets were ironed on the bed every day by a maid (a tip Pamela had learned from Wallis Simpson). At bedtime, there would be an imported chocolate bar or homemade cookie on the pillow. Particularly favored guests found a Gucci handbag or luxurious bathrobe in their room. In the garden a large tree was grubbed up to let in more sunlight and the beds planted with 2,500 pastel-colored tulips personally selected by Billy Baldwin. Even the Duchess of Devonshire—formerly Debo Mitford and accustomed to the glories of Chatsworth—thrilled at the "masterly arrangements." "It is wonderful to arrive tired & stupid and find such a haven."[18] It was Averell's house but Pamela quickly made clear whose hand was on the tiller. The three maroon-colored cars in the garage—a Jaguar, a Bentley and a Cadillac—had the numberplates PCH1, PCH2, PCH3. The impact on every visitor, however grand, was one of awe at her focus and drive.

Pamela was out to impress the right people—Henry Kissinger was granted a key to the garden gate so that he could swim whenever he wished—but she knew she also had to be political. She avoided the term "servants" as a nod to a more egalitarian world. "We don't have servants here," she claimed, "we have a team. Young college girls come here for a year or two, very bright people, interested in politics, and then they go on to something else." One female cleaner, Pamela loved to inform everyone, had left to become a biochemist in Chicago.[19]

Until the late 1960s the grandest restaurants in New York and Washington banned women from wearing trousers—which were fit only for working in the garden. When that changed, the *New York Times* thought it so significant it ran a lengthy piece in 1972 on the latest stage of "women's liberation." In a nod to her own growing emancipation Pamela wore trousers in many of her first photographs with Averell but in most other ways her marriage appeared traditional, even if it was not. "It never occurs to me that I've lost my identity or that I've never had any identity," she told a journalist. "This may sound arrogant" but "I've always been me."[20] The national mood shifted further. Just a month after her wedding, Congress passed the landmark Equal Rights Amendment forbidding discrimination on the grounds of sex, thanks to the determination of Bella Abzug, a Democratic congresswoman of New York, Gloria Steinem and Betty Friedan. Pamela admired their pluck but knew that Averell was old-school. She would have to be more subtle in the ways she shaped their marriage.

Averell was in the process of transferring Arden as a tax-deductible gift to Columbia University, although the family would retain part of the 25,000-acre wooded estate, and she persuaded him to sell the Manhattan townhouse too. She wanted their lives to revolve around politics in Washington. To be the ultimate political hostess, she needed a country house near the capital to entertain at weekends. After persistent lobbying on her part, Averell agreed to buy Willow Oaks, a manor house at Middleburg in Virginia, looking out to the foothills of the Blue Ridge Mountains and referred to as "the Farm" (although little was grown there except more flowers). A short drive from Georgetown, the Farm reminded Pamela of Dorset even more than Haywire, especially after she imported dozens of her father's favorite rhododendrons. She had a hill bulldozed to create a better outlook from her bedroom and the swimming pool moved to another site where, to the astonishment of Clarissa Churchill, it was "heated to ninety degrees giving off clouds of steam in the freezing Virginian winter."[21] The $740,000 purchase price was nearly matched by Pamela's spending on improvements to connote comfort, wealth and most of all power to the senior politicians showered with invitations.

Willow Oaks also felt like Pamela's domain and it allowed her in her mid-fifties to resume hunting, her enthusiasm undimmed by a string of bone-breaking falls. Her favorite horse was a small mare bred in Dorset called Prospect, who she thought "tremendously fast and clever as a cat." Members of the Middleburg Hunt soon learned not to underestimate their new member as she zipped past them over the biggest fences.[22]

It was fun spending Averell's money, but she instinctively knew the dangers of privilege unless shared. She was a generous contributor to charities, notably for victims of domestic violence, but she also occasionally supported individuals she thought deserved a kick start. Through hunting Pamela met the professional show jumper Katie Monahan, who asked her if she would help her career in a male-dominated field by buying horses for her to enter international grand prix events. Pamela admired Katie's boldness and agreed. She called the first horse they acquired the Governor—although this alarmed Averell, in case it performed poorly and reflected badly on him. Thankfully, in its first twelve months the Governor won three major titles, $100,000 prize money and was named Horse of the Year, for which both Katie and Pamela received Mercedes cars. "Here was a lady who gave all her life," Katie says of Pamela's munificence. "When I got married, she hosted the wedding reception at her house for three hundred people."[23] "She wanted to be gracious," Emma Soames agrees, "but she needed the means for her graciousness." And now she had them. This *noblesse oblige* to a chosen few would inevitably intensify the bitterness of others.

Peter Duchin for one felt betrayed by the changes that Pamela was imposing. Devoted to Marie's memory, the Manhattan house had been the nearest he had known as a child to a proper home. Worse still was news that Averell's Florida residence at Hobe Sound was also to be sold without him having made good on his offer to let Peter build himself a house there. Peter began to believe that Pamela was intent on cutting Averell off from his past, and that included him. The final straw, though, seems to have been money and Winston.

Egged on by Marie, Averell had traditionally given Peter handsome gifts at Christmas, such as a drawing by a famous artist. The first year after the marriage to Pamela it became clear how Peter's stock had fallen when he opened his far more modest gift before hearing about Winston's Piper Seneca. Pamela was "pushing me aside and bringing Winston in with Averell," Peter complained. "I get a tie and Winston a plane."[24] With Marie's death, Peter had lost his champion while Pamela was intent on drawing in her own son, hoping to create a semblance of a happy family. Yet in her desperation to assuage her own maternal guilt, Pamela had—just as with the Haywards—become blind to the effect on others.

Thankfully, Bill Hayward (if not his sister) had changed his mind about her and dropped the lawsuit. He even admitted that his views of Pamela had been "tainted by what we'd heard about her" and that he now realized how, after living his life to the full, Leland had left her in the lurch. "I probably appeared like a vulture to her."[25] Pamela was willing to forgive, later even persuading Averell to set up trust funds of $50,000 for Bill's children. But her experiences with the Haywards made her fear another unseemly battle with Peter, a man described by one of his wives as "wild but polite."[26] Pamela's instinct was to set their relationship on a formal footing she thought she could control. She took away Peter's N Street key and meetings would thereafter be planned in advance.

Averell had been diagnosed with prostate cancer so perhaps, as with Leland, she thought she had to protect her aging husband's health. Or perhaps it was because the families of her men had so often caused her heartache. Her insecurity at first was palpable but as her marriage became increasingly solid her methods were no less blunt. When his marriage to Cheray later broke down, Peter's resentment would be fueled by Pamela's bitterest foe of all.

28

Three months after her wedding, in December 1971, Pamela was sworn in as an American citizen by a federal judge in New York and immediately set out her objectives. "I want to vote and participate in the election," she announced. "I think everyone knows which way I will go."[1] Given her upbringing as a Conservative, her Churchill background and Leland's possible Republican leanings, her allegiance was not in fact clear to many. It became more so the following night at a supper party for 140 people to welcome her as an American citizen, hosted in Georgetown by the Bruces. The heavily Democratic guest list included Ethel Kennedy and Robert McNamara, defense secretary under Presidents Kennedy and Johnson. Wearing a long black chiffon dress, Pamela told reporters waiting by the line of black limousines and gray Rolls-Royces that politics was her main interest in life, but she knew that it was necessary to keep within tight feminine constraints. She would, she said, be attending the Governor's lectures—to take notes.[2]

Her arrival in Washington coincided with social and political turbulence and Averell's obsession with ousting Nixon. The first manned moon landing had taken place in 1969 but there was mounting concern about environmental devastation on Earth. Racial tensions had barely lessened since the torrid violence of 1968—indeed Nixon's regime seemed intent on delaying desegregation as well as imposing a vicious crackdown on civil rights. Meanwhile, suspicions of corruption were beginning to encircle the president even if no one had yet firmly linked him to the break-in at the Watergate headquarters of the Democratic National Committee (the party's governing body). Finally, Nixon had failed to end the bloodshed in Vietnam and protests continued with four unarmed students killed by the National Guard during an anti-war demonstration at Kent State University.

At the start of the election year of 1972, Pamela had followed Averell's lead in backing Senator Edmund Muskie as the right Democratic candidate to depose Nixon that November. Seen as an establishment figure, he shared Averell's passion for nuclear arms control and an internationalist outlook in which America was morally obliged to assume a global leadership role, a position Pamela had of course wholeheartedly backed since her involvement in dragging the United States into the Second World War. Averell was hostile to the "prairie populist" contender Senator George McGovern because of his pledge to "cut and run" from the Cold War conflict in Vietnam—unilaterally pulling out American troops without first extracting Soviet concessions. Both Harrimans believed it would signal weakness to Moscow—and that dealing with the Soviet Union was effective only from a position of military strength—but the idea garnered passionate grassroots support from a war-weary nation.

The Harrimans joined Muskie on a whistle-stop election tour of Florida. Averell had previously been reluctant to make sizable donations (Bill Walton used to complain that it had been a Herculean job to extract a check for the Kennedy campaign[3]) but Pamela persuaded him to underwrite one of Muskie's campaign broadcasts in the hope that it would give him more say in the party. Such involvement allowed her to witness presidential campaigning up close and personal, including the dirty tricks played by the Nixon side. Pamela began to doubt whether Muskie had the force of personality to withstand the attacks after he was accused of crying under pressure—although he famously claimed his cheeks were wet from melting snowflakes. Averell still wanted to run as a Muskie delegate at the Democratic National Convention in Miami in July (where the presidential candidate would be chosen) and was "very hurt" when he was rejected despite his investment.

Undeterred, he decided to run as an independent delegate and Pamela dutifully campaigned for him as well as for Muskie across New York State. She drove thousands of miles, knocked on doors and buttonholed voters in grocery stores but although she adored the political theater Averell failed to pick up enough votes. She was surprised that "we ran and lost,"[4] as the Governor had attracted sizable crowds. It turned out that most of them had come to catch a glimpse of her. She was a glamorous celebrity and infinitely more box office than the wooden elder statesman who had failed to inspire as governor of New York nearly two decades previously.[5] It was yet another electoral defeat for Averell, who struggled to win the status he thought his long history of service justified. The snub was made even more painful when one local group pushed past him to ask Pamela to run for the city council. She declined but was thrilled to have the recognition—even if she also appreciated the potential perils for her marriage. She accompanied Averell to Miami but they left as soon as McGovern was nominated as the candidate.

It was already becoming clear that this was an unusually political marriage, and that Pamela was perhaps even more eager to be engaged than her husband. There was soon a *Harriman* position rather than an *Averell* one—"he" became "they." The Harriman position was that McGovern was no match even for a president increasingly embroiled in controversy. Nixon duly won his second term in the White House, the last time an American presidential candidate scooped more than 60 percent of the popular vote. In her first election in Washington, Pamela had followed her husband to back the defeated candidate of the defeated party and seen a man unfit to occupy the

Oval Office return triumphant. In future, she would make up her own mind.

The experience was a crash course in American politics and Pamela noted the power of charisma over crowds. Up-and-coming figures such as McGovern's campaign manager Gary Hart had it, but Muskie and Averell did not. Soon afterward, she finally tasted the sweetness of political victory. Robert Strauss, a flirtatious Texan with a love for the political game, was running for the chairmanship of the Democratic National Committee and asked Pamela to help. After the Nixon victory, the party was divided and barely able to pay its phone bill. Strauss needed to convince Democrats he could hold their "patchwork party" together and saw just the operator he needed. "Pamela had a knack," he observed, and "Averell knew it."[6] As she once said, Averell was "not a politician really. He was a staunch Democrat . . . but party politics didn't really interest him. He was much more of a statesman. That was why he never got reelected as governor. He wasn't prepared to play politics."[7] But, it turned out, she was.

29

It was not only crowds on the stump in New York State who wanted a piece of Pamela but anyone who liked to hear about Churchills, Kennedys, FDR, Harry Hopkins, de Gaulle or most of the other towering figures of the previous thirty years. That included almost anyone in public life, and she was much in demand as a guest. It would have been an unfortunate lacuna in her history if she had not had Hitler on her list—and it seems likely that she at the very least exaggerated her encounter with him for that reason. Averell certainly regretted that he never met him—feeling his historical roster was somehow incomplete—and was impressed that she had. It was all part of Pamela's stardust and the denizens of Washington leaned in to catch every historical insight. "No one else was left," remarked the lobbyist Tony Podesta on both Harrimans, "with such eminence, authority, historical reach, social class, and policy credentials."[1] She exercised discretion, however, even obfuscation when necessary. She knew instinctively not to criticize the Kennedys—not even Joe. When Arthur Schlesinger asked about him, incredibly she claimed that he had been "endlessly kind" and excused his defeatist dismissal of Britain's chances during the war as "honestly believed." When Schlesinger asked what Churchill thought of him, she replied that she could not recall Winston mentioning him. Averell interrupted gruffly with the truth (which Pamela knew but was avoiding): "Winston despised him."[2]

An invitation to the Harrimans' N Street home trumped almost all others in Georgetown except possibly Kay Graham's. One young newcomer, David Lane (who went on to become an ambassador under President Obama), found his first visit a little overwhelming. When he asked the butler if he could use a phone, he was told, "Oh yes, Mr. Lane, go straight to the Van Gogh and turn right."[3] There was a shrinking band of women who had the time, setting, wealth and determination to entertain at this level. To host was to exert power over who met who and when, and perhaps even what they talked about.

Most prized of all was Pamela's eggnog party before Christmas, the chosen ones proudly displaying their invitations. Hobnobbing with British aristocrats was popular but even more of a draw was mixing with Hollywood royalty—few others in Washington had the stars as friends. "Theater and politics are very much alike," Pamela would say. "It's success or failure. You either have a big hit play or it folds. You win the election or you lose."[4] Jack Nicholson and Warren Beatty made appearances and when Robert Redford turned up at a Pam party in May 1974, Kay Graham gushed with excitement at her "wish come true" of meeting him.[5]

In the vipers' nest of Washington, Pamela courted few women as friends and even fewer successfully—Kay never became quite the ally that Pamela had hoped. She continued to rely on the sage counsel of Bill Walton but he was not the only one from the old times whom Pamela still saw, in part because they enlivened Averell's mood. Martha Gellhorn came to the Harriman ski lodge in Sun Valley, Idaho—a resort built by Averell in the 1930s to boost traffic on the family's Union Pacific Railroad—to go hiking, soaking in the rustic feel including the bear skins on the wall.

Another favored guest Pamela had known since the 1930s was Anthony Eden, who had resigned as prime minister over Suez fifteen years previously with his reputation in tatters. Eden had since been plagued by ill health and by the winter of 1976 had been diagnosed with uncontrolled prostate cancer. Pamela invited him and his wife, her friend Clarissa Churchill, along with Dr. William Cahan, in case the oncologist could come up with "something helpful."[6] Pamela was often accused of being mercenary but showed particular care for those who were ill or down on their luck. When he joined the party, the *Sunday Times* Washington correspondent Henry Brandon was forbidden to upset Eden. Pamela took him to one side to whisper, "Please, Henry, don't mention Suez!"[7]

Brandon marveled how Pamela had Eden ensconced on a wicker chair by the pool, dressed in a bottle-green robe and straw hat, looking "almost as handsome and dashing as ever."[8] When Eden suddenly deteriorated and was determined to go home to die, no airline would fly him given the severity of his condition. Pamela asked Winston to contact the British prime minister Jim Callaghan, who sent an RAF hospital plane to pick Eden up. Ten days later he was dead. Averell and Eden had adored reminiscing about the war but Pamela began to feel eager to take an active part in the future. She had reached the point where she longed to surround herself with younger people.

Pamela had been in residence in Georgetown barely three years when the Watergate scandal shook Washington to the core. Facing certain impeachment—and with the stench of political scandal engulfing the city—in August 1974 Nixon became the first American president to resign. His vice president, Gerald Ford, succeeded him. He too had served in the Second World War and was yet another commander in chief to take an interest in Pamela. In those less partisan days, the Harrimans were A-list even under a Republican administration and were regularly welcomed at the White House. It was gratifying to be invited in July 1976 to the state dinner for Queen Elizabeth II (even if

Pamela was only on table seventeen with the wife of Senator Bob Dole). Kissinger was also eager to invite them into the State Department—as when the blue-blooded president of France, Giscard d'Estaing, whom Pamela knew from her Paris days, visited Washington aboard the presidential Concorde. Consequently, her own guests were of both political parties, even if the majority were Democrats.

Pamela's primary enterprise appeared to be to help her husband feel like he was, even in his mid-eighties, still relevant, by having Washington's power players dining at their table or mingling in their library. There was still a united Harriman position on politics and she did not diverge from it publicly. Yet as he aged so she increasingly but discreetly became the driving force at gatherings that were serious attempts at pursuing an agenda, forging an alliance, developing a policy or winning the support of a newspaper. Camelot was long since over but Pamela shared Kissinger's view that "the hand that mixes the Georgetown martini is time and again the hand that guides the destiny of the Western world." Averell's friend Richard Holbrooke spoke for many other (male) politicos—and the occasional pioneering woman such as Barbara Walters, the first female cohost of an evening TV news bulletin—when he praised Pamela for making such events "so much fun."[9] Under her direction, N Street was becoming a Democratic hub looking to a return to power. Young party thinkers were offered the Harrimans' adjacent building at number 3034 to draft policies for the next manifesto. Pamela also hosted a buffet supper for two hundred Democratic officials. "My garden is going to be ruined by tents and people," she fretted to Jock,[10] but in reality she could not have been more pleased at how she was being accepted into the crowd preparing for the 1976 presidential elections in six months' time.

No one could manage Averell like Pamela but even she was finding it ever more difficult. She took notes of conversations that might be of interest because he often did not hear them, a frustration that prompted outbursts of temper. He made little allowance for inexperience, even berating a young secretary for not placing a paper at a particular angle for him to sign. To younger men he was known as the Crocodile, for the way he seemed half-asleep one moment and the next snapped off their comments with a curt dismissal. Woe betide anyone who questioned his good office. Averell slapped a woman who had effectively accused him of being a war criminal for his early support of war in Vietnam.[11] Even children learned to comport themselves as if in the presence of royalty. The young sons of one assistant, Pie Friendly, were reprimanded for having their hands in their pockets. Pamela gently chided Averell with a wounded look and tried to make amends with smiles and good cheer. Her influence gradually made him nicer.

Persuading him that women should take a more active part in politics and affairs of state was a bigger challenge. Even though he knew she had operated at the highest levels during the war, he was rooted firmly in the idea of his generation that in peacetime women could gather people but not govern. So when she invited politicians and editors to dine, it was understood that they were court dinners for him. Incredibly, he still expected Pamela to lead the women upstairs to her study before coffee, to allow the men to talk about serious issues without them. One night in early 1976 the glamour couple of DC, the *Washington Post* editor Ben Bradlee, who had overseen the Watergate exposé, and his journalist wife, Sally Quinn, were at N Street for a dinner in honor of Senator Frank Church, who was considering a run for the presidency. The meal ran the course of many Pamela had previously arranged for senators, congressmen and senior officials, the candlelight glancing off the hand-painted eighteenth-century blossom and peacock wallpaper. After dessert, she tinked her water glass and announced that the ladies should follow her upstairs.

The other women left the room but Quinn, who was writing a profile about Church for the *Post*, followed the men into the library, knowing that was where the senator would be most forthcoming. Averell fiddled with his hearing aid in astonishment and asked her to join the other women. Quinn went to stand over by her husband. Turning puce at what he saw as female impertinence, Averell bellowed that it was his house and in his house the ladies went upstairs after dinner. Defiant, Quinn said she was leaving. She marched down the hall to the front door, hoping in vain that her husband would follow "to protect my honor." Pamela did not intervene, torn between alarm for Averell and sympathy for Quinn's position. She was no more interested than Quinn in the traditional female topics of children and pets. Even interior design was, for her, about setting the stage for serious purposes. She was also embarrassed by a custom she knew to be outdated, and had hoped to befriend Quinn. "She was apparently horrified," Quinn recalls. "She wanted to be part of the young, hip crowd and this crusty old man . . . was ruining her social standing in Washington. After that she was even nicer to me." Quinn thinks Pamela's motives were suspect, however, and to this day judges her an "appalling person." "Nobody could stand her. She wanted to be a close friend of mine but she was just the biggest climber."[12]

Another well-connected Georgetown figure, Polly Fritchley (whose second husband had once dated Pamela), harbored similar feelings. "She admired Pamela's energy, guts and determination," according to her son Frank Wisner, "but felt that Pamela walked on other people to go to the next level on the ladder."[13] In truth, she was being judged through a female prism at a time when women were not supposed to show rugged ambition (a quality often admired in men). In the ruthless environment of Washington, success also inevitably led to mistrust.

Quinn might have left the house in defeat, but she had awakened something in her hostess and emboldened her to move on from mere convener. News of the incident spread and the ritual of separating the sexes faded away altogether after Kay Graham also refused to oblige in another Georgetown house three weeks later. Thereafter, Pamela sought to earn her place with the men by recounting her own historic role—even reading out loud extracts from Mary Soames's new biography of her mother, Clementine, in which Pamela emerged as a mainstay of both Churchills.[14] The message was clear: she wanted a political role as of old and no longer wished to be seen as Averell's "little wife."[15]

Society was rapidly changing. Old customs were being ripped up. As Averell's health weakened, so Pamela began to see that women's liberation could help her in making her own political choices. Like many of her generation, Pamela publicly claimed she lived through her men and adopted their outlook for her own. Yet Quinn's defiance and Averell's outburst that night spurred her more than ever to modernize her marriage and her life.

30

A few months later, in July 1976, Pamela astonished Washington, Averell and perhaps even herself. Under the name Mrs. W. Averell Harriman—a custom she had not yet abandoned—she announced her support for Bella Abzug as the Democratic Party nominee to become senator for New York. Having watched her as a progressive feminist congresswoman delivering sexual equality legislation and taking a bold stand against the Nixon regime, Pamela believed Abzug should become the first woman Democrat to be elected to the Senate in her own right. "I admire her independence and courage," Pamela stated.

Five years into her marriage, Pamela was striking out on her own as journalists were briefed that the Governor had not taken a position. And she had chosen Abzug (famous for big hats and calling a staff member a "cocksucker") in place of Averell's more conservative political associate Daniel Patrick Moynihan. Pamela held a fundraising party for Abzug at Kitty Carlisle Hart's Manhattan apartment, where she told guests, "We would like to show a lot of people who feel she's brusque and aggressive [that] we feel she is aggressive in the right way."[1] Gloria Steinem, Elizabeth Taylor and Barbra Streisand were also fans (although Jackie Onassis stuck with "Pat"). Privately, even Averell had dramatically changed tack. Now it was he who was following Pamela's lead and he abandoned Moynihan. "I believe in discrimination—for women," he wrote to an astonished Edgar Bronfman, their neighbor at Haywire.[2]

"We all know Bella for her strong, courageous and early opposition to the war in Vietnam," Pamela told her guests in her first political speech. She also lauded Abzug's fight to clean up the environment and for her being one of the first in Congress to support gay rights, issues not yet considered mainstream. Abzug was surprised at her prominent new backer but no less enthused, telling her the "press may not have known that you can speak as well as throw parties [but] I never had any doubt."[3] Pamela still did not think of herself as a feminist, however, merely viewing Abzug as an exceptional candidate rather than the vanguard of female force. At a press conference, Pamela told of how she had been sizing up the many members of Congress who had come through her door and she had been "tremendously impressed" with how the once-ridiculed Abzug had gone on to achieve "more than most." If "Battling Bella" succeeded—and to that end, Pamela encouraged Abzug to lose thirty pounds and ditch the kaftans—it might prompt a sea change in old-fashioned Washington attitudes. Including toward Pamela herself.

In her excitement, Pamela railed to Sally Quinn about Moynihan spending his nights "wisecracking" in pubs and claimed he would be a liability in the Senate "with that amount of alcohol in his head." Quinn published Pamela's unguarded comment in the *Post*, prompting a furor.[4] Moynihan still won the primary—although only just—and duly won the vote in November. He had long been a heavy drinker and now he became a committed enemy of Pamela's. Yet the saga ultimately benefited her as it brought her wider attention while teaching her greater circumspection with the media. Her backing of Abzug also reflected her intuition as to where the tides of history would eventually flow.

Once she thought him likely to win the primaries, Pamela donated $1,000 (the maximum then permitted from an individual) to back

Jimmy Carter, a peanut farmer and former governor of the southern state of Georgia. Averell duly followed her lead a couple of months later—although both were underwhelmed by the choice. Soon afterward, her fundraising reception for Carter's 51.3 Percent Committee for bringing more women into public life—another step in her embrace of women in politics—caught the eye of newspaper editors. Under the headline THE AMERICANIZATION OF PAMELA HARRIMAN, the *Washington Star* hailed her work for Abzug and the 51.3 Percent Committee plus her frequent high-level Democratic gatherings, as a remarkable political coming-out.[5] She was winning a deserved reputation in some quarters for working tirelessly to answer the party's calls for help.

If Pamela was moving toward support of women's liberation, she was increasingly concerned about the way the Grand Old Party was veering to the right. The hotly contested Republican primary came down to a battle between the incumbent President Gerald Ford and an insurgent from the conservative wing, a Hollywood actor she had met when married to Leland, called Ronald Reagan. Most Democrats dismissed Reagan as a lightweight but Pamela sensed early on that one day he might win, a thought she considered "terrifying." "I just hope the President doesn't lose in his own home state," she told Jock.[6] In the end, Ford won the nomination, but it had been a close-run thing.

Pamela was thrilled at having finally backed a winner when Jimmy Carter squeaked past Gerald Ford in November's presidential election—even if she found him remote and unimaginative. Pamela had nursed hopes that Averell might be appointed Secretary of State, but Carter thought the eighty-four-year-old too old and patrician and gave the job to Averell's protégé Cyrus Vance instead. Pamela switched her energies to connecting her husband to events through other friends now ensconced at the State Department's headquarters at Foggy Bottom. She offered Vance's senior assistants Richard Holbrooke and Marshall Shulman free accommodation at 3034 so that they would keep Averell in the loop. Over time, these "lodgers" inevitably "coalesced" around Pamela rather than the Governor, who found them increasingly difficult to hear. Just as Churchill had once coached her in the conduct of war, they came to act as her high-level tutors in American statecraft over drinks and sometimes dinner. By the time they left for bed, she had thoroughly debriefed them on their day.[7]

Holbrooke was the antithesis of Averell, whom he had assisted in the 1968 Vietnam peace talks in Paris, in his wild brand of genius. He would become one of the most important peacemakers of his generation, but his aggression made him an uncomfortable colleague and had trashed friendships and marriages, leaving him grateful for a free room. A self-described "blatant sexist," he and Pamela became unlikely friends. She brought out his warmer side and saw through the bombast to his talent. He craved her moneyed life, but as he mentored her, also came to admire her not merely as a glamorous hostess but as a potential political force.[8] Shulman came to Washington as special assistant to Secretary Vance, bringing his wife, Colette, who had made a name for herself reporting from Moscow. She refused to become "just some Washington wife" but continued to conduct research into Soviet living conditions. Pamela was intrigued by such a prominent career woman known for her weekly 1960s television program on the Soviet press. Colette in turn took the chance to study Pamela and came to understand her better than most. If Pamela said that in her world men were more important than women, Colette observed, it was simply because it was still men who held the positions of power.[9]

Pamela's political and media friends, including television anchor Diane Sawyer, often came to the Farm at weekends but Pamela kept them separate from her horsey crowd who gathered for hearty hunt breakfasts and balls. Averell disliked these events as he did not know anybody, another drawback of an elderly husband. Pamela asked a handsome younger man who helped run the stables to escort her instead. He kept a dinner jacket at the ready in the tack room, prompting a new round of rumors. Even so, the Harrimans enjoyed "a comfortable relationship given depth by the fact they had known each other many years ago," according to Colette. "I don't remember them arguing even once."[10] Pamela created a relaxed atmosphere and "a real community there on N Street." She knew the lodgers' official salaries were comparatively modest and that the Shulmans' son was battling a serious brain illness. She paid for their tickets for a holiday and refused rent. "She was very kind . . . to people she liked," remembers Colette. "Some didn't like her simply because they felt neglected by her."

The N Street community's inside track was particularly useful on Russia. In 1979, one Soviet official who came to dinner at the Shulmans' apartment even tipped them off about the imminent invasion of Afghanistan. Relations with Moscow had been Averell's specialist subject since he had served as ambassador there during the war and his exalted status in Washington had rested on his perceived understanding of the Kremlin mindset, a subject many found bewildering. Throughout the Cold War it had been his mission to help forge better relations with the Soviet Union and back in early 1971 he had traveled to Moscow on behalf of President Nixon. Age in no way diminished his desire to try to do more, even if it meant paying for the trips to the Soviet capital himself. He had been visiting Russia since the age of seven, in 1899, when Nicholas II was tsar, later negotiated the sale of a manganese mine with Leon Trotsky and during the Second World War spent more time with Stalin than any other American. Memories of war were still fresh in Russian minds and Averell retained a special place as the man instrumental in arranging American aid for the fight against Hitler.

After the bloody embroilment of Vietnam, America was more open to the idea of a rapprochement with Moscow. As she established herself as Churchill's living representative, Pamela liked to point out that while warning of their aims to subjugate much of Europe in the Iron Curtain speech back in 1946, he had also stressed the need to negotiate with the Soviets.[11] In 1974, she had accompanied Averell to Moscow, where he embarked on a series of meetings with senior officials including general secretary Leonid Brezhnev, then presiding over a country at the height of its power but eager to ease tensions with the West. Pamela had been excited about the trip, but in a country where politicians' wives were rarely seen let alone heard, she was carted off for traditional female pursuits and excluded from the meetings that mattered. Since then, she had devoured reports and articles in the hope that in the future she could get properly involved and now that she had America's Soviet experts lodging with her she threw herself into her studies with redoubled energy.

Pamela's self-education paid dividends of sorts. In March 1978 President Carter invited her to sit on the top table at a state dinner in honor of the Yugoslav revolutionary fighter Josip Tito—the first time a communist leader had been welcomed to the White House. Yet again, her Churchill heritage was magnetic and the aging figure who had once led the most effective resistance in Europe looked delighted to be with her.

The Harrimans also believed that it was essential to make use of this period of détente with Moscow to restrict the development of newer, ever more deadly warheads. Always driving both Pamela and Averell was their shared terror of a new world conflict. "The Hiroshima bomb is trivial compared to the bombs we have now," Averell thundered. "We can't let anything stand in the way of a good [arms control] agreement. And we had better act while Brezhnev is still around!"[12] In May 1978 Averell served on the American delegation to a United Nations session on disarmament but his access to the Oval Office was hampered by a feud with Carter's national security adviser Zbigniew Brzezinski over his hardline attitude, which the Harrimans feared would strengthen the hawks in Moscow and leave little room for negotiation.

Pamela and Averell never really found the way to reach through to Carter on this or many other of their favorite issues. From the start the peanut farmer from Georgia had brought out the worst of Averell's snobbery, eliciting the snipe, "I don't even know Jimmy Carter and as far as I know none of my friends know him either."[13] Pamela also struggled to "get on Carter's wavelength." "He wasn't a people's person," a Harriman intimate observed. "Though he was a very bright, clever man, it was sort of technical cleverness."[14] There was no "cornpone Camelot"[15] for Pamela to preside over as she had hoped but a spartan regime reflecting America's economic woes and Carter's personal style. Voices began to hark back to the days of FDR and JFK, both exceptional communicators. "Jimmy Carter was one of those outsider presidents," Kay Graham judged, "who found it difficult to find the right modus operandi for Washington."[16]

Averell was fobbed off with ceremonial duties such as leading delegations to funerals. One, in February 1979 for the Yugoslavian vice president, included a young senator from Delaware called Joe Biden, whom Pamela had grown to admire. "Traveling with both of you was a privilege that I will not soon forget," Biden wrote in thanks after the trip.[17] Like many who did not know her well, the senator had perhaps not yet appreciated Pamela's role went beyond traditional maternal preoccupations. "I am not sure which impressed me more. Your concern for my cold, Mrs. Harriman," Senator Biden wrote, "or your concern for my political development, Governor."[18] He added a postscript, though, offering Pamela his services with her fundraising efforts. It was not long before he too came to realize her full worth.

Bob Strauss already did. When President Carter appointed him Trade Representative with a seat in the Cabinet, Strauss was obliged to give up his commercial directorships. Averell asked him if he could find a company board for Pamela to serve on and Strauss duly "nudged" her into his former seat at Braniff Airlines. Her first and last corporate role—she turned down another offer from Philip Morris because of the smoking link to cancer—reflected her growing status in America as a "can do" person with impeccable connections. She put in the hours, flying to plane factories, giving speeches and having Winston host a cocktail party for Braniff directors in a green-and-white striped marquee on the riverside terrace at the House of Commons. In truth, however, she was not really suited to it and the job was a distraction. The world of business was no substitute for government and she still focused most of her attention on hosting political events with an energy, reach and cachet that thrilled Washington.

In 1980, Pamela was named Democratic Woman of the Year—an honor typically granted to First Ladies or congresswomen. At a dinner in Washington, Rosalynn Carter did her duty and described Pamela as a "wonderful person." "Generally speaking, everyone was quite ladylike about it," observed the *Washington Post*.[19] "Almost everyone." One unnamed member of the Woman's National Democratic Club reflected the surprise of some by saying, "I don't know what she's done." Club president Carol Williams claimed that out of two thousand members she had received "maybe two or three" protest notes (although Pamela thought it was probably far more[20]). Williams insisted that Pamela deserved the award as the "one muckety-muck who gets in there and works. Sure, she married the right fellow but she's the only class act we've got."[21]

More to Pamela's taste as a friend was vice president Walter Mondale, a man eight years her junior with twinkling eyes. When she and Averell joined Mondale's May 1980 delegation to attend Tito's funeral so many other dignitaries, including President Carter's plain-speaking mother, known to all as Miz Lillian, wished to attend there was no room for them at the front of the plane. While Averell slept at the back of the aircraft, in one of the bunk beds that pulled down from the cabin ceiling, Pamela sneaked forward to join the vice president. Their animated conversation did not go unnoticed. "Did you see her sitting on the arm of that attractive Walter Mondale's seat? Close up like that?" Miz Lillian asked a rising staffer at the National Security Council called Madeleine Albright. "She has to do that," Miz Lillian ventured, "married to that old coot."[22]

In the morning, when everyone was preparing for landing, the eighty-eight-year-old coot was nowhere to be seen and Pamela trod up and down the aisle asking fellow passengers if they had seen him. Every seat and bathroom was searched and Pamela became frantic. Only then did a crew member think to unlatch the bed above Averell's seat to find the statesman unaware that it was morning or that his bed had mistakenly been pushed back up into the ceiling. He emerged bewildered but unhurt. It was further proof that Pamela was heading back to carer mode.

It was of course the price to be paid for marrying someone thirty years older, but she rarely admitted to frustration over Averell's increasing infirmity, confiding to the writer Christopher Ogden that the traveling kept boredom at bay. One year, she sent a birthday note saying how "wonderful" her life was with him. "I have always loved you from the first moment in the Dorchester Hotel in 1941. Happy Birthday and lucky us." They were not especially lucky, however. The prostate cancer diagnosed not long after their wedding had metastasized into Averell's bones and he stoically battled pain while refusing treatment. Averell "must not refuse to be ill," a concerned Pansy wrote to Pamela. "He has made you so happy & been so sweet to me, that he must take care of himself for all our sakes."[23]

Pamela was herself struck down on several occasions with viral pneumonia and painful attacks of diverticulitis, which confined her to her room on weak tea and chicken soup. At one point in the early 1970s, she feared that she too would need an operation if the pain did not subside. Just as she had been brought up not to mention illness, she kept her ailments from Averell. After she once fell and hurt her arm, she carried on that evening attending to him without complaint. Only on the insistence of Averell's doctor the next morning did she finally get it X-rayed. It was broken in two places.[24]

Pamela's old admirers respected Averell—Maurice Druon declaring himself "completely seduced" by him. Bill Paley, though, wondered how a highly sexed fifty-something woman coped with marriage to a doddery old man, telling her that he still found her "particularly saucy."[25] Perhaps it was no wonder that Pamela secretly engineered to see Gianni alone as he battled through a turbulent few years. Fiat was losing hundreds of millions of dollars and he and his executives were under constant threat of kidnap and murder by the Marxist-Leninist terrorist group known as the Red Brigades. His son Edoardo's erratic behavior as a mystic who publicly criticized Fiat was also troubling. Gianni, looking sexier than ever with his gray-flecked hair, leaned on Pamela at such times and there remained an eternal frisson between them. As Averell became less of a fully-fledged husband, so Pamela sought excitement from the man who had always thrilled her.

One morning, one of the Harrimans' assistants, the obliging Pie Friendly, was asked not to come into the office in the next-door building as usual but to go to the petit salon behind the dining room in the main house. Here, sitting on the blue sofa next to the Degas ballerina, she was instructed to occupy the Governor until lunch and on no account let him go to his office. Only later did she discover that Pamela had spent several hours with Gianni and "did not want Governor Harriman to see her former lover or know he had come."[26]

Pamela never spoke about the full nature of her relationship with Gianni during the latter stages of her marriage to Averell. In all probability, she was still in love with the Italian while conceding that she depended on the security that Averell was finally able to give her. Later, on their twelfth wedding anniversary in 1983, Averell wrote: "These have been the most rewarding years of my life. I can't find adequate words to express how grateful I am to you."[27] At a large celebratory dinner that night, Averell declared that they were marking their fortieth anniversary, as if there had never been a twenty-five-year gap.[28]

Pamela retained Gianni's affections through the decades but continued to harbor doubts about her appearance and took to heart a piece celebrating Marella's beauty in *Women's Wear Daily*. In what seems to have been a veiled attack on her rival, Marella took the chance to deplore women who cared more about the decor of their house than their grooming or clothes. For "a woman who is not beautiful," she pronounced, "elegance is indispensable . . . Often you see a dreary little woman with little gray shoes and a skirt who has a delightful house and charming flowers." Most inelegant of all, she ventured, was to wear too many jewels.[29] Pamela instantly stepped up her regime. She dieted and swam, walked and rode until she got down to a tiny size four (or size eight in the UK). Diana Vreeland was enlisted to select her wardrobe, and her jewelry once paraded with pride in Paris, was pared right down. Pamela was gratified when she made an international best dressed list for the first time and a women's magazine asked her for beauty tips for their readers.[30]

As much as her appearance, she wanted to upgrade her public image. For a woman who wanted more than ever to leave her racy past behind her, there was no interest more improving than high art. Pamela started with a speech in November 1979 to launch a membership drive at the Toledo Museum of Art in Ohio—she was keen to expand her presence beyond Washington. Perhaps it was a slightly risky move to have arrived by helicopter in the midst of an economic downturn, but her efforts were rewarded with the attention of the Washington art elite—notably Carter Brown, who was leveraging the capital's National Gallery from repository of a few Old Masters to a world-class institution vying with the Metropolitan Museum of Art in New York. In return, she introduced a grateful Brown to her Paris "intellectual" friends such as Gerald van der Kemp, now curator of Versailles. Such was her growing reputation as an aesthete that on a visit to Washington in 1977 Queen Margrethe of Denmark asked an ecstatic Pamela to accompany her to the ballet. Busy with fundraising, diplomacy and the arts, Pamela's different worlds were all coming into focus in her role as DC's newly anointed grande dame. She had risen further socially than anyone had envisaged but her ultimate goal of real political influence still eluded her. And it was not about to get easier.

31

If the early 1970s saw the peak of second-wave feminism, including the *Roe v. Wade* ruling protecting women's right to an abortion, there came the inevitable backlash. Pamela anxiously watched the rise of conservatives such as Phyllis Schlafly—who famously saw no irony in making a career out of campaigning for women to stay in the home—and staged a tactical retreat. Pamela "shuns interviews," the *New York Times* declared in 1977, "just as she shuns ostentation and anything that hints at frivolity or shallowness." While the piece celebrated her as a Washington figure, it also described her as a "very quiet" wife. Pamela was repositioning herself, not as Bella Abzug's champion but, in the era of what became known as the Moral Majority, as a traditional spouse.[1]

There was another reason Pamela wanted to downplay suggestions of "unfeminine" ambition. Brooke Hayward had secured a large advance to write a portrait of her family, to be called *Haywire*. Now publication was imminent and fearing it would be devastating, Pamela had already changed the name of her Mount Kisco home to the more commonplace Birchgrove. When the book came out in February 1977, Brooke described it as an "exorcism" of anger about her parents' "carelessness and guilt and the wreckage they can make of lives."[2] They were no longer alive to hear Brooke condemn them as unfit for parenting, but she reserved some of her most venomous attacks for Pamela, who came across to reviewers as "vain, grasping and acquisitive."

Brooke revived her accusation that Pamela had stolen her pearl necklaces, portraying her as a Cruella de Vil figure, her "face a phantasmagoria of white against a background of black sable and beyond her an enormous black limousine, hovering curb-side like a sleek bird of prey."[3] "Some people might think it best to leave a few of these family skeletons in the closet," the *New York Times* suggested, but "Miss Hayward drags them out into the open and rattles the bones for the world to hear."[4] It asked the question "why?" No doubt Brooke wanted to top up the "small income" she drew from her mother's trust funds but she also made it clear she was intent on "revenge."[5]

Pamela swung into action to downplay the row, telling the *New York Daily News* that "sometimes stepchildren and stepmothers don't get along but I think Brooke is a wonderful, really talented writer."[6] She claimed that she was more hurt about the attacks on Leland, who was not able to defend himself, than the allegations against her. That may not have been entirely true. Tom Brokaw of NBC's *Today* interviewed Brooke on his show and his invitation for Sunday lunch at Birchgrove was promptly rescinded. Pamela knew she was being talked about wherever she went, even at a State Department lunch for Audrey Callaghan, the wife of the British prime minister, where she was doorstepped by reporters. One observer thought she looked "flushed"—matching the hue of her flame-red dress—but determined to "bear up in a dignified manner."[7] Pamela's courting of newspaper editors may have earned her some respite. Her "accolade" to Brooke's writing talents was hailed as "generous" by the *New York Daily News*, which also stated that Pamela had no "need to purloin two sentimental but not very valuable necklaces having fantastic jewelry of her own." Unnamed "family friends" were helpfully quoted as insisting she had performed "a difficult stepmother role with charm and grace" and "made Leland very happy. It is too bad his children can't appreciate that!"[8] Even so, *Haywire* was a bestseller read by millions, praised by the counterculture writer Joan Didion and serialized in *Esquire* and *Vogue*.

Pamela privately raged at the injustice but had taken on board how a woman who wanted to get on had to conduct herself in late-1970s America. She engineered for a syndicated interview to paint her as a demure housewife who "sets a nice table." She "listens more than she talks with an attitude of attention and sympathy," the piece added in helpful vein, preferring the "less harsh glow of the reflected spotlight" of a wife and mother figure "who likes to take care of people." Her only "real regret," Pamela now claimed, was that she did not have more children.[9]

Some key Democratic figures were also wheeled out in support. Robert Strauss was quoted saying "no one else comes close" in the league of political hostesses and that she possessed a "high grace and humanism." Underneath this super-feminine veil, though, he conceded that "Pamela loves power and politics is power ... A lot goes on at dinner parties here. You never know what they're talking about over there by the fireplace but it's probably not the weather."[10] Most likely it was the presidential election in 1980, which Pamela feared Carter would lose after a series of missteps on the economy and overseas. She desperately hoped for a Democratic candidate she felt she could back fully—one who could better tap into voters' everyday concerns while strengthening America on the world stage. The search for one would dominate the next chapter of her life.

In the meantime, opinion gradually turned in Pamela's favor, in large part thanks to her media savvy. When news came a year later that Brooke was planning a full-blown biography of her stepmother, Bill Hayward recalled that "Everyone said if she did it, no one would talk to her, so she dropped it."[11] Pamela had become a real power not to be tackled lightly. "A lot of people," he observed, "are quite scared of her."[12] Brooke would not, however, cease her campaign. War broke out again in 1978 when CBS bought the rights for a movie based on *Haywire*. Pamela hired a forceful DC lawyer, Edward Bennett Williams, to ensure she barely featured. "The descriptions of you have been toned down," Pamela was assured.[13] And yet while waiting for the movie to come out in 1980, Pamela was "really upset." "She always felt," her associate Peter Fenn remembers, that "she had tried her hardest to be the mother the kids really didn't have."[14]

Perhaps as a result, Pamela hardened her attitude toward Marie's family through her first marriage—apparently fearing that they might also stand in the way of her happiness with Averell. She banned them—including Marie's granddaughter Alida Morgan, whom Averell had supported financially all her life—from popping into N Street on a whim as they had done when Marie was alive. "I never saw [Averell] alone again," Alida complained.[15] Pamela was more accommodating of Averell's blood family, especially his daughters Kathy Mortimer and Mary Fisk. Both women had endured heartache—Kathy's philandering husband suffered from bipolar disorder and early onset Alzheimer's while Mary's was battling muscular dystrophy. Neither Harriman daughter, though, had reason to work. They had inherited from their mother and Averell had set up trust funds for them worth $1 million each.[16] Since 1960 he had also provided trust funds for his six biological grandchildren as well as gifts of Union Pacific stock at Christmas with the stern instruction for the gifts to be treated as "capital, not income." The idea that they might rely on unearned Harriman money rather than supplement it with worthwhile careers appalled him.

How the grandchildren showed respect to Averell dictated Pamela's attitude toward them—if they made him happy, they were handsomely treated. In 1975, Kathy's son Averell Mortimer sent what Pamela thought a beautiful letter of fealty that she read out as an example to the others.[17] His cousin Averell Fisk, by contrast, came a cropper when he arrived sweaty and mud-splattered straight from a game of polo. "The minute I entered the house, Pamela said in front of my grandfather, 'Oh my God, you smell like a damned horse!'" She instructed him to bathe and change into fresh clothes—and he never forgave her.[18]

Pamela increasingly found she had little in common with Kathy, who shunned public life for an earthier existence. On one occasion, she arrived with Averell for lunch at Kathy's cottage at Arden just as she was arranging the hors d'oeuvres. One of Kathy's dogs wandered in and snatched some pâté off a plate, so she grabbed the animal and extracted the food from its jaws before casually offering it to Pamela, who refused it with horror.[19] From then on, Pamela was reluctant to visit Kathy at home and Averell did not go on his own, adding another source of tension. "She dictated his every movement," railed Averell Fisk. "By controlling him, she could control his money... She was infected by greed." He believed that his grandfather would never have made Pamela his wife had he been younger and not bereft over the loss of Marie.[20] The man himself saw it differently. When a friend suggested that marrying Pamela had been one of the best decisions he had ever made, Averell smiled. "No," he replied, "not one of the best. It was *the* best."[21]

32

There were two Winston Churchills in Pamela's life. The legend of the great war leader was a huge asset to her in Washington. The other, her son, was a growing liability to her persona as true-blue Democrat—notably on race. President Carter relied heavily on the black vote and had created a relatively diverse Cabinet. Pamela was intent on making her own contribution to racial justice. At a time when Washington was still struggling to emerge from the deep divisions of its past, she held a fundraising dinner for the black mayor of DC, Marion Barry, only for her butler, an ex-police officer, to see fit to remove her gold trinkets from display. Coming downstairs just before the guests arrived, Pamela asked him, "Where are all my things?" "We don't know this crowd," he replied. Utterly horrified, she told him: "Michael, put them all back!"[1]

It had been painful to read in the newspapers in January 1977 that the extremist MP Enoch Powell had delivered an anti-immigration tirade to young Conservatives in Winston's constituency. Powell had been an incendiary figure since his notorious "Rivers of Blood" speech in 1968 calling for immigrants to be sent "home." After widespread uproar at his latest prediction of racial violence, Winston issued a statement claiming not to have been informed of Powell's appearance beforehand but complained to his agitated mother that he had received "a flood of hostile and in some cases abusive letters—more than 100 in fact!"[2] Pamela had once nurtured dreams that her son would follow his grandfather into Downing Street but Margaret Thatcher had sacked him in opposition as junior defense spokesman for voting against renewing sanctions on the minority white government in Rhodesia. When she became prime minister in 1979 she refused to have him in her government.*

Such was her craving for a happy and united clan, Pamela still spared no expense or effort when it came to her son but now there were other calls on her generosity. Like many members of the upper class, the Digbys were struggling to maintain the lifestyle they had enjoyed for generations. Inflation and soaring taxes had chipped away at their income, while since the early 1970s the British economy (labeled the "sick man of Europe") had been beset by strikes, forcing the Conservative government to introduce a three-day working week and rolling power cuts. Henry Kissinger referred to Britain's plight as a "tragedy."[3] Pansy, who lived in ancient splendor at Cerne Abbey, was down to her last few servants when Pamela came in as fairy godmother. "Would you like me to send her $1,000?" Pamela asked Eddie, whose son she also sent a handsome financial gift, as she could "well afford" to.[4] It was perhaps a surprising outcome that Pamela was coming to the rescue considering her brother had inherited virtually all the family wealth. Pamela's generosity extended to Mrs. Martin, her favorite member of staff—sending her cash, paying her doctors' bills and inviting her over to America. In 1972, when after thirty years she finally retired, Pamela sent Mrs. M more money and a telegram thanking her "for everything you have meant and been for me."[5]

If Pamela was once again falling into the trap of hoping to buy love or loyalty, then Pansy sensed the danger. She felt it necessary to stress to her daughter that she did not love her for the cash, clothes

---

* In May 1993, Winston was reprimanded by prime minister John Major for calling for a halt to the "relentless flow" of immigrants—a furor that once again drew headlines in the U.S.

and trips she had given her and the rest of the family, but just for "you yourself."[6] Despite their divergent outlooks on life—and geographical distance—the two women remained fond of each other. Toward the end of her life, bursting with pride, Pansy told her, "You always make me feel I must have been a good mother."[7] After she died in March 1978, Eddie sold Cerne Abbey, which had been in the family for generations, marking yet another retrenchment in the Digby estate while Pamela carried on as if Averell's fortune was almost infinite.

Clementine Churchill was too proud to ask Pamela for money but Winston did not hesitate on her behalf. In February 1977 he sent his mother details of "Grandmama's very unsatisfactory financial situation," showing that after staffing and medical costs, her income was £15,000 a year less than her outgoings and she would run out of capital in two years, and had already sold her silver candlesticks. "It is most kind of you and Ave to say you would like to help," he wrote.[8] In the end, Clementine, who Pamela had continued to cherish as a mother figure even if she no longer addressed her as "Mama," died that December at the age of ninety-two. Pamela's assistance was therefore not needed.

Pamela was nevertheless anxious that Winston was being reckless with the huge sums she was giving him—especially his plans for a ski chalet in the French Alps called La Colombière but nicknamed Pie-in-the-Sky. Winston thought his largely self-drawn plans for the new build near Chamonix were "avant-garde" but they were impractical and expensive. She informed him in early 1977 that it had cost $562,000 in gift tax to set up a $1 million trust for him and that she had been forced to sell thirty acres of the Birchgrove estate and take out a loan against future income (presumably her expected inheritance from Averell). She warned her son not to "deplete" the money "rashly."[9] Winston reduced the chalet's living area by a third. "What do you think?" he asked his mother, adding that it was "wonderfully kind of you and Ave" to pay for it.[10] The Harrimans were appalled, sending back the plans with their critique scrawled in red ink. The kitchen was tiny, the hall too big, the double-height reception room too cold and—most bizarrely for a ski chalet 3,000 feet above sea level—there was no provision for heating. Finally, with Averell's backing, Pamela warned Winston that he was spending "family" capital on "a very extravagant house without any of the advantages of extravagance."[11]

Averell was certainly unimpressed by what he saw as Winston's profligacy but was "pretty sloppy" about the health of his own finances, leaving them in the charge of William Rich at the family bank Brown Brothers Harriman in New York.[12] A rather buttoned-up thirty-four-year-old lawyer, Rich wielded enormous power over the Harriman fortune from the choice of investments to paying staff and settling bills. Averell delegated supervision of the estate to seventy-two-year-old Washington powerbroker Clark Clifford and his law partner Paul Warnke. Smooth-talking Clifford had built his name on advising four Democratic presidents, including Kennedy. The fact he had little experience in managing complex family fortunes seemed of less importance to either Harriman than his connections and prestige.

After several changes were made, Pamela and Averell visited La Colombière in August 1979 and finally seem to have approved of it. Minnie thanked them for "giving us the Pie" but her cheeriness was not to last. Revelations later that year of Winston's long-standing affair with Soraya, the former wife of Saudi arms dealer Adnan Khashoggi, prompted a media firestorm in Britain and awkward questions for Pamela on arrival at a state dinner for Margaret Thatcher at the White House. Minnie found the saga "very difficult" but stood by her husband. "She's rather like Clemmie," Pamela privately remarked, deeming her "much too good" for Winston, whose entitlement appalled her. "I see a lot of Randolph in him," Pamela observed with mounting dismay.[13] Being his grandfather's namesake—inviting constant and unflattering comparisons—was turning out not to be such a blessing after all.

33

"Have you heard the wonderful joke going around about Reagan?" Pamela asked a startled magazine interviewer during the countdown to the 1980 presidential election. "Asked what he would do with the abortion bill, he replied, 'I'd pay it!'"[1] Pamela erupted into "deep velvety laughter" that filled the house. If her off-color wisecrack reflected a lifetime in male company, it also revealed widespread underestimation of the Republican candidate and the appeal of his "New Conservative" anti-choice agenda. Several state legislatures were introducing new bills to restrict access to legal terminations again and although Pamela had found him "charming as a person" she despaired at Reagan's support for this turning back of the liberal social trends of the 1970s. As a politician, she said, "he's everything I disagree with."[2]

Two weeks later the Harrimans held their election-night party in the library at N Street, where they had hired a large television screen to track the results. The buffet of hot chicken hash stayed virtually untouched as their guests watched the Democrats go down in flames, losing the White House and, for the first time in twenty-six years, the Senate. Many sloped off to bed early in despair.

The B-movie actor had won by a landslide on the back of discontent fueled by high inflation, energy prices and interest rates; a backlash against galloping social change on race and sex; and frustration that Washington looked weak abroad. More than fifty Americans had been held hostage for a year by the revolutionary ayatollahs in

Iran beyond the help of President Carter's inept rescue attempt that cost eight U.S. servicemen's lives. Communism was also on the march again with the Soviet Union's invasion of Afghanistan on Christmas Eve 1979 to crush the American-backed mujahideen, leading the president to withdraw a strategic arms limitation treaty from the Senate. Carter's departure after one term was seen as a tectonic and potentially permanent political realignment to the right.

Teddy Kennedy had tried to woo the Harrimans to support his bid to become the Democratic presidential candidate, inviting them to a lunch of poached salmon at his Senate office where he was "very generous" in his promises.[3] They did not rate his chances, however, believing him less suitable than his two brothers for the Oval Office, and refused to abandon the president. Their loyalty helped to see off Kennedy's challenge and prompted a phone call to Pamela from Rosalynn Carter herself to say thank you. Carter was a well-intentioned man but an unlucky leader. And now that he was gone the Democrats were despairing of finding a contender capable of reversing such an electoral calamity. Pamela compared the shock to Churchill's defeat in 1945.

As the Democratic salons of Georgetown entered their darkest hour, and after nine years as an American citizen, Pamela saw her chance. Even as the losses came flooding in, she had been on the phone to political friends to call a council of war. Churchill had bounced back, returning as prime minister in 1951, and so could the Democrats. Adversity galvanized her; here at last was an exit from a shrinking life with an elderly husband. Most important of all after four decades of frustration, however, was the prospect of finding the excitement and perhaps even access to power she had enjoyed as a young woman in London. "Not to have peaked at the age of twenty-five was important to her," says Stuart Eizenstat, Carter's domestic policy chief.[4] As she approached her sixty-first birthday, he and other supporters realized that she embodied something the Republicans had in Reagan but which the Democrats lacked: star power.

A few days later, Pamela gathered her favorite Democrats, including Richard Holbrooke, Stuart Eizenstat, Clark Clifford and Robert Strauss, to discuss the party's future over dinner. Holbrooke later described the pervasive "sense of disaster" but the Harrimans struck an upbeat note and suddenly hope, however faint, was in the air. "The Governor ignited it" but "Pam gave it form and structure."[5] The challenge was not just how to raise more money and organize better to win back seats but to create an attractive alternative to Reaganism—not from the left as had failed under Carter but from the center, where Pamela felt most comfortable. She was brimming with ideas on policies to appeal to the middle classes but was still widely viewed as a "foreign ornament" to her illustrious husband. It was clear she could not yet take the lead because "no one present would have taken her seriously."[6]

Before the election Pamela had employed a chief of staff well versed in the ways of Washington. A brusque Texan, Janet Howard moved into a small apartment at 3034. "We just clicked," the fiercely loyal Janet recalled.[7] She showed Pamela how she could achieve her aims by setting up a political action committee, or PAC. These were routinely created by trade unions, pressure groups or professional organizations as an effective way to raise and distribute money to advance their political agenda, but the idea of an individual establishing one was new. Pamela had of course already fundraised—on a smaller scale—but she doubted whether she was qualified for a high-profile role on policy. She feared the prospect of regular public speaking and television appearances pitting herself against opponents with the university education she lacked. Janet enlisted Jesse Calhoun, leader of a powerful maritime union (the Marine Engineers' Beneficial Association), to pile on the pressure. "He called her and shouted CHICKEN! CHICKEN!" Pamela asked who was on the line, and Calhoun replied, "It's Jesse. You'd better do this PAC!"[8] Pamela chuckled but took his message to heart. She would not be painted as a coward.

The idea was that the Harrimans would jointly head the PAC—to be called Democrats for the Eighties—and publicly Pamela gave the impression it was Averell in the driving seat. In fact, he doubted her chances of success and although supportive was too frail to take on more than a nominal role. Averell "didn't do a damn thing except show up," Strauss noted. "She did everything herself."[9] "Her marriage had put her in touch with leaders of the party. Without that, it wouldn't have been possible," explains Eizenstat. "But she then did it on her own."[10]

PamPAC—as it became known, derisorily at first—was a watershed in Pamela's marriage, with Averell's political ambitions making way for hers. He had talked to friends about Pamela keeping busy after his death, but he had hardly envisaged a project on this scale. Pamela herself was unsure as to how PamPAC would evolve but was determined to push it as far as she could. Some thought it the "fantasy of some would-be Georgetown Joan of Arc," a ridiculous conceit that an aristocrat could save the party of the dispossessed. Even the normally loyal Strauss "pooh-poohed" Pamela's plans, telling her no one would want to donate money to her rather than directly to the candidates or the party.[11] The *New York Times* pointed out that political groups came and went "faster than tour buses," rarely coming to much.[12] Why should hers be different?

Averell's name lent the enterprise gravitas in the face of such widespread skepticism but Pamela gave it celebrity rocket fuel. She depended heavily, however, on her fixer-in-chief, admitting "It was our baby—Janet's and mine."[13] Janet sharply divided opinion—many admired her abilities, others disliked her as Pamela's "rottweiler," given to outbursts when she thought her boss not well served. "She was quite abusive," says one former staffer. "She was a negative force who reduced people to tears." Janet was, however, rewarded for her dedication with a good salary and gifts such as a Cartier watch.

Pamela shored up what she knew were her weaknesses. She hired two outstanding writers—Alfred Friendly and Bob Shrum—to help craft speeches and comment pieces. Within three weeks of the election defeat, the woman who had once struggled with spelling had a rousing article published in the *Washington Post* headlined REBUILDING THE PARTY FROM GRASS ROOTS UP. The Democrats had, over fifty years, succeeded in making America more "humane," she wrote, but time had run out. Yet she saw hope in the magnitude of the defeat as it contained "seeds of opportunity" to find a new generation of leaders. Making it clear she intended to steer that process, Pamela referenced her Churchill heritage with a familiar finale: "This was not the beginning of the end," she declared, "but only the end of the beginning."[14]

Her next step was to appoint a blue-chip board. Only one woman made the grade, the Woman's National Democratic Club president Carol Williams, who had supported Pamela so assiduously for her award. Sandy Berger, a former speechwriter for Cy Vance and rising foreign policy expert, came in as chairman, tutor and connector. Considered one of the party's "first-rate thinkers" and "strategists,"[15] Berger spotted Pamela's potential and set about immersing her in the practicalities of government. "Pamela was a little funny about her education," says Peter Fenn, former chief of staff to ex-senator Frank Church, who joined as PamPAC's first executive director. "With her it was all street smarts,"[16] but she was a quick study. "They had far more serious discussions than people imagined," adds Sandy's widow, Susan Berger, who saw how Washington underestimated Pamela. Sandy "made sure she knew everything he could tell her. He was a great teacher and she was an equal."[17]

Berger introduced Pamela to a thirty-four-year-old Washington outsider who had failed to win reelection as governor of Arkansas. "Sandy told me she was trying to help the Democrats get reorganized after we all got whacked including me," Bill Clinton recalls.[18] Probably the youngest ex-governor in U.S. history, Clinton was in a "depressive funk," believing he had blown his political career.[19] Even his wife, Hillary, thought he might never recover. Pamela saw it differently. "It's very important in life to have success but it's even more important to have failure," she repeatedly advised. "And to know how to handle it." With a prescience that would come to change American politics and her life, she saw beyond Clinton's rookie mistakes. His critics, including Averell, viewed him as "cocky" and "provincial" but she marveled at how he worked a crowd, synthesized policy ideas and deciphered the bigger political picture, and invited him to dinner to persuade him to join the PamPAC board.

For a while—until he decided to run again for governor in 1982—Clinton became the other public face of Democrats for the Eighties and she projected him around DC as much as she could. The benefit was not one-way. "Inviting him to join her board gave him credibility," says Fenn. "She was very, very helpful to him."[20] Clinton was not too proud to acknowledge her belief in him at a time when "I wasn't always able to believe in myself."[21] He wrote to thank her for giving him the opportunity to work together "to regain the political leadership of our country and to correct some of our past errors."[22] He was one of the few who had no problem with taking her seriously, just as she did him.

They met for lunch soon afterward but Pamela was obviously distracted. She was preparing to give her first television interview, on the prime-time show *Good Morning America*, and Clinton remembers the typically composed Pamela as "amazingly nervous." No one doubted her impact one to one or in intimate groups, but Pamela balked at the challenge of courting a huge audience she could not even see. She was convinced that she would bomb. Clinton urged her to forget the stylized Churchillian oratorical style she had adopted for her speeches because "TV is more conversational." "You need to relax and speak in the same tone you have used over lunch," he advised her, offering to accompany her to the studio. He thought "she did just fine and then we became friends."²³ Clinton would regularly take the time to praise her public appearances, including a speech in March 1981 to Democratic Congressional Wives. "You did a very good job on it," he wrote encouragingly, "as you have on everything associated with Democrats for the Eighties."²⁴

Pamela's stentorian delivery was more suited to the event in January 1982 marking the centennial of Franklin Roosevelt's birth, when she became one of only very few women to address the Joint Session of Congress. Averell had "pleaded laryngitis"—illness was often now an excuse—so she delivered the speech in his place. Winston wrote to say how "proud" he was of her "admirable" performance. "Few can claim to have a grandfather who addressed a Joint Session, but I venture to think that I am alone in having a grandfather and a mother!"²⁵ Soon after, he received another handsome check.

Despite his misgivings, Strauss joined the PamPAC board as *consigliere* largely for Averell's sake but was astounded by Pamela's unashamed use of her assets in pursuit of her goals. She instinctively knew how to flex her own reputation to draw in the crowds. She appreciated how N Street—the Renoirs, Picassos and the Van Gogh, plus the photographs of Averell with the giants of recent history—would appeal to a party enthralled since the Roosevelts by "enlightened" aristocrats. She had seen how Jack Kennedy had set the tone with the line "to whom much is given, much is expected." Peter Fenn believes that Pamela felt the same way and "never denied who she was or was defensive. There was an attitude of 'be who you are, do what you can.'" Soon she was photographed attending meetings looking purposeful in 1980s power suits and pussy-bows. Or in the *Post* dashing out of her front door with a flurry of maids, secretaries, butlers and chauffeurs in attendance, one holding an umbrella to protect her coiffure for the ten steps to the car. The keen-eyed might spot Averell waiting in the hall for a hasty peck on the cheek before she disappeared for a day packed from breakfast to bedtime with political speeches, fundraisers and confabs interspersed with the odd visit to a couturier and requests for her autograph. In her briefcase, "Washington's most improbable political operator" (as the *Post* dubbed her[26]) kept a stash of fresh turkey sandwiches handmade by her chef (with lettuce, without crusts) and mints in a monogrammed silver box.

The British newspapers picked up on her new role, with the *Mail on Sunday* running a piece on how she was "rekindling the fire and spirit" of the party.[27] It turned out that the "voice in the Democrat wilderness" had a cut-glass English accent; the savior of the party for the poor might just be an aristocrat with five homes and a safe full of jewels. "Yes, I lead a very privileged life," Pamela conceded, aware that Averell's political aspirations had been constrained by his patrician image. Yet she could do more to give everyone "a fair chance" where she was, than by going to "live in a hovel."[28] She never advertised it but was secretly practicing what she preached. Her work with bomb-blasted children during the war had left a lasting impact and now every summer she invited forty severely disabled youngsters and their carers to enjoy a day of games and picnics at Birchgrove. She—and the one outsider invited, William Cahan—would talk to each in turn, play with them and pitch in to help with their food. Her generosity came to light only when Dr. Cahan wrote to the *New York Times* about it after her death.[29]

These occasions were private but supporters such as Eizenstat saw how she was capable of transcending her background in a way Averell could not. She "brought in the common touch"[30] by talking to labor leaders just the same way as she did well-heeled donors. She also set out to prove that someone with the money to be a lady of leisure could work harder than anyone. An awestruck John Kerry, Vietnam hero and a rising Democratic star battling for a seat in the Senate, wondered at her willingness to toil so tirelessly for the party. Eventually he put it down to a belief that as a superpower America had a duty to its own people as well as the world. "She is extraordinary. Her motives are selfless," he told a reporter. "She believes in the larger meaning of our country."[31]

The doubters thought her a closet Republican who had donned the Democratic mantle purely to ensnare Averell, but she was genuinely agitated by Reagan cutting social security. "I believe things should work from the bottom up," she explained, "the opposite of the Republican trickle-down theory."[32] She insisted it had "never occurred" to her to join the Grand Old Party. Her allies claimed she found Republicans stodgy and boring, and that her Democratic allegiance stemmed from her friendship with Kick Kennedy back in the 1940s. Privately, she cast herself as influenced by old-fashioned one nation Conservative notions of responsibility for the poor, sentiments she thought would appeal to a modern middle-of-the-road Democrat. What she said was crucial was the idea of respect and responsibility for the less fortunate through creating a universal "safety net"[33] and striving for a "more fulfilling life for all people."[34]

Pamela was canny enough to know her wealth could be a problem, however. She worked hard on her image but also enlisted others to help her. The ever-loyal Bill Walton was drafted in to write pieces in *Architectural Digest* (beloved by "liberals with large wallets") that presented her as a serious player determined to make a difference. "By their own definition, both the Harrimans are 'political animals,'" he dutifully wrote, who were "less interested in ordinary social goings on than parties with a purpose."[35] The combined effect was as if she had created a political love potion. Soon after setting up PamPAC she threw a reception mobbed by eighty-five excited labor leaders, and two dinners for equally enthralled party leaders on Capitol Hill. Tom Foley, the House majority whip, attended one and compared it to an invitation to the White House. "Normally to have fifteen people at a Democratic gathering, you have to invite forty," he observed. "Tonight, we invited fifteen and there are forty here."[36] Pamela's supporters joked that it was easier to get a Senate quorum on N Street than on the chamber floor and relished her special knack for lifting spirits and calling in favors. Pamela "had this way with the senators," smiles Sven Holmes, who came in later as director of PamPAC. "She did a strokey, strokey of their forearm, saying, 'I'd love it if you could do . . .' and they all promised to do it and came away feeling terrific."[37]

Yet Pamela's serious intent was obvious. She was "warhorse . . . instigator" and "disciplinarian," according to one of her board members, Washington lawyer Berl Bernhard.[38] "When she wanted to get things done," Peter Fenn adds, "she was on that phone the whole damn time."[39] Her efforts were noted early on when the *Washington Post* ran an admiring piece headlined PAMELA HARRIMAN'S PLAN TO SAVE THE DEMOCRATIC PARTY.[40] To that end, PamPAC took over most of the bedrooms on the top floor of 3034 and turned them into offices for her growing team. She kept overheads as low as possible and when she splashed out on a newfangled word processor for mass direct mailings, she instructed Fenn not to tell Averell how much it cost. Every time Fenn heard the trademark *clomp, clomp, clomp* of Averell slowly climbing the stairs he stood in the doorway of the office to hide it. Pamela chipped in $5,000, the maximum allowed of her own money, to kick off her campaign, followed by (a rather stingy) $1,750 from Averell and $5,000 from her friend Jesse Calhoun's own PAC.[41] Kathy Harriman also wrote a check for $5,000. Soon Pamela and Janet were pulling in much larger sums, totaling $1.3 million in the two years up to the 1982 midterm elections. The money came from donors including Jay Rockefeller, Democratic senator for West Virginia, and the Wall Street investment bank Morgan Stanley. This was impressive but not the chief reason that Washington was taking notice. In May 1981, Pamela astonished friend and foe alike and revealed a readiness for risk that Averell had always lacked.

The Republican-supporting National Conservative PAC was

running a scurrilous $400,000 campaign designed to intimidate the Democratic senator for Maryland,[42] Paul Sarbanes, a figure who assiduously avoided controversy. Fenn's old boss Frank Church had been brought down by similar attack advertisements and he despaired of the Democrats' "wimpish" reluctance to fight back. Fenn suggested PamPAC intervene by spending $20,000 on radio slots branding the NCPAC as an extremist right-wing organization deliberately peddling untruths. To his surprise Pamela replied, "Yes, let's do it!" Sarbanes knew nothing of what was being done on his behalf until he jumped in a cab and heard the PamPAC counter-ad on the radio. It ended with a stirring ultimatum to NCPAC: "We're the Democrats for the Eighties and we've paid for this radio time to give you fair warning. We're going to fight your lies and your distortions with a political tactic you might find amazing. It's called the truth."

"Sarbanes and all these Democratic senators who thought there was nothing to be done were ecstatic," Fenn remembers with glee. "Pamela loved the fight. She didn't want PamPAC to be some society thing. The more we got involved in the hard stuff the more she liked it."[43] Despite having just broken a vertebra falling off her horse, Pamela held a press conference. Struck by her usual nerves, her delivery was halting but she seized media attention—including CBS, the *New York Times*, the *Baltimore Sun* and *Newsweek*—at a time when Reagan's folksy charm was "blocking the sun" for everyone else. Democrats for the Eighties, she said, had a "responsibility to stand up to those purveyors of politics of negativism and fear" and the whole democratic process was under threat from a "maverick" organization playing to the "dark side of human nature."[44] She provided background material so that journalists could see for themselves the falsehoods perpetrated against the senators under attack. The NCPAC chairman admitted inaccuracies but called the PamPAC accusations "the most vitriolic, vicious, mean untrue stuff I've seen." Fenn countered that somebody had to "get down in the gutter" to fight back. "I was young and it wasn't one of my best quotes but she loved it."[45]

Pamela's courage had quite an impact. Clinton vowed never again to "practice unilateral disarmament" against the Republicans' "verbal assault weapons."[46] Strauss was also impressed by Pamela's combination of blue blood and backbone, and excited about what she might do next (such speculation leading to reports, vehemently denied, that she intended to run for office in Virginia).*

PamPAC was making the news and the opposition was taking note. Jesse Helms, an ultraconservative senator from North Carolina who was anti-choice, civil rights, feminism and gay rights, railed against this "wicked woman" who had been on trips to Moscow and had paintings on her wall by Picasso, who was a "communist!"[47] At first Pamela was upset by the Republican volleys but soon realized they meant that she was making her mark. And yet her bravado was undermined by a constant trickle of self-doubt, perhaps even a touch of impostor syndrome. When *Architectural Digest* asked her in early 1983 to write a column and stipulated that she should write it herself, she refused to believe she was capable. When she submitted her copy, she wondered if it had "any potential" and asked if professional writers "might consider polishing it."[48] The editors were delighted with her version and there was no need.

By 1982 PamPAC had given $600,000 to congressional candidates Pamela had largely chosen herself. She took good advice but ultimately the decisions on who to back were her own rather than the

---

* Strauss began to flirt outrageously with her—a lot of men found it hard not to—and there were rumors that they were in the throes of an affair, a notion his ego enjoyed. When doorstepped by a reporter asking him about the relationship, that was another matter and he rushed out a statement denying the reports and declaring his love for his wife.

party's. Her choices were informed by pragmatism (was the seat winnable?) and personality (was the candidate a winner?). She had backed enough outliers and losers in the past—including Bella Abzug—to know the signs. When West Virginia's senator Robert Byrd's reelection bid appeared to need help, she thought it worth funneling $10,000 into boosting his campaign. "She's an indefatigable worker," said the grateful Byrd on his reelection,[49] and he later became Majority Leader and stayed in the Senate for a then record fifty-one years.

Her strike rate was phenomenal. In 1982, the Democrats gained twenty-six seats in the House in significant part down to her. Thereafter she switched her attention to the Senate, making more progress in 1984. One of the three candidates she had given the maximum to early on had been George Mitchell of Maine, but she had also hosted special evenings for other favorites including Al Gore and John Kerry. Her contributions to Joe Biden's campaigns in Delaware since 1983 elicited effusive letters from the young senator whom she considered "very, very bright," keeping a file of newspaper cuttings to track his progress. "It is wonderful to have friends who are always there when you need them," he told her.[50]

In truth, Pamela disliked calling people up and asking for cash. She also resented being corralled away from the almost exclusively male talk of new ideas. "She wanted it to be more than a fundraising enterprise because she knew people weren't buying what we were selling," Clinton says. She saw that change was needed in "personnel and policy" and was not interested in a "vanity project." Clinton was thrilled when she hired as an adviser his old professor from Georgetown University Jules Davids, as that "showed me that underneath all that 'let me bat my eyelids and watch your knees buckle' stuff she was . . . very serious."[51] "It was the strategic stuff that really turned her on," Fenn agrees. Even now, she needed to prove it to others.

34

Pamela's Issues Evenings might have been mocked by some as a "drawing-room farce" but over the coming years they established her as kingmaker and political queen. She held the first in March 1981, basing the occasion on her old Churchill Club model of gathering people of affluence and influence in beguiling surroundings. The idea was for up to forty potential donors to pay $1,000 each to listen to a star or Democratic hopeful—names such as Ted Kennedy or John Kerry—who would be invited to the N Street library to talk on issues from the economy to defense. The antithesis of a soulless bun fight in a hotel ballroom, the evening would offer a reverie of style and cosseting combined with hardheaded fundraising and policy discussion.

With precise choreography, guests would arrive at seven to be ushered through the glossy front door into "Pamelot," where they would mingle over cocktails and mini soufflés served by the white-gloved butler under the Van Gogh. When Pamela shimmered into the room in couture, the effect was complete. "That whole business model was very important to the resurrection of the party," says Eizenstat.[1] When he first saw the *White Roses*, Robert Stein, a senior party official, "practically collapsed. It was so powerful."[2]

The company would then take to rows of gilt bamboo chairs to hear Pamela talk about the purpose of the evening being to raise money for Democrats fighting marginal races, find leaders of the future and identify policies that would rejuvenate the party. She then took her seat on a sofa at the front next to Averell. She pretended the company had come for the Governor—who by now could barely see or hear—but it was no longer true and often he slipped out of the room after toasting his wife.

After an introduction by Strauss or Clifford the speaker had the floor for an hour or so until a candlelit dinner at round tables in the sun porch, laid with starched white tablecloths with the PCH monogram and handwritten place cards stamped with the Digby ostrich. Young senators or promising governors would be seated next to donors with money or party elders with advice. "I learned from Pamela that someone should always meet someone new at a dinner," says Kiki McLean, the prominent campaigner who started her political career as an N Street assistant, "and someone they already know."[3] Another rule was that the cuisine should be of a standard virtually unknown elsewhere in the city. A typical menu started with a light green turtle soup, followed by raw Chesapeake oysters, fresh jumbo shrimp and creamed Maine lobster, then rum raisin cake, Colombian coffee, cognac and cigars.[4] After dinner, the speaker took questions before everyone left at 10:30, passing a basket placed strategically on the hall table on their way to the door. Averell counted the takings—which on average reached $100,000 a night.

The ninety or so Issues Evenings held over the next ten years amounted to much more than fundraising. Pamelot became the "gathering place for the party in exile," Tony Podesta said.[5] "Pamela had a magnetic charm that came from her beauty," recalls Stuart Eizenstat, who adds that she picked up the tab herself. "She also had an understanding of how power works." "Her detractors were wrong" that her charms were a "substitute for intellect and insight," says Bob Shrum. "She was widely read and mostly self-educated,"[6] and she knew who to invite, the topics to discuss and the tone to set. Major donors found a call to arms from Pamela irresistible. She exuded a compelling optimism despite the bleak Democratic Party outlook. "Pamela learned about leadership from Winston Churchill," says Stein. "She too had tenacity, willfulness, and a *joie de vivre* in the midst of devastation. Churchill's public image was that we can do this, we're greater than this. And Pamela provided that spirit to American politics."[7] "She was a personality you gravitated to," Fenn agrees. "She wasn't cocky but she was confident she could make a difference."[8]

She managed the evenings with "delicate skill," reported the *New York Times*, circulating constantly, effecting introductions or quieting the room with a tink of her wineglass to announce that the senator next to her had said something "I'd like him to share."[9] Pamela read up on her donors as she had once studied lovers and they were unutterably flattered. By the end of the evening, many had lost their hearts and were opening their checkbooks to make another donation. She had once again cast her spell over powerful and wealthy men accustomed to the best of everything but feeling privileged to have been admitted to something entrancing and intimate. A few misguided souls mistook her professionalism for something else and wondered if she would go out to dinner with them—one even venturing she might sleep with him. They were charmingly but firmly disabused.[10] Pamela rarely invited women because she found them reluctant to donate to political causes. "They don't get it," she complained. "When they're asked, they say, 'gosh, $5,000 is a lot of money' and these are the women on yachts in the Mediterranean."[11] That gradually changed as more women entered politics and female donors gained more confidence[12] but the Pamela of the early 1980s made her preference clear: "I like to feel I'm at the side of a real man, a man you know is a man because he gives you the feeling you're a woman."[13]

Journalists were also rarely invited but the mystique of what happened in the N Street library every month prompted a media quest to find out more. At one Issues Evening in September 1981, Clark Clifford introduced the speaker, New York financier Felix Rohatyn, who Pamela had invited to outline the flaws in low-tax low-spend

Reaganomics on the usual off-the-record basis. In his preamble, Clifford described the president as an "amiable dunce"—as Pamela, confined to bed at Willow Oaks that night after being kicked in the ribs by a horse, read soon afterward in a transcript of the proceedings. Intriguingly, the *Wall Street Journal* also obtained a copy, and such was PamPAC's fame it ran a front-page article picking up on Clifford's comments.[14] After the story broke, Pamela proclaimed herself "mortified." "This has never happened in our house before," she said, "be sorry for me."[15]

There was no reason to be. The rumpus boosted her profile even more, with the *New York Times* describing her evenings as "gems of the genre."[16] Some wondered if it had been an opportunistic leak. As she herself conceded to *Newsweek*: "It is better to be talked about than not talked about."[17] When Peter Fenn admitted he had supplied the *Wall Street Journal* with the tape—the journalist had broken his word not to quote from it—Clifford demanded he be sacked. Fenn never let on that Pamela had authorized him to do so and was in return grateful to her that she remained loyal: "The more you knew her, the more the respect grew."[18]

Such fame—and Pamela's rise from hostess to a more actively strategic role—brought a new round of criticism. "Ben [Bradlee] used to say that everything about Pamela was about her own gain," says Sally Quinn. "And that her politics were between her legs."[19] "The attacks on her were very personal," Eizenstat confirms. "There was a lot of jealousy."[20] When Pamela thought the press was treating her unfairly, she called the editors directly. "Pam was not one to take criticism lying down," Eizenstat continues. "It takes a lot of guts and I didn't expect it." Pamela saw it as a question of looking out for herself and that she had "never relied on anybody or anything outside of me. It may have to do with not having a lot of friends when we grew up."[21] But if Pamela had missed out in younger life the Democrats were her tribe now.

Her mission was to identify, nurture and fund fresh faces with electoral pizzazz. N Street became a sort of "paddock where the best horses for the electoral races were paraded" and "tested for their ability to jump political hurdles."[22] Pamela formed her opinion of contenders—including possible presidential candidates—on their performance in her house. Some fell at the first fence. When Pamela selected Senator Bill Bradley to address an Issues Evening, a crowd flocked to N Street excited at the thought of hearing a famous basketball player and distinguished legislator pitch himself as a possible runner for the 1988 presidential election. At 7:30 precisely, the six foot five Bradley took to his feet, rested his arm on the mantelpiece, "opened his mouth and"—as told in Bob Strauss's inimical fashion—"the fire went out." "He was very smart," explains one prominent Democrat treated to Strauss's "biting" account of the evening, "but boring."[23] Bradley's campaign for the presidency went out too.

Pamela also saw through the eventual nominee, Michael Dukakis. Before his Issues Evening, Dukakis's staff made what Pamela thought a "ridiculous" demand for a dais, threatening that the five foot eight Massachusetts governor (one of that year's Democratic contenders lampooned as the "Seven Dwarfs") would pull out at the last minute unless he got one. "So we had to go and get made an eighteen-inch platform right against the Van Gogh," an unimpressed Pamela complained. "I was terrified he'd teeter over and fall through it."[24] Dukakis went on to lose emphatically (as she had feared) to George Bush after being portrayed as an out-of-touch East Coast liberal. After that, more Democrats took notice of how the contenders fared in the N Street "paddock." Even the *Washington Post* judged that "clever politicians" asked Pamela for her judgment and were unwise if they did not take heed.[25] She was introducing a new professionalism to her party's political processes, as Democratic strategist Tom O'Donnell remembers: "She's a Brit, she's a woman, but if she says jump, we say how high?"[26]

Bill Clinton did not remain on the PamPAC board for long. He ran again for governor in 1982 and won—the first time a defeated governor had come back to be reelected. Pamela's friend Cynthia Helms, wife of former CIA director Richard Helms, watched with amazement how she continued to devote herself to introducing "a rather obscure young governor from Arkansas to the Washington elites."[27] A turbulent childhood in the South immunized Clinton from the elitist tag attached to Dukakis—although he had studied at both Georgetown and Oxford. The flipside was that he was perceived in some DC circles as an upstart from a "hick" state with an erratic electoral record. The un-grand Clintons were not a hit with the grand hostesses of Georgetown. Pamela thought that no longer important. "The whole thing has changed," she told the *New York Times*, and the concept of the hostess was dead. "Women aspire to be political leaders, not social leaders."[28] Herself included—woe betide anyone who now called Pamela a hostess. As her views changed about what the women of Washington could do, it was a term she had come to loathe.

Pamela knew from Jimmy Carter's misfortunes that being a Washington outsider was "a sure way to fail in this town"[29] but it seemed that her regard for Clinton was unshakable. She was already wondering whether one day he might become a presidential contender. Four months after he returned to the governor's mansion in Little Rock, he and four other governors attended an Issues Evening, where his mastery of his briefs outshone more experienced figures. Afterward they repaired to Pamela's study upstairs as Clinton was staying the night. Under the gaze of Romney's *Lady Hamilton*, Clinton pressed both Harrimans for recollections about Stalin, Churchill and the war. Averell eventually retired but Clinton, an habitual night owl, kept firing questions at Pamela until at least 2:30. Pamela finally asked Clinton what time he needed to leave that morning. He replied 4:45.[30]

Clinton's boundless energy was in stark contrast to politicians who had gone down to defeat such as Edmund Muskie. He became an N Street regular and made a vivid impression on party elders. Pamela recognized in him a resilience and hunger for success combined with charm and guile similar to her own. She was prepared to speak out in defense of someone she considered a real kindred spirit. When the media branded her friend an "ersatz" JFK she pointed out the difference: "where Jack Kennedy was born to power, Bill Clinton got there all by himself."[31]

Eizenstat was another struck by Pamela's nose for a future star. "She spotted Clinton very early," he says, and also thought them alike. "When he came into a room of five hundred people for a reception, while he was talking to you for fifteen seconds you had his full attention. It was like a magnetic field. She had the same. A royal presence, a grace."[32]

Reaganites were also charmed and Pamela thought there was "something to be said for being friendly with the enemy," sometimes inviting GOP figures to N Street. "She was the Democrat who didn't disappear," said the wife of a top Republican. "She courted Republicans as well. They all had to deal with her."[33] Even First Lady Nancy Reagan, eager to attract stardust to the White House, set out to befriend Pamela. She resisted several invitations, then yet another arrived, this time to an intimate White House ladies' luncheon. She came away disappointed by the lack of serious political discussion. "Nancy's as shrewd as a fox," Pamela said afterward, "but all she talks about is Hollywood. I had my fill of tinsel-town while married to Leland."[34]

Pamela saw how the Democrats desperately needed a professional television studio to record campaign advertisements to the same production quality as the Republicans. She granted a $400,000 interest-free loan toward the $1 million cost and once she thought

Averell too detached to notice, turned $150,000 of it into a gift. When the new studio opened in April 1986 it was named the Harriman Communications Center in her honor, putting her into a whole new league on the Hill.

She had also thrown herself into the substance of party policy by funding and presiding over the hugely popular *Democratic Fact Book* or "bible," as it soon became known. It was compiled by a team of policy staffers she recruited to the top floor of 3034 to gather facts on Reagan policies and the best alternative Democratic thinking so that every candidate would in effect have a "walking research staff" on some twenty key issues. Money speaks loud in American politics but the need for well-briefed candidates was just as clear-cut. Many politicians were in awe of the different ways Pamela "got stuff done" to turn around Democratic fortunes. Grateful officials found that she had filled a vacuum and become "this substitute party leader."[35]

Pamela learned how to run a household to regal standards from Wallis Simpson. They became friends in the 1950s and attended Christian Dior's funeral together in 1957. Dior had given Pamela clothes and tips on how to dress

No 1950s party in Paris or New York was complete without Pamela's presence. The wives and mistresses of wealthy men across the world feared her genius for seduction

Leland was sexy, funny and eventually available, but despite the warnings, Pamela had no real idea what she was letting herself in for

Pamela was thrilled to get involved in the US version of the 1960s satirical show *That Was the Week That Was*. At the time, it offered her a rare if temporary foray into her beloved world of politics. Here she discusses ideas with presenter David Frost, while sporting an unusual hat

Pamela's friendship with President Jack Kennedy was the envy of Washington. Here he and Jackie find the time to support Leland's ill-fated production, *Mr President*, in September 1962 even as tensions with the Soviet Union were reaching a perilous crescendo

Pamela with young Winston and his fiancée Minnie at Haywire. Watching her son betray his mild-mannered wife with multiple affairs eventually helped to transform Pamela's ideas about women and the feminist cause

Bored by her role as traditional wife to Leland, and unable to play any significant role in American politics, Pamela set up shop in New York. She sold the 'Pamela look' to an initially enthusiastic clientele, such as Bobby Kennedy's wife Ethel, but many were slow to settle their bills

Peter Duchin and Brooke Hayward in New York in 1986. Duchin later claimed that their 'common hatred' for Pamela had cemented their marriage

Pamela's marriage to Averell gave her what she had always wanted: 'love, lovely things and the political arena'. Here she is attending her first Democratic Party convention, at Miami in 1972

Pamela gave her support to a grateful President Carter, but only reluctantly. She never thought him right for the White House and saw how an outsider struggled to make inroads in Washington. She had an instinctive understanding of power – and how to win and lose it

Pamela backed the feminist Bella Abzug as senator for New York. It was the first time she publicly took the lead in politics. Pamela still eschewed what was then known as 'women's liberation' but her latest reinvention had begun

Nuclear conflict terrified Pamela, and she and Averell made great efforts to try to re-open communications between the West and the Soviet Union during the Cold War. When the Gorbachevs came to Washington in 1987, Raisa visited Pamela at her Georgetown home, where they symbolically held hands for the world's cameras

Pamela was one of the first to spot Bill Clinton's potential as a president even if she was aware of his flaws. She was cheerleader, fundraiser, counsellor and confidante as well as critic – and he in large part attributed his rise to the White House to her

Her victory party for the Clintons at home in Georgetown after the presidential elections in November 1992 was a triumph but there was no word on her longed-for job in the administration. Her enemies and even her friends thought she might have fallen out of favour

Pamela's butler informed guests at N Street that they would find the downstairs bathroom by going past Van Gogh's *White Roses*, then one of the most prized paintings in private hands. She adored her art collection but in the end it brought her heartache and ultimately to the brink of financial ruin

President Chirac of France had 'uncommon personal relations' with Pamela when she was ambassador in Paris. She played a secret but historic role as interlocutor between him and Clinton during the Bosnia war

Pamela's coffin arrived at Andrews Air Force Base, Maryland, on 8 February 1997 in a driving snowstorm. Her death in Paris and its aftermath was as dramatic as her life

President Clinton tried to silence Pamela's critics with an emotional eulogy at one of the grandest funerals Washington had seen in years

Pamela *in excelsis*. Her last glorious hurrah in a 1995 photoshoot by Annie Leibovitz for *Vanity Fair*

35

Pamela was running a textbook campaign of reinvention—for herself as well as her party. She knew any major political player in Washington needed impressive foreign policy credentials, particularly on the Cold War. It was hardly helpful that in 1981 Winston published a book pushing what she considered an ultra-hard line against the Soviet Union, entitled *Defending the West*, in stark contrast to her own position. She tried to persuade him to cancel speaking at a New York lunch in his honor—he refused, not wanting to forfeit an order from his hosts for four thousand copies.[1] Pamela thought it vital for world peace to be able to counter the hawks but she knew what she had garnered from her high-level lodgers and her Issues Evenings was still not sufficient for her views to be taken seriously. The $11.5 million donation she and Averell gave to the Institute for the Advanced Study of Russian-American Affairs at Columbia University in 1982 bought her the chance—in her early sixties—to remedy that, with what was effectively a top-flight university education. "She was a student educating herself, constantly enhancing her qualifications," says the director Robert Legvold, who witnessed her peppering the institute's experts with questions about the Soviet Union. "Her reputation was as a socialite, a dabbler, an unserious person. But she was not flighty or aggrandizing at all. The reputation was not the reality."[2]

That Cold War tensions had reached their highest level since the Cuban Missile Crisis of 1962 was a clear driver in Pamela's efforts.

Both the U.S. and the Soviet Union were once again engaged in a massive arms race and by 1983 the two superpowers had amassed 18,400 nuclear warheads between them. America's siting in West Germany of Pershing II missiles capable of reaching Moscow in six minutes was considered by the Kremlin particularly inflammatory. So too was Reagan's call for a new "Star Wars" Strategic Defense Initiative, a program intended to shield America from Soviet missiles thus making it possible to launch a first strike of nuclear weapons without fear of retaliation. Such protection (although no one knew if really possible) would undermine the notion of mutually assured destruction or MAD, then seen as a bleak deterrent to starting a nuclear conflict. Well known in his Hollywood years as an anti-communist crusader, Reagan dialed up the rhetoric by dubbing the Soviet Union the "Evil Empire," fanning the flames and terrifying Pamela that a Third World War was a real and imminent threat.

The Harrimans had made friends with the larger-than-life veteran Soviet ambassador Anatoly Dobrynin and his wife, Irina, who had become a useful channel to the leadership in Moscow. Hoping to improve relations between Washington and his own country, in June 1983 Dobrynin helped organize one last trip to Moscow for Averell, with Pamela in attendance. Both Harrimans strongly felt it their duty to try to reassure the Soviets that not all Americans had succumbed to foolish hyperbole—indeed, there was growing support at home for the Nuclear Freeze campaign to stop the testing, manufacture and deployment of all nuclear weapons. Paying for a doctor and a delegation of experts including former lodgers Colette and Marshall Shulman as well as Peter Swiers from the State Department, the Harrimans flew to Moscow in the hope of sizing up the new Soviet leader Yuri Andropov. He was barely known in the West and as the *New York Times* put it, it was essential to understand "the personality and background of the man with whom President Reagan must share responsibility for war and peace in a nuclear world."[3]

The omens were not encouraging. The few details available were that Andropov was a former KGB chief (where he was the ultimate boss of one Vladimir Putin) who had been involved in the bloody suppression of the Hungarian uprising in 1956. And while ninety-one-year-old Averell had sought assurances that he would be granted an audience if he made the arduous journey, doubt lingered until the last moment. Averell's hopes were pinned on his long-term popularity with Russians but it was likely Pamela's celebrity that finally secured the meeting as, on hearing she was in Moscow, Andropov expressed his wish to meet her. Like many of his compatriots, Andropov was steeped in the folklore of the Second World War, including stories of Churchill's unforgettable daughter-in-law. "That clearly played a role," said Swiers. A gap was found in Andropov's diary—for them both.[4]

The state television news service, TASS, picked up on the excitement with footage of the couple arriving at the Communist Party's offices on Staraya Square. For eighty minutes, Pamela sat across a green baize table from the enigmatic Andropov, his hooded eyes behind old-fashioned spectacles. The only woman in the company of five men, she studied him for signs of ill health. Dr. Cahan had spotted worrying symptoms in a television clip of him in Red Square and had told her what to look out for. She observed how the pale and stooping Soviet leader spoke in staccato sentences, constantly pausing to take sips of water. He was clearly seriously unwell.[5] Not only did she do the looking—Averell's frontal vision was now so bad he could barely see his Russian host—Pamela also did much of the talking as Averell struggled to hear.

More formal than his predecessor Leonid Brezhnev, Andropov nevertheless displayed promising signs of openness to the idea of negotiations with America. The world was entering a new "very dangerous period," he warned, and his deepest concern was that the West and the Soviet Bloc had lost the ability to communicate. "Normal relations," he said, had to be urgently reestablished to avoid the risk of a conflagration far worse than the Second World War, when they had been allies. Four times he mentioned the prospect of nuclear conflict. "This war may perhaps not occur through evil intent," he feared, "but could happen through miscalculation." To the Harrimans' relief, he wanted them to relay to Washington his desire for "peaceful co-existence" and the end of the arms race, and that Moscow was "interested in joint initiatives" to restore East-West relations.[6] Toward the end, Averell informed Andropov that he hoped Pamela would continue working with the Soviet leadership "when I am no longer able to."[7] It was the moment when Averell definitively passed the torch of helping to maintain world peace to his wife.[8]

The Harrimans could not have known that, although there were still near-cataclysmic flashpoints to come, their conversation contained the seeds of the eventual end of the Cold War. It was, according to Swiers, the first time that a Soviet leader had not been "ideological" about the West—and indeed it later emerged that he had been the protector of the reformer Mikhail Gorbachev. Neither Harriman had official status and their trip perhaps achieved little beyond satisfying their curiosity and instilling a sense of hope. Even so, it was significant that the Kremlin had indicated a new receptiveness to concessions that eventually led three years later to the historic Reagan-Gorbachev summit at Reykjavík and in 1987 a treaty banning land-based short- and medium-range nuclear missiles. Pamela had also proved herself worthy of a seat at the high table and Averell had given his blessing to her as his successor. Coverage of the trip sparked the interest of a Ukrainian schoolboy, Dmitri, who wrote to Pamela in Russian about how he admired her efforts to help the East and West understand each other. She had his letters translated before copying out handwritten notes in Russian in response, and they continued their correspondence in one form or another until her death.[9]

When the Harrimans returned to Washington, they found their

meeting had sparked worldwide interest and Pamela was in hot demand for her Soviet insights. Privately they briefed an apparently receptive Secretary of State George Shultz—others in Washington simply thought them naïve when it came to Moscow—and also gave evidence to the Senate Committee on Foreign Relations. *Women's Wear Daily* ventured that a Soviet-American entente "would be reached immediately" if Pamela were in charge. On David Brinkley's Sunday morning politics show, Pamela reported that Andropov was a "very impressive-looking man," but "I wouldn't want to play poker with him."[10] She avoided mentioning Andropov's health in public—a courtesy noted by the Kremlin in a country where only a strongman with a fist of iron is deemed fit to rule. Pamela heard later that the Soviet leader had liked her and Averell very much and thought they had been "very good" to him. "I am a very sick man," Andropov said, "but they have never told the press."[11] Part of Pamela's power had always been to know when it would pay to keep secrets.

Later that summer, Pamela gathered a group for dinner at Birchgrove. Tensions with Moscow still dominated the news and over coffee Pamela read out her record of the Andropov meeting while Averell sat silently in an armchair. Someone asked her a question about the Soviet leader. Suddenly, Averell snapped alive. "This was my meeting," he roared. "I should tell it. I just took Pamela along."[12] If it was occasionally painful to readjust, there was no doubt that Averell reveled in Pamela's rising prominence and that in Moscow he had formally ordained her as his successor. "He loved her with a burning passion concealed under that Victorian exterior," a friend remarked. "He wanted her to succeed, and he gave her everything, not only money, but training, access and tutelage. He watched her pick it up slowly and carefully as he declined."[13] The thought that she wanted to surpass him in influence never occurred to him but her thirst for—and understanding of—power would ultimately prove greater than his.

A few weeks later, on Monday, September 26, 1983, forty-four-year-old Lieutenant Colonel Stanislav Petrov was the duty officer at the Soviet nuclear early-warning center when the system picked up the launch of an American missile. With exceptional courage, Petrov disobeyed orders to alert senior officers immediately, preferring to search for corroborating evidence. He found none and so there was no retaliatory action, which could well have resulted in nuclear war. Later it was confirmed that the radar had malfunctioned—just the sort of incident Andropov had feared (although it remained unknown to civilians on both sides for years). Two months after that the world came to the brink again when a vast NATO military exercise, code-named Able Archer, triggered fears in the Kremlin that it was a guise to cover U.S. preparations for a nuclear strike. The Soviets put their nuclear arsenal on maximum alert, preparing to launch dozens of missiles, each one a hundred times more powerful than the Hiroshima bomb. Again it was a calm decision by Lieutenant General Leonard Perroots, the U.S. Air Force's assistant chief of staff, to monitor rather than escalate in kind that may have prevented a full nuclear exchange. Without talks, the survival of the world rested on a hair trigger.

Shortly afterward, Andropov died from kidney failure. As the new voice on U.S.-Soviet relations, Pamela wrote a newspaper comment piece and gave a television interview to Diane Sawyer on CBS. Pamela criticized Reagan for not attending Andropov's funeral—despite now saying he wanted to improve relations with Moscow—as it was more important than ever to "start a serious dialogue." "I think the Soviets, as much as, or perhaps even more than, ourselves, are scared of nuclear war," she said in her slow clipped voice. Sawyer highlighted Pamela's authority on the subject with "I believe that with the exception of Indira Gandhi you were the only woman we know of to meet with Yuri Andropov." "I believe I was," Pamela replied, judging him "a man that gave you the impression you could negotiate with him."[14]

Konstantin Chernenko took over but he too was ill and died soon after. The Soviet Union turned to Andropov's protégé Mikhail Gorbachev. This time, Pamela was well briefed about the new leader from her Russian friends. Thanks to Andropov, Gorbachev was equally knowledgeable about her, as the Reagans would discover.

36

Averell had been Pamela's doorway into American politics but now his poor health was in danger of holding her back—particularly after Christmas 1983 when a large wave crashed over them on the beach in Barbados. Pamela scrambled to her feet but Averell clutched his right leg in agony. She desperately dragged him away from the surf and X-rays later showed that he had a fracture above his ankle.[1] Pamela had a lift installed in N Street but it was clear his bone cancer was on the march and "he was doing less and less," Pie Friendly remembers. "Most of the people who really wanted to see him now were just after money."[2]

Isolated and depressed, Averell bemoaned Pamela's absence at political events at the same time as encouraging her to go. She returned home as soon as she could but if she was going to be out more than a few hours enlisted friends to provide him with stimulating company. Averell told Clayton Fritchey on one such occasion: "I know why you came here. She asked you to come. It's like that every day. You know, I really love her."[3] In intense pain, Averell was increasingly bad-tempered even with Pamela. Yet if he could not see or hear her, he bellowed her name and when she reappeared at his side reached out for her hand. If she returned home late, she woke him up to reassure him, kissing him and saying, "I'm back, sweetheart."[4] The journalist John Chancellor, a Birchgrove neighbor, had "never seen anyone work so hard to keep an ancient oak alive."[5]

Pamela took the arrows with grace, even if she had already

endured a similar decline with Leland. Still mentally sharp, Averell moved their tax residence to Virginia where the inheritance regime was more favorable but Pamela was convinced that, despite the accident, the flower-scented air of Barbados would help him live longer. It could also provide the perfect retreat for political discussion while he was looked after by a nurse close by.

A few months later, they bought Mango Bay, one of the most beautiful houses on the island, for $1.2 million. Pamela arranged for Averell to sleep in a two-bedroom bungalow in the grounds surrounded by papaya and mango trees, so he could rest away from the constant buzz of visitors and avoid the stairs. Her bedroom was behind pea-green shutters on the first floor of the main house, which had been created in the late 1960s by Oliver Messel, who designed Princess Margaret's home on Mustique. Pamela often had dinner served in the gazebo down by the beach but despite the relative informality she liked to emphasize that here, as at N Street, she was now in charge. She insisted on always being served first.

"It was sheer heaven," thought Colette Shulman, who came every year with Marshall. Yet Pamela never just relaxed and was seldom spotted on a sun lounger. She was constantly on the phone, receiving faxes and asking for updates from the N Street staff. Visits were vacations in name only. Aside from Russia, her focus was on exploring ways of countering Reagan's free market economics—particularly tax cuts for the rich and reductions to social programs for the poor. In the recessions of the early 1980s, nearly twelve million people lost their jobs and by the end of his first term homelessness was sweeping across America. And yet Reagan controlled the language and scope of debate and had driven a divisive wedge between Democrats, who seemed welded to a plethora of special-interest groups and incapable of becoming "a unifying force with a national message."[6] The talk around the pool was about how to rebuild the party to oust Reagan before he could do more damage at home or overseas.

Streams of Washington figures from Speaker Tom Foley to Richard Holbrooke and Bob Shrum took up her invitations—some were given first-class return tickets as Christmas presents. Pamela was not the usual grand foreign houseowner on the island, though, as she made a point of inviting Barbadians to join in her New Year's Eve parties with their jolly singalongs around the piano. "It reminds me of how inclusive she was," says Colette.

It was a challenge to keep Averell involved but at least flying to the island was no longer an ordeal. Pamela had been working on him to buy a private plane for almost a decade, but it had proved a long road to persuade Averell the outlay was justified. On her sixty-third birthday in March 1983, however, he had dispatched Janet to New York on a secret mission to pick up a $2.8 million ten-seater Westwind jet and a group of Pamela's favorite people including Kitty, her cardiologist friend Dr. Isadore Rosenfeld, Schlesinger and Holbrooke. Together they flew down to DC and awaited Pamela on the tarmac before giving her an aerial tour of her home city in her new plane. Back at the house, Averell reassured himself that she would make good use of it for her work. Most of all, it would ensure she got home after a day's campaigning so that he would not be alone at night. Pamela had the plane repainted in a white, brown and beige livery with an outsize Digby ostrich on the tail. Embossed on the fuselage was the call sign N-PH-84—representing her initials and the year of the main focus of her life: the next presidential election.

37

Reagan's first Cabinet was entirely composed of men* and ushered in a new conservative era of disapproval. Women were banned from wearing trousers in the Reagan White House and now that free love was old hat Pamela became ever more defensive about her private life, putting off a stream of writers wanting to write her biography. She feared her political career could not survive a book of salacious tales of her past. "If Pamela slept with everyone she is supposed to have slept with," one wag remarked, "she wouldn't have had one free night in the last three decades."[1] Bob Shrum pointed the finger at many who wanted to come to her PamPAC sessions but were not invited. They "derided her past," he says with dismay. "It was all right for men to live as she had; for them there was . . . a kind of macho admiration. But not for a woman." And particularly not one who had failed to come to a tragic end like courtesans were supposed to. "There was a sense of envy about how it had all seemed to turn out."[2] Pamela was "suitable mistress material," sniffed Joan Braden, a hostess, former State Department official and mother of eight, "but not someone to bring home to Mother."[3] Her detractors also thought she exaggerated her experiences during the war, doubting whether she had really lived through the Blitz or that she had been close to Churchill. They could hardly know that the little she told (or could tell) barely touched on it.

---

* Although Jeane Kirkpatrick held the Cabinet-level job of ambassador to the UN.

Consequently, Pamela tried to sound out reporters as to whether they were more interested in her Then or her Now before granting an interview, always striving to steer the conversation toward her political life. She became known to journalists as nervous and coy, and taped every media conversation with two recorders. On camera, she developed a technique of looking down as if deep in thought and then raising her eyes with a smile to disarming effect.

The one she would have liked to have written up her life—her son, Winston—showed no inclination. Yet in large part thanks to his mother, Winston and his family owned horses, a thirty-two foot yacht, the plane (later traded in for a Portuguese apartment), the French ski chalet and a London flat as well as his country house with tennis court and swimming pool—all on an early 1980s parliamentary salary of £13,950, albeit supplemented by American lecture tours, journalism and book royalties. Even if the yacht finally tested Winston's finances and was sold, the family lived almost fantasy lives and later the country house was upgraded for a grander one. The eldest son, Randolph, was still at Harrow (Pamela paid all four children's school fees) when she gave him a VW Golf costing £6,000, a gift replicated for the others when they reached seventeen.[4]

Pamela's largesse—which accelerated as Averell's health faded—was both welcomed and resented by Winston. The signs are that he wanted his mother's attention but begrudged her disapproval of his recklessness with his career and marriage, seeing the money as an attempt to control his life through her purse strings. Averell railed at his ingratitude. When Winston did not call Pamela on her birthday, he eventually phoned his stepson in a fury to ask if he had forgotten. "Winston said that he was going to call later," according to Janet Howard. "But I always wondered."[5] It did not help that Winston's political career declined as hers continued to soar, although she made a point of praising him when she could. His measured comments in the Commons on the Falklands War in April 1982 earned an effusive note of congratulations: "Darling Winston, Thank you for your speech in the House . . . I am proud of you."[6] In Washington she arranged special dinners to introduce him to the great and good, from Al Gore to the Senate Defense Committee. Perhaps it was jealousy that drove Winston to denigrate her in public, telling the *Sunday Times Magazine* in 1982 that "I don't see how she'd have ever carved out a political role on her own." She was, he decreed, simply a "political consort" proving herself "the best possible wife" by espousing "her husband's causes."[7] Later he informed the *Washington Post* that "My mother's not a politician. She married a politician,"[8] and on another (most unhelpful) occasion that she would have been a Republican had she married one.

Pamela did not let on she was hurt—she simply redoubled her political energies and decided to flex her Churchill heritage in the Democratic Party cause for the 1984 presidential elections. After one brainstorming session with Clinton, she penned a *New York Times* comment suggesting that Reagan might meet the "same unexpected fate" as Churchill in 1945. Britain's war savior had been personally popular but had "lost control of the political narrative," she wrote, developing a theme she would return to often. Reagan offered no real hope for an exhausted nation and also had nothing to say about the future, so might well suffer a similar "democratic dispatch."[9] "The *Times* piece was great!" Clinton exclaimed.[10] Unfortunately, the comparison turned out to be one historical parallel too far.

Pamela's main problem, though, was that she was not inspired by any of the party's presidential hopefuls. None seemed to offer the right mix of personality and policy. She liked Walter Mondale as a friend, and allowed herself to imagine that becoming his envoy to Britain would be "a fun idea."[11] (Pamela went as far as quizzing the British ambassador Antony Acland about British labor laws.) Yet since Mondale's turn in the N Street paddock, she had thought he lacked the charisma for the fight against Reagan. He had been so unexciting that Janet Howard had asked Clinton to give an impromptu after-dinner talk to liven things up. Of course, when Mondale was nominated Pamela rallied behind him and the first female vice presidential candidate, Geraldine Ferraro, but was still unenthused.

Mondale had hoped his running mate would exploit the gender gap—female voters liked Reagan less than male ones—but Pamela believed Ferraro's failure to convince the electorate as well as questions about her husband's finances made it even harder for women in politics. "That's why," she said, "it is so important for us to push good women into high spots." The notion of a female president was, however, "just not on the cards"—although Pamela would have liked to have seen the Republican Jeane Kirkpatrick have a go. For now, although there were more women on the lower slopes of politics, they were rarely able to climb toward the summit. Pamela almost always found herself the only female at high-level political meetings.[12] Once that had pleased her. Now she began to see how it left her exposed.

Pamela's first speech at the 1984 Democratic National Convention in San Francisco was hardly a ringing endorsement of the Mondale-Ferraro ticket but focused on the fight for the Senate. Unfortunately, if she had improved as a TV performer over the previous few years (she could try to forget the invisible audience to focus on the interviewer alone), addressing a huge but half-empty hall was a test too far. Once again, the ponderous cadences of a Churchill tribute act failed to penetrate the hubbub of conversation—not even her neat line that she was an "American by choice and a Democrat by conviction." Yet what she had to say was important and set out her own progressive priorities: "Never again will the highest offices in the land be labeled For Men Only or," she vowed, "limited to one race."

Thereafter, Pamela remained semidetached from the presidential campaign. Her view of Mondale's chances had long been clear. As far back as 1983, she had kept him waiting for ten minutes for a lunch appointment at the Four Seasons Hotel in Washington, a discourtesy spotted by the *Washington Post*.[13] A self-effacing figure, he forgave her and shortly before his death sent the author a message that he had liked Pamela "very much." As she expected, he lost by a landslide. Her political antennae had been all too accurate.

Despite her mother's warnings, Pamela's insecurities still drove her to earn affection or approval through money. She tracked down Hudson, her old butler from the Attic days, to help him, and when she heard that Leland's secretary had angina she transferred her social security payments to her. Even when Peter Duchin announced that he was to marry again and that his bride was—of all people—Brooke Hayward she persuaded Averell that they should give the couple $10,000 of Union Pacific stock and a case of expensive wine. This did little to improve relations, Duchin later claiming that it was his and Brooke's "common hatred" for Pamela that had cemented their marriage.[14]

In January 1982 Averell transferred his art collection to Pamela to reduce later tax liabilities—it was his wish that she would eventually leave it to the National Gallery. Averell's daughters were incensed. "Can't you leave me just one picture?" Kathy asked her father, observing the vast sums of money going to Winston and his family. "I can't afford it," he replied.[15] In 1984, Averell signed a new will appointing Pamela his primary beneficiary as well as sole executor and trustee. Pamela balked at the responsibility but Averell reassured her that she could rely on Clifford and Rich. The following year, Clifford duly reported that 1985 had been "good" for the Harriman family trusts, but he was intent on acquiring new assets to provide "even higher yields" in the future.[16] Pamela assumed she was receiving the best possible advice. The course was now set for disaster.

38

When the end was near, Richard Holbrooke asked Averell whether he had any regrets. "Yes," he shot back. "Not marrying her the first time."[1] Soon afterward, Averell whispered that he was "hurting so badly" before slipping away on a tide of morphine in the same room at Birchgrove where Leland had died fifteen years earlier. This time there was none of the bitter drama of Leland's death, just a hollow sadness. Holbrooke expressed his admiration of how Pamela had coped for so long and in a tender nine-page letter told her that Averell's "one true regret was the years apart from you." His farewell gift had been his encouraging her to "step out" into politics on her own.[2] Winston related how much he "appreciated" the fact that Averell had been "wonderfully generous" to him and his children.[3] President Reagan put out a statement that the world had "lost one of her most respected statesmen" while the *New York Times* went into full praise mode, dubbing him America's "plenipotentiary supreme."[4]

The funeral was held three days later but had been meticulously planned by Janet for years. Seven hundred mourners filed into the French Gothic splendors of St. Thomas's Episcopal Church on Fifth Avenue led by Pamela in heavy black veil and mantilla. With appropriate grace, she had invited Peter Duchin, and with Winston and Averell's grandsons he carried the coffin out at the end as the congregation sang "The Battle Hymn of the Republic." Flanked by state troopers, the cortège crossed the George Washington Bridge to travel up to the Harriman burial ground at Arden. Shaded from the blistering mid-July heat by tall hemlock trees, sixty family and friends gathered on a knoll next to Marie's grave for the blessing. After Bishop Paul Moore uttered "ashes to ashes, dust to dust," thudding a handful of dry summer sand onto the coffin, the throng repaired to the big house for a buffet lunch.

After a few minutes, Averell's daughters beckoned Duchin to join them at a window overlooking the forest. "Averell was not in that coffin," Kathy told him in her matter-of-fact manner. Peter reeled and asked her what she meant. Averell had requested that he and Pamela should be buried together, three miles away from the rest of the family on the edge of Forest Lake. His corpse was being stored in a funeral parlor deep freeze until the new grave could be prepared. Peter thought it "macabre and very, very weird" and a betrayal of his beloved Ma (and no doubt Pamela *was* opposed to allowing Averell to be reunited with Marie in death). Quivering with emotion, he hitched a lift back to New York with Kay Graham and poured out what he had just learned. Graham thought the whole saga "ghastly" but to Peter's bitter frustration nothing appeared in her paper for weeks.[5]

Then, two days after Averell's memorial service in Washington's National Cathedral in mid-September, word reached Pamela that a story about a "sham" burial was to run in the *Post*. Pamela and Holbrooke bombarded Graham with calls pleading with her to pull the piece but she refused to overrule her editor, who was gleefully promoting the story. The next morning, Pamela was distraught at the "vicious, vicious, vicious"[6] article under the headline HARRIMAN NEVER BURIED, but her allies quickly rallied, with Mario Cuomo, governor of New York, calling to say, "Don't let the bastards get you down." Winston was also sympathetic, writing that he was "so sorry" the press were "making beasts of themselves."[7] Bishop Moore insisted to the *Post* that Averell had been buried "liturgically" if not physically.

Not all of the Harrimans shared Duchin's horror—particularly after Averell was finally laid to rest in the spot he had chosen under a headstone engraved "Patriot, Public Servant, Statesman." Robert Fisk, Mary's son, announced that the first burial ceremony had been the "logical" thing to do while the family waited to lay him to rest in a "place he loved."[8] "There was no intention to deceive."[9] There was always someone unnamed yet "close to the family," though, presenting the affair as proof of Pamela's controlling nature. The fuss died down soon enough but Duchin continued to rage. He blamed Pamela for the fact that Averell had not left him anything. Nor had she thought to send him "even the smallest memento of Averell's—no set of cufflinks, tie clasp, anything," he complained. "She's finally gotten it all for herself—even his bones."[10]

Averell had indeed left Pamela a wealthy widow. The woman who had once had to retire early to bed to stay warm now owned art valued at up to $100 million (albeit informally pledged to the National Gallery). Averell had dispersed much of his fortune to good causes but although the value of the estate was never released it was believed to have been $65 to $75 million (and wilder estimates had it up to $125 million). Pamela, however, insisted she was "not as rich as you think."[11] A conservative investment regime had provided little growth and much of the fortune was tied up in property or trusts for his children and grandchildren.

Averell's daughters were left just $4,000 cash each and the interest from a separate $30 million trust fund to be controlled by Pamela, and specifically had no claim on the art collection. The omission—which shocked them—was "not from any lack of love and affection," Averell had written, "but because I know them to be otherwise provided for." Kathy and Mary gathered their families to discuss the possibility of suing but the two sisters decided to avoid the inevitable publicity. Yet under the surface of civility and discretion, anger was quietly simmering.[12]

Pamela didn't collapse as she had done after Leland's death—and perhaps there was even a sense of relief. She had developed a wide circle of friends and had won the respect of many prominent Democrats. At sixty-six she was at last her own woman with her own money, and determined not to show her age. After a newspaper described her as "a bit chubby" Pamela was "so stung that she just stopped eating," Cynthia Helms remembered. "She served delicious food . . . but sipped on a cup of bouillon herself."[13] Pamela installed an exercise bike on the top floor of N Street—well before the trend for home gyms—but preferred to swim in Barbados, ride at the Farm or hike with friends in Sun Valley. "She'd ring us every day at nine and say, 'Where are we going today?'" recalls Mallory Walker, who with his wife, Diana, saw her in Idaho every summer. The evenings were cool on the mountain and on occasion they would slip into a hot tub on the terrace. Pamela liked to spice things up by joining them nude[14]—but even then her talk revolved around politics.

Most effective of all was a facelift. Early in 1988 she booked in with Dr. Sherrell Aston, plastic surgery chief at a hospital in Manhattan, a decision that would make her doctor a society legend. She "radiates health" and has "an energy in her step," *Time* magazine observed.[15] "Boy, her plastic surgeon did a good job!" confirms a close friend. "Pamela looked fabulous even in sunlight." Bill Manchester, a biographer of Winston Churchill, told her that someone had asked him what she was like. "One of the sexiest women I've ever met," he replied. "At her age?" the friend inquired mercilessly. Manchester declared that her "kind of beauty is timeless."[16]

The rejuvenated Pamela admitted she was "very lonely being a widow" but Gianni continued to call her every day, visit her regularly and drew hearts and kisses on his letters. On one occasion, he was spotted having breakfast at N Street with Pamela by the British diplomat Sir Robin Renwick, who formed the impression he had stayed overnight.[17]

One of her other male consorts seemed more regular than others. Curly-haired and gangly, Carter Brown was not her physical type but was erudite and ambitious. Pamela had given generously to the National Gallery but his goal was to secure a formal endowment of *White Roses* as the crown jewel of the collection. He courted Pamela, who was flattered by the attentions of a man fourteen years her junior and a titan of the culture world. A scion of the family who had endowed Brown University, he was notorious even among his own relatives for being tight with his money.[18] Soon he was instructing sales staff on expensive shopping trips to "send the bill to Mrs. Harriman's attention."[19] She flew him to London on Concorde, rode with him on the Orient Express and cruised with him down the coast of Turkey. Carter claimed that marriage was on the cards and that he expected to inherit Willow Oaks plus a $1 million bequest to maintain it,[20] yet Pamela's friends thought of the match more as a "relationship of convenience." Even if she valued Carter's companionship Pamela was determined to die as Averell's widow. "I've had a wonderful life . . . I have been married to wonderful people. I couldn't top it," she told a journalist.[21] That might have been so but at quiet moments she admitted she relied heavily on her work to fill her life.[22]

39

On the evening of November 5, 1986, Pamela mounted a stage bedecked with red, white and blue balloons, dressed in a neat blue suit and a wide smile. The Democrats had just recaptured the Senate and increased their majority in the House in the midterm elections, and during the jubilation afterward three pillars of the party lavished praise on the woman standing beside them for what she described as a "political earthquake." George Mitchell thanked her for making victory possible; Paul Kirk hailed her as the first lady of the Democratic Party and Tony Coelho declared: "We are indebted to her and we love her." Barely four months after Averell's death, Pamela had proved she had the electoral firepower that had eluded her husband all his life. It was payback for an incredible six years during which she had given the party confidence that it could be as tough, professional and determined to win as the Republicans—a feat celebrated in a newly composed song called "Pamela Harriman Is Indestructible."[1] It was a moment to savor. PamPAC had once been considered "a boondoggling idea," she informed a reporter, "but I don't think they think that now."[2]

Soon after, she gave a dinner for the new Democratic senators, having worked with them all to win their seats. Between April and July 1986 Pamela had hosted seventeen events at N Street for Senate candidates, including Joe Biden, raising an average of $150,000 a time. Telling Biden that her aim was to see key Democrats chairing powerful Senate committees, she added "including you as head of

Judiciary!"* Biden's tragic past—in which his first wife and baby daughter were killed in a car crash—meant he had particular reason to get home every night to Delaware to be with his family so Pamela made special arrangements. Not only would she love to have his second wife, Jill, attend (an unusual concession), but she offered a lift home in her private plane after the event, which she would ensure ended by 10 p.m. sharp.[3] "We are proud of you," she told a grateful Biden.

A few months earlier Pamela had promoted Janet as the first female director of PamPAC, positioning her even more as the lynchpin of her life. Janet had become "almost an extension of Pamela," said Eizenstat,[4] and seemed to have magical powers. When Evangeline Bruce was writing a book, *Napoleon & Josephine*, she boxed up the results of months of research to be dispatched from Paris to America but the container went missing. Pamela put Janet on the case and within hours the bosses of the courier company, the New York Port Authority and the governor of New York had between them managed to find it.[5] "Mrs. H would even call her in the middle of the night," recalls Pie Friendly, "and one time Janet had no paper by her bed to write down a list of complex requests, so she had to write across the inside of a book."[6]

Janet's promotion reflected a slow if steady feminist awakening over the previous few years, although Pamela would never have called it that. Back in 1981, Pamela had pronounced that she liked to "feel I'm at the side of a real man" but now she admired Margaret Thatcher for bestriding the global stage—if not for most of her politics—and had her locks whipped into a comparable 1980s power helmet. Their views on female advancement were also not dissimilar. Neither believed that they as women should be stopped from doing anything men did, though they still expected men to occupy most positions of power (indeed, Thatcher appointed only one woman to her Cabinet in eleven

---

* Senator Biden became chair of the Judiciary Committee in 1987.

years). Pamela never seriously considered elected office for herself, preferring to acquire power behind the throne without subjecting herself to the media intrusion of the ballot box. True, she supported talented female candidates for the Senate such as Barbara Mikulski and Dianne Feinstein, but she found it a "problem" that she was expected to back female candidates because of their sex—they had to be exceptional, probably more so than equivalent men.[7] Pamela "ignored a lot of women," Janet confirmed, "but she developed over time."[8] After Averell's death, she began to seek out more female company, even shortening the legs on the chairs at Willow Oaks to make them more comfortable for women guests.

One female interest she came to champion—drawing on her own experiences as a young woman—was the "crucially important matter" of birth control. In October 1985 she lobbied the Catholic Joe Biden to vote against an amendment that would prohibit the District of Columbia from using public money to pay for abortions (he had previously voted against the use of federal funds). She warned him of the "severe impact" the amendment would have on health care for poor women. While Biden battled with the conflict between his faith and his generally progressive politics—which would lead to a career-long back and forth on the subject—Pamela had become so disillusioned with what she considered the "narrow-mindedness" of Rome that she decided she no longer considered herself a Catholic.[9]

Yet in common with many privileged women of her generation, she had a blind spot on some issues. In 1991, when the attorney Anita Hill accused her former superior Clarence Thomas, who had been nominated to the Supreme Court, of sexual harassment, Pamela was appalled at the way she was treated but was otherwise unsympathetic.

While she thought Thomas unqualified for the Supreme Court, she believed at first that women bringing such claims to the public realm were "naïve and unsophisticated" and should get used to what she called "men making advances."[10] It was a stance that perhaps accounts for her public silence on Joe Kennedy. Over time, she reflected that she had probably been "unfair" and that because of an imbalance of power these women had "good reason to feel threatened." Finally, she decided she would not pull her punches against Democratic senators who had backed Thomas. She told a reporter that one of them, Charles Robb, son-in-law of Lyndon Johnson, had "dug his own grave."[11] Gloria Steinem cheered her on, once hailing Pamela as "the woman who proves that not all feminists have to wear combat boots."[12]

The 1986 victory in the Senate gave Pamela kudos but Averell's death that year had liberated her politically. "She wanted to play a more hands-on role in the political process, something she couldn't do while Averell was still alive," explained Carter Brown.[13] And she was willing to pay to progress her career via her control of two Harriman foundations giving out over $1 million a year. She chose to donate to august organizations that would put her on the board, such as the Brookings Institution, a liberal think tank where in 1988 she was named a trustee. She also donated to the Atlantic Council, a bipartisan organization promoting alliances between the U.S. and Western Europe, and became vice chair in 1989. These board positions added to her seriousness and stature and were followed by learned op-eds in the *Washington Post* and the *New York Times*. Overall, she donated to and served on the board of nearly a dozen bodies including the Council on Foreign Relations and the Commission on Presidential Debates. Such prominent positions went a long way in filling an otherwise painfully empty CV.

Next on Pamela's self-improvement mission came several high-level overseas trips, including one following up on a prior invitation to Averell as head of a delegation to China. She bankrolled her entourage, bringing along Sandy Berger and Arthur Schlesinger and meeting up with Holbrooke in Beijing. Eager to promote her Harriman family, she invited her step-grandson David Mortimer—she also claimed to have pulled strings for him to be nominated for the Council on Foreign Relations.[14] Pamela asked questions, took notes and gave her Chinese hosts a dinner with six past and present American ambassadors, punctuated by rounds of toasts. There followed other sorties to Japan with the governor of Virginia, the Middle East with the Council on Foreign Relations and Turkey with the Atlantic Council. Her efforts were eventually noticed in the way she had hoped. "She has become," the *Chicago Tribune* reported with a hint of disbelief, something of "a foreign affairs expert."[15]

40

Mikhail Gorbachev spotted Pamela in the ballroom at the Soviet Embassy in Washington in December 1987 and made his way through the crowd of politicians, policy wonks and ambassadors. "Your name is very well known in our country," he told her through an interpreter, to the envy of the room. "Your husband contributed greatly to the good causes of the century. We have a documentary at home of the times when he worked with us and when we were allies." Then he looked her in the eye and said, "He was the best-looking man I ever saw." When Pamela took her seat at table one, his wife, Raisa, grabbed her hand and declared, "I am so looking forward to coming to your house. Thank you so much for having me."[1] Pamela's glory was complete.

The charismatic Gorbachevs—the closest to Soviet rock gods the West had ever seen—were in the American capital on a historic first state visit. Sales of vodka soared and the capitalist bastion of the Marriott Hotel renamed its coffee shop Café Glasnost. When "Gorby" stopped his boxy Russian limousine to shake hands with the crowds on the junction of Connecticut and L Streets NW, they surged forward to catch a glimpse of his famous bald pate with its strawberry birthmark. "It was like the coming of the second Messiah," one DC woman exclaimed and as the *New York Times* reported, "If a spaceship had landed in the middle of Washington, it could not have caused more commotion. Pedestrians quivered with excitement."[2] The unscheduled stop made Gorbachev an hour late for his meeting with Reagan at the White House, leaving the American president in no doubt that here was a rare world leader possessing charisma and a way with crowds rivaling his own.

Talk of the "Evil Empire" had given way toward the latter stages of Reagan's administration to fresh thinking. Especially after Gorbachev (taking up what his former protector Andropov had started) had made overtures to America and begun reforms in his own country—under the banners of glasnost (openness) and perestroika (restructuring)—that would bring down communist rule and ease tensions with the West. For many, the Soviet leader embodied the end of forty years of Cold War fears of nuclear obliteration.

Now Gorbachev—whom Thatcher had hailed as "a man one could do business with" (a phrase uncannily similar to Pamela's about Andropov)—had come to Washington to sign the treaty eliminating an entire category of nuclear weapons. It was vindication of the Harrimans' stance since their visit to Moscow in 1983 that the Soviets were willing to compromise and that East-West relations should be "normalized."

Raisa Gorbachev was of special fascination as a female symbol of glasnost. As the first personable wife of a Soviet leader—predecessors had largely presented as hatchet-faced miseries—Raisa dressed with style, smiled strategically and wielded enormous power as her husband's closest adviser. Her schedule in Washington was almost more sensitive than her husband's and she was flooded with invitations. Nancy Reagan had hoped for a friendly powwow over tea and a tour of the White House but she had to press for two weeks for a response. When it finally came it was at best lukewarm, declining the offer of tea and accepting only a brief visit to the Executive Mansion that was evidently frosty, even tense. Their first meeting in 1985 had sparked a so-called "personal Cold War"—Nancy had been unable to disguise her contempt for the way Raisa snapped her fingers at her KGB bodyguards or lectured her on the glories of Leninism—and now diplomats were concerned that antipathy between the women might undermine the whole summit. Matters took another turn for the worse when it was discovered that Raisa had asked to be invited for coffee at Pamela's house even as she was deliberating as to whether she would join Nancy at all.

At a lunch at the State Department for two hundred guests, Gorbachev again homed in on Pamela and held her hand while asking what she thought of his meeting with Reagan and adding, "We must work together."[3] Immediately afterward, an abrasive "youngish" man who had watched this exchange marched up to her without introduction as if he knew her well. "How nice to see you," he exclaimed, trying to grab her attention. "Isn't this a great day!" Later he pushed himself in front of Kay Graham and again made determined conversation, ending with "I'd like to take up your invitation to lunch." Both women were baffled as to who this presumptuous man was, only to be told by a journalist that he was Donald Trump, developer of the four-year-old Trump Tower in Manhattan and now lobbying for Soviet permission to build a Trump outpost opposite the Kremlin. Pamela thought his bumptious manner "hilarious."

Afterward, Pamela went on to a more intimate dinner with the Gorbachevs at the Soviet Embassy, another significant marker in the end of the Cold War. Over drinks in an anteroom beforehand, Admiral William Crowe, chair of the Joint Chiefs of Staff, revealed that the Embassy had long been out of bounds to serving American military personnel. "So do you have special permission to be here?" she inquired. "I didn't ask," he replied. "This is a new era."[4]

They adjourned to a larger salon for dinner, to be joined by the Reagans and vice president George Bush and his wife, Barbara. Pamela steeled herself. She rarely drank but noted no fewer than six wineglasses at each setting and dozens of iced bottles of premium vodka. The Russians were settling in for the long haul. The ingredients, cooks and waiters had been flown over from the Kremlin that morning and the starter was "big grey caviar," served twice. The courses kept coming—some were unidentifiable, others included fish soup, crab with lobster, brochette of lamb and finally an eleventh course of strawberry ice cream shaped like sandcastles. Pamela presumed that mercifully marked the end but soon afterward the waiters returned with blueberry tart and then a huge collection of candies. She was amused to spot her neighbor, Charles Wick, head of the United States Information Agency (whose job included pumping out anti-Soviet propaganda), pocketing a few of them when he thought no one was looking. After a singer from the Metropolitan Opera performed nine songs it was time to give thanks and bid her exhausted goodbyes to the Gorbachevs. She also took her leave of an unsmiling American First Lady in the knowledge that the White House was "miffed" by her success with Raisa.[5] Unnerved by Nancy's evident displeasure, Pamela found herself saying "thank you so much" to her too.[6]

However late the hour, Pamela had much to do as Raisa was due at N Street the following morning. She had been given only five days' notice that there would be twenty Secret Service, ten KGB and six members of the Protocol Office attending. When the KGB poured into the house in advance of the visit, they checked every room and found a photograph of her with Andropov—"Ah, ex-chief of KGB!" they exclaimed in surprise. Two more security cars were parked down by the swimming pool, where they churned up Pamela's beloved lawn. In the meantime, Raisa had asked to meet distinguished American women so Pamela had been landed with the job of finding five who could drop everything to attend. She had managed to gather Barbara Mikulski (the sole female Democratic senator) and Nancy Kassebaum (the only female Republican senator), Kay Graham, the president of the University of Chicago Hannah Gray and Justice Sandra O'Connor, the first woman to serve on the Supreme Court. Pamela acknowledged criticism that they were all white and privately vowed to do better.[7]

On the day, Raisa was running late but finally at 11:30 they heard the sirens announcing her arrival in a ZIL limousine flanked by police motorcycles. Pamela greeted Raisa at the door and whisked her down the hall to the library, where she showed her the Van Gogh. Pamela's chef Gretchen had spent days preparing the food laid out on Pamela's George III silver dishes but it remained untouched as the women repaired immediately to the dining room, where the round table had been set with pens and pads—the only man in the room was the interpreter. Raisa sat next to Pamela and talked passionately about the threat of nuclear weapons, joint collaborations on cancer and alcoholism, and her mixed emotions about being thrust onto the world stage. After an hour and a quarter, Raisa came to the front door with Pamela to face the crowd of reporters outside. Soviet women rarely spoke in public—not even Raisa—and Pamela thought her guest "very nervous," so they grabbed each other's hands and stepped out in unison to a wall of cameras and reporters yelling Raisa's name. "I have now visited the house of Mrs. Harriman," the Russian said through her interpreter, describing her host as connected to the time "when we were allies." "Mrs. Gorbachev is doing a fine job," responded Pamela to a barrage of flashbulbs.

The talks with Andropov, the long years of studying, the friendships with sympathetic Russians and the drafting of op-ed pieces on finding common ground had paid off. There were, of course, far greater seismic forces at play but Pamela's highly personal part in the rapprochement of two wary superpowers—hailed by Robert Legvold as "earnest, impressive and consistent"—had been publicly acknowledged on the Russian side at least. Afterward, Raisa sent Pamela a warm message of "most sincere thanks."[8] It simply marked "a legacy for Averell," Pamela insisted to those who thought she was getting too big for her boots. "Not because I decided I wanted to project myself as me" but working for world peace through dialogue, "doing things . . . I believe in, he believed in."[9] *Women's Wear Daily* branded the meeting as "an incredible confirmation" of Pam Power.[10] She had been singled out by Gorbachev, whose actions in the next few years would transform the world stage. His decision to loosen the Soviet yoke over the countries of Eastern Europe—including the withdrawal of Red Army troops—created a democratic momentum that led to the dismantling of the Berlin Wall in November 1989 and the drawing aside of the Iron Curtain. The following year Gorbachev agreed to the reunification of Germany and even raised the prospect of it joining the Soviet Union's longtime enemy NATO. In 1990, he received the Nobel Peace Prize.

Pamela was delighted with the new East-West understanding and, of course, the boost to her status from such visible endorsement by Gorbachev. Soon after the state visit, Georgetown University's Institute for the Study of Diplomacy asked her to give the prestigious annual Samuel D. Berger Memorial Lecture. A lectern was brought into her office so she could conquer her nerves by practicing with Sandy Berger and Bob Shrum. Stuart Eizenstat knew how significant the event was in Pamela's career, a moment when she "burst out" from Averell's shadow as "someone who is identifying leaders [and] shaping policy."[11] Pamela was so intent on perfecting her "diplomatic coming out"—effectively her job application for the next Democratic administration—that she almost made herself ill.

On the night itself in April 1988, she arrived on the arm of Edmund Muskie to address a packed auditorium of handpicked ambassadors and politicians—dubbed the "Grecian Formula set" (a reference to aging men who dyed their hair) by the *Post* in a piece mocking Pamela as "the only Washington hostess with her own foreign policy."[12] Dressed in a tight-fitting black silk cocktail dress, she warned of the perils of Washington's excessive political rivalry and in a deep "Churchillian"[13] voice called for nonpartisan cooperation to protect

America's reputation abroad. "Tell the truth . . . and tell it early," she exhorted her audience in a list of six dos and don'ts. The *Post* reported "scores of stifled yawns" but Eizenstat—considered a "very serious man who was not going to be bowled over by frippery"[14]—was one of several admirers to call her performance "wonderful." Another wished out loud that Pamela could be president.[15] Yet a reporter chose to point out to her that she had never held a government post and was "best known through her association with powerful men." Pamela reeled while the journalist turned to Sandy Berger to ask whether he had written the speech for her. With growing irritation, Berger replied that it was "characteristic of Pamela to ask lots of questions and for lots of ideas and to synthesize them in her own way."[16] It was in any case entirely normal for such a major address to be the work of many hands.

Afterward, Bill Clinton was supportive, describing her words as having helped him "clarify" his own thinking,[17] but saw the hostile reaction of others. He dismissed her critics as envious of her achievements, noting that his mother had brought him up to believe it a "fool's errand to be jealous of other people's successes. You should cheer them and then make your own."[18] Melissa Moss, a senior Democratic official, was appalled by the flak. "She was reinventing herself, something men have done for years and no one raises an eyebrow." The naysayers "downplayed her intelligence and knowledge," recalled Carter Brown, "but I can say with certainty that she knew what she was talking about."[19]

It was certainly true that the Soviets continued to see her as an important contact in Washington. When Gorbachev's special envoy Yevgeny Primakov flew into town in October 1990 to discuss Saddam Hussein's invasion of Kuwait with President Bush he reserved a forty-minute slot for a meeting with Pamela. "They were very impressed with each other," remembers Pamela's friend the foreign affairs expert Judith Kipper, who accompanied her. "The relationship continued."[20]

Shortly afterward, Pamela told the Soviet government's official newspaper, *Izvestia*, that she finally considered herself an "emancipated woman." The writer of a lengthy, admiring feature suggested she could become a second iron lady in the mold of Margaret Thatcher. "Why a second one?" Pamela asked.[21]

Pamela liked to say that she did not care what people said about her—although she knew that such bravado gave people "another reason" to think her a "bitch!"[22] The worst assault at this point came from British journalist Henry Fairlie, who had nursed a grievance since Averell had thrown him out of an N Street party for mocking the Kennedys. Trailed on the front cover of the August 2, 1988, issue of the *New Republic* (a Reagan White House favorite), Fairlie had written a lengthy piece entitled SHAMELA. Describing Pamela as a Washington widow of "vivid repute . . . her name inflated with each husband," Fairlie wrote that she had viewed the Democratic Party as a "charity" to adopt merely for the purpose of seeming "serious and useful." Since then, "the fable of Pamela Harriman's ascendance" had reflected the willingness of Washington to "prostrate" itself "before great wealth and glamour." "The nature of her trade with Washington, which takes place across the corpse of her most recent husband, is concealed by her elevation as a Very Serious Person." Claiming that this new status had been bought with Harriman money—"Washington easily detects wisdom in $75 million"—he went on to ridicule her lecture on corrosive political rivalry as an exercise in "lapidary unction." Finally, Fairlie (or Unfairlie, as she thought of him) even turned on her father as "a caricature of a minor peer." No one could doubt the precision of Fairlie's darts or the distress they caused their target.

Pamela had powerful allies swiftly marshaled by George Mitchell. Over half the Senate, including Barbara Mikulski, Paul Sarbanes and Lloyd Bentsen, signed his letter on official Senate stationery to the *New Republic*'s editor. "We cannot recall an article as mean-spirited and degrading," they wrote, and were "distressed at the viciousness of the attack." Pamela Harriman "is a woman of extraordinary wealth and ability" who "could have chosen idleness and self-indulgence. Instead she chose to devote her life to public service," for which she deserved praise not vilification. Sandy Berger wrote to her privately that he cared "intensely" about her and that although the article was "garbage" he knew that she was hurt and "that enrages me." Most gratifying was this: "There is no one else in America who could get fifty-four senators to agree overnight on <u>anything</u> and that reflects their genuine respect, affection and gratitude." Finally, he added that he would "<u>always</u> look back on . . . working together as one of the most cherished experiences of my life."[23]

Janet was, however, still concerned and contacted Eddie to talk over "serious and disturbing matters concerning . . . your sister."[24] Pamela canceled her public engagements to consider if she wanted to go on.

41

In the end, she was lured back into the game by her evergreen hopes of high office if the Democrats won against George Bush in November 1988. "Of course, I expect to do something," she had told the *Chicago Tribune* in January,[1] and she genuinely felt her experience of high-level politics and diplomacy qualified her for such a role—perhaps even ambassador to the United Nations. Having raised millions for the Democrats and with the Senate in the bag, "Queen Pamela" had her dreams painfully dashed.

Initially she had thought Gary Hart had the "spirit and image"[2] to regain the presidency and threw a $250 a head fundraiser for him. Shortly afterward he became embroiled in a sex scandal (in which the married Hart was alleged to have slept with the model Donna Rice and a string of other women) and Pamela never spoke to him again. "He nearly put me out of business," she said.[3] She then thought it had to be forty-year-old Clinton. "Why don't you come to Barbados for a week or so?" she had cabled him. "We can talk about when you will run."[4] Within ten days he had bailed out, claiming over dinner with Pamela that he wanted to be around as a father for his seven-year-old daughter, Chelsea. Also Hillary did not think the Democrats could win.[5] Others claimed he had been deterred by the media frenzy over Hart's dallying and Pamela was herself worried about Clinton's sex life. He often stayed at N Street when he was in Washington, in the room directly above her own, and on one occasion it became obvious that he had smuggled a woman in for the night. Though hardly a prude, Pamela was livid at Clinton's disloyalty to his wife but also the obvious political recklessness.[6]

Joe Biden was another contender but pulled out amid accusations that during a debate in Iowa he had plagiarized the "thousand generations" speech given by the Labour Party leader Neil Kinnock about his family's humble background. When others dropped Biden in embarrassment, Pamela sent a note saying she admired him for the way he had faced the furor. "You have stood tall. With admiration & respect, Pamela."[7] Publicly dismissing the affair as just a "wrinkle,"[8] she also helped with efforts to retire his campaign debt. "I truly appreciate your support and friendship," he replied, "and I will not forget it."[9]

Pamela's hopes were now pinned on Al Gore, a regular at her Issues Evenings and a handsome young senator she thought qualified to handle international affairs. Pamela also liked his wife, Tipper. But Gore got involved in his own ruckus over negative comments against his rival, the Reverend Jesse Jackson, and he withdrew too. So the party had ended up (to Pamela's dismay after the dais kerfuffle) with Michael Dukakis, and Clinton was to nominate the Massachusetts governor at the 1988 Democratic convention in Atlanta. Unfortunately, he gave a speech that was almost comically tedious. "Delegates on the floor began yelling at Bill to finish," recalls Hillary.[10] "Thirty-two minutes of total disaster," was how Clinton himself saw it.[11] Pamela immediately stepped in, taking Bill and Hillary out to dinner to talk over a media rescue plan.

Eight days later Clinton appeared on Johnny Carson's *Tonight Show*. With a giant hourglass on the table to help him keep track of time, Carson asked Clinton what had happened in Atlanta. He replied that he wanted to make Dukakis, not known for oratory, look good and "I succeeded . . . beyond my wildest imagination!" By the time he had played the saxophone and flown back on the red-eye to Little Rock, an almost mythical star had been born and a crowd had gathered to cheer him home.[12] Pamela admired how Clinton had been "very gutsy" on the *Tonight Show*, turning failure into a media triumph.[13] It was, however, embarrassingly late for Pamela to endorse Dukakis and offers of help were rejected. She was so fed up she packed her bags and fled to Italy.[14] When Dukakis lost, even in the once-solid South, dreams of an ambassadorship were shattered.

"I'm tired of getting up at 5 a.m. every day and banging my head against a wall," Pamela told Doris Lilly after George Bush succeeded Reagan in the Oval Office.[15] At sixty-eight, her reserves of energy seemed finally to be dwindling. She had barely allowed herself to grieve after Averell's death, working long days ever since and the constant sniping made her unwell. The attacks took many forms. For more than a decade, Daniel Patrick Moynihan had been planning his revenge for Pamela's comments about his drinking. When she applied to join the Century Club, a prestigious literary salon in Manhattan famed for its house martini, he did his utmost to block her.[16] Other members, including Bill Manchester, came to her rescue. "It is the world's best club. But," he teased, "never drink an entire Century Martini at one sitting. The consequences don't bear thinking about. You may wake up in jail, in a hospital, or in bed with a Republican"![17]

In the end, Pamela rallied and simply changed tack, diverting PamPAC funds to her new National Polling Project to provide selected candidates with drilled-down data on messaging—testing Democratic as well as Republican policies. Pamela was collecting vital information no one else had and there were constant demands for it: Tom O'Donnell was just one grateful party strategist who found Pamela "very willing" to help and Clinton described it as yet another "terrific idea."[18] And yet despite all she had achieved she was often still treated as a lightweight. "She had worked very, very hard and had reinvented the Democratic Party all by herself," says Judith Kipper. "She didn't get credit for it, she wasn't appointed, she wasn't paid, she wasn't recognized except by some. At that time of course women had a certain place. But instead of writing about parties and gossip, there should have been a proper profile of her work."[19] The distinguished State Department lawyer Nancy Ely-Raphel also thought Pamela widely misunderstood. "It wasn't just her money" that was useful to the Democrats, as people thought, as that was seen as an acceptable female contribution: "It was her brain."[20]

By the turn of the decade, by Janet's account, they had raised $12 million, but as the novelty of glitz wore off her fundraising efforts faltered and Pamela had once more to be persuaded to keep going. Clinton felt a particular debt of gratitude, once writing, "A lot of water has flowed since we went together to your first TV interview in 1981—thanks for everything."[21] In early 1989 he threw a $1,500 a head dinner in her honor at L'Enfant Plaza Hotel. A tribute song had been commissioned from the British-born satirical composer Christopher Mason and in unison the crowd sang "Just Wild about Pamela Harriman" with a verse predicting that her "awesome" energy would propel a Democrat into the White House again. "How can I thank you for that wonderful evening of flattery!" she wrote to Clinton afterward. "It was fun & I felt spoilt."[22]

Success meant less without anyone to share it and failure hurt more too. Winston came over to stay from time to time but made himself unpopular with his mother's staff. "He treated me as lower than dirt," Pie Friendly complains.[23] Nor did she think him that close to his mother. "He and Pamela didn't see much of each other. He never stayed long."

Although he sometimes looked uncannily like his mother, Winston saw himself as true-blood Churchill, the bearer of his grandfather's name and the rightful tribune of his legacy. His aunt Mary Soames, the sole survivor of Churchill's children, had her own views. She was appalled by what she saw as Pamela's "hypocrisy" in having annulled her marriage to Randolph just "so she could marry Agnelli, while intending to keep the Churchill moniker right through her life."[24] "There's not a great deal of love lost between Mary and me. Her children are not called Churchill and I'm sure she resents it," Pamela countered territorially. "My child and grandchildren are all Churchills."[25] Mary was the undisputed family matriarch and had made a success of being an ambassador's wife, first in Paris and later Rhodesia (now Zimbabwe), for which in 1980 she had been made a dame. She had also written an award-winning biography of her mother, Clementine, and by contrast with her siblings had led a fulfilling life. But in truth, Mary had not pursued a high-flying political career and in America at least, Pamela was now established as Churchill-in-chief. When it came to the fortieth anniversary of the great man's Iron Curtain speech in 1986, she was invited to give the keynote address in New York and to write a prominent comment piece in the *Washington Post*.[26]

Winston's decision to pen an autobiography, called *Memories and Adventures* and published in 1989, promoted his own Churchill pedigree but opened a painful rift with Pamela. She sent him a grief-stricken letter in which she told him that an outsider reading the book would wonder if he had any "affection or relationship" with her or that she had played any part in bringing him up. "I find this strange & somewhat hurting," she wrote, restraining herself as much as she could. "I have been hit so hard by Brooke's book & various articles by the Duchins and I had assumed that this would not be so in any book you wrote." She was sure his slights had been unintentional but Winston had credited Randolph with parental love she felt had come from her. Packed with fond accounts of his father and grandfather, Pamela found the only description of her was that she was "generous"—a word she began to detest.[27] The book left her bereft. "She's been clobbered for so long," an intimate revealed, "she's given up on anybody ever understanding her point of view."[28]

Pamela nursed a worrying suspicion about Winston's conduct: "I've financed a lot of his life. I suspect that deep down that's quite tough for him." Perhaps this dependence had sparked an unhealthy rivalry and resentment. She gave Winston and his family "really a lot"—now including flats for his children in fashionable London postcodes and spending tens of thousands more on decoration and furnishings. "Obviously if I can do it, there's no harm and anybody would do it," but she wondered if "he must hate . . . the fact it's me giving [them] apartments rather than him."[29] "The only subject we argued about," recalled Carter Brown, "was her indulgence of young Winston. Whatever he wanted in the way of money, he would get. He played his mother like a harp, pushing her buttons and sweet-talking her to death."[30] Pamela was sending Winston money regularly but in early 1988 he put the Alpine ski chalet on the market. "We felt we had to make some economies," he told his mother, having rejected her suggestions he rent it out as it was "much too nice."[31] Winston was not to go without, however, and intended to buy an apartment in the Swiss resort of Klosters (favored by the British royals) before selling the Pie. He was consequently after a bridging loan, but Pamela felt that if he needed more money he should sell other assets she had funded. "I'm terrified he's going to come to me," she confessed, as she was no longer minded—or able—to oblige.[32] The costs of running her own houses, the plane and her work for the Democrats were draining her resources while investments had been hit by the stock market wipeout of 1987. It was a sign of her quiet financial distress that in 1988 she sold her beloved Degas ballerina for $10 million.

She seems to have ruled out selling any further pieces. But the following year Carter Brown, who was consumed with launching a spectacular celebration of the National Gallery's fiftieth anniversary in 1991, persuaded Pamela to make the official pledge of her Van Gogh as its centerpiece (which would at least give her a useful tax break). "I think it very important a work of art of this quality," Pamela announced, "is kept within the United States."³³ The Harrimans thought it more important it was kept within the family and a furious row broke out between Pamela and her stepdaughters, who suspected she had been bamboozled by Carter (although it had always been Averell's wish that she bequeathe it to the gallery). Carter was relieved when the deal was signed as he knew about Pamela's "financial difficulties."³⁴

On trips to London, she no longer stayed at Claridge's but had swapped to the lower-budget (although still luxurious) Stafford Hotel in St. James's. One family source suggested she was overspending her income by more than $1 million a year and dipping deep into capital.³⁵ Winston had long worried about the management of the Harriman estate, especially the trusts set up for his children, and even mentioned his concerns to his mother. Yet, unwilling to challenge Clifford and Rich because they had been handpicked by Averell, Pamela continued to assume that the problems would solve themselves. The *Chicago Tribune* had found her "vague" when asked about the details of her financial affairs.³⁶

She trusted Clifford to supervise the Harriman money even after he resigned in disgrace in 1991 as chair of a holding company that turned out to be owned by Bank of Commerce and Credit International. Clifford claimed he had not known of the BCCI connection when the bank was revealed to be a criminal enterprise funding terrorists and drug barons but Bob Strauss was just one who dropped him like a stone, claiming he had always been "greedy as hell."³⁷ Yet Pamela stood by him. With Jackie Kennedy Onassis, she even lobbied John Kerry, who was chairing a congressional inquiry into BCCI, on behalf of their "good friend."³⁸ Their loyalty was misplaced. Clifford was charged with fraud, conspiracy and taking bribes. The criminal proceedings were eventually laid aside because of his declining health but his reputation as the ultimate safe pair of hands lay in tatters.

When Pamela gave Winston a dark gray horse as a typically

generous birthday present in 1992, even he worried about the cost and canceled the Fortnum & Mason hamper she had also ordered. Further gifts to the National Gallery seemed improbable and after Carter unexpectedly left his job they parted ways. Almost uniquely for Pamela, they did not stay friends. "Basically," Janet Howard thought, "he had been after her paintings."[39]

After a decade at the coalface, Pamela felt unappreciated by the party's men in gray suits despite constant requests for her to do more—if always as a volunteer. Women largely went unrecognized, with still only one female Democrat in the Senate (and one Republican) and not a single women's bathroom in easy reach of the chamber. By the end of 1990, Pamela had had enough, telling the *Washington Post*, "I think I've paid my dues." She disbanded PamPAC, saying she hoped to be called in as a "sharpshooter" if the leadership "want it."[40]

Bush's victory in the Gulf War in February 1991 seemed to make a Democratic White House more distant than ever but Pamela was a rare believer that the cracks in the economy might yet do for him. Passing the seventy mark, she saw the 1992 election as her final chance to help bring a Democrat to victory and "to do something" in the administration before she was "too old."[41] In a post–Cold War era, she recognized that America would need to recast its international role in the face of new threats to peace from the breakup of the Soviet Union and the violent nationalism unleashed in Yugoslavia. From having watched the devastation and turmoil of the postwar years, she knew new world orders bring new world dangers. She wanted to put her experience to good use (and was conscious that other wartime survivors were starting to leave the political stage) but beyond her circle of party admirers she still struggled to be heard.

It was no wonder Pamela was in a hurry. Exhaustion, stress, loneliness and frustration were taking their toll, and her health was beginning to let her down. She underwent tests including a biopsy and what seems to have been an exploratory operation. Her friend and sometime escort Thomas Quinn, a wealthy donor, remonstrated with her that her politics workload was "too much" for her. "Don't let those fellows take advantage of all of your time."[42] It hardly helped that Slim reopened old wounds by publishing a memoir—*Slim: Memories of a Rich and Imperfect Life*—portraying her once again as a power-crazed stepmother, gold digger and man snatcher. Pamela's marriage to Leland continued to cost her dearly. Doctors were worried about her "latent" hypertension—her blood pressure rose with stress, and she had plenty of that—and prescribed Norvasc to reduce the risk of strokes and heart attacks. She was also taking Premarin, an estrogen-only form of hormone replacement therapy (unusual at seventy), suggesting she was possibly suffering from night sweats or even loss of libido.[43]

She dealt with her concerns by returning to skiing. "It is great to see you on the boards again," Winston told her after a holiday together at Sun Valley in 1991, "after a break of at least 35 years!" And she stepped up her campaign for a purposeful foreign policy role. Russian expertise was still highly valued in Washington and she decided to finance two trips with a group of experts led by Robert Legvold from Columbia to see the real-life consequences of the Gorbachev reforms for herself. "She was trying to understand a country and its institutions before they fell apart," Legvold explains.

On the first visit, in May 1991, Pamela went with Judith Kipper, Colette Shulman and Strobe Talbott, who had been a Rhodes scholar with Clinton. While the group stayed in the National Hotel on Red Square with views of the Kremlin, Pamela was keen to meet those living in very different circumstances to hear their hopes but also fears of the chaos that such dramatic change might bring. "I could see how moved Pam was," says Legvold, particularly when talking to young Russians.[44]

Three months later, tanks rolled onto the streets of Moscow when hardliners staged a coup against Gorbachev. Although unsuccessful, it humiliated him and saw Ukraine and Belarus become the latest of twelve Soviet states to declare independence. On Christmas Day, Gorbachev resigned (Pamela immediately sent him and Raisa an invitation to use Mango Bay for a holiday). The first democratically elected leader in Russian history, Boris Yeltsin moved into the Kremlin, where the Soviet hammer and sickle was lowered for the last time, to be replaced by the Russian tricolor introduced by Peter the Great. Pamela had met Yeltsin when he had visited America in 1989 and come under attack from the Communist Party newspaper *Pravda* as a hard-drinking demagogue who embarrassed his country on the international stage. Most undignified, the report continued, was that he had dozed off in front of Pamela. She had given a "motherly smile," according to the dispatch, when Yeltsin's head dropped down on the table between them—although when approached by the *New York Times* Pamela insisted he had been "very much not asleep."[45] Once again, she personally knew the new occupant of the Kremlin even if the country he presided over had dramatically changed.

President Bush hoped that the center of the Soviet Union would hold to avoid "another Yugoslavia but with nuclear weapons" but Pamela saw that a breakup was inevitable. Now she was eager to be one of the first to inspect new states as they declared independence, to explore pressing questions: after Soviet repression was lifted, would they also descend into ethnic violence? Would they join the West or eventually be reabsorbed under Russian control? How should America react to the collapse of the Soviet Union as its only rival superpower, one that had justified so many of its actions at home and overseas? What would happen to the vast Soviet nuclear arsenal and was it in safe hands? And what role should America play in this rapidly changing world?

For the second trip, Richard Holbrooke joined the seventy-two-year-old Pamela and her team on a chartered Tupolev plane as it flew around the different states undergoing potentially explosive transfers of power. At Tashkent, the pilot flew them down onto the tarmac to what looked like a possibly hostile reception. After a nervous wait, he came into the cabin and took a huge rubbish bag full of rubles out of a locker to bribe the Uzbek officials newly in charge of the airport. Pamela seems to have been unperturbed. "She understood the turbulence," Legvold recalls, "of new countries struggling to create or reinvent themselves."

They drove on to the official residence of President Islam Karimov, a leftover from the Soviet era where the party were effectively kept prisoner by armed guards.[46] "Pamela soldiered through it, expressing gratitude," says Legvold. That a meeting with the president later took place was a personal coup. "Karimov didn't put on a show like this for the average American—he even gave gifts. The primary reason he and other similar leaders agreed to these meetings was Pamela."

She had to be rescued in Kiev when a crucial document went missing and the Ukrainian border guards refused to let her leave the country. Fortunately, Holbrooke had retained the visiting card of the feared security service chief and the problem was resolved. In Tblisi, Georgia, where even the most seasoned travelers in the Soviet Union thought the Intourist hotel the dirtiest they had seen, Pamela emerged unruffled in a peach woolen couture suit after sleeping on sheets gray with sweat and taking a stomach-churning filthy shower. "Pamela always kept calm," remembers Kipper, however surreal their visit became. Even when the party visited Zviad Gamsakhurdia, the "rabid" Georgian nationalist, surrounded by guards with automatic weapons "and these really, really scary attack dogs got out. She was really somebody."[47]

By the time they reached Kazakhstan, Pamela had done twelve

days straight of back-to-back meetings. One afternoon, she was scheduled to visit the state university when she developed a severe headache. "She never complained but Dick Holbrooke was insistent she miss this one," Legvold says. The others went in her place, to discover that the university's president, faculty and hundreds of students had all turned out to meet her. Even in a country until recently closed off on the other side of the Iron Curtain, "they knew a lot about . . . this famous personality." Pamela was mortified that she had let people down and, to make amends, established a fellowship for two young Kazakhs to study in America.

While extending opportunities for others, "she was still constantly enhancing her qualifications," Legvold says, for the role she had no intention of giving up even if it killed her.[48] "She and Averell were the most ambitious septuagenarians you'll ever meet," her friend Eizenstat notes. As Clinton also observes with admiration, Pamela "lived as a permanent self-improvement project."[49]

42

In 1989, Pamela stuck her neck out for Ron Brown to become the chairman of the Democratic National Committee, and he won. It was a seminal moment—the first time a black person had been elected to head a major American political party—and her example had persuaded others to rally behind him when a prominent group of Jewish donors refused.[1] Even Clinton, coming from Arkansas, was initially nervous,[2] and the *New York Times* greeted Brown's victory by suggesting that the Democrats' choice of a black man "risked damage" by making whites feel "fearful" and "unwelcome."[3] Appalled, Pamela put her hand on Brown's arm and said, *"I'm* with you." "The Democratic Party wonder gave him her blessing," remembers Melissa Moss, the DNC's finance director. "That was huge and Ron was grateful. He couldn't have done it on his own."[4] "Ron adored Pamela," confirms Brown's campaign manager Rob Stein. "We all did." Despite his Harlem upbringing—spliced with an urbane prep school education—Pamela and Ron recognized in each other a similar sense of purpose. They were seducers, maybe chancers and certainly believers. Both, for different reasons, constantly had to prove themselves to the doubters.

Pamela worked with Brown to strengthen the DNC into a more efficient and aggressive operation through young stars but also by posing difficult and practical questions. "She would arrive at a meeting and ask, 'What are we trying to achieve here? Who are we trying to convince of what? How does that coordinated campaign work?'"

remembers Mark Steitz, Brown's director of communications and research. "These were questions it was useful for me to answer."⁵ Wealthy outsiders coming into politics was nothing new, but Pamela was different. "A lot of people think of campaigns like a Washington miniseries," adds Steitz. "They think, What's Logan Roy [the all-powerful tycoon in *Succession*] going to do in these grand drama terms—where they imagine they have control that nobody has . . . Whereas Pamela was level-headed on the realistic scope of the campaign. That was a surprise."

Over time the Harriman-Brown double act became the first to think a 1992 victory in the White House was a real possibility—but only with a candidate who could command a winning coalition of poor and minority voters with the middle classes. There was no clear frontrunner so Brown asked her if she would host a showcase of presidential contenders for high-level donors at Willow Oaks in June 1991—an Issues Evening cum "PamPAC-DNC summit."⁶ In what became known as the Middleburg Meeting, the idea was to present a strategy to win back the Oval Office the following year and raise the first serious tranche of money to fill up a party machine running on empty. No one else could pull it off—no one else had such social capital to burn. She was a "happy warrior," says Steitz, and she obliged.

On the afternoon of June 13, just after her return from Moscow, Pamela stood up and in her deep, resonant voice welcomed forty guests to the drawing room, where the French windows had been left open to the Minterne-style gardens. Many had been drawn by the glamour of spending time in the bucolic home of a legendary British aristocrat who even now made male knees go weak. "It was a special moment," agrees Melissa Moss. "We deliberately kept it intimate with only people who could play at the highest level. They didn't know it yet but we wanted $250,000 each from them." The big-ticket donors sipping tea from fine china cups were also attracted by the opportunity to rub shoulders with potential runners (including Clinton but also Senators Bob Kerrey and Jay Rockefeller, although not the prevaricating Mario Cuomo). The politicians came because they knew Pamela could make or break their careers and that this was their best chance to recruit backers for a potential campaign. Almost all were skeptical of the chances of victory but understood that this was a gathering of a sort never attempted by either party. "We were at an inflection point," remembers Moss. And there was no Plan B.

Pamela thanked the group sinking into her squishy white linen sofas and reminded them that the stakes could not be higher. Bar the four years under Carter after Watergate, the Democrats had been out of the White House since 1968. Yet she assured them they could win and that Bush's 90 percent approval ratings at the end of Operation Desert Storm (expelling Iraqi forces from Kuwait) would not last. There was a feeling that if she had confidence in the plan, her guests were at least willing to listen.[7] Brown stepped up, dressed exquisitely as always, briefly complimenting each guest in turn. By the time he finished there was a sense of "family in the room." "That was his great talent," says Stein, "to bring people together and make them feel good about themselves. Ron and Pamela had similar personalities."[8]

The strategist Paul Tully sweated heavily as he ran through a series of Harvard Graphics slides (forerunners of PowerPoint) on a precariously balanced projector, detailing where the money was needed in the search for swing voters. Earlier Steitz had set up the equipment on a "perfect" table but Janet had almost "tackled" him to the ground declaring it to be a priceless antique. A perennially disheveled chain-smoker, Tully looked out of place in Pamela's immaculate drawing room but made a compelling case that Bush was beatable if the right Democrat sold the right message to the right voters in the right states.

Pamela intervened to remind the audience, who had watched the Democrats lose five out of the last seven elections, that Clement Attlee had sensationally beaten Churchill in 1945 because voters were shifting away from the war to personal concerns: they had wanted to hear about new homes and health care, not international treaties. It might be "surprising," confirms Steitz, but some of the Democrats' analysis at this point flowed directly "from Churchill."[9] And so American voters of 1992 were similarly expected to refocus from military success to, in this case, falling real wages (the notion that eventually led to the campaign mantra "It's the Economy, Stupid"). Then Bush would be vulnerable. By dinner that evening, when wines from Pamela's vineyard were served, contenders and donors were in ebullient mood, flushed with excitement that victory really was in reach.[10]

Clinton, Brown and Pamela made a formidable trio and their resilience and optimism were infectious. There was a special electricity between them. Eizenstat enjoyed watching Clinton and Pamela walking arm in arm like "a supernova . . . two stars reflecting on each other. It was something to behold."[11] But all three were "joyous figures" who had triumphed over tough times and used their charisma to achieve things. They were "like those life-size Joe Palooka dolls," agrees Peter Fenn. "You punch them and they come right back at you—sometimes harder."[12] Ron's battles with racism as an African American striving to rise through the ranks of U.S. politics were only too obvious. Clinton grew up in the small Arkansas town of Hot Springs, surrounded by gambling dives and coping with an abusive stepfather. Pamela might have been raised in Dorset splendor, "but had seen in the 1940s the profound ugliness and danger of authoritarian war machinery and many of the world's problems in the decades since," explains Stein. "She was a privileged woman but she had a soul."[13]

Over brunch the following day Brown informed the donors that the party needed $3 million to implement Tully's plan to organize big and to organize early—well before the candidate was chosen. When the team asked the donors to donate $250,000 each, several obliged on the spot, handing over checks worth a total of $1.5 million. The same amount flooded in from others shortly afterward, reaching the fundraising goal effectively in one swoop. That was the point, Pamela noted later, when "we topped the Republicans" in fundraising.[14] Many believe that without that timely investment, the GOP would have fought their way to another victory. And yet there was one giant piece missing: a candidate. Clinton dazzled some but continued to annoy others with his "aw shucks country-boy self."[15]

Reporters had got word that an important event was taking place and gathered at the foot of a hill just down from the house. Brown and Pamela went to meet them, confirming that there had been a significant meeting but refusing to be drawn further. In its first edition, the *New York Times* ran a photograph of Pamela flanked by four presidential contenders; the men were all named, while she was tagged "unidentified." By the second edition that had been corrected. Febrile talk of a "secret strategy" rattled President Bush back at the White House. He lashed out at "frantic Democrats" who "all go down to Pamela Harriman's farm," which he mockingly described as the new "bastion of democracy." The fact he chose to attack Pamela—rather than Brown or the candidates—was seen as ultimate proof of her pivotal role in reviving her party.[16]

Clinton sent Pamela a fulsome letter of thanks. She too had been impressed by his performance but hesitated to commit to someone whose peccadillos might destroy him at any moment. She had gone off Al Gore as a presidential candidate ("hasn't grown in four years, can't connect with people"[17]) but had high hopes for Jay Rockefeller, who as great-grandson of the oil tycoon John Rockefeller hailed from her own social circles. When he pulled out two months later—with the rather lame excuse of a lack of time to prepare for government—she fell into a "deep depression" about his "spinelessness" and after "eleven years in the field" she felt she "wanted to take a pass."[18] Yet the contenders continued to jostle for her support, with Bob Kerrey ringing to tell her he was announcing for president and asking, "What do I do next?"[19] She knew Clinton was the best but despaired that he still did not even have a campaign manager—phoning her twice in one day for advice on who to hire—and mistakenly, in her opinion, wanted to run the show from Little Rock. "He keeps asking what is my reluctance," she said privately. "I don't know why he doesn't understand."[20] Already, there were rumors of a string of affairs and whether they were true or not they were only going to get worse. While she dithered, so did he. Where were the candidates, asked the *Washington Post*, of "commitment, audacity and imagination"?

Clinton formally entered the race in October 1991 but as Hillary knew, "the mainstream media didn't give Bill much hope of making it through the primaries, let alone being elected president."[21] While still nursing her fears, Pamela arranged N Street dinner parties for him to be tried out by key Washington figures such as James Woolsey, a senior arms control negotiator for both Democratic and Republican presidents, who came away "impressed." She had given Clinton a $1,000 donation and eventually threw her full weight behind him, saying he was the best and most likable candidate for the job. Her declaration was "timely enough to be persuasive with others," remembers Melanne Verveer, a close aide. "For him it was a big deal—a lot of people until then were saying that there was no way this guy from Arkansas can do it."[22] "Whether she believed in me or not," says Clinton, "she sure convinced everyone else that she did."[23] As well as filling the election coffers, he thought her greatest contribution was giving him that mainstream "credibility" not only with Democrats in Washington but "people all over America."[24] Clinton was grateful for her spreading the word that he was far more than just some small-state governor. Pamela had decided to make him, in the words of Carter Brown, her "last great political project."

Three months later, a supermarket tabloid ran a story on an Arkansas woman called Gennifer Flowers, who claimed to have been Clinton's lover for twelve years. The common wisdom was that that was probably the "end of Bill" and that at best the campaign would be a dry run for the elections in 1996. Yet Clinton was not judged like others and many warmed to him out of sympathy, particularly after Hillary agreed to give an intimate TV interview at his side on *60 Minutes*. Clinton's affability and Hillary's forbearance beguiled the audience. The Comeback Kid's flaws became part of his appeal. "I had already said I hadn't lived a perfect life," Clinton said later. "If that was the standard, someone else would have to be elected president."[25] At seventy-one, Pamela could not wait another four years, but was in a constant state of alarm in case "another shoe falls."[26] Still, Clinton seemed to be back on track although many party elders were disgruntled by the emphasis on youth in his team. Pamela was old enough to be Clinton's mother—and even a grandmother to many of his staff.

Pamela claimed she had not suggested Al Gore as Clinton's running mate—"You mustn't ask that question," she said teasingly to the *Washington Post*[27]—but she certainly knew about his appointment weeks before others.[28] When Clinton won the nomination at the party convention in New York in July 1992 she called for the party to unite behind someone whose charisma, pragmatism and intellect gave him "the best chance since Robert F. Kennedy of rebuilding a coalition that rallies both white and black voters" and of meeting the "problems of the post–Cold War world." And then several more shoes fell with suggestions that Clinton had dodged the Vietnam draft, engaged in antiwar activities at Oxford and smoked marijuana (even if he did not inhale). Even his close aide and fellow Rhodes scholar George Stephanopoulos asked him whether it was time to withdraw. Pamela's choice was not going to make her life easy but what she "liked most about Clinton was that she saw a lot of herself in him," noted Joe Klein, author of *Primary Colors*. Both were masters of reinvention, while Pamela also compared Clinton's "resilience and inner strength to the determination" she had witnessed in her father-in-law. "Clinton may not be Winston Churchill yet," wrote *New York* magazine, "but give her a chance" to make him so.[29]

Pamela threw her last major fundraiser, the Day in the Country for Clinton, at Willow Oaks on September 13, 1992, hoping to raise $1 million. Seven hundred donors were expected, requiring fifteen full-time staff led by Janet working through the night. Such was the demand for tickets, Janet collapsed with tremors in her right arm and Melissa Moss had to take over. By the time Janet returned from the hospital with her arm in a sling, twelve hundred people were on the list. On the day itself—pleasantly cool and autumnal—more than 150 elite donors pledging at least $10,000 sat down to lunch at the nearby Red Fox Inn. They alone donated $1.7 million. Wearing a black and white dress and diamonds, Pamela had them for early evening cocktails at the house with Clinton and Gore but some of her guests thought she looked a little distrait. It turned out that vast queues of people had formed outside the gates and as far down the lane as the eye could see, huge convoys of cars banked up against the hedgerows. More people than anyone had imagined (over thirteen hundred) had turned up for dinner in a marquee on the lawn. The prospect of mingling with Clinton, Gore and Pamela—and the whiff of impending victory—was too heady to resist. Tempers had started to fray as the caterers searched for extra food. Staff were dispatched in a desperate hunt for more tables and chairs. Seating plans were redone and then abandoned. A false calm reigned in the drawing room but outside there were scenes of near chaos and Pamela began to fear her reputation for flawless organization was about to be trashed—and her chances of a job with Clinton's administration with it. She also knew that Barbra Streisand was hosting a fundraiser a few days later and was horrified in case hers was overshadowed.

"The Middleburg Event was overwhelming," remembers Moss. "Janet had a picture of a beach on her desk. When things got too crazy she would say, 'Let's pretend we're on that beach for a moment.' But that also meant success."³⁰ The event raised $2.2 million at a time when the Republicans were struggling to drum up the dollars. With seven weeks to go Bush was also failing to narrow Clinton's lead in the polls. A fortnight later Pamela was finally rewarded with a title: national cochair of the Clinton-Gore campaign. "Everyone," national chairman Mickey Kantor wrote to her, "is honored to have you working so closely with us."³¹

Pamela hardly dared believe the polls leading up to the elections on November 3. On the day itself, she flew to Little Rock to watch the results with the Gores. When they saw Clinton had won Kentucky—a stunning upset for the Republicans—the euphoria of victory began to sink in. At 43 percent, Clinton's was the lowest popular vote for a winning candidate since Woodrow Wilson eighty years earlier—in part because a third candidate, the independent Ross Perot, had taken a slice of the vote—but it was still a clear win.

Clinton came to believe that if he had not been defeated in Arkansas in 1980, he would "probably never" have entered the White House. "It was a near-death experience but an invaluable one," he said, "forcing me to be more sensitive to the political problems inherent in progressive politics."³² It was "almost as if," noted the *Los Angeles Times*, Pamela's philosophy of needing to learn from failure had "rubbed off on the 42nd president of the United States."³³ Other tributes poured in from those who knew how hard she had worked. Her efforts had led to the "direction that Clinton took the party," Eizenstat responds to those claiming Pamela had raised money but was devoid of political thinking. "I can't emphasize how important she was in moving the party to the center: a tougher defense policy, the focus on the middle class, the self-examination of where and why we'd gone wrong." If Bill and Hillary Clinton were now the Democratic king and queen, he would call Pamela the "queen mother."³⁴ The best Winston could do was tell his mother that he hoped her reward was more than a "fat tax increase" and that at least Clinton had attended the "right university—the first Oxford man in the White House."[35] Pamela informed the *Post* her son had once guffawed at the idea of her as a politician. "He laughs less about it now."[36]

The next day, Pamela flew back to Washington wearing dazzling green crocodile shoes for a low-carb lunch in the N Street sun lounge with Artemis Cooper, granddaughter of Diana and Duff. While they chatted the phones rang constantly and coffee in the library was interrupted by the butler. "It's Mrs. Gore on line thirty, madam," he said. "Oh, Tipper, isn't it wonderful!" Cooper heard her cry down the line. "Everybody you've ever known and ever disliked is looking for a job!" Pamela asked her what she could do to help, and Cooper heard Pamela give advice on recruiting teams for her and her husband. "But what you've really got to do is talk to Janet," she said. "She knows where all the bodies are buried, and she'll do everything for you." Pamela put down the phone, but then picked it up again and asked, "Janet, did you get all that?"[37]

Two weeks later, blue-and-white squad cars blocked off N Street to traffic. Throngs of spectators were corralled behind yellow police tape, their breath hanging in the crisp night air. Viewed from inside 3038, black Secret Service wagons stood in silhouette against the lights of the TV crews opposite. Filling the hallway and library were the Gores and a hundred hand-selected lawmakers, activists and off-duty media stars whose excited hubbub quieted as the blare of sirens drew closer. Just before eight, an agent in a trench coat with one hand pressed to his ear turned to the butler Clive to warn "One minute!" Clive passed it on to his boss hovering near the entrance. At the signal sixty seconds later, Pamela's front door swung inward in perfect unison with the armored limousine drawing up outside. Dressed in Manolo Blahniks and her beloved sequins, Pamela stepped out into the volley of flash bulbs, shouts from the journalists and applause from the crowd. Hillary and Bill Clinton turned and waved before climbing the couple of steps to their beaming host. "Hi Pamela," Clinton said, embracing her. "Hello Mr. President," she replied in triumph, "and welcome. I am so glad you could come this evening." Splashed across news bulletins and the next day's front pages it was a scene out of a Hollywood blockbuster. Pamela could hardly have wished for better recognition.

Inside, the president-elect raised a champagne glass and with a further dramatic flourish, "To Pamela," he grinned. "The First Lady of the Democratic Party." Pamela clasped Clinton's hand and steered her "pink-faced and smiling" trophy through the crowd in view of her Georgetown rivals. So many had "clawed and scratched" for an invitation that three days earlier Pamela had had to arrange for a tent with space heaters to be erected on her terrace to accommodate the extras. Asked later why her gathering had triggered such an overwhelming response, Pamela replied that she assumed it was because "twelve years has been a long time in the wilderness, and the joy and the hope and the feeling we have now does excite people."

Fueled by delicious chicken in puff pastry, guests looked around them to see who else had made the grade that night. Those schmoozing under the Van Gogh hoped the party signaled a rosy future and there was wild speculation as to which jobs they were destined to win. The chosen felt they were part of a new chapter in America's history—helped by a then still unusual smattering of black faces including Ron Brown and transition chief Vernon Jordan but also Jesse Jackson, Congresswoman Maxine Waters and Washington mayor Sharon Pratt Kelly. (Pamela had always hoped that Ron Brown's election would bring more people of color into the highest level of politics or "out of the woodwork," as she put it.[38]) In another corner, Joe Biden could be heard trying to recruit the newly elected Senator Dianne

Feinstein—California's first female senator—to join the hitherto all-male Judiciary Committee.[39]

Of equal interest was who was absent, such as Clark Clifford. He continued to plead his innocence but was now a "tarnished prince"[40] and Pamela could not countenance him near the new president. Others who had hoped but failed to get the call had left town to avoid humiliation. Some of them claimed that it was the smaller Vernon Jordan gathering the previous evening that had been the real power hub, not Pamela's showier extravaganza. Those lucky enough to attend were effusive, however. "WOW. Thank you for one of the greatest nights of a guy's life," Kay Graham's son Donald, president of the *Washington Post*, wrote to her afterward. He had sensed "deep gratitude and love from so many to you, as the person who started them on their way or extended a hand when a politician was down."[41]

Kay also attended Pamela's event and declared that Clinton would not have been elected without her.[42] But the *Washington Post* quoted an unnamed "non-invitee" describing it as the "The Night of the Living Dead," a party full of "pooh-bas" soon to be put out to pasture and resembling the waxworks at Madame Tussaud's.[43] Pamela began to worry. Clinton's election heralded the shift from her generation to baby boomers born in the late 1940s and 50s. At the age of seventy-two, was she too old for Clinton's fresh-faced team working twenty-hour days as they transitioned into government? Was the N Street supper the start of something exciting or a fancy farewell? Clinton sent her a handwritten note thanking her for the "wonderful" evening and declaring "we're off to a good start after twelve years of preparation."[44] He and Hillary flew back to the governor's mansion in Little Rock, where they summoned many of Pamela's closest political allies, including Berger and Holbrooke, to offer high-flying positions in the new administration. James Woolsey, whom she had got together with Clinton at N Street back in September 1991, took on the CIA. On Pamela's future, the weeks passed in silence.

Pamela took up the "power seat" on the richly upholstered banquettes of the Jockey Club, a Washington establishment rekindling the fashionable glow it had last enjoyed in the days of Camelot. In the lead-up to Christmas 1992, she held court here looking, according to one of many prominent newspaper profiles, "the very model of a modern Democrat and a very important one at that."[45] On her right breast she sported a gold saxophone pin sent her by the jeweler Kenneth Jay Lane with the note "You really should be able to blow your own horn."[46] Others had taken to wearing a similar brooch to denote their status as a FOB (Friend of Bill) but Pamela's was the first and the biggest.

Yet she remained without a job, despite making her wishes clear to Clinton directly and also through Berger. She still hoped to become an ambassador, she had told her confidant Robert Shrum on a walk through the Middleburg woods that Thanksgiving.[47] Not to London but to France, where her old sexual adventures might be appreciated rather than providing fodder for the tabloids. In the meantime, she had to affect public indifference, knowing that betraying either overconfidence or impatience could be fatal. "I certainly don't want to leave Washington," was her stock response when asked. "I haven't waited to get a president elected for twelve years to then leave."[48]

Word of Pamela's role in Clinton's triumph had traveled the globe. The call from South Africa came out of the blue on January 9, 1993. Would Pamela speak to Nelson Mandela? South Africa was going through momentous change as it abandoned apartheid rule. Mandela had been out of prison since 1990 after serving twenty-seven years for conspiring to overthrow the state and was a revered international figure—in 1993 he would win the Nobel Peace Prize with the reforming white leader F. W. de Klerk. As president of the African National Congress, he was preparing for the first elections under the country's new constitution that would give all races the vote for the first time, and which would be held the following year. Clinton had invited Mandela to the inauguration celebrations in Washington and he would "very much like" to meet Pamela during his visit to discuss the problems of "getting his people to the polls" when the old white National Party had the infrastructure, money and experience he lacked. Without funds and advice from outside, he believed the ANC might be on course to lose.[49] Nine days later they spoke in person for the first time at an inauguration dinner. The next morning—the day of the inauguration ceremony—Mandela called her at 8:30 to request a formal meeting. Pamela invited him for lunch at N Street that Friday and despite the obvious distractions was able to enlist the help of Peter Tarnoff, the undersecretary designate at the State Department, and the ever-willing Berger to draw together within hours a small group of people she hoped would be "useful contacts."

Pamela once again came to her famous front door to greet Mandela, who cut a regal figure in his multicolored batik shirt. She showed him around the art collection—he was most taken by the depictions of ostriches—before the group sat down to talk in her dining room. "Mr. Mandela seemed very pleased," Pamela noted afterward, "and felt there would be support coming to him from this meeting." There followed several further conversations and when they met again, Mandela (by then voted in as the first black president of South Africa) gave her a token of his appreciation: a lithograph of a fast-moving and elegant ostrich.

By the time of his inauguration, Clinton had made hundreds of high-profile appointments including Secretary of State and the national security team. Pamela's critics crowed that she had been sidelined—perhaps the president-elect did not want to be associated with too much glitz. Perhaps she could not fit into his plans for the most diverse administration in history. "There was some nervousness that she had fallen out of favor," confirms Melanne Verveer. "Nothing was said for quite some time."[50]

43

In a male-dominated press pack in supermacho Washington, the notion of hostilities between Hillary and Pamela prompted feverish speculation. Here were two ambitious and powerful women counseling an inexperienced incoming president, surely leading to friction behind the throne. Pamela's past and Clinton's wandering eye made it all even more plausible and rumors began to swirl that Hillary was trying to shut Pamela out from her husband.[1] "There was speculation about that all the time," recalls Verveer. "The two women thing in his life was more fabricated than real . . . I never saw any sign of jealousy."[2]

Pamela had nonetheless taken some time to warm to Hillary. Sensitive about her own lack of formal schooling, she felt outclassed by Hillary's intellectual confidence garnered at top-flight Wellesley College and Yale Law School. Hillary did not share Pamela's flair for fashion and interior aesthetics or her success as a seductress—indeed, the new First Lady's Methodist beliefs and somewhat severe reputation had once earned her the nickname of "Sister Frigidaire."[3] If Hillary was a proud feminist—dubbed "feminazi" by early Republican culture warriors—then Pamela was still sometimes equivocal about the cause. And yet Pamela had come to admire Hillary and recognize how, far from her intellect and strength undermining her husband as the critics claimed, they were key to his success. By different routes, they had climbed to the top of the ultimate boys' club through self-discipline and hard work. They respected each other for it. As *New*

York magazine observed in January 1993, the pair were remarkably alike in that neither played "by ordinary rules."⁴ Pamela sensed it was best to work on both Clintons, writing to Hillary in the New Year, "93 is going to be a turning point in History thanks to Bill & you."⁵

Winston might not have cared to write about his mother but elsewhere there was ever more interest in her life. "A book on Pamela, regardless of how wonderfully it's crafted," decreed *New York* magazine, "would still be high gutter."⁶ Comments such as these, combined with the Fairlie saga, had convinced Pamela that she urgently needed to shape her narrative, so she cast around for a writer to help her produce a serious assessment of her achievements. She settled on the *Time* journalist and Yale man Christopher Ogden who had published an admiring biography of Margaret Thatcher. Pamela considered Thatcher the "outstanding woman of this century"⁷ and a figure who had outshone her male counterparts—as she had written to the former prime minster to tell her.* A stream of other writers who approached Pamela— even Doris Kearns Goodwin, who had written on the Kennedys—were given the brush-off. In September 1991 Pamela had negotiated a contract with Random House for a then huge $1.65 million,⁸ for a "neither coy nor salacious" biography that would track how Pamela had become "one of America's most influential citizens."⁹ Pamela orally agreed generous terms with Ogden, including paying him half the advance and picking up half his expenses. The literary agent negotiating the deals, Morton Janklow, told Ogden that with worldwide rights he could expect to make a million dollars.¹⁰

Ogden taped fifty hours of interviews and was given a key to N Street so he could come and go as he pleased. The deal was that Pamela would speak freely—although she insisted that nothing must be said

---

* Thatcher responded a week later: "The admiration is mutual. You have done wonders for Britain as well as America."

about her relationship with Jock Whitney as his wife was still alive—and they would decide what to use later. In New York, Random House publisher Harold Evans could scarcely contain his excitement about a book detailing the life of a fabled courtesan. When news broke that Sally Bedell Smith, another prominent author, had embarked on a rival, unauthorized biography, it became even clearer what Random House expected in return for its "awesome" advance. (Janet, meanwhile, found Bedell Smith in the sun porch at an N Street party and threw her out.[11]) Pamela had previously been relaxed with those she trusted about talking about her sex life but now feared her hopes of high office could end up trashed by tales of her libidinous past. "People didn't want to know about a little freckled Britisher," said Peter Duchin. "They wanted to read about the size of Aly Khan's member."[12]

Pamela had not signed the contract (perhaps she had never entirely quelled her doubts about the project) and in a panic she asked Ogden to return the tapes. He refused—he had already invested months in the book, resigned from his job at *Time* and on the back of the promise of a substantial cash sum was looking at buying a bigger house. As usual in a crisis, she reached for someone reassuringly expensive—this time Theodore Sorensen, the lawyer Jack Kennedy had called his "intellectual blood bank." Yet a summit in October between Sorensen, Evans and Ogden at the Knickerbocker Club in New York failed to reach agreement on the style and content of the book. Pamela returned her copy of the contract unsigned and retreated to Barbados before summoning Ogden to her study on her return to N Street in December. "Have you brought the tapes back?" Pamela demanded, stating they were hers. Ogden replied that the tapes belonged to them both and he was effectively keeping them hostage until they agreed terms and he had been paid $305,000 for work done to date. The mood soured. Pamela declared his stance "ridiculous," warning she would turn the dispute over to her lawyers. "This story is out on the street and it will be very ugly," he warned as he walked out, and he would write a book without her.[13]

Pamela had been naïve and now she was cornered. Two books were being written about her out of her control and her blood pressure was soaring.[14] Ogden appealed for another meeting to try to come to a fair settlement by themselves but Sorensen advised her to take a hard line: "Winston Churchill's daughter-in-law should never submit to blackmail!"[15] A team of three partners and several associate lawyers threatened Ogden with an expensive legal battle. Eventually he backed down, agreeing not to press his claim for the $305,000, to surrender the tapes, transcripts, notebooks and diaries and not to quote from them. He could, however, use certain background information subject to her agreement and there was nothing that could stop him writing an unauthorized book. Pamela recognized that it was unlikely to be flattering. "We don't have a friend out there," she wrote regretfully to Sorensen.[16]

She continued to entertain the idea of writing her own biography but her sister Sheila strongly advised Pamela to "keep quiet." Nothing could stop "that woman"—Sally Bedell Smith—writing "what is better left unsaid" but it would be "better for you and the family if you didn't write a book [as well]!"[17] Perhaps it was meeting Jacquetta at a wedding in March 1992 that finally changed Pamela's mind. She had not seen her youngest sister for so long that she failed to recognize the plump white-haired figure in tweeds and sensible shoes. Although Jacquetta was eight years her junior, as a quietly spoken widow with six children struggling to keep a tourism business afloat on the Isle of Mull, she looked some fifteen years older.[18] Pamela drew back from adding further stress to her sister's life.

Sorensen said he "regretted" the high cost of legal services when he sent Pamela his bill in June 1992, but no one could have predicted the twists and turns over eight months of this "unfortunate imbroglio." He hoped she would find it reasonable as it was, he claimed, less than the cost of litigation. The amount is not detailed in her papers but was said to be $3 million,[19] ten times the amount Ogden was asking for. Absorbed by her duties with the Democrats, perhaps Pamela had not realized how fast the meter was ticking. Maybe Sorensen presumed such an amount could hardly bother the widow of Averell Harriman. How wrong he was. And there were more bills to come, until the final amicable agreement with Ogden was reached in 1993. That moment would almost certainly have come earlier—and cheaper—if Pamela had not brought in big-name lawyers but dealt with Ogden herself. By February 1993, she had sold Mango Bay for a reputed $3 million and laid off the staff, writing in the green leather-bound visitors' book in classic unsentimental style "everything in life must end . . . no regrets." She also put her plane on the market for $1 million. She needed the cash.

44

President Clinton came out all guns blazing in March 1993 when he finally appointed Pamela as ambassador to France. Those involved with the Democratic Party, he said, were already "familiar with Mrs. Harriman's talent for diplomacy." Two of the "many qualifications" she brought to the job were "years of dedicated service" to America and "unceasing devotion to the cause of world peace." The fact was, though, as Pamela was painfully aware, she had no *formal* qualifications at all. The president listed her eleven board appointments and stated that she had "attended Downham School, England, and performed postgraduate work at the Sorbonne" (which sounded considerably more impressive than the reality). The only degree to her name was an honorary doctorate of law from Columbia University, where she was of course a major donor.

The backlash was instant. Ross Perot, who had waged an antiestablishment campaign during the election, denounced her appointment as embodying "what's wrong with the system." She was "deficient as a scholar, diplomat and public official," ran one newspaper article that described her selection as a "bad joke."[1] Ultraconservative senator Strom Thurmond from South Carolina, a supporter of segregation, thundered about her past life with, "They're sending the Whore of Babylon to Paris!"[2] Ted Sorensen's view had long since been "let he who has not sinned cast the first stone"[3]—but the stakes could not have been higher. Pamela had had to wait until her seventy-third birthday for real recognition and her first proper job and could barely sleep with wanting not to mess it up now. (She was even reticent on her official health statement to the State Department, not admitting to having had at least one abortion, perhaps fearing the consequences.[4]) "I don't have to defend her record or appointment," the president declared at a press conference. "She will succeed."[5]

Pamela's instincts about London (which were shared by Clinton) were confirmed when the *Daily Mail* attacked her for having "no diplomatic experience," sneering that it was "late in the day" to start an important career. The paper sought to inflame ancient sensitivities—thereby undermining Pamela's standing—by questioning whether the French could trust her. As an English-born aristocrat and former daughter-in-law of Winston Churchill, surely she would be too British to be able to represent American interests.[6] The idea took hold in certain quarters, the American actress Gayle Hunnicutt buttonholing Pamela at a funeral demanding to know "How can you be American ambassador when you're English?"[7] Rarely did she confess to self-doubt but in a letter to Jackie Onassis, Pamela wrote: "I hope I can handle it."[8] Jacquetta thought her sister "quite mad" to take on such a big job but wished her "all the luck in the world." "I am too old for my liking," Pamela replied. "But what can I do?"[9]

As *Time* magazine noted, she "spared nothing" in her studies of foreign affairs, aware that her predecessor Walter Curley had previously been ambassador to Ireland and had also graduated from Harvard and Yale.[10] Pamela took the course for new envoys and continued her studies at Willow Oaks at the weekend on such esoteric subjects as corn gluten quotas and copyright violation. She also set up extra seminars with experts from Harvard and on trade and economic issues at New

York University with Boris Johnson's cerebral stepfather Nicholas Wahl, whom she pummeled with such questions as "Who in the present French government will be friends?"[11]

Clinton is adamant that, although her appointment was in part in thanks for her support, he considered her the "best person in the country to do that job."[12] The prominent French newspaper *Le Figaro* seemed to agree, hailing Pamela on its front page as the "most powerful kingmaker" and "legend on both sides of the Atlantic."[13] Yet no one was in any doubt that Franco-American relations were prickly—indeed, there had been precious little warmth since President Kennedy had famously taken Jackie to Paris to a euphoric reception in 1961. Washington rarely understood the thinking in France and was often dismissive of it in a fashion unthinkable with Germany or Britain.[14] In the age of phones and faxes, American ambassadors were not unfamiliar with being cut out of the direct loop between leaders but Pamela saw how someone on the ground could do more at a time of global flux to reset the Franco-American relationship and foster mutual understanding. Wahl came away from their sessions impressed with her "inborn intuition about power and what's on people's agenda."[15] Pamela also quizzed Curley on how much she would need to spend personally to run the embassy.[16] Under the American system, political appointees are expected to meet many of the costs of their posting themselves, including entertaining. His answer was alarming—the Fourth of July party alone generally cost an entire year's State Department allowance and certain former ambassadors had left Paris practically ruined.

The Senate Foreign Relations Committee had to approve her nomination and the usual suspects expected Pamela to fail under a barrage of technical questions. *New York* magazine even suggested that French politicians had lobbied Joe Biden, one of its members, against her.[17] It was unusual for there to be much interest in such a hearing but Pamela had just been proclaimed one of *People* magazine's

"Fifty Most Beautiful Women in the World," the only seventy-something on the list. And shortly afterward Barbra Streisand had slid into the seat next to her at the White House Correspondents' Dinner to ask her what many women wanted to know: "What *is* your secret?"[18]

A crush of TV cameras, photographers, journalists and socialite spectators in sunglasses poured into Committee Room 419 at the Dirksen Senate Office Building and Pamela's slot was brought forward by seventeen minutes to limit the chaos. She entered wearing a tailored green suit and a gold eagle brooch on her right breast, flanked by Janet carrying her briefcase and Peter Swiers and Wendy Sherman of the State Department. Together they had prepared "murder board" answers to every conceivable hostile question in the knowledge that two of Pamela's deadliest foes were members of the committee. Pamela looked nervous as she scanned the room. To her relief, she saw that Daniel Patrick Moynihan was not present, though Republican Jesse Helms—whom she had repeatedly tried to dislodge in North Carolina—was.

The first moments were promising. Senator Charles Robb—with whom she had crossed swords the previous year over Clarence Thomas—greeted her with a kiss and Biden, who was chairing that day, opened with "Madam Ambassador, how are ya? It will be a piece of cake." As Pamela surveyed all the Democratic senators she had funded, she gave a four-minute opening statement outlining her membership of policy organizations, and her speeches, articles and meetings with foreign leaders. When she finished, she beamed with relief. Rather than question her on policy detail, senator after senator poured praise on her—"she will do a superb job" said Paul Simon of Illinois, whose reelection campaign had received $6,000 in 1989 from Pamela and her PAC.[19] Paul Sarbanes, whom she had helped in 1981 with the fight-back ads, declared Pamela brought "serious qualifications to the post." After throwing her a few easy questions about

French politics, Biden declared himself unable to think of a "better-suited" nominee.[20]

When it came to Helms's turn to speak, Pamela stiffened. He had blocked nominations of ambassadors he thought too liberal before—earning him the nickname Senator No—and could do so again. Helms suggested she had been nominated because of her fundraising. "Yes senator, I think that was part of it. I do not think it was the whole."[21] The Republican then made great play of reading out the long list of Democratic senators she had supported over recent years. It was a dangerous moment, but one prominent name was not mentioned. "Where's Biden?" the future president piped up, with mock dismay. "I'll have to reconsider my position here!" "You didn't ask, Senator," Pamela came back with a playful chuckle (although he had asked, but not since 1989). Helms, a man capable of Southern courtliness, thereafter seemed to soften. He declared Winston Churchill to be his hero and—finally—that he too thought she would do a "good job." A few days later the floor of the Senate endorsed Pamela with a unanimous vote, Republican leader Bob Dole declaring himself a "longtime admirer."[22]

That night Pamela attended one of a string of farewell parties in her honor, hosted by Sandy Berger at a basement Mexican restaurant. Treasury Secretary Lloyd Bentsen gave a rhapsodic toast recognizing that "no one on this globe has seen war and peace" as she had and describing her as a woman of remarkable fundraising abilities. "There have been days at Treasury when I've gotten so tired of figuring out how to reduce the deficit," he joked, "I wanted to call Pamela to ask 'Could you get your friends to write a check?'"[23] Afterward she climbed up the steps to street level when suddenly "her legs melted under her." Frank Wisner, now Under Secretary of Defense, rushed her in his official car to George Washington Hospital where she was treated overnight for exhaustion. Pamela made light of the episode ("she did not want to display any infirmity," according to Wisner[24]) and with less than three weeks to go before her departure, resumed her normal frantic pace. "If I'd had time to think about it in depth," she confessed, "I'd have probably been too scared to take the post."[25]

Five hundred guests assembled under the eight chandeliers of the Benjamin Franklin Room at the State Department to witness Pamela's swearing-in ceremony, prompting vice president Al Gore to joke about the crush. "To paraphrase Voltaire," Gore told them, "if Pamela Harriman did not exist, we would have had to invent her." Joining him at the lectern, Pamela was thrilled that the family was out in force—various Harrimans as well as Winston—to witness her triumph. "I have had a blessed and wonderful life but this is a singular moment," Pamela told them, "one I never expected." "Now my home in Paris will be your home too. Please come—but not all at once!"

There were plenty more parties thrown for her, including one by Kay Graham for old-timers struggling to make inroads into the younger Clinton crowd. Sir Robin Renwick threw an event for 120 in the Lutyens ballroom at the British Embassy, where she had been a regular visitor and now appeared in a bright red cocktail dress. Sir Robin was impressed by how many senators came. "They only turn out for something special."[26] Renwick knew how special Pamela was—and how powerful she had become through her connections to the Oval Office. In fact, he had already secretly sought her help with Clinton after it had emerged that the Home Office had complied with President Bush's request to look into his activities as a student at Oxford, including whether he had sought British citizenship to avoid the draft. The inquiries drew a blank but when the story broke that the British government had helped Clinton's opponent in this way, prime minister John Major feared that the Special Relationship might have been irreparably harmed. Renwick had sent Pamela a copy of a confidential letter on the subject from Major to the president marked "for your strictly personal information"[27] in the fervent hope that she, if anyone, could help reestablish trust with the Oval Office. Pamela was needed back in the center of events where she belonged.

Clinton had told her that there was "no doubt" in his mind that he would not have been "fully prepared to stand before America and the world" as president had it not been for her support. "I will never forget all you did," he wrote.[28] He and Hillary marked their appreciation with a private dinner in her honor at the White House. Twenty-eight friends including the Gores, Vernon and Ann Jordan, the Bergers, Tom Foley and George Mitchell gathered in the Blue Room for cocktails, with a pianist playing in the corner, but in tune with the more informal Clinton era, they were asked to wear business dress rather than black tie.

It had been a rocky time for the president and the Clintons arrived a little late. That week alone he had made the headlines for supposedly delaying traffic at Los Angeles airport while receiving a $200 haircut on Air Force One. Staff in the White House travel office had also been fired and then reinstated, raising questions over the judgment of inexperienced Clinton staff. Hillary's biographer Carl Bernstein described this early period in the administration as "resembling a car barreling downhill with failing brakes" and in need of seasoned old hands capable of "preventing a fatal wreck."[29] Pamela had already been urged not to leave for Paris as "Clinton's in enough trouble: he shouldn't be letting his wisest adviser stray that far away."[30]

By the time Pamela emerged immaculate from the overnight plane at Charles de Gaulle airport early on Thursday, May 27, 1993, Paris was in ecstasies about its new American ambassador. "We love glamorous people," exclaimed one French government official. "And her past, well, for us it's a sign of vitality!"[31] Comparing her to a cross between Lady Hamilton and Moll Flanders, *Paris Match* hailed her as "one of the most subtle seductresses of the century" who had "turned the scandal of her past into an ornament."

Pamela already knew her distinguished deputy chief of mission

Avis Bohlen (her father, Chip, had been Kennedy's ambassador to France and Averell's deputy in Moscow) who ushered her into the airport's *salon d'honneur* to meet her private secretary and security detail of three. It was surely reason for celebration that the two women formed the first all-female team to head a Class One American embassy yet it seems Pamela felt otherwise. Pamela had known Avis since she was a child and had lent Hobe Sound to her mother as a retreat for six weeks when she was widowed. The *Washington Post* claimed, however, that she had objected to a female second-in-command, preferring a man. Pamela had immediately phoned Avis to reassure her that was not the case—but Janet thought that there had been "some truth" in the story. Either way, it meant Pamela had no choice but to accept Avis, although the piece had inevitably raised questions about how they would meld as a team. "I was on tenterhooks because she didn't have a reputation of liking other women," Avis says, "although I remembered how kind she had been to my mother . . . [and] it was nice of her to call me."[32]

In the event, both were a revelation to each other and Janet—whom Pamela had brought with her—believed that Avis's finesse finally convinced her boss that women could perform the most serious jobs as well if not better than men. "It was an embassy of women," Avis remarks. "The head of the economic section and the head of the consular section were women too. It was luck of the draw."[33] "I had no idea before how really good these people are," Pamela gushed to an interviewer from *Vogue*.[34] She had found out the hard way that big-name men were not always what they were cracked up to be.

The low-slung official limousine, a small Stars and Stripes fluttering atop its radiator, swept through the stone archway at 41 rue du Faubourg St. Honoré into the large courtyard outside the ambassadorial residence called Hôtel de Pontalba. Pamela climbed the steps into the marbled hallway with its bubbling fountain flanked by the American and State Department flags and no doubt allowed herself a moment to reflect how life came around in circles. She had never married her Rothschild lover back in the 1950s or presided over his mansions and was shunned by much of his family. Yet here she was now, taking possession of a sixty-thousand-square-foot early-nineteenth-century palace (with a ballroom decorated with saucy depictions of cupids) that had until the war been a Rothschild family home. Now it was hers. Élie had sent a handwritten welcome card with "love and kisses," saying that he knew she would be a "great success."[35] Hundreds of other friends and admirers had dispatched the roses, peonies and lilies filling the palatial state rooms.

Up on the second floor her private quarters (with spectacular views toward the Eiffel Tower) had been overhauled for her arrival—she had sent in the interior designer Mark Hampton within hours of being confirmed. At a reported cost of $500,000, most of which came from Pamela's pocket, Hampton had sought to create a sense of "calm and permanence" with English country house chintzes, oriental rugs and art.[36] *Architectural Digest* described this "tonality" as "patrician rather than ponderously rich."[37] Pamela had added practical brown sofas and her nesting items such as a silver-plated ostrich car mascot from Gianni and a comforting Churchill painting of a drinks tray called *Jug with Bottles*. In pride of place was a favorite Paul Helleu painting of his red-haired wife at her secretaire, which she had acquired in Paris with Élie.

Her major artworks were also already in place. Five days earlier, Charles Moffett, curator at the National Gallery in Washington, had flown over to hang them in the public state rooms and to have them wired up for security. The Van Gogh was set in a huge panel edged with beautifully restored gold leaf in the Louis XVI Salon above a long gold damask sofa, its profusion of whites and pale greens lighting up the room under cavernous gilt and cream ceilings. Most of the other works, such as her Picasso's haunting depiction of *Mother and Child*, Matisse's *Blue Hat* (a study of a scowling courtesan) and Renoir's laughing *Portrait of Mademoiselle Demarsy*—Pamela joked that she sat in front of the right picture depending on her mood[38]—were hung in the more intimate Blue Room, the smallest of the three ground-floor salons. Some of her more modern works by American artist Walter Kuhn were displayed in the ballroom and elsewhere visitors spotted a painting of Sun Valley by Eisenhower. She had created her stage and was ready for the show.

Pamela was now a double Honorable—once as the daughter of an English baron and the second time as an ambassador. As the first *female* American envoy to France she faced a novel question of whether to be addressed as *Madame l'ambassadeur* or *Madame l'ambassadrice*, the feminine version but typically attached to ambassadors' wives. *Madame l'ambassadeur* carried the authority she desired and—knowing that here too her reputation could undermine her—she became a stickler for it.[39] "French people would say to me, 'Why are they sending this woman? She doesn't know anything about diplomacy. She's a courtesan,'" remembers Avis. "I replied, 'You'll see. She's way smarter than you think.'" From the off, "she was avid for briefing papers, we could hardly give her enough."[40] Pamela "talked about how it was still a battle to be taken seriously and she had to prove herself all the time," says CNN correspondent Christiane Amanpour. "I heard some horrible diplomat say that she saw the world laying on her back. It was so crass and ignorant."[41] None of these voices apparently paused to reflect on how they might have viewed her erotic feats differently—perhaps with admiration rather than scorn—if she had been a man.

The following day Pamela had appointments from breakfast to lunch, took dozens of calls and at six dropped in for cocktails with the British ambassador Sir Christopher Mallaby at his residence next door, where in less favored times she had famously been barred by Cynthia Jebb. Now with a new name and nationality it was glorious to stride in as the American ambassador but after a few minutes of "chitchat" on the terrace, Mallaby made a mistake from which he would never fully recover. He leaned forward, and with a knowing look, informed her that he was friends with someone who knew her intimately: Maurice Druon. Pamela's smile faded and she made her displeasure clear by plunging her hand into her Thatcher-style handbag to draw out a United Nations resolution on Bosnia to suggest alterations to the wording. Mallaby interpreted this as Pamela's way of demonstrating that she intended "to deal with the substance of the work and not to seek social stardom." Incredibly, he seems to have been surprised that she "wanted to be a real diplomat."[42] His attitude bespoke a widespread presumption among British officials. Indeed, according to Tom Pickering, one of America's most eminent emissaries, many thought she was "operating above her station," an attitude he attributed to "jealousy."[43] Ray Seitz, the American ambassador to London, a career diplomat, also underestimated her. He admitted to having been "skeptical" that there would be enough of "substance" to discuss at a meeting she convened the following year and was reluctant to attend. "I was wrong," he confessed, and "we ran out of hours." Not only had he learned "a lot" but she had given him unparalleled access to key French figures including soon-to-be prime minister Alain Juppé.[44]

"People often tried to catch her out," says another ambassador, "but she had this undeniable presence" and knew her subject.[45] The more astute realized she was not only well informed but ruthless—even if she veiled her maneuvers with twinkling charm—and did not forget slights even if she pretended to. When Princess Diana came to town in September 1995, Pamela saw her chance to right the wrong of being barred from the royal presence in Paris back in the 1950s. She inveigled herself into a small room at Versailles where the princess was chatting with Madame Bernadette Chirac before an opulent dinner for 250 to mark the opening of an exhibition on Cézanne. Mallaby watched with astonishment as "Pamela placed herself right beside the princess just as the photographers entered the room." Having ensured she would feature next to Diana in the media, Pamela slipped away, leaving the place reserved for her at the dinner empty. She had done what she set out to achieve.[46]

Visits to the British residence—another opulent palace furnished with treasures acquired from Napoleon's sister Pauline Borghese—also roused her competitive spirit. After paying for a magnificent six-year restoration of Pontalba, Congress had balked at the cost of suitable antiques and while some Louis XVI pieces had been donated there was a leftover feeling from its use as offices for twenty years. It did not do that the Brits—whose power and prestige had diminished since the Big Three days of the Second World War—had the slight edge in the grandeur stakes. Spending her own money, securing donations and using her well-honed style, Pamela began to upgrade the VIP quarters of the residence to a level befitting its rank.

Over her first week or so she hosted four American Cabinet members, presided over dinners, lunches and receptions, threw a huge party for the Paris air show, and took the lead over a staff of a thousand. Soon nine or ten meetings a day with French and American officials and businessmen became her routine, often ending in two separate "cocktail hours" (perhaps with TV anchor Larry King, Ron Brown, now Commerce Secretary, or her old friend Lauren Bacall) and a working dinner (only Cinderellas left before midnight). Then when the Europeans retired to bed, Pamela returned to her desk to make and take calls from America and read official cables in "very very small print" until 1:30 in the morning.[47] She was up again after an average of five hours' sleep for a working breakfast, often with a White House official who had stayed overnight. Not long after her arrival, she addressed the Foreign Relations Committee of the French Senate—in French, for twenty minutes, and followed by questions. "It was the most terrifying thing I had ever had to do," she told friends.[48] She cut a starkly different figure from many political appointees. "A good share of them have simply bought their office," Pickering reveals. "The going rate used to be $200,000 in donations, now more like $1.5 million. Then they often don't want to do the job, they just want the title and go there once or twice a year."[49]

A few of Pamela's staff could not keep up the pace or were in her view not good enough and so were bypassed (such as the embassy's speechwriters, whom she ignored in favor of drafting in Bob Shrum either remotely by fax or occasionally in person). Others asked to extend their stay because of the excitement and the way she trusted them to do their job. "Some political appointees are dastardly to the diplomatic service," notes Verveer. "But she worked well with them."[50] "She ensured her team kept a high profile," remembered staffer Donald Bandler, comparing her favorably to other ambassadors who wanted to be the sole public face of the embassy.[51] "Her laugh sounded happy," says Nancy Ely-Raphel, who visited her. "She was satisfied with her life. She was finally in her own place. She was finally in charge."[52] She was a "perfectionist," Holbrooke observed, "determined to present a flawless façade." When he was appointed Assistant Secretary of State for Europe—becoming at least nominally her boss—he tried to persuade her to take more time off. Even as the oldest member of Clinton's administration, she refused: "I'm not built that way."[53]

Pamela's in tray was crowded with Franco-American spats over international trade—then being dubbed the new post–Cold War global conflict. First off, the media were in high dudgeon over allegations that Paris had been spying on American defense and aerospace companies. The French were meanwhile trying to downplay the row as simply a ruse to discredit them. Tensions were further heightened by contrasting French and American approaches to commerce that often proved inexplicable to the other side (something that Pamela became particularly good at resolving). She conveyed Paris's fears that a country as *hyper-puissant* as America could weaken the European Community (emblem of French power) as a trading bloc, while Washington worried that France was tipping Europe (a burgeoning economic superpower) toward protectionism. One acrimonious dispute had broken out over France defending its film industry from American "cultural imperialism" by blocking U.S. cable channels and decreeing that at least half of television programs should be made in Europe to avoid "destroying French culture." The Hollywood movie *Jurassic Park* was even denounced by one minister as a "threat to French identity."[54] Another flashpoint came with French reluctance to open up to American agriculture exports—requiring Pamela to explain to baffled Washington officials her host country's attachment to ancient (if highly subsidized) farming traditions with the battle cry *La France pour La Ferme!* It was less a case of French "cussedness" than emotional resonance, she spelled out, but once that was understood there were areas where Paris might be persuaded to yield.

Much of Pamela's year was dominated by the GATT world trade negotiations that had been going on for seven tortuous years in an effort to avoid such disputes descending into a full trade war. She identified the key French players, got to know them and their goals, and arranged one-to-one meetings with the American Trade Representative Mickey Kantor, who was the principal in the marathon GATT talks in Brussels. "I knew what I was getting was careful and considered advice," recalled Kantor, who had worked with Pamela on the Clinton campaign. "If someone else had been there, I might have worried about the quality of the information, about the access or what filter the information was coming through."[55] "I was a sort of messenger going back and forth," she confirmed of the final tense weeks of bargaining, "explaining to Washington why the French think and argue the way they do and also in the other direction."[56]

The Hollywood lobby wanted Pamela to leverage their frustrations but she declined. Kantor says she was right and that it would have been an "act of irresponsibility" to derail a worldwide trade agreement over movies, particularly after the Americans made ground on agriculture. She "knows when to hold 'em and when to fold 'em," he said.[57] "In this fraught climate, putting across the Clinton administration's agenda is a Herculean job," reported *Town & Country* magazine but Pamela had "tackled it with gusto."[58]

Her experience as special back channel between the Americans and Brits during the war could not have been more instructive for what to say, when, how and to whom, and to understand key players' emotions as well as ambitions. The Downing Street years were a "key part of how her whole life had been preparing for this moment," confirms Pickering. Her Churchill heritage added "luster and gave her an entrée."[59] It also gave her a role model: Harry Hopkins, the wartime figure beloved and trusted by Churchill as much as by his boss Franklin Roosevelt—a point she drove home to Clinton by sending him a recording of a documentary on how FDR's envoy had worked tirelessly to keep the 1940s Anglo-American alliance alive. Pamela had witnessed how "Harry had that extraordinary faculty of making the prime minister think he was working for him at the same time as he was working for the president. President Roosevelt was very attached to Harry so that made the relationship much easier." Fortunately, Clinton was "very attached" to Pamela, allowing her the space to work on the French. She shared Hopkins's knack of lending a sympathetic ear to politicians harried by great power and responsibility—in two different nations at once—and to make them both feel she had their interests at heart.

Indeed, the French administration under President Mitterrand also soon became "very attached" to Pamela. The epitome of *gauche caviar* (the French version of champagne socialist), Mitterrand led a cultivated if colorful life with a secret mistress and family and was enchanted by beautiful women. "Crazy, incredible" stories about Pamela were doing the rounds at the Élysée Palace and, according to the leading intellectual Bernard-Henri Lévy who knew him well, even the typically inaccessible Mitterrand was "eager for word about the beautiful ambassador's previous escapades."[60] Some, including Mallaby, complained that Pamela was "visible all the time" only because of "playing that card" of a tinseled past and that her beauty had made it "easy for her." Avis thought that it might help but was clear that Pamela's achievements were principally down to "a political savvy and an ability to size up other people . . . She really made a difference."[61]

The French realized with relief that Pamela was a different proposition from Evan Galbraith, who had been sent over by Reagan as ambassador in the early 1980s when Mitterrand had first come into power. Relations had not fully recovered from that time of suspicion and friction. Pamela wanted to change that. She spoke well but she paid heed too. "She has got the French and the U.S. talking and occasionally even listening to each other," a senior State Department official observed with awe. "That's no mean feat."[62] Hoping to improve mutual understanding still further, Pamela arranged a lunch for Reagan's former Secretary of State George Shultz with several key Paris figures, when he found himself "dying to join an animated exchange" in fluent French between her and former president Valéry Giscard d'Estaing. "I enjoyed that lunch because the talk was substantive," Shultz said afterward, with Pamela providing both "the spark and the sparkle."[63]

Pamela's sparkle was in hot demand. In his early forties at the time, Christopher Dickey, Paris bureau chief for *Newsweek*, was seated next to her at a dinner party on the Left Bank. "The idea of her as a courtesan made sense that evening," he recounted. "Younger men fell for her all the time."[64] The historian Antony Beevor, also then in his forties, talks of sitting next to Pamela on a Parisian sofa and finding himself "mesmerised" by her eyes. And Bernard-Henri Lévy, again of a similar age, was smitten by how she pretended not to know things as a way of skillfully persuading others to divulge useful information. He found "her habit of staring at men, then looking down modestly, the sign of an accomplished seductress."⁶⁵ She also had a reputation for fun—softening her ambassadorial grandeur with a playful chuckle; arranging her imposing residence with inviting chairs, sofas and cushions; leavening business talk of trade quotas with a delectable snippet of gossip. When her young friend David Sulzberger dropped by in his brand-new Bentley, she knew she could not take it out on the road but drove it round and round the courtyard at speed. Her name was linked to Prince Rainier of Monaco, a coterie of handsome French businessmen and even one or two particularly personable sports coaches. Occasionally, she imported Thomas Quinn, her Washington man about town, to escort her but there was no one she wanted to marry and sometimes she would take another woman such as Nicole Salinger (divorced wife of JFK's former press secretary Pierre) as her plus one instead.

Equally keen to meet her was the notoriously buttoned-up Gaullist prime minister Édouard Balladur. The ever-devoted Maurice Druon, by now Sécretaire Perpétuelle of the Académie Française, was the one to arrange their first meeting, only ten days after her arrival, over a "family dinner" (code for knee-length cocktail dresses rather than long gowns for women and men in black rather than white tie). Pamela dazzled Balladur that night with her knowledge of events past and present and the meeting paid dividends almost immediately. The prime minister traveled to Washington soon afterward to be given a bipartisan congressional lunch—then a rare honor for a visitor from Paris. If the old Washington hands had feared that dispatching a woman as envoy to France would present extra difficulties, it was early proof they were mistaken. "France takes women in powerful jobs much more in its stride than we expect," Pamela observed, while expressing dismay at the attacks on Hillary back home. "One lovely thing is that women [here] are pulling for me. It matters to them how I do."⁶⁶

If the 1970s had started her awakening, working in a powerful female environment obliged Pamela to open her eyes to the sisterhood. *Time* magazine found her "surprisingly eager to get aboard the feminist bandwagon."[67] She ensured that more women were invited to her gatherings, spotting such future stars as Christine Lagarde, then head of Western Europe at a U.S. law firm, who went on to head the IMF and the European Central Bank. It was a conspicuous change of tack, the moment when she pivoted to "spearhead[ing] women's affairs in Paris," according to senior diplomat Don Bandler.[68] She was also "transparently proud" of her granddaughter Marina Churchill, a London barrister. When asked if she would lead an independent life like Marina if she were starting out now, the blue eyes blazed: "Would I? *Would I?*" she responded, making it very clear she would.[69]

One of her first tests arrived with an invitation from the grand men-only Travellers Club of Paris. Normally the American ambassador would be made an ex officio member and a lavish dinner would be held in his honor. As Pamela was a woman, the club wrote saying they could offer only a lunch and she must go in through the side entrance. "What should I do with this?" she asked Avis, who was still feeling her way with her new boss. "I think you should tell them to go jump in the lake," she dared to reply. "Good, that's exactly what I wanted to do!" exclaimed Pamela.[70]

The invitations were endless and Pamela resorted to inventing excuses—illness, trips, pressure of work—to turn many of them down without offense. Janet, ensconced in the residence as executive assistant, ran five appointment books and a computer-generated schedule to keep track of it all. Pamela strongly believed in "face to face rather than fax to fax" and Janet prepared cards printed with that day's appointments and profiles of people Pamela would be meeting, small enough to fit in the side flaps of her Chanel shoulder bag. If Janet sometimes flared up under the pressure, Pamela retained her composure. Once asked how her father might have reacted to her success, she replied: "He'd be surprised, I guess. But Daddy was always surprised by me."[71]

Equally, invitations to Pamela's residence became prized by French and Americans alike. "Everybody seems to come through Paris"[72]—and everybody wanted something. Those Pamela liked she would treat like royalty, arranging private tours of museums, meals and parties, and coming into their rooms at 7:15 in the morning to throw open their curtains. There was a loneliness in her full days and full house, though, and she welcomed Evangeline Bruce, telling her onetime foe afterward that it had been just "great to have a friend I could trust & therefore talk with."[73]

She did not like being taken for granted, however. Donald Trump demanded Pamela's help with the launch of a new hotel in Paris but although she kept up appearances, according to Peter Fenn since that first bizarre meeting in Washington she had come to think of him as "phoney and tacky."[74] When Bill Gates asked her to put on a big dinner for him he rejected her philanthropic overtures—he was not yet the great donor—so she refused. "She was frustrated," reports Christiane Amanpour, who came to know Pamela well, "that he wanted something but wasn't willing to pony up."[75]

In October 1993 Bob Shrum arranged for the businesswoman Linda Wachner to drop in, prompting the start of an unusually intense friendship with someone described by *Fortune* as one of the "seven roughest, toughest, most intimidating bosses" in America.[76] The appeal of "this small woman with honey-colored hair"[77] and no family of her own, who had become rich on revolutionizing the selling of bras, was to confound Pamela's other friends and eventually cause ructions. Also the widow of a much older husband, Wachner had made connections with a number of celebrities including Barbara Walters and other ambassadors such as Renwick by flying them around in her Gulfstream III, holding parties in their honor or taking them on her chartered yacht. Now she was devoting her attention to Pamela, who impressed fellow guests including Charles Powell (formerly Margaret Thatcher's chief foreign policy adviser) by gracefully diving into the sea from the yacht's upper deck.[78] "Linda embodied brashness," thought David Sulzberger. "But Pamela and she seemed to be very close friends. She began to take over her life." Pamela was grateful for Wachner's interest in her legal and financial problems, hoping her business acumen would help guide her through. "Linda paid her lawyers to look at them," recalled Janet.[79]

The French also wanted a piece of Pamela. "You should see the faces of young Gaullists," one embassy official noted, when she begins "'When I had dinner with General de Gaulle . . .'"[80] She was always "a very interesting person," confirmed Carter Brown. "She could converse about virtually anything from French wines to the details of the last Panama Canal treaty. And when she told a story she had a real kind of thespian's gift to re-create the voices of the people in the story, so it always sounded very dramatic."[81] Her mature voice was velvety and now rated on the internet as an ASMR experience.* People loved to hear her laugh too. "It was so nice," says Avis, "melodious and soothing like everything about her."[82] Nicolas Sarkozy, the youthful minister for the budget and mayor of Neuilly, was another high-flying Frenchman who was entranced. "Monsieur le ministre," she addressed him, "I lived in Neuilly before you were born." "Madame," the future president of France replied, "that you have lived in Neuilly I can well believe. But that you lived there before I was born is impossible."[83]

There was one notable figure who was left unthrilled. "I will have to say goodbye to this house for four years," Élie's wife, Liliane de Rothschild, had declared to the previous ambassador at a reception at Pontalba before Pamela's arrival. "I won't come again while *she's* here."[84] Pamela did her best to avoid Liliane too—although there was a tense

---

* An autonomous sensory meridian response voice is said to prompt a tingling sensation on the scalp and neck likened by some to "low-grade euphoria."

moment at an exhibition one evening when she spied her on the other side of a glass display case. Pamela grabbed her companion, David Sulzberger, and quickly steered him away. It was more tricky that Madeleine Druon apparently sought to put the past behind her by inviting Pamela to the family's converted abbey near St. Émilion. Pamela invented an excuse for not leaving Paris—while making other plans to do so—and on other occasions claimed illness. Madeleine eventually lost patience and perhaps even began to become suspicious. The Druons were regulars at the British Embassy and on one occasion when they turned up to a grand dinner Madeleine spotted her old rival's name on the seating plan. "Pamela!" she cried. "I wasn't sure whether she was just exclaiming her name," says the butler Ben Newick. "Or a horrified *Pam est là!*" (Pam is here!)[85] Clarissa Eden was also present but when Pamela spotted her talking to Druon, presumably concerned about what might be being discussed, she "crossed the room and broke it up."[86]

Pamela's entertaining style combined American clout with European finesse and was certainly demanding. She fell out with the long-standing housekeeper and replaced the butler with her old one from the last time she lived in Paris, who had since been working for Gianni. Within weeks the chef was also dismissed, having committed the error of complaining that Pamela never made time to discuss menus. Tartly, he was reminded that he was talking about *Madame l'ambassadeur* not *Madame l'ambassadrice*.[87] The household staff totaled sixteen and Janet ensured that the highest standards were met for the round of breakfasts, brunches, luncheons, teas, dinners and private Sunday night prerelease screenings of the latest American movies. Pamela was spending $250,000 (equivalent to $520,000 now) a year on hosting, dwarfing her official budget of some $20,000,[88] but she can perhaps be forgiven for wanting to show off to those who had once looked down on her as déclassée. Stella de Rosnay was fascinated when invited for cocktails, crossing the Pontalba courtyard under a smart new red awning. "Considering how she was shunned by the British Embassy back in the 1950s," de Rosnay says, "it is remarkable she bore no grudge. She talked very nicely of my parents and seemed to think it should all be forgotten."[89] It was fun to invite people who had once thought her "not fit to be seen"[90] to the palace where she was now queen. Sandy Bertrand, director of Condé Nast and friend from the 1950s, told Pamela how he was "terribly happy" to see her return to Paris in "such glory."[91]

At one typical gathering in the state dining room, her staff served Laurent Perrier champagne or crème Chartreuse cocktails as aperitifs and fine Bordeaux wines from Château Tanesse with dinner. (Pamela rarely delved into her Napa Valley stocks sent by friends because she believed French guests preferred their own wines.) Dinner (prepared by a new chef hired from a royal palace) began with a vol-au-vent stuffed with turbot, followed by veal Orlov with a truffle sauce. A cheese board came next—in the French tradition—and then charlotte russe. Even her invitations—on thick ivory card—were superior to State Department standard issue. Pamela was named "First Lady of Paris" by *Vogue*,[92] and "when she entered a room it stopped," recalls Amanpour, a regular invitee. Some claimed her media coverage was surpassed only by Princess Diana's. "It's taken fifty years," Pamela reflected privately, "to realise I can't have been all dumb and ugly."[93]

Just three months before she died from cancer, Jackie Kennedy Onassis wrote that "everyone here is so PROUD to see the magnificent way you are breezing through your life."[94] Jackie had bought into the Pamela legend, a life that was almost too good to be true. Where other American ambassadors typically flew on normal commercial services across the Atlantic, Pamela took Concorde at her own expense and the crew ensconced their special passenger in prestige seat 1A.

Keeping it up was hard work. Pamela spent thousands on her

wardrobe, an artful mélange of French and American couture. Givenchy sent her garments to try on at home and Karl Lagerfeld expressed his gratitude with huge bunches of lilies while Bill Blass said of his famous client: "She did more with a scarf than any woman I ever met."[95] Every morning before breakfast she applied a light makeup before being driven a few minutes to a salon to have it removed and replaced with a professional *maquillage*. She developed her own look of highlighting her blue eyes with blue eyeliner, had her eyebrows skillfully shaped and wore diamond earrings to add luminescence to her skin. In some ways she had never looked so good—and occasionally she would allow herself something a little racy, once making an entrance in a tightly tailored floor-length gown in leopard-skin print.

Janet, though, was worried. At one of Pamela's receptions, while Pamela was glad-handing the room, a guest had taken Janet to one side and whispered that there could be problems with the Harriman investments. But Pamela trusted in Averell, and that everything was fine. "Nobody," Janet observed, "wanted to believe it."[96]

45

Seven months after Pamela arrived in Paris, the honeymoon came to an abrupt end. Kathy boarded an overnight flight from New York in December 1993 and did not come in peace. At seventy-six years of age, she and her sister Mary had been outraged when the large remittances they received from the family trust funds every year suddenly stopped. When he was alive Averell had waved aside his daughters' concerns, instructing them to leave it to Pamela and his handpicked advisers. Now they felt they had no choice but to intervene.

Mary's son-in-law Charles Ames, a Boston lawyer, had spent the previous year trawling through the trusts' accounts and had discovered a financial "cataclysm" that had all but destroyed one of America's great fortunes, in one case reducing funds worth $25 million to less than $3 million.[1] The 1987 stock market crash had been painful but, seeking to repair the damage, Rich had plowed $20 million (via a loan taken out against family trust funds) into a rundown hotel, and former Playboy Club, in New Jersey, which was part owned by a notorious felon. The hotel with its worn shagpile carpeting turned out to be a dud and had been revalued at just $50,000.[2] The trusts were set to be all but wiped out when the loan had to be repaid, leading to questions as to whether appropriate fiduciary standards had been met by all those involved. There were other doubtful investments and Pamela had also borrowed heavily. Incredibly, she had signed off the New Jersey loan and was guarantor if there were insufficient funds to repay it.

The Harriman family had gathered at Arden to discuss the next steps and now Kathy and Ames intended to force Pamela to meet her legal obligations.

Driving from the airport in sheets of rain they arrived at the dazzling grandeur of the residence lit by Christmas lights and, after dropping their bags, the pair walked briskly toward Pamela's office in the separate embassy building around the corner. She had only the previous day received by fax a thirty-page outline of their findings. "These are *some* accusations," she said from the other side of her desk, no doubt hoping it might protect her from the confrontation she dreaded. "Have you asked Bill Rich about this?" she asked, insisting there must be a misunderstanding. Ames simply listed the family's demands: Pamela must restore the $20 million loan money to the trusts; Rich must be sacked and Clifford replaced as trustee; and details of all future transactions regularly reported to the family. Pamela seemed shell-shocked. She promised to resolve the problem and had already hired Lloyd Cutler—yet another expensive lawyer, former presidential counsel and soon an adviser to Clinton on the Whitewater affair—to look into it. The three avoided further money talk over a somber dinner but Kathy was so tense she rushed to the bathroom to vomit.[3]

Pamela again doled out Union Pacific stock that Christmas but when Cutler discovered that the losses were broader and deeper than anyone had feared, amounting to at least $30 million, she insisted she was in no position to repay the hotel loan. The Harrimans were forced to liquidate their trust funds (although they did have other sources of income) and in May 1994 hired a notoriously tough litigator to sue Pamela, Clifford and his legal partner Paul Warnke, and Bill Rich. The case made the front pages of the *New York Times* and *Washington Post*. "She's got a real sickness about money," a vindicated Peter Duchin growled to *Vanity Fair*. The loyal Kitty leaped to her defense, pointing to Pamela as a "victim in all this. I know she knew nothing at all about these financial matters" and had lost more than the rest of the family.[4] She had also been "very, very fond of some of them."[5] Cutler insisted Pamela had not known where the money was going, simply "signing things Bill Rich told her to sign."[6] Further support came from a former associate of Rich, Tom Richardson, who accused the six grandchildren of "amazing greed." He branded them "typical remittance children . . . always stomping their feet and crying 'Why don't we have more money?'"[7]

That same month, Christopher Ogden's unauthorized biography *Life of the Party* was published with considerable fanfare. As she had most feared, Pamela's life was cast by reviewers as a tale of "the vanities of an international courtesan" and the book itself a "sniggering account of her successive liaisons." Almost all of the chapters were named after her lovers—"Ed," "Gianni," "Élie"—as if each man defined her life. The *New York Times* inferred from Ogden's five-hundred-page tome that Pamela was a fantasist who had abandoned the notion of motherhood "except in name."[8] In Britain, the *Independent*'s coverage referred to her as the "scarlet lady of half the Western world" and a "party-circuit gold-digger."[9] In her defense, Pamela's lawyers (incurring yet another bill) claimed that the book contained an "extraordinary number of inaccuracies and falsehoods." And as Ben Macintyre later noted of his fellow author, Ogden had approached his "subject with a hatchet and a blunt one at that."[10] Some thought his work so hostile it represented a Republican plot to undermine Clinton in the lead-up to the midterm elections.

Holbrooke saw how she was "upset" but determined to push on.[11] That July, Pamela scaled down the all-day Independence Day celebrations at the residence to a small cocktail party for trusted friends. She also culled anyone who gave Ogden or his book house room, including the scion of a famous Chicago family who was made to resign as director of the Terra Museum of American Art (where Pamela had served on the advisory committee) because he had "demonstrated disrespect" by hosting Ogden for a book signing.[12]

Pamela's friends nevertheless grew concerned. The Democratic donor Walter Shorenstein urged her to rely on her "good deeds" to "transcend the matters" for which she was being "unfairly pilloried." Pamela was not about to show weakness to Shorenstein or virtually anyone else. She thanked him for his "kind" words but added, "Believe me I do not worry."[13] The truth was, though, that Pamela was bleeding money. If she had failed to take sufficient notice of what was going on before, on Cutler's advice she now brought in yet another adviser, Felix Rohatyn, to investigate the full picture. Her trust in Averell to hire the right men to place her finances on a secure footing before he died turned out to have been disastrously misplaced. Rohatyn discovered "as messy a financial situation as any I've ever seen"[14]—a morass of loans, mortgages, missing documentation, wild overvaluations and penalties for previous late or underpayment of tax.[15] So muddled were her affairs, Pamela was reduced to asking for an extension for her annual financial submission to the State Department. Her own investment losses of at least $25 million turned out to be worse than any family member's and she was forced into a fire sale of Union Pacific stock to pay off millions of dollars in loans. She also quietly put her Georgetown houses on the market but although the smaller 3034 eventually sold in May 1995 for $990,000, she struggled to offload the main house even at a reduced price of $3.3 million. Times had moved on—the bathrooms did not have showers, the kitchen was outdated and for those without chauffeurs, parking was in an inconvenient garage around the back. Perhaps most of all, without her presence and artworks the house seemed almost ordinary. She was down to her last reserves and told Kathy she was considering bankruptcy.

Over the summer—after half a century of friendship—all contact between Pamela and Kathy ceased. She and the other Harrimans believed Pamela had betrayed them by acting recklessly with their money. In September 1994 trustees on behalf of the Harriman daughters and grandchildren filed a 118-page complaint in the Manhattan Federal District Court seeking up to $90 million in damages. They charged Pamela, Clifford, Warnke and Rich with being "faithless fiduciaries who betrayed a trust and squandered a family's inheritance" and claimed that more than $30 million had been lost. All four defendants denied the allegations.

Pamela was "hoodwinking us," claimed Mary's son Averell Fisk, and "using Mafia-like tactics to defraud us."[16] "The story on the street was that Pamela had squandered all of Averell's fortune but that wasn't true," Avis insists. "The money went in bad investments not on her lifestyle. These claims really, really upset her."[17] "People felt no compunction about suing her," Susan Berger remembers, "because they thought she had more money than God."[18]

Pamela still made light of her troubles. Thanking a fellow diplomat for the gift of a knife in December 1994, she quipped "I may use it to cut my throat, but hopefully not!"[19] Janet was so concerned about Pamela's plight, though, she summoned Holbrooke to come for a weekend to give support. "He was appalled at how lackadaisical Lloyd Cutler and Clark Clifford had been," Avis recalls.[20] Even the White House was alarmed. America's most visible diplomat was engulfed in a bloody and escalating legal battle that was taxing her time, energy, resources and health. Ultimately, she risked humiliation.

46

Pamela's private woes sent her into overdrive to prove she could do her job. When the wife of an American tycoon on holiday on the Riviera had her jewelry stolen over the Bastille Day holiday weekend, Pamela abandoned dinner with friends to make calls and soon the most senior police officer on the Côte d'Azur was on the case. Former diplomat William van den Heuvel, watching her take action even on a Saturday night, advised her to be "careful." "The pressures and ... substantive demands of your post," he warned her, "are so compelling that someone just has to protect you."[1] When appointed ambassador to the United Nations, Madeleine Albright had decided she needed a "wife" and her sister Kathy took a long leave of absence from her job to help her.[2] Others such as Antony Acland, onetime British ambassador in Washington, had hesitated before taking his dream job because his wife had died and he was not sure he could cope alone (and soon remarried). It was an extra irony that back in 1982 Pamela had set up and funded an award for the wives of foreign diplomats in recognition of their strenuous unpaid work for husband and country. It was in the name of Avis's mother (also Avis Bohlen), who had of course been a diplomatic wife herself.

It was accepted that ambassadors with spouses, and especially children, should be given sacrosanct family time. Pamela would say she did not have another life outside work—her only sanctuary was taking a break to swim fifty lengths with Janet at the Hôtel Ritz either first thing or skipping lunch if she had no official engagement. The strain of running the embassy without a partner caused enough concern in the White House for Clinton to write, "Can you handle it solo?" "What," she replied, "are my alternatives?"[3]

On a trip back to Washington that October—via a day in New York visiting doctors—Pamela made quite a splash. She injected a shot of glamour now missing from the capital, despite efforts by women such as Arianna Huffington, who admitted she had been inspired by Pamela to chance her arm as hostess and grande dame.[4] And Pamela had already also proved herself as an ambassador. "Congratulations," her mentor Nicholas Wahl said to her, on what "everyone" said had been a "brilliant" start.[5]

Pamela was taken so seriously—even by the *Washington Post*—that on a later visit not only did Kay Graham come down to greet her but she was flanked by ten others, including the editorial board. Commentary in her birth country remained hostile, however. Pamela resorted to her trusted technique of inviting the proprietor of an unfriendly title—in one case Conrad Black of the *Spectator*—to the residence to be systematically charmed. He swiftly promised to pursue an "abatement" in his magazine's "infantile and irritating . . . crusade" against her.[6] There was nothing Pamela could do, though, to prevent a new book about the sexploits of Jane Digby. Where once she had relished comparing herself to her amorous forebear, now as ambassador she deplored how the author Mary Lovell described her "ability to attract and fascinate" to be as "legendary as that of her ancestor."[7] And yet the prospect of dying a similar death to Jane—alone and abandoned—started to haunt her. Pamela was grateful when David Sulzberger offered to visit Jane's tomb in Damascus and arrange for it to be restored.

Even so, coming home to America ranked as a feat of endurance, plunging her back into the distressing fallout of the Harriman lawsuits and Ogden's book. There was also "indefinable sadness" in the Washington air over the White House staggering from one crisis to another.[8] Interminable investigations into the Clintons' investment in the Whitewater holiday home development had failed to unearth lawbreaking but the president's opponents were relentless, leading Clinton's biographer Nigel Hamilton to brand it the "ultimate example" of 1990s media "madness."[9] Further trouble came in 1994 when a young Arkansas state employee Paula Jones filed a lawsuit claiming Clinton had exposed himself to her in a hotel room. Clinton denied wrongdoing—and initially even having met Jones—but she pushed ahead with her claim for $750,000 damages for sexual harassment and the stain of scandal seemed indelible.

In such circumstances, Pamela was keen to help the beleaguered president at least to live up to his potential overseas. The upcoming commemorations in France for the fiftieth anniversary of D-Day offered the opportunity for him to prove himself statesmanlike on her patch. "It was Clinton's first visit to France as president and Pamela wanted it to be given great play," Avis explains. "She made that happen."[10] Yet "Bill's relationship with the military had gotten off to a rocky start," Hillary recalled, after the allegations over avoiding the Vietnam draft and his "Don't Ask, Don't Tell" policy of banning discrimination against closeted gay servicemen and -women. Although now widely criticized for blocking the out LGBQT community, it was seen as too progressive by many at the time. Even Clinton's ability to salute properly had been called into question. A lot was riding on how soldiers, sailors, airmen and the audience back home judged his performance on the beaches of Normandy.

It was clear that Clinton was to lean on Pamela and her historical associations. Discussions in the White House had revolved around the concerns of the Second World War generation she embodied as to whether younger world leaders had taken on board the "lessons learned in the thirties and forties." As the son of a veteran and having listened to Pamela's and Averell's memories of that conflict, Clinton took the point seriously and wanted to remind "today's youth that they are the beneficiaries of Normandy and to inspire them to service."[11] On his way to the commemorations, Clinton thrust Pamela into the spotlight by quoting her saying that "history will look upon the twentieth century as a century of war. What we and our allies do in the next few years will determine if history regards the twenty-first century as the century of peace." TV anchors from Katie Couric to David Brinkley queued up to interview her on the significance of the event. She hoped, she said in a lightly Americanized accent, a slight crackle in her voice, that the ceremonies would give U.S. veterans a chance to see how appreciated they were in France. She also privately hoped that her role in such a historic occasion would once and for all stop the references to "that scarlet woman."

Two days before the president was due to arrive, Pamela was driven to Normandy to oversee the final preparations after six months of intense work. She made her way to Château de Balleroy for a private dinner hosted by its American owner Robert Forbes. Pamela had arranged for Hillary's mother, Dorothy, to be put up at the château—a Renaissance masterpiece—as well as her friend Stuart Eizenstat, now ambassador to the European Union. Eizenstat remembers the evening as magical and was fiercely grateful that Pamela had made sure he and his wife, Fran, were invited. Even a display of Forbes's colorful hot air balloons could not compete with Pamela's stories of the war, though. She was the star.

On the anniversary itself, June 6, Pamela left at 5:40 a.m. by helicopter to join the president on the USS *George Washington* out on the turbulent waters of the Channel. It made for a treacherous landing on the aircraft carrier. Nonetheless, "Pamela arrived looking absolutely beautiful and looked glorious all day," says an admiring official traveling with the president, who compared her favorably to Hillary "looking dreadful in a hat."[12]

Clinton had spent the night on board after dining on the Royal Yacht *Britannia* with the queen and now presided over a sunrise service with the six thousand crew. "They sang 'Those in Peril on the Sea' and Clinton threw a wreath onto the water," recalls the official. "There wasn't a dry eye." The president took off on Night Hawk One helicopter for the start of his day of engagements on land, followed by Pamela in Night Hawk Two. Later Pamela rejoined the American and French presidents for an emotional ceremony at the U.S. military cemetery at Colleville-sur-Mer, where Clinton told veterans that "We are the children of your sacrifice." Television cameras captured Pamela's somber face looking out to sea, reliving the agony of waiting for news and the faces of friends who never came back. For her it went to the heart. The lines she often recited about that day were written by John Maxwell Edmonds as an epitaph for his fallen comrade: "Went the day well, we died and never knew, but well or ill—freedom—we died for you."*

The moment was so poignant it enraptured the president and nearly derailed his schedule. Any delay could cause chaos and ultimately it was down to Pamela to ensure that Clinton kept on track and left for Paris. "The helicopter was waiting and waiting," the White House official remembers. "The tension was mounting but Pamela handled it so well." Nicholas Wahl later told Pamela he thought her "one of the stars of the show." "Whether in English or in French, whether at a round table discussion or a formal speech, you were terrific."[13]

With the president safely under her roof at the residence, Pamela could finalize the preparations for the next day's itinerary. She wanted Clinton to have the chance to win over a group of thirty French and American CEOs and had arranged a meeting in the Louis XVI Salon. "They were all pretty skeptical," Avis remembers. "They'd heard stories that everything in those early days was so disorganized, and heads of state would be shut outside the White House and nobody

---

* She repeated these lines in a speech on January 10, 1995.

was ever on time. Pamela wanted to create the chance for them to appreciate what a really smart guy he is. And he just blew them away, he knew so much and he could talk on all these issues without any notes."[14] Pamela also persuaded a reluctant Clinton to meet the unusually pro-American mayor of Paris, Jacques Chirac,[15] whom she had spotted as a likely future president willing to work closely with Washington. It was gratifying to see the two men forming a rapport in the cozy environment of the Blue Salon, a meeting more significant than any could have known.

Later, Mitterrand hosted a candlelit state dinner at the Élysée Palace, where Pamela turned out to be the toast of the evening. "I was at a table with some of Mitterrand's group, perhaps one of his brothers, all men," remembers Verveer. "Each and every one said they were in love with Pamela." Mitterrand escorted the Clintons out of the dinner at 10:30 and insisted Pamela come with them to see I. M. Pei's famous new glass pyramid at the Louvre, where the architect himself was waiting to act as their tour guide. In the morning Verveer informed Pamela how she had enchanted all of Paris. "Darling," she beamed in reply, "that is delicious!" Verveer realized she had not told the ambassador anything new. She was already aware "she was captivating and doing a good representative job for the country."[16] The Clintons' visit had been a triumph, a light in the darkness surrounding his presidency, in which he had been able to show the best of himself at home and overseas. Two weeks later, the president wrote to say he and Hillary "could not have hoped for better results," much of which had been "directly due" to Pamela's "ability and energy."[17]

Those memorable few days in June had stirred up unfathomed emotions. They also reinforced Pamela's trust in America's sacred destiny, probably the strongest conviction of her life, as the leader of a transatlantic partnership vital for safeguarding world peace. Still fired up six months later, she issued a call to arms to her adopted country and perhaps specifically her president. The D-Day commemoration had, she said in a speech on America's role in the modern age, been a reminder that Uncle Sam had saved Europe fifty years ago but also that "Europe still looks to the U.S. as the pillar of strength . . . If democracy and freedom can prevail, it will come from the United States. We have a responsibility to continue to help Europe, a responsibility to . . . our veterans who gave their lives so Europe could be free."[18]

By the 1990s, Pamela was one of only a few survivors from the Second World War generation left in government anywhere. So when she had pronounced on another occasion that Washington shared responsibilities with Paris "to create a world where peace can rule" her words carried weight.[19] Even more so because of her privileged access to the president. She used it sparingly but if she called Clinton at the White House, he picked up.[20] When she returned to Washington, he made time to see her, as did the First Lady.[21] It was this that gave her genuine clout in Paris, as well as in the U.S., and something she made no bones about. The problem was that even if she had an innate feel for Clinton's politics, he remained an inexperienced and hesitant president on the international stage and one distracted by sagas—some of his own making—at home. Pamela insisted that it was simply not widely understood "just how broad-gauged a man" he was.[22]

A month after the D-Day events, Pamela returned to America and again found it "very depressing." Over lunch at the Knickerbocker Club, Arthur Schlesinger pressed her to explain what was going wrong with an administration that had begun with "such radiant hope and high expectation." Some of it was down to bad luck or "unforeseen external troubles," she said, on top of an opposition determined to dig into Clinton's past. She also placed some blame on the president himself. He was bright, well briefed and "pointing the country in the right direction" but he caved in too quickly, was prone to indecision and lacked presidential dignity. She particularly disliked "those awful jogging photographs." "Much of the disorganization," she concluded, "spills down from the top."[23] She went to see Clinton, to be "very blunt" about the scale of his problems. It was testament to the strength of their friendship that she could challenge him in such a way but it was, she reported back to Schlesinger, "very difficult to know how much it really penetrates. He feels so terribly hurt and frustrated . . . and sees himself as the object of persecution by the press." "You say how successful my European trip was, but why the hell does no one write this?" he had complained to her.[24] Clinton confirmed to the author that he and Pamela had the "occasional argument" but that it was "never personal, just over whether we should do x, y or z." And because he trusted her, he enjoyed "an unusual straightforward relationship with her" that he "treasured."[25]

If Pamela thought of the president as her last great political project, then she still had work to do. Carl Bernstein has talked of Clinton's capacity for self-absorption and "tendency to throw it all away when he was on the edge of greatness."[26] And that he "often needed to be managed, pushed, reassured, guided or scolded . . . to perform at the level of which he was capable."[27] Most often this role fell to Hillary, of course, but Pamela would also weigh in. Sometimes through hints such as the "symbolic scissors" she gave him to remind him to "cut through red tape,"[28] but also on occasion speaking in a way that only very few dared. The November 1994 midterms highlighted the urgency. The Democrats lost eight Senate seats and fifty-four in the House, creating the first Republican Congress for forty years.

On January 26, 1995, the French Interior Minister Charles Pasqua, an ally of Balladur, summoned Pamela to his office. It was an unusual move. It was election year, however, and Pasqua knew what he was doing. He had previously showered Pamela with gifts of wine from his home region in the South of France but this time Pasqua was curt. He presented her with a dossier containing damning evidence on operations out of her embassy from a two-year sting by French secret agents staked out in a nearby hotel.[29] They had tracked a plot to bribe French officials for information about their GATT negotiating position on movies and entertainment. Pasqua showed her a list of names and incriminating photographs of clandestine meetings, hotel bookings and credit card imprints, and even a stash of 500-franc bills. "The CIA station was not well-managed," concedes Avis. "It was out of control and doing a lot of stupid things." Low-level economic espionage was commonplace on both sides but immediately on Pamela's return to the embassy she headed straight to the secure space known as the "bubble"—a hot and sweaty room within a room encased in transparent plastic to guard against bugs—to interrogate CIA station chief Richard Holm on what was a shameful breach of security. Such matters—although embarrassing and provocative for supposed allies—are typically resolved behind closed doors between the relevant intelligence agencies but after a month Pasqua leaked the affair to the French press. The spectacle of one ally publicly accusing another of full-scale spying plunged Franco-American relations into an unprecedented crisis. By casting America in a woeful light, it also pandered to widespread Gaullist antipathy to *le Goliath américain*—and the belief that the CIA was intent on destabilizing the French economy—just as voters were preparing to choose their next president.

Pasqua put out a statement in which he branded the affair as a major scandal, and one only to be expected when two women were left to run such an important embassy. Pamela issued an official line in response denouncing Pasqua's account of their conversations as "inaccurate and incomplete"[30] and the State Department dismissed the whole affair as "overblown." Pamela had been kept in the dark before the storm broke—and indeed Holm later commented, "I assumed she did not *want* to know what we were doing."[31] Yet the front page of the *Washington Post* described the debacle as a "rare public humiliation" for her.[32] Close friends, including her cardiologist Dr. Rosenfeld, were increasingly worried about the way she was fighting on so many fronts. "I think she's a great woman, I'm very fond of her," said Brooke Astor, but "she sounded dreadful when I spoke with her last."[33]

Pamela would not let the matter rest. Always keen to seize opportunities presented by a crisis, she knew "what needed to be done," recalls Bob Shrum, who was staying with her at the time. On first-name terms with key figures in the French media, she dropped hints that they should raise questions about Pasqua's motives for the leak. She wanted them to plant the thought in French voters' minds that this was a political game but without saying so herself. And the media duly started speculating whether Pasqua's move had been a desperate attempt to boost his boss Balladur's presidential campaign, which was struggling against Pamela's pro-American favorite and his deadly rival, Jacques Chirac. "It was sticky, very sticky," remarked Bandler, who assisted her, "but she handled it with aplomb."[34]

Balladur furiously backpedaled and banned his ministers from making further comment.[35] Fearful of the effect on relations with Washington, he tried to make amends with Pamela by assuring her that he wished to reestablish mutual trust.[36] In the end, it was Balladur who was humiliated. Two months later he was forced out of the race in favor of Chirac, whose polling had benefited from the way Pasqua's maneuvers had backfired. Keener than ever to see Chirac win the presidency, Pamela had meanwhile secretly dispatched Shrum (by then the most sought-after consultant in Democratic politics[37]) to coach him for his upcoming debate with his remaining rival, the socialist candidate Lionel Jospin. "Chirac had been a mediocre debater in the past," Shrum remembers, and this performance could be decisive in the neck-and-neck race. "I'm not sure I made any difference," he adds modestly, looking back at Chirac's victory, "but the new French president knew that she had tried to help and Jospin never needed to know."[38]

. . .

Pamela felt hounded by the Harriman lawsuits. They kept her up long into the night after her work was done. In desperation, in January 1995 she offered $10 million to settle the case but the family turned it down. She then had the U.S. chairman of Christie's, Christopher Burge, fly over to value her art collection and reluctantly put three of her most valuable paintings—the Picasso, the Renoir and the Matisse—up for auction to raise an expected $20 million. Despite calls from the Harrimans and her friends to solve her difficulties by selling the Van Gogh—her pledge to the National Gallery was almost certainly not enforceable—she refused to part with it. (Perhaps she could not countenance the humiliation of a forced disposal of her biggest trophy.) Christie's staff sported a white orchid, Pamela's signature flower, at a glittering celebratory dinner in Paris before the sale but in the end her chosen paintings sold for a "disappointing" $17 million. *Blue Hat* went for half the base estimate.[39] The main N Street house had also still not sold.

She had been relying on these sales to fund her revised offer of $20 million, which was accepted by the Harrimans in the summer after months of negotiation. The settlement was derailed at the last minute when Clifford declined to contribute the final $3 million. Accusing her of acting in bad faith and seeking to protect her lavish lifestyle, the Harrimans' lawyers signaled a return to the "trenches."[40]

With exquisite timing, Winston became embroiled in accusations of greed of his own after reaping £12.5 million from the sale of his grandfather's papers. Many in government—and nearly 90 percent of the public in a poll—felt he should have donated Winston Churchill's archive or sold it for a modest sum.[41] Distinguished historians thought half of the collection, which included drafts of his Second World War speeches, already belonged to the state as it pertained to Churchill's duties in office.* It transpired that Winston junior had waged a "stroppy" campaign for twenty-five years to persuade the government to pay £20 million[42] before accepting a lesser offer extended by the new National Lottery (which critics pointed out had been set up to fund good causes rather than enrich private families). Labour was to exploit Winston's windfall in its successful 1997 general election campaign.

Winston had continually claimed, according to government documents, that he needed to sell the papers for a large sum as he had "very little money of his own."[43] True, he had lost money as a Lloyd's Name (an investor in the famous London insurance market) but now he was most likely wealthier than his mother. It was not only his own lifestyle, however, that he needed to maintain. Winston faced what was set to be an expensive divorce after years of affairs. Pamela's sympathies were with Minnie, whom she described as an "angel" in her unwavering support of her husband.[44] Equally displeased was Winston's constituency association, which canceled a silver jubilee celebration for his twenty-five years as their MP, at which Pamela had agreed to be guest of honor. A "large number" of members had pulled out in protest at Winston's betrayal of his wife. Pamela wrote to a Mr. Harding, CBE, who had regretfully canceled the event, that "I, too, am very disturbed about what is happening to my family."[45]

By this point Pamela's legal and financial fees were reported to have topped $4 million and the losses $41 million, and she had no real option but to take to the law herself. In September 1996 she sued Brown Brothers Harriman for "alleged looting," claiming that the firm had allowed Rich "to sell securities and to transfer millions of dollars out of trust accounts for his own purposes."[46] Pamela had already taken the painful step of suing her onetime friends Clifford and Warnke for failing to supervise the money managers who had

---

* American presidents donate their papers to the nation for free.

ruinously mismanaged Averell's estate.⁴⁷ Washington took comfort from the fact that Pamela had turned out better at negotiating with the French than picking financial advisers.⁴⁸

Jacques Chirac's election as president of France on May 7, 1995, confirmed Pamela's nose for political winners—and love of the game. His victory sparked a new energy in Paris and afforded her an intensely envied entrée to the Élysée Palace (famously once the home of the courtesan Madame de Pompadour), just two hundred meters from her front door. "She was the only ambassador to have access to Chirac," confirms his diplomatic adviser Jean-David Levitte, "because she was Pamela Harriman."⁴⁹ A Frenchman who had in his youth studied at Harvard and fallen in love with an American, Chirac spoke good English and (thanks to Pamela) already knew Clinton, and crucially had seen firsthand her influence over him. Most unusually, Chirac called her up to invite her to the Élysée for talks—"they shared uncommon personal relations," states a former senior official.⁵⁰ When she entered the huge first-floor Salon Doré, the courtly Chirac kissed her hand and showed her to a sofa in front of a tapestry emblazoned with *Don Quixote Guérit de la Folie par la Sagesse* (Don Quixote recovered from folly with wisdom). He took his favorite armchair by the door and in English explained he needed her help to reset relations with Washington on the most pressing issue: Bosnia.

Fighting had broken out in the Balkan state in 1992, a product of resurgent nationalism in Yugoslavia in the vacuum left by the death of Tito and the collapse of communism. Clinton's two years in the Oval Office had been overshadowed by the mounting genocide. Neighboring Serbs and, to a lesser extent, Croats and their ethnic warlords within Bosnia had sought to divide most of the country between them by expelling or annihilating the remaining Bosnian Muslims through ethnic cleansing and incarceration in concentration camps. Consumed by his problems at home, Clinton held back from intervention. Few in Washington saw Bosnia as a priority—most of Congress, with the odd exception such as Joe Biden, was set against America taking the lead. And looming over it all was the ghost of Vietnam and most recently October 1993, when the U.S. had twice been humiliated by mobs within a week. In the Black Hawk Down fiasco in Somalia, two American military helicopters had been shot down in Mogadishu and eighteen Americans died in the firefight that followed. Several of their bodies had been dragged through the streets as trophies. In Haiti, an armed crowd on the docks of Port-au-Prince had chanted "Somalia! Somalia!" and prevented an American warship from carrying out a UN mission to help return the country from military dictatorship to democratic rule. In both cases, warlords had humiliated the world's only superpower, and Clinton himself. Thereafter the president faced rigid opposition from the military to further excursions overseas and especially the tangled conflict in the Balkans, where there were no direct U.S. interests. "With the possible exception of ancient Rome," as Madeleine Albright put it, "no society has ever auditioned for the role of world policeman."[51]

The situation in Bosnia was rapidly deteriorating, however. A ceasefire negotiated in 1994 had broken down and Serbs had been bombing Muslims in western Bosnia in violation of a no-fly zone, as well as tightening their blockade around the capital Sarajevo where their snipers picked off innocent civilians including children. Half-hearted NATO air strikes on a Serb stronghold—later compared to pinpricks—had led to Bosnian Serbs seizing lightly armed UN peacekeepers (known as Blue Helmets) as human shields against further attack. Reports of French Blue Helmets chained naked to trees incensed Chirac.* After others were killed when Serbs seized a UN outpost, his patience with the European Union's dithering response ran

---

* Reports of the troops being stripped were later disputed.

out. Europe lacked political and military cohesion—compounded by competing national loyalties to the Serbs or Croats—to mount an effective response. A "numb confusion" reigned "in the face of the Bosnian Serbs' brutality."[52] Where the Cold War had united the West in opposition to Soviet communism, it was now fractured.

No one European nation could or would take charge; no ceasefire had held; no peace plan had worked. There was a growing recognition that only America could provide the leadership and military muscle required but Chirac also spotted the chance for France to star on the international stage by working in tandem with Washington. He found a willing and powerful go-between in the American ambassador—and she promised him she would "call the president directly to explain" the French position. "It was most useful we could rely on Pamela to call Bill Clinton to convey our message," says Jean-David Levitte. "She would get through to the Oval Office immediately."[53] The bloodshed on European soil haunted Pamela and her own experiences of war gave her a particular clarity. (Chirac himself had been only six at the outbreak of war and Clinton had been born after it ended.) Then, America had eventually come to save Britain and the rest of Europe from tyranny; Pamela made it clear she thought Clinton had a similar obligation to act now. The end of the Cold War was no excuse to turn inward; it merely presented different problems. But nor should Europe, as Clinton saw it, walk away from its "responsibilities."[54] America could not act alone.

Pamela understood "how the position had changed since Mitterrand," recalls another of Chirac's senior aides. "She explained to President Clinton directly and the people around him the need to become more aggressive diplomatically but also on the ground. It was very unusual to see someone like that play a very political role." "We had confidence that she had the capacity to exert strong influence on Bill Clinton personally," agrees Levitte, as initially "Clinton was not in favor of any U.S. involvement in the Balkans . . . [but] she was very clever . . . and we knew she had this personal relationship with him." The pressure on her had never been greater—she had finally reached the place she had worked for over the fifty long years since Germany surrendered in May 1945. And yet this was also the moment rumors swept Paris that she wanted to give it all up, that the lawsuits and hostile coverage had taken their toll. She threw everything she had into opening the channel of communication between Chirac and Clinton but wondered how much she had left "in the tank."

In June, Pamela helped set up a meeting for Chirac at the White House on his way to a G7 summit in Canada. Clinton disliked altercations, preferring "to conciliate in other people's squabbles," according to Deputy Secretary of State Strobe Talbott, "and to boost leaders whom he liked."[55] Thanks to Pamela, he already liked Chirac, otherwise what was always going to be a tough meeting might have been even tougher. The Americans in the Oval Office that day soon learned why the French president had earned the nickname *Le Bulldozer*. He threatened that unless America supported a UN Security Council resolution to send in a well-armed Anglo-French Rapid Reaction Force to protect the UN peacekeepers, he would withdraw his troops from Bosnia altogether. Alarmed American officials, knowing that it would still be an uphill task to win Congress backing for intervention, asked Pamela whether Chirac meant what he said. Knowing him well, she was able to inform them that, in her view, he did. It was a decisive moment, when Washington appreciated that Chirac was a more forceful leader than traditional allies in London, and America's obvious European partner. (Although relations became cordial and the Brits were equal partners in the Rapid Reaction Force, John Major never became as personally close to Clinton.) Pamela knew "all the finest details on trying to end the Bosnian war," Clinton remembers, and she was also aware of "how desperately the United States had to keep France in the fold."[56] American—and congressional—opinion began to shift. "There was a change of attitude by the U.S. after Chirac's meeting," a senior French official claims. "They decided it was time to stop turning the other cheek." Chirac's blunt statement that "the position of leader of the Free World is vacant" had also focused minds.

Back in Paris, Pamela saw the power of the media in pumping up the pressure on the White House by reporting the atrocities in Bosnia night after night—a phenomenon that became known as the "CNN effect." Footage of Serbs taking women away to be raped and men to be slaughtered had a visceral impact on audiences across the world. It was at this point that Pamela befriended the station's trailblazing correspondent Christiane Amanpour, who was "intensely involved in telling the story," inviting her up to her chintzy bedroom at the residence, rows of perfume and potion bottles lined up on the glass-topped dressing table, to discuss how to ratchet up the case for massive intervention. Just as in the 1940s, Pamela was convinced that only America's might could stop the bloodshed. "She really identified with the need to stop the genocide," remembers Amanpour, who had even had a row on live television with Clinton over America's ineffectual position. "She'd sit on an armchair applying her makeup and briefing me. As a very visible young woman on television, I felt like I had a very special relationship with her. I really loved her for what I could see she was doing. She was a superhero. With her experience from World War Two she was providing the moral compass."[57]

In July, the Bosnian Serb general Ratko Mladić, known as the Butcher of Bosnia, shelled three towns (Srebrenica, Žepa and Goražde) crowded with starving Muslim refugees reduced to scavenging tree roots, all humanitarian aid having been blocked by the Serbs. The towns had been declared among six UN Safe Areas but were protected only by a poorly armed force of Blue Helmets who did not even have a clear mandate to fire. News came out that the Serbs had corralled thousands of men and boys into a football stadium in Srebrenica and massacred them. A UN arms embargo had left the Bosnian government virtually powerless to fight back, giving the

Serbs in Bosnia (amply supplied by arms-rich Belgrade) almost a free run to conduct further atrocities against the Muslim minority. A vast tragedy was unfolding while America still hesitated and Chirac had to repeat to Clinton on the phone that France would withdraw its troops from Bosnia unless the U.S. took decisive action to stop the genocide in which three hundred thousand people had now died.* "We cannot allow ourselves to be accomplices," he warned, according to newly declassified papers.[58] There needed to be a credible threat of force.

Under immense pressure, Clinton finally issued an ultimatum to the Serbs from U.S. Strike Command and its French and British counterparts, warning of a huge retaliation unless attacks on safe areas stopped. The world waited to see whether it was an empty threat. In the meantime, he dispatched Richard Holbrooke to Paris to construct a plan. Holbrooke made his way to Pamela to brief his friend on the new American position before she took him in to see Chirac. Holbrooke shared Pamela's view that America should be playing a far more decisive role—he saw the U.S., according to his third and last wife, Kati Marton, as "the last best hope of mankind"[59]—and was gripped by Pamela's experience of history. Holbrooke understood that as a trusted Hopkins-style confidante of both Clinton and Chirac—and he was not close to either—Pamela's ability to help cement a forceful alliance was "unique."[60] From the failure of the first Paris negotiations on Vietnam back in 1968, where he had assisted Averell, he knew that finding the road to peace is all but impossible without the full backing of the principals.[61]

Holbrooke had the unyielding personality for a hardball negotiation with the merciless warlords of the Balkans—or "junkyard dogs," as one American official called them.[62] "He was brutal, an egotist, the kind of person who was perhaps useful," a senior French source puts it,

---

* This number is used by Chollet and Power's *The Unquiet American*; however, it has since been disputed. The International Center for Transitional Justice suggests 140,000 deaths; the United States Holocaust Memorial Museum an estimated 100,000 deaths.

"but he could upset people." Holbrooke himself appreciated that Pamela could soothe wounded egos (including his) but also raise red flags when necessary. "Dick pushed things, saying he was smarter than anyone else. She calmed him," says Tom Pickering, "but she was also a corrective."[63] She did not seek to dominate conversations, and largely left the technicalities to senior staff and the overall strategy to Holbrooke, but crucially she ensured that the Americans and French did not fall out by providing, as Levitte puts it, "a little drop of oil every now and again."

"Believing France the key to Europe . . . and using her ability to reach almost anyone in Washington by phone, she gained greater access for French officials to important members of the U.S. government than ever before," Holbrooke noted, "despite the aversion of some American officials to any event held in France."[64] He conceded that the "French could be famously difficult," but they now had the strongest stance, in part because they had suffered the heaviest casualties in Bosnia with more than fifty killed. It was obvious the Americans "needed French support to succeed."[65] "Holbrooke was like this light and all the moths of the diplomatic, academic, journalist and political worlds all convened," recalls Amanpour. "It felt like this was the most important thing facing the world at that time. And it was." Pamela would walk in, one senior official remembered, and say, "How can I help?"[66] Holbrooke shared Pamela's view that results required the right people, environment and mood—diplomacy, to his mind, was theater—and she provided them. The mood soon changed for good.

At 8 a.m. on August 28, Pamela was waiting on the hot tarmac at a military airport outside Paris to welcome Holbrooke off an incoming plane. "It was typical of her that she would meet us, even at such an early hour, as a sign of support," Holbrooke remarked, "and to brief us immediately on the French point of view. Some ambassadors never made such an effort, no matter what the circumstances."[67] As they drove into town through heavy traffic she took him through a schedule of meetings, most crucially with Alija Izetbegović, the embattled seventy-year-old Muslim president of Bosnia, whom Chirac had invited to Paris for talks. For the past three years, he had lived under fire in his unheated presidential palace in besieged Sarajevo, even its inside walls pockmarked with bullet holes and, reminiscent of wartime Downing Street, its windows replaced by heavy plastic. And yet he betrayed no sign of yielding territory, despite his hopes being dashed again and again that the West would save his burning country from Serb aggression. Distrustful of the EU and impatient with American inaction, the battle-hardened Izetbegović had sought help from fellow Muslims in other countries, including volunteers known as the Bosnia mujahideen. No peace agreement could be worked out without his cooperation. Holbrooke knew that the "key voice" on how to shape a future Bosnia had to be "primary victims of the war."[68]

Shortly after Pamela and Holbrooke reached the residence, the news came through on CNN. Five Serb mortar shells fired from the hills above Sarajevo had landed in a busy marketplace killing thirty-eight and wounding far more. It was, Holbrooke angrily declared, the final outrage. There could be no further delay. Decisive and immediate action by the U.S. in leading "a massive air campaign" with NATO allies—in other words devastating military force against the Serbs—was vital.[69] The residence became a storm of activity. Makeshift offices were set up in the grand salons, maps and folders strewn over the priceless furniture, urgent talks took place on the big cushioned sofas, while Holbrooke paced up and down on the thick gold and cream carpets in his socks, barking into one phone after another. (Only when he put his feet up on the table did Pamela's indulgence run out.) He knew that the atrocity gave him and Pamela their best, and perhaps final, chance to win White House backing for the decisive attack to cow the Serbs into coming to the negotiating table. All eyes were now on Clinton and what he would do but even at this frantic hour Holbrooke paused to tell Pamela how "extraordinary" it was that he was working with his friend of twenty years to deal with "the most important test of American leadership since the end of the Cold War." "Of course," she replied. "Averell would have been so proud of both of us."[70]

Holbrooke dashed out to meet Izetbegović and his foreign minister Muhamed Sačirbey but it did not go well—the mood was too tense, too frenetic. The Bosnian president was entirely focused on the need for NATO bombing and suspicious of the whole idea of talks, which had thus far resolved nothing and resulted only in broken promises and more bloodshed. "His eyes had a cold and distant gaze," Holbrooke thought. "After so much suffering, they seemed dead to anyone else's pain."[71]

This time *was* different, though. Preparations were secretly underway for a huge and sustained NATO precision-bombing campaign against the Serbs, called Operation Deliberate Force, although as yet there was still no green light from the White House. General Wesley Clark joined Holbrooke and Pamela in the residence the following day to help with the military planning. Multiple phones were ringing, embassy staff were running in and out with news bulletins and maps, coffee was made and remade, meals were brought in. That night tensions mounted still further as Holbrooke repeatedly beseeched Izetbegović to join them, but he had tired of what he saw as the American's bombast. Following an after-dinner speech, he had left his hotel with his bodyguards and planned to fly back to Bosnia in the morning. As night fell Pamela had a buffet dinner served on two round tables laid out under the Van Gogh, windows open onto an unnaturally peaceful Paris scene, a few side lamps casting small pools of light in the corner. She had brought in Sačirbey, who had invited Bernard-Henri Lévy, a dedicated advocate of American intervention in Bosnia, but crucially Izetbegović was still missing.

Excited to be spending the evening with Pamela, Lévy was told nothing about what was being planned and took exception to the way Clark and Holbrooke left the table nine times during the meal. He had no idea that they kept being called away to discuss last-minute hitches in starting the bombing with leaders in Washington, Brussels and New York. Lévy found Pamela the "perfect host," however—or at least until just before midnight, when she started pointedly looking at her watch as if she thought it time for everyone to leave. After an aide came in to whisper in her ear she dashed out through the ornate double doors.[72]

Pamela had decided to try her own brand of diplomacy. Holbrooke referred to the way she "weaponized" the power of her notoriety and splendor of her residence and fervently believed that "if she could get the right people together in a room she could get them to agree, or at least reduce their disagreements."[73] He had also seen how "she was so often right."[74] And so Pamela had sent trusted members of her staff to fan out across the Paris night to try to track down the Bosnian president. It was past 11 p.m. when they found him walking through a light summer shower in the park bordering the Champs-Élysées. They cautiously approached him to issue an invitation to dinner with Pamela at the residence. When he not unreasonably pointed out it was too late to eat, they changed tack and insisted she had important information. "I followed these unknown men," he recounted, with some surprise.[75] Where Holbrooke had failed, Pamela's legend succeeded.

Soon afterward, Izetbegović's car was making the short distance to the residence where Pamela had just taken her place at the top of the entrance steps. A scrawny figure dressed in khakis and a paramilitary beret, he stepped out to be met by a vision in Courrèges silk who in her designer heels towered over him. She fixed her famous blue eyes on his and escorted him into the scented opulence of the Samuel Bernard Salon where Holbrooke was engaged on another call. Izetbegović angrily remonstrated with General Clark, repeatedly demanding immediate bombing and denouncing American failure to intervene as a "dishonour." And yet there was nothing the general could report from Washington; all this could still be in vain.

Finally, after another call came in, Holbrooke pulled Izetbegović aside. Clinton had come through. "Mr. President," he said, "we have some good news . . . NATO planes will begin air strikes in Bosnia in less than two hours." Pamela's and every other face in the room lit up with relief. Not privy to the momentous news, Lévy was in the hallway about to leave as he watched Pamela lead Izetbegović up the stairs to the sitting room on the first floor where a television had been set up to watch the attacks. His last glimpse was of Pamela looking "very dignified, strangely earnest. They all followed her in silence, even *they* seemed in awe of her, lit by a soft light that gave them the look of conspirators caught in the act."[76]

At 2 a.m. local time, Operation Deliberate Force began. More than sixty aircraft from bases in Italy and the aircraft carrier USS *Theodore Roosevelt* in the Adriatic pounded Bosnian Serb positions around Sarajevo. They were supported by French and British artillery in what was the largest NATO military action in history. Izetbegović said of what he called that "famous night": "The world has finally done what it should have done a long, long time ago." The *Financial Times* judged that "Western policy would not have had a shred of credibility left if there had not been a tough response."[77] The *International Herald Tribune* declared: "The United States today is again Europe's leader; there is no other."

The strategy worked. The psychological balance changed. The Serb aggressors reeled from the intensity of the bombing.* Izetbegović came under pressure to trust the Americans and particularly to agree to redrawing the Bosnian map—previously rejected as an unthinkable reward for ethnic cleansing—on the road to peace. "A lot of those pre-negotiations," remembers Levitte, "took place on Pamela's drawing-room sofas." Within a week the foreign ministers of Bosnia, Croatia and Serbia would meet in Geneva and agree an outline peace plan. A

---

* The twenty-two-day operation struck 338 Bosnian Serb targets. Civilian casualties were comparatively low, with one estimate of twenty-seven.

month later there was a countrywide ceasefire. In November, Holbrooke convened the warring factions in Dayton, Ohio, in a vast U.S. air force base hangar—as dramatic a stage as Pamela's residence—to negotiate compromises on all sides. By Thanksgiving an agreement had been reached and the war in Bosnia was over. An international force commanded by NATO would supervise the peace. Holbrooke was rightly praised but Clinton hails Pamela—whose contribution has remained largely unrecognized—as a "big piece in our effort."[78]

Clinton was also correct in saying "American leadership was decisive in pushing NATO to be more aggressive and in taking the final diplomatic initiative."[79] But when he flew to Paris on December 14 to sign the agreement in person, Pamela reminded her president that while America had done the "job" he must be sure to "acknowledge the role" of France.[80] Chirac was grateful that she had helped to ensure that the ceremony took place in the Élysée Palace to recognize the sacrifices of his country.[81]

Shortly after Clinton's arrival, the key figures gathered in Pamela's residence, reflecting just how important a role it and she had played. Looking around her she took stock of the momentous gathering. Along with Clinton there was Holbrooke and Secretary of State Warren Christopher but also the "junkyard dogs" themselves—Franjo Tudjman of Croatia, Slobodan Milošević of Serbia and Izetbegović. "Welcome," Clinton began, sizing them up. "You have all taken significant risks in getting to today's peace agreement."[82] Pamela saw how Clinton was trying to get the measure of Milošević and whispered in the president's ear, "I hope you like your lunch seating as you'll be right across the table from him."[83] "She always paid attention to things like that," he remembers with gratitude, and he indeed used his chance to observe the Serbian leader at close quarters, finding him "intelligent, articulate and cordial" but in possession of "the coldest look in his eyes" he had ever seen.[84] (In 1999, Milošević became the first sitting head of state to be charged by an international tribunal with war crimes.) An hour later, they reassembled on the stage in the Salle des Fêtes at the Élysée for the signing, Pamela a rare woman in a sea of men. The agreement has held—if imperfectly and with obvious strains—for nearly three decades.

Pamela had helped Holbrooke forge Clinton's greatest foreign policy win—and arguably the last successful U.S. military intervention, even the high-water mark of Washington's postwar global supremacy and the so-called Pax Americana. It was one of the final acts of what has become known as the "American century," when the thinking (following the liberation of Europe from the Nazis) was that the U.S., as a beacon of liberal democracy, had earned its status as the world's natural leader. As the world shifts once again, few Americans now talk about their country being the "indispensable nation" but Pamela, who lived and died in the twentieth century, believed that a superpower that did not protect the vulnerable was not worthy of the name. She "played an invisible but decisive role," insists Levitte. "Without her [peace in Bosnia] would have been a lot more difficult." Eight years later, during the international rifts over the Iraq crisis of 2003, *Le Monde* hailed her ambassadorship as a golden era when American and French presidents understood each other via their mutual trust in her. "Her skill in defusing tensions and maintaining communications lines," the paper harked back fondly, "had gone a long way in achieving peace through joint action."[85] Without her, it declared, relations had become tense, misunderstandings rife and the world more dangerous.

So many of the twentieth century's horrors had touched Pamela personally—the bloodshed and destruction of the Second World War, the political assassinations in America, and the near-Armageddon of the Cold War. She wanted lessons to be learned and Stuart Eizenstat, a world authority on Holocaust issues, believes she also helped to smooth the path for Chirac's momentous announcement of July 1995, in which he acknowledged for the first time the culpability of the French in dispatching Jews to the Nazi death camps. Pamela "didn't press him on it but she was a factor," he says. "He, like her, wanted history to be more accurate."[86] Few outsiders knew or understood how she had proved a force behind a powerful sense of ambition and optimism in those last years of the century. It was a collective drive to make the world a safer and better place that had already toppled the Berlin Wall and ended apartheid in South Africa. Now it had brought peace to Bosnia and would also eventually deliver the 1998 Good Friday Agreement in Northern Ireland.

Pamela, meanwhile, was about to sign a document that marked a personal defeat. She had offered new concessions to bring the Harriman lawsuits to an end, both sides realizing that to continue would wipe out everything they had. After Christmas with Minnie and the grandchildren, she flew to New York to sign a settlement. Kathy and her son David Mortimer—once Pamela's favorite members of the family—went to meet her at her lawyers' twenty-ninth floor offices, uncertain as to whether they had a deal until the moment they stepped out of the lift.

The contents of the documents laid out before them have been kept secret—and to this day the family refuse to comment—although plausible accounts have Pamela paying $9 million to the family outright and more than $2 million to the Harriman charitable trusts and foundation as well as forgiving $2 million of loans made from her funds to the Mortimers and Fisks. She would have to sell Willow Oaks if she could not pay up and would be left with comparatively little in cash to sustain her lifestyle, with most of her remaining wealth tied up in property and art.[87] Several million more would be paid to the Harrimans on her death. Pamela's lawyer Roy Reardon put out a statement that the settlement "corrected inequities" resulting from losses on investments recommended by professional advisers chosen by Governor Harriman before his death (thus removing the suggestion of wrongdoing by Pamela).[88] Some close to the deal said that it was little different from the terms Pamela had offered at the outset.[89] The tragedy was that the heartache and turmoil had wrecked the last few years for everyone concerned.

"In a true sense, it killed her," said Mary's son Averell after she succumbed to a massive heart attack nine days later.[90] Winston agreed that Pamela could never return to "happy families" with the surviving Harrimans. "It was quite an unpleasant case all round."[91] They united only through their lawyers in their joint case against Clark Clifford and Bill Rich.[92] The litigation rumbled on but the money finally retrieved was relatively minimal (an estimated $1 million) despite Pamela personally pleading for more from Clifford. Without the protection of a rich, powerful family she felt lonely and exposed. Both Gianni and her brother, Eddie, had also suffered heart attacks. Bill Walton had died in 1994 and Martha Gellhorn (by then eighty-seven, nearly blind and suffering from ovarian cancer) wrote to Pamela that they were "the only ones left of the old London wartime gang."[93] Pamela thanked Stavros Niarchos for a weekend in St. Moritz (where they were joined by Gianni and Dr. Rosenfeld) and for a friendship that meant "so much" to her but he too was failing. He died in April 1996. Ron Brown, a regular visitor to Paris, was killed in an air crash in Croatia the same month. At his memorial service in Washington, she was unable to contain her grief at the loss of another close friend.

Gianni still called every day—even more remarkable considering how quickly he tired of everyone else—and when he came to Paris they dined at Caviar Kaspia restaurant, tucked away on Place de la Madeleine. "She'd always be late getting dressed when he called so I would give him a drink and olives and talk to him," remembers Janet. "He was fun, good-looking, always tanned. He had wanted to marry her, no question, and she loved him." "He loved her too," David Sulzberger believes. "There was a complicity of intimacy between them. He was the great love of her life." But whatever their regrets about the past, Marella was ill with Parkinson's, his own health was under strain, and it was all too late.

Fortunately, Pamela found congenial company in the gentlemanly new British ambassador who arrived with his wife, Sylvia, in the summer of 1996. A more gracious character than his predecessor, Michael Jay was yet another surprised—even now—by the contrast between the reality and the widespread public perception of Pamela as seductress, fortune hunter and "flibbertigibbet." "People joked to you that you would have to take care in her presence because of what she might get up to," he remembers.[94] Jay quickly realized, however, that she was supremely well briefed and "very effective." That was not to say that she was not sometimes "coquettish" with her neighbor, twenty-six years her junior. There was one memorable moment—"one of the most extraordinary" of Jay's illustrious career—when Pamela invited him up to her private residence alone. He followed her up the stairs, not entirely clear what was going to happen next. "She showed me the view of the garden," he recalls, a little wistfully, "with a twinkle in her eye."[95]

While others had faded or passed away, Linda Wachner became a regular presence in the residence. She attended receptions, the Sunday evening film shows and even organized a new kitchen back in N Street. "It was a very surprising match to put it mildly," says one observer. Janet had worked tirelessly for Pamela in Washington and Paris for nearly seventeen years and had been trusted even to sign papers on her behalf (becoming adept at reproducing her signature). She had given up her own life to run Pamela's but felt herself being pushed out in favor of Wachner.

Relations with Winston were still strained after he moved into a new apartment with his new partner, Luce Engelen, a Belgian jewelry designer, in Belgrave Square, one of London's swankiest addresses. Luce resented Pamela's suggestions for redecoration, seethed when she tucked her feet up beneath her on the sofa and began addressing her as "Madam." Pamela continued to try to help, giving a speech in Winston's constituency in December 1996 and setting up savings accounts for his three grandchildren. She also had him and Luce to stay for a week at the residence in November 1996.[96] Despite being taken to dine at L'Ami Louis (one of the most fashionable restaurants in Paris) Luce remained furious at the way she thought Pamela had treated Winston in his childhood, seemingly making clear her views of her as a mother. A month after the visit, without telling anyone, Pamela altered her will.

Pamela's fourth year as ambassador was as busy as ever. In July, she was able to revive her friendship with Nelson Mandela, now president of South Africa, when he came to Paris on a state visit to coincide with Bastille Day. It was yet another reminder that diplomacy at the highest levels relies on mutual trust and understanding—as Churchill had vividly demonstrated during the war—although the Republicans denounced Clinton for what they deemed his administration's wrongful "personalization" of American foreign policy. It worked for Pamela and she continued to sort out Franco-American spats by spending private time with Chirac.

In June 1996, she had to prepare for another presidential visit when Bill and Hillary Clinton returned to France for a G7 meeting. One night Clinton took her alone for a memorable two-hour tour of the city in his car and as they passed her old haunts, the lights shining through the rain, she told him "what it was like to be young in Paris after the war" after years of being bombed and when "everybody you know is in danger of dying." Her youth had been deferred to those years in the late 1940s and 1950s and she confessed to the president that she had been "a little bit indulgent and done things she might not otherwise have done" but who wouldn't? She confessed that that was why she had wanted to return to Paris, because she owed it "so much."[97]

As Clinton geared up to fight for a second term, Pamela informed him that she wanted to leave her post as soon as a replacement could be found. Those on the ground—such as the veteran *New York Times* correspondent Craig Whitney—hailed her time in Paris. "She has done good work here," he told *Le Monde*, even if he knew only a fraction of what she had done.[98] Pamela was well-known but "not her total persona and especially not her achievements," confirms Verveer, "or how significant those achievements were." Tom Pickering ranked her as a "master of diplomacy" who was a "very clever, very capable, significant and well-managed person." "I don't know how anyone who met her," he says, "could forget her."[99] The White House and the State Department had "ultimate confidence in what she was doing," Susan Berger reports.[100] And yet Pamela feared her achievements would be drowned out by the forthcoming biography from Sally Bedell Smith entitled *Reflected Glory*.

Carter Brown denounced both Ogden's and Bedell Smith's works as "distorted and unrealistic volumes" that dwelled "on the negative, because that . . . is what sells books."[101] Bedell Smith's "dislike of her subject boils on the page," noted the *New York Times* review, and some of her "knifework is not for the squeamish."[102] The bestseller depicted Pamela as a "promiscuous social mountaineer and naked self-promoter" who had floundered as an ambassador—with one unnamed source claiming that she "may be in the room when issues are discussed but her views won't count because there is no merit in what she says."[103] The problem was that Pamela's greatest feats were the least known and she was not one to shout. Ultimately it was public judgment that mattered and here, at least, it was damning.

Pamela was overjoyed when Clinton won again in November 1996, the first Democrat to be elected to a second term since FDR sixty years earlier. He had benefited from an improving economy but also a more stable world, thanks in large part to the resolution in Bosnia. Yet distraught at what she saw as Bedell Smith's hostile account of her life and her work, Pamela saw matters in black and white terms as she had with Ogden. Anyone who did not condemn the book was not her friend; anyone who facilitated it her enemy. Just before Thanksgiving, the banker Felix Rohatyn and his wife, Elizabeth, invited her to dinner at a candlelit restaurant on the Right Bank. Rohatyn had been speaker at that famously leaked Issues Evening and a latter-day adviser on her finances but Pamela was furious, particularly with Elizabeth, and her tone was "decidedly undiplomatic."[104] Elizabeth was chair of the New York Public Library, where Bedell Smith had just appeared to promote her book. "It was your responsibility to prevent this from happening," Pamela raged.

Gradually, Pamela retreated and by dessert the three once again seemed on friendly terms. The following day she invited Felix to the embassy, where she talked about her decision not to seek reappointment. Rohatyn had made his fortune in banking but had always thrilled to the idea of public office. So far, he had been denied his dream but knew that Pamela would be expected to recommend a replacement to Clinton on a visit to DC the following week—and there were few public offices more enticing than envoy to France. "It should be someone like you," she said, according to Rohatyn's account.[105]

There was no promise to back him in the contest and in the end, along with many senior State Department officials, Pamela decided to recommend Frank Wisner, then ambassador to India. Yet a disappointed Rohatyn seethed for years that Pamela had been "devious," claiming she had acted out of fear that he would outshine her socially and diplomatically.[106] Pamela had in fact decided that the Paris job required a professional envoy, recognizing that it would take a certain expertise to follow her without her personal connections. When she returned to Washington and saw Clinton in the Oval Office, she made her preference clear. "She sat on the edge of the Resolute desk next to the president, showing those most gorgeous legs of hers and insisted in her charming manner that I succeed her as ambassador," Wisner was later briefed by Sandy Berger. "When she wanted to engage, there wasn't anyone who could resist her entreaty. Clinton couldn't refuse." "Did she know how to use her feminine wiles?" smiles Clinton in agreement. "Yes . . . but was it on balance good for other people too? You bet it was . . . it was good for America."[107]

On the same visit Pamela spent time with Hillary discussing other upcoming appointments. "Despite four years in Paris . . . she was still in the thick of Washington society and gossip," Hillary recalled with amazement, "and buzzing with curiosity about Madeleine." Albright's was one of the names in the frame for the next Secretary of State and Pamela was intrigued. "I've been talking to *everyone*," she said to Hillary in her "wonderful smoky British accent."[108] It may have been more accurate that the two front-runners had been talking to her. Christiane Amanpour remembers Pamela sitting in a sheer flowery silk bathrobe in her Paris bedroom while she took one call from Albright and another from Holbrooke. "They were lobbying her to be Secretary of State—and I'm sitting in the room while it's happening. They knew she was hugely influential." Despite her close friendship with Holbrooke, Pamela fretted that he broke "too much crockery," hinting that she was in favor of Albright becoming the first woman in the role. Public interest came first. "It all looked so peachy," remembers Amanpour, "but she had a core of steel."

47

Pamela flew to Washington for the inauguration on Linda Wachner's plane. It was time to plan the rest of her life. Even on her historic first day as Secretary of State, Madeleine Albright set aside time for Pamela to discuss her future role in the administration. She intended to keep "very active" on foreign policy, Pamela assured her,[1] and told friends, "I don't want just to sit on the porch at Willow Oaks."[2] Only intimates such as Bob Shrum and his wife, Marylouise, thought her uncharacteristically melancholic. Pamela was desperate to finish the merry-go-round but not as much as she feared it coming to an end. Where would she live? What would she do? Who could she trust? So pivotal to her life had Linda Wachner become that there were suggestions that once the N Street house was sold they might buy a smaller Washington home together and use Linda's apartment in New York. "This sounds lesbian," says a close source. "But it wasn't." Wachner does not care to comment but Peter Duchin brutally put it down to "Pamela saw Linda, Linda had a plane. Linda saw Pamela, Pamela had class."[3] A more sympathetic view would be that despite her prominence, success and fame, Pamela was embattled and fearful, and at night she went home alone.

Back in Paris, Pamela slotted straight back in with a business breakfast with Michael Jay on European defense. As ever, she arrived dressed immaculately and fully briefed for a detailed and weighty discussion. Yet there was a new sense of vulnerability about her so Jay and Sylvia invited her to family dinners as often as possible. "It's difficult being the head of an embassy," Sylvia explains. "You can't talk to anyone in case it looks like favoritism."[4] One evening, Pamela invited the Jays to hers for supper. The three were chatting afterward in her drawing room when Pamela took down from a shelf a copy of *The Dream*, Churchill's short account of his life written in 1947 as told in an imaginary meeting with his late father. Her voice cracking with emotion, she read the ending where Churchill is about to tell of becoming prime minister but then wakes, leaving his father to believe that his life had been a failure. From her long late-night talks with Churchill, Pamela knew how the notion that he had been a disappointment to Lord Randolph had consumed the war leader all his life. It was as if Pamela, like Churchill, was now reflecting on her own record and finding it wanting, that the attacks had in the end reduced her successes to dust. If only she could go back and start from the beginning.

As she talked, her guests noted that her "American accent retreated and she sounded like a young girl from Dorset." "We were all being very English," sitting in her armchairs and nursing a final drink, says Jay, but when they returned home both felt shaken and pondered on how people at the end of their lives often want to return to what they knew best and the happiness they thought they once had. "I'm not sure she wanted to go back to the U.S.," Jay says. Indeed, Pamela had begun to wonder whether she would not after all have ended up happier marrying "a wonderful man, having ten children and never moving away from Dorset."[5]

Jay considered it an "extraordinary privilege" to be working with her but where had ambition and drive got her? The great courtesan, the peace broker, the Democratic Party queen, the kingmaker who had nurtured so many others was stranded in that great mausoleum of a house and "terribly lonely."[6]

Only the thought of the christening on February 1 of her great-granddaughter Arabella Repard seemed to animate her. She flew over to Britain for the service and the following day put on a bravura performance in the saddle. "Mother led a pack over five miles at a very brisk pace," Winston recalled. "We were leaping five-bar gates and she was in top form."[7] Late that night she flew back on the last commercial flight from Gatwick for the usual Monday morning meeting with Don Bandler, who had won "very fierce" competition to take over from Avis as her deputy.[8] After lunch with Élie's cousin David de Rothschild, she was engrossed in a lengthy phone discussion on destroying excess weaponry in the Balkans. It was a knotty technical matter of the sort most other ambassadors left to their staff but Pamela took pride in handling such issues herself.[9] Arthur Schlesinger called to tease her about being a great-grandmother, and she had sounded cheery about returning to Washington in a month, regaining "control of her life" and finding a pied-à-terre in Paris.[10] And yet the upbeat talk had felt a little forced and after putting down the phone Pamela complained to Bandler of a headache. Sensing something was not right, he closed the door to her office and told her quietly that she seemed tired. "Why don't you take a little time?" he asked. "Everything has been taken care of."[11]

Pamela summoned her chauffeur to take her to the pool at the Ritz. Once she had taken Janet swimming with her, but her onetime lynchpin had returned to America, distressed at Wachner's leverage over her boss. Bandler was horrified when "Linda and Janet had had a big fight on Linda's plane. They both wanted to be Pamela's best friend. It was one of the hardest things I had to steer during the whole period." Even Pamela's greatest supporters were aghast at how Janet had been cast off, being told that there was no money left to employ her back in Washington. She had gone home to search for a new job, crying on the plane all the way across the Atlantic. The estrangement had cut both women more deeply than either had possibly imagined and before leaving for her swim Pamela left a conciliatory message for Janet to call her that evening.

Less than an hour later, the Ritz phoned the embassy with news that Pamela was "in trouble." She had collapsed in the water after twenty lengths and was being dashed in an ambulance, sirens blaring, to the American Hospital at Neuilly-sur-Seine. Bandler urgently summoned the embassy car and shot through the streets to her bedside. He found Pamela "all wired up in a plastic oxygen tent" but he took her hand and kept repeating her name. When there was no response, the supreme professional broke down and cried. Bandler later admitted he had "loved" working with Pamela and he had been bowled over by how "horrible" it was to see her unresponsive and alone.[12] Gianni jumped on the first plane to Paris. Pamela's secretary also phoned a tearful Amanpour, but she was on her way to Serbia to interview Milošević and could not come to say goodbye. Phones were buzzing all over Paris and by now around Washington too. At the White House, Press Secretary Mike McCurry told reporters that he thought "much of the whole world will be thinking of her."

Shortly afterward, Winston walked in to the sight of his mother lying lifeless, her hair uncannily neat, her fingernails painted her favorite cherry red. Just the previous day she had been at his side, galloping across rolling Kent countryside; now she was in intensive care, being kept alive by an array of beeping machines. Dr. Rosenfeld boarded an overnight flight from New York to see if he could help, but there was nothing he or anyone could do. Pamela had suffered a massive brain hemorrhage. She would never come back. Winston gave permission for life support to be turned off and a priest came in to give Pamela the last rites, ending with "May the Lord who frees you from sin save you and raise you up." As the heart monitor faded to zero, a nurse reported that President Chirac was on the phone. "I told your mother that before she left French soil," he said to Winston, "I would award her the Grand Croix of the Légion d'Honneur." Now he would clear his diary for a posthumous ceremony. She would be the first foreign female diplomat to receive the honor, the most prestigious in France.

Winston phoned the White House with the news of her death and within seconds was put through to Clinton. "Mr. President, have you heard what President Chirac proposed?" he asked. The American president could hardly be shown up by his French counterpart and, according to Winston, "suddenly, the Atlantic Ocean became a poker table." "We're not going to be outdone on this," Clinton responded.[13] A week later, he signed off on awarding Pamela the Presidential Medal of Freedom, America's highest civilian honor,[14] with the words: "Let history record this nation's pride—and this president's gratitude—for Pamela Harriman's service to our alliance with France and our common cause of liberty."[15]

Clinton did not order flags to be flown at half-mast like he did the following year for Barry Goldwater, the former Republican presidential candidate, or Lewis Powell, the Supreme Court justice. But he stood on the frozen ground of the South Lawn of the White House and with genuine emotion said that Hillary and he were "very sad to learn that our good friend and America's outstanding ambassador to France" had passed away in Paris. She was, he said, "one of the most unusual and gifted people I ever met" and she had been a "source of constant good humor and charm." They would both miss her "real friendship" "very, very much." He concluded: "America has lost a great public servant and another immigrant who became a great American." Privately, Clinton still talks of how he was "heartbroken. I just expected her to be there. I thought her love for life would keep her alive."

Madeleine Albright described Pamela as a pioneer and "one of this century's most exceptional women" whose remarkable past meant she "understood better than anyone" the need for America to remain engaged in the world. A more socially awkward character herself, Albright also noted that "amidst the high-tech gadgetry of the Information Age" Pamela had been "a master of the personal touch that separates simple communications from true diplomacy." The State Department's official spokesman took five minutes of the daily news conference to "say on behalf of the Foreign Service officers she really was one of the finest ambassadors that many of us have seen . . . and if you talk to the embassy staff as I did this morning she was loved. This is not true obviously everywhere in the world." He found it necessary to add: "She was a very serious person."

Arthur Schlesinger could not believe such a life force had gone. "She was such a dear and generous friend and so vital a part of our lives," he wrote in his diary. He found consolation only "in the fact that she died at the height of her career."[16] Rob Stein thought there had been "nobody like her." "Pamela was *sui generis* in the world from the 1940s to the mid-1990s. That's a hell of a run."[17] Having watched her boss trying for years not to buckle, Janet was convinced that Pamela had been "swindled" and that the lawsuits had caused her death. Others who knew her well felt the same, Peter Fenn judging that the stress and upset of the litigation "killed her, no question."[18] Tributes poured in from both sides of the aisle in the Senate, and in the House it was a Republican, Don Manzullo of Illinois, who sponsored a resolution commemorating her life and giving "heartfelt thanks" for her work for her adopted country.

The *Daily Mail* marked her death with a tribute—of sorts—to her significance: "When historians look back on the twentieth century," it said, "they will find traces of Pamela Harriman's lipstick all over it." The verdicts on her life were by no means universally complimentary— one dismissing her as expert only in the subject of "rich men's ceilings."[19] Brooke Hayward was quoted as remarking she was sorry that "Pamela did not linger, preferably in pain. She . . . tortured me for thirty-seven years. Thank God I outlive her."[20]

The president of the French Republic made his first and last visit to the American ambassador's residence the following Saturday. Walking out onto the marble terrace overlooking the gardens Pamela had had remade in the English style, Chirac looked halfway down the stone steps to the catafalque ringed by a protective guard. In the rows of seats on a blue platform below sat Élie de Rothschild and Maurice Druon looking gray and forlorn. Gianni's mouth was "distorted in grief."[21] Winston on the verge of tears, his family, Pamela's staff and colleagues, French officials and friends filled the other couple of hundred places, faces upturned in shock in the pale winter sun, the air full of birdsong. Often considered haughty, Chirac was pale and visibly emotional as he placed the Grand Cross of the Légion d'Honneur on the casket decked in the Stars and Stripes. Trumpets played the plaintive notes of Taps, the American army's signal for "lights out."

The Archbishop of Paris gave a prayer followed by a martial dirge from the band of the French Presidential Guard in their red and blue uniforms. It seemed appropriate that for the first time the guard included a woman. "I regret infinitely that this ceremony today takes the form of a final adieu," Chirac said in French, in a speech he had largely written himself. "She was elegance; she was grace." Placing Pamela in the stellar lineage of American ambassadors to France that began with Benjamin Franklin and Thomas Jefferson, he declared that Franco-American relations would have been considerably more turbulent without her. "This great lady was a peerless diplomat," Chirac concluded. "She was, for President Clinton as well as for me, an irreplaceable interlocutor, perfectly attuned to our thoughts and expectations." A sorrowful Michael Jay watched the "cardinal and the president presiding over the ceremony for one of the greatest courtesans of all time. And it was an entirely appropriate way for her to go."[22] Finally, Sandy Berger, who had flown in to represent the president, stepped forward to say, "We have come to take her home."

Pamela crossed the Atlantic for the last time, touching down in a driving blizzard at Andrews Air Force Base on the outskirts of Washington to be met by Secretary Albright and a military gun salute. There had been discussions about whether the president himself should attend, but protocol issues got in the way.[23] Janet's estrangement had not stopped her flying to Paris with Berger and organizing a bus with a police escort to ferry Pamela's friends to the base. As the guard of honor lifted the coffin and carried it solemnly through the snow to the hearse Shrum leaned over to Berger to whisper, "I can hardly believe that the person I laughed with on inauguration day is in that box."[24] "She was a friend to each of us," says Susan Berger, who also met the plane. "We all loved her." "She became an American by choice," Albright declared from a lectern inside the huge aircraft hangar. "Nobody loved this country more." Winston noted that "No ambassador from any country has ever had such a homecoming."

Five days later twelve hundred people from forty countries climbed the hill to the National Cathedral for Pamela's memorial service—or as the *Washington Post* tagged it, the "Last Cocktail Party." The bells started ringing for the service for an hour before it began, but everyone in town already knew. The majesty of the occasion—with both the president and vice president taking part—reflected how Pamela had achieved a prominence that eclipsed all but one Churchill and surely made her worthy, as she had hoped, of continuing to bear his family name. Clinton's wish for a full state occasion had been felled only by advice that it would set the wrong precedent for a "mere" ambassador.[25] Even so, a major government announcement on drugs control had been postponed to clear the decks. Extra chairs had been brought out to accommodate the crush. Those without an invitation had to queue up and squeeze in at the back. Some came to mourn, others to network, the mood was somber more than sad. "The running joke was," remembers Sally Quinn, "that there wasn't a wet eye in the house."[26] Other critics described the event as the gathering of a "cult."[27] Rob Stein saw it differently: "It was the loss of a family member."[28]

Hillary Clinton, Tipper Gore, Kay Graham, the ambassadors of France, China and Britain, most of the Cabinet, a clutch of Kennedys, numerous senators, White House veterans from the Kennedy,

Johnson and Carter eras and former Speaker of the House Tom Foley were present. The ever-loyal Holbrooke and Berger came—as well as Don Bandler and Vernon Jordan and an array of her favorite Russia experts. Bob Shrum and Arthur Friendly joined Janet, who was in floods of tears, as was Judith Kipper. Lloyd Cutler turned up and so did Kathy Harriman, Robert Fisk and Felix Rohatyn (who would achieve his wish of succeeding Pamela as Frank Wisner turned the job down). Brooke Hayward and Peter Duchin stayed away. Gregory Peck and Kitty Carlisle Hart formed part of the Hollywood pack—and all three siblings flew over respectively from England, Ireland and Scotland. Donald Trump annoyed her friends by making the "big entrance." Some were surprised to spot Sally Bedell Smith and Christopher Ogden.

Pamela's coffin was dressed in simple white cloth with a stripe of red and gold while the choir wore green, Pamela's favorite color. Like the Allied troops who died on D-Day fifty-three years earlier, Mrs. Harriman had given her life for freedom, said the Very Reverend Ernest Hunt, Dean of the American Cathedral in Paris. Al Gore read a passage from Ecclesiastes with the line "the quiet words of the wise are more to be heeded than the shouting of a ruler among fools." Pamela's eldest grandson, Randolph, cited his great-grandfather's 1932 essay "Thoughts and Adventures": "Life is a whole, and good and ill must be accepted together. The journey has been enjoyable and well worth making—once."

All eyes were on the president as he stepped up to the pulpit. Few expected the next eight minutes to unfold quite as they did. Such speeches are normally built of platitudes and congregation pleasers. Clinton told the author that he had wanted to defy her critics and set the record straight on her substantive achievements. First, he picked up on Churchill's theme with the tribute that "throughout her glorious journey, Pamela Harriman lightened the shadows of our lives . . . she left us at the pinnacle of her public service, with the promise of her beloved America burning brighter because of how she lived." Like Chirac before him, the president (wearing a fawn and black tie given to him by Pamela on his last visit to Paris) bade farewell to a "cherished friend" whose remarkable qualities were much more than her "unforgettable elegance," the lilt of her voice or her "luminous presence." "I can see her now," he said, "standing on the windswept beaches of Normandy on the fiftieth anniversary of D-Day." She had been there "as an active life force in the greatest continuing alliance for freedom the world has ever known" and had "felt to her bones America's special leadership role in the world." "History," he said, looking increasingly moved, "had come full circle."

Yet she contributed much more: notably a "vibrant sense of history and the wisdom that came to her from the great events" that "she had helped to shape" including, he chose to highlight, the "peace accord in Bosnia." What she had done in the face of adversity, he said as his eyes raked the rows of her critics sitting before him, was prove herself "indomitable." Seeking to crush the reports of a female rift, Clinton talked of how Pamela had been there for both Hillary and him throughout the turbulent 1992 election as "wise counsel, friend, leader" who seemed never to doubt that success would come. Afterward, her appointment to Paris had been "one of the easiest" he had had to make as her whole life had been "preparation for these last four years of singular service and achievement in Paris." To those who still scorned, the president who had finally reversed the Democrats' interminable losing streak delivered his verdict on her role in his own journey to the White House: "Today I am here in no small measure because she was there."

The next day, the *Washington Post* questioned why the "femme fatale of World War II who spent the Blitz . . . dodging bombs and wrecking homes" had been lauded in such a way.[29] Another piece in the same paper observed that "you would have thought she had actually done something momentous."[30]

When Pamela altered her will fifteen days before she died, she made two major changes. Winston discovered he was no longer her sole major heir. In her last act as convert to the female cause, Pamela had decided to express her displeasure at his deserting his wife of thirty-one years by leaving half the estate to Minnie. "Winston saw it as the last insult from his mother," according to a family member. "He was never good enough for her." The other alteration, that Janet would receive nothing, shocked Pamela's friends as much as her foes. "It was inexplicable," says Melissa Moss, that Pamela failed to "take care of Janet after all her years of loyal service."[31] She had, however, just a few days earlier discussed plans to put that right by giving Janet an immediate tax-free gift to mark seventeen years of service. Her death meant they were never completed.[32] By contrast, Pamela left $250,000 to each of Winston's four children, $100,000 to her brother Eddie and gifts of up to $20,000 to two gardeners, her butler, cook and chauffeur. The Van Gogh, as expected, was to go to the National Gallery in Washington—Pamela's last gift to America. Linda Wachner was one of the executors of the estate, which in the eleven years since Averell's death had fallen from an estimated $65 million to less than $10 million, mostly property, art and jewelry. News of the will came at a tough time for Winston, whose political career was running into the sand. His constituency had disappeared in boundary changes and, with a general election only months away, no other wanted him.

Linda took charge of clearing Pamela's effects from the residence and within weeks put them on public display in Paris before shipping them to Sotheby's in New York for an auction in May. The sale included her remaining artworks and also intensely personal items such as two heart-baring notes from her friend Louise Vilmorin, giving those who had been fond of her, including the Jays, an uncomfortable feeling of voyeurism. Others were excited at the chance to rifle through the life of a *grande horizontale*—in death Pamela was being compared to Violetta, the unfortunate courtesan in *La Traviata* who seeks true love—and a few wanted to own a part of it. But for the Jays there was a feeling of sadness and surprise that Pamela's intimate life seemed to be open to view and up for grabs. She had, Pamela once reflected, "sipped deep at the well of life"—but now everyone was peering in.

Sotheby's produced a green-covered catalog with Digby crest endpapers to curry interest in the eleven hundred lots but, perhaps fearing controversy, there was little publicity. On the day, the auction room was busy but not crowded, although the phones were buzzing with bids from afar. Actress Whoopi Goldberg sat in the third row bidding for several items and ending up with two: a two-foot-long leather-covered figure of a donkey, for which she paid $1,495, and twelve silvered-metal coasters (at $2,875, six times the high estimate). Aretha Franklin acquired three silver cigarette boxes and three occasional tables for $8,395. Lots relating to Pamela's success as a seductress fetched up to twenty times their original estimates. One unnamed Hollywood denizen wanted her Pamela trophy—a chintzy boudoir screen with matching armchair and footstool—to create an "intensely feminine chamber in LA."[33] Perhaps inevitably, there was fevered interest in Pamela's four-poster bed, which went for $41,400. Romney's *Lady Hamilton as a Vestal* sold well, but with her best pieces already gone, only half a dozen items of Pamelabilia fetched sums in the six figures. One was Pamela's beloved Helleu, which made $431,000 (surely her best investment as she had bought it for less than fifty francs). The silver-plated Digby ostrich car mascot from Gianni attracted little interest.

Some $2 million of the final proceeds of $8.7 million went to finalize the settlement with the Harrimans and the rest was divided between Winston and Minnie. Although a third higher than the original best estimate, Pamela's sale had not matched Jackie Kennedy's the previous year, which had raised $34.5 million, and curiously did not include Pamela's jewels (these were quietly auctioned later). Sotheby's had not bothered to send a catalog to the comedian Joan Rivers, who had bought at the Jackie sale. "Why, after all, would anyone want a piece of Pamela Harriman?" Rivers parried. "Anyone that wanted it, believe me, has already had it."[34]

Eventually 3038 N Street was sold at a reduced price to Pamela's dermatologist, Dr. Nigra, who was excited to buy his famous client's house. The real estate agent instructed him to wire the money immediately to Winston as "he was concerned that as an asset in the United States, the Harrimans might do something to reclaim it."[35] Winston and Luce were allowed in briefly beforehand to collect personal papers. In the vault, they found documents on Pamela's annulment but also neatly tied bundles of letters from her lovers. Far from dumping her, as has been the common wisdom, "they all wanted to marry her, every single one," says an intimate who saw them. As ever, the perception of Pamela was not the reality. What she really wanted—and what those men were unable to give her—was to live a life on her own terms. As a woman born in the early twentieth century to parents who wanted a boy, who was raised only for marriage, who never had the chance of a formal education or proper career, that meant changing her name and her nationality, wrecking her health with work and worry, and waiting five decades for her second break.

President Clinton looks back on his friend with affection and awe. "Was she calculating?" he asks a quarter of a century after her death. "Yes, tell me someone in politics who isn't. Was she ambitious? Yes, she was a child when she married the [soon to be] prime minister's son and found a way to make herself useful during the war at some risk to herself. Did she have a good time living? Yes, she did. Good for her."[36] And yet he never got around to awarding her the Medal of Freedom—"I absolutely meant to and regretted it"—another occasion when she found herself overlooked. Her ambitions for her four years as ambassador in Paris gave, as her other great admirer Richard Holbrooke observed, a "different meaning" to all the choices she had made over the many years before. They had turned out to be the ultimate preparation for the role she had played so effectively right at the end. "After a life, in which she was identified closely with a series of important men," he said, "she did something important so splendidly on her own."[37]

Acknowledgments

This book is one of many voices—some of whom sadly left us during the many years I spent researching Pamela's life. Often it felt as if I was rushing to record a pivotal passage in history before we lost more of its key players. I remember them all with gratitude and give thanks for their recollections and thoughts—and in many cases their sense of fun and wonder at Pamela's extraordinary life. Some were friends or admirers of hers, others much less so. Their insights are equally valuable. No one could possibly forget her. I am fortunate that a number of these sources have subsequently become friends of mine.

Firstly, I am grateful to President Clinton for our hugely enjoyable discussion—which went on for three times the allotted slot. He was a mine of fascinating memories and analysis, and thanks too must go to his staff for their help and patience.

Peter Fenn, Robert Legvold, Avis Bohlen, Christiane Amanpour and Colette Shulman not only talked to me about the life and times of Pamela but were kind enough to cast their expert eyes over passages of the book. I am so grateful.

I was honored also to have Peter Caddick-Adams and Misha Glenny read respectively the extracts on the Second World War and Bosnia, and Allen Packwood, director of the Churchill Archives at Cambridge University, read the entire typescript. I hugely value their time and all their comments.

Particular thanks must also go to David Sulzberger, with whom I

ACKNOWLEDGMENTS

have shared many entertaining lunches and who has helped in countless ways. Frank Wisner also went above and beyond as did the late Janet Howard, even when she was obviously frail due to her final illness. Melissa Moss has been my lodestar and an excellent and generous raconteur and Ambassador Lord Jay and Lady Jay charming and helpful interviewees. The renowned Jean-David Lavitte (President Chirac's chief foreign affairs adviser) was of wonderful assistance in explaining the French experience of Bosnia. His account—and that of others both privately and publicly—shed light for the first time on what he called Pamela's "invisible but decisive" contribution to the tortured process of finding peace. I have not attempted to write a full blow-by-blow analysis of events in the Balkans and the reactions in Western capitals, but specifically an account of her role according to those who worked most closely with her on the crisis. I am aware, as so often in these circumstances, that this may not tally exactly with those who watched from a different vantage point.

I have been extremely fortunate in the access I have been granted during the course of researching this book. A few key sources did not wish to be named because of continuing sensitivities (including a prominent French politician) and certain intimates of the Churchills. In such cases, I have quoted them without names or specified material as "private information."

I owe huge thanks for their testimony, and also to Ambassador Tom Pickering, Emma Soames, Celia Sandys, Peter Duchin, Melanne Verveer, Rosamée de Brantes, the late Jane Portal (Lady Williams), Stella de Rosnay, Gill Ross, Ambassador David Lane, Ghislaine Graziani, Didi d'Anglejan, the late Robert Stein, Tom O'Donnell, Katie Monahan-Prudent, the late Clarissa Churchill Eden, Sally Quinn, Lally Weymouth, Susan Berger, Sven E. Holmes, Jonathan Powell, Pie Friendly, Amanda Downes, Ambassador Lord Renwick, Stuart Eizenstat, Mallory Walker, Diana Walker, Ambassador Nancy Ely-Raphel, Paul Kirk, Dr. Simon Mollan, Judith Kipper, Mark

ACKNOWLEDGMENTS

Steitz (who gave kind permission to quote from his papers), Artemis Cooper, Antony Beevor, Robert Shrum, Shelagh Montague Browne, Ben Newick, Lord Charles Powell, Dr. Thomas Nigra and Kiki McLean. Special thanks must also go to Sidney Blumenthal who opened doors for me, and Jane Thayer, Mandy Grunwald and Kitty Kelley for teaching me about the ways of Washington.

In exceptionally trying circumstances during the pandemic, the staff at the Library of Congress managed to remain cheerful and helpful. And as always it was a pleasure to dig into the new and old treasures of the Churchill Archives and it was a welcome experience to research at the New York Public Library—again despite all the hurdles. Because of travel restrictions I conversed with many other archivists online including several presidential libraries and custodians of the Beaverbrook Papers at the House of Lords. I am full of gratitude to all for their guidance in tracking down vital documents.

A special treat was to enter both the British and American ambassadorial residences in Paris. The then British ambassador Edward Llewellyn was gracious to chat over coffee with me about the duties of a modern ambassador and to allow me a tour of the official residence, the Hôtel de Charost. Candice Nancel from the State Department was kind to give me a thorough and knowledgeable tour of Hôtel de Pontalba, just the other side of the wall. So much made sense as a result. It was also a privilege to be a guest at the magnificent Grand-Hôtel du Cap-Ferrat on the Riviera—how lucky Pamela was to live such a life in such places!

Those eager for earlier accounts of Pamela's life—taken from a different perspective—should of course turn to Sally Bedell Smith's and the late Christopher Ogden's biographies as mentioned in the Prologue. Both are highly readable. In the notes, I have also directed readers to other books that might prove particularly useful as background as well as a fuller bibliography.

Thanks also go to the industrious Rosa Haworth, who assisted

ACKNOWLEDGMENTS

marvelously with a month of fact-checking. My sons, Laurie and Joe, were also a great help with researching, transcribing and urging me to hurry up with finishing. They have put up with long absences from a preoccupied mother and I hope they don't mind too much! I'd like to say a big thank-you, too, to Lizzie Maggs and Alice Cappell for their support. I am also grateful to Peter and Hilary for providing a writer's retreat for a week; to Gordon and Babeth Marsh for their reminiscences and endless delicious suppers when I was in full writing mode; for the cheer and encouragement of Peter Gatley, Anthony Quinn, Jenny Liddiard, Dave Cooper and Alison Ewbank, Anthony Marks and Tom Barry, Susannah Herbert and Jane Dyball; Sarah Morgenthau and her wonderful family for their friendship and putting me up in Washington; the thoughts and encouragement of Jonathan Maitland; the editing haven provided by Jana at Mykonos; to Ela, thanks for making my life so much better; and for the kindness and support of Jane and Christian Brocard, Jan and Nick Light, Caroline and Georges de Costa, Laurent and Sofya Pattenotte, Sylvie, Annie, Bibi and Miguel, Didy and John, Gaëlle and Dominique, Steve and Lorraine. All the Otaries—my phenomenal multinational wild swimming group in France—need to know how special they have been to me in the past few years. This book is dedicated to them.

Mark Bergman, Gregg Collins and Lee Pollock have also been stalwart in their encouragement. And I have lost count of the number of friends who have regularly said, "Please hurry up, I'm dying to read it!" I also want to thank the BBC film archivist—whose name I never caught—who once came up to me at a festival to say, "The one I really want you to write about is Pamela." Well, this book is down to you!

Of course, none of this would have been possible without the best of all literary agents, Grainne Fox of United Talent Agency, who has changed my life entirely for the better. Huge thanks too to Sarah Savitt of Virago in the UK and Emily Wunderlich and Andrea Schulz of Viking in the U.S. for their enthusiasm, vision, backing and

ACKNOWLEDGMENTS

patience. Zoe Gullen of Little, Brown pushes and pulls a book into shape like no one else and I always enjoy working with Linda Silverman on putting the pictures together. Thanks also to Marie Hrynczak and Hannah Wood, as well as proofreader Elizabeth Dobson. I am also thrilled that the redoubtable Grace Vincent is handling the publicity in the UK in tandem with Lucy Martin, with Rebecca Marsh adding her own spark and sparkle from the U.S. together with Carolyn Coleburn.

The pandemic and losing my mother and brother within four months made this book particularly difficult to write. It was in any case a monumental task to piece together Pamela's life—a life that was lived as if each day was her last. If the challenge was sometimes overwhelming, I got through in large part thanks to Jon.

London, 2024

Notes

The restrictions of the pandemic shaped the research of this book, notably at the Library of Congress, which houses Pamela's only recently fully opened collection of papers. On my visit in December 2021, access (when granted at all) was severely limited to a few hours a day with regular breaks for deep cleaning. It was not possible to record exact box numbers. Those wishing to locate specific papers can consult this guide: https://findingaids.loc.gov/exist_collections/ead3pdf/mss/2018/ms018013.pdf.

Unless otherwise indicated, much of the direct speech from Pamela in the text is derived from the transcripts of Christopher Ogden's extensive interviews with her. He, of course, was not permitted to use them during her lifetime but they are now finally open at the Library and provided a rich resource.

Other items in this vast and astonishing archive include hundreds of letters, financial statements, appointment books, diaries, her own notes of important occasions. In the notes section, Pamela Harriman Papers is abbreviated to **PHP**.

Also at the Library of Congress are Averell Harriman's Papers (**AHP**) and Rudy Abramson's collection.

Visits to the following libraries were impossible because of Covid so my research was conducted online with valued help from the archivists: the Kennedy Presidential Library, the Franklin Roosevelt

NOTES

Presidential Library, the Richard Nixon Presidential Library and the William J. Clinton Presidential Library.

Antony Blinken's Papers were also useful both within the Clinton Presidential Records and at the National Archives and Records Administration (**NARA**).

Fortunately, I was able to visit the Churchill Archives at Churchill College, Cambridge, in the UK before and after the restrictions. The following abbreviations have been applied:

- **RDCH**—Randolph Churchill Papers
- **MCHL**—Mary Churchill Soames Papers
- **CSCT**—Clementine Churchill Papers
- **BREN**—Dr. Piers Brendon Papers
- **DIAC**—Diana Cooper Papers
- **CHAR**—Chartwell Papers from the Winston Spencer Churchill Collection

Given the possible confusion arising from the numerous books written by different Churchills, I have referred to them by their title rather than the author.

The Beaverbrook Papers (**BBK**) are lodged with the House of Lords Library.

The Foreign Office (**FO**) papers quoted are at the National Archives at Kew, southwest London.

Lastly, interviews were recorded and transcribed and the quotations used were double-checked with interviewees whenever possible.

NOTES

1

1. PHP
2. Spinney, p. 76. Read Laura Spinney and Catharine Arnold for more about the pandemic
3. *Time*, July 5, 1993
4. Bedell Smith, p. 23
5. PHP
6. PHP; *Vanity Fair*, July 1988
7. PHP
8. Jenkins, p. 213
9. *Architectural Digest*, June 1984
10. PHP
11. PHP
12. PHP
13. Lord Digby quoted on *Churchill's Girl*, Channel 4, November 30, 2006
14. PHP
15. Bedell Smith, p. 29
16. PHP
17. *Churchill's Girl*, Channel 4, November 30, 2006
18. PHP
19. PHP
20. *Memories and Adventures*, p. 47
21. C. L. Sulzberger, *The Last of the Giants*, March 7, 1958, p. 454
22. For more on Jane, read Mary Lovell's *A Scandalous Life*

2

1. *Sunday Times Magazine*, October 31, 1982
2. Clarissa Churchill, interview with author
3. PHP
4. C. L. Sulzberger, *The Last of the Giants*, p. 455
5. PHP
6. Abramson, p. 308
7. PHP
8. PHP
9. *Washington Post*, June 12, 1983
10. PHP
11. PHP

3

1. *Tatler*, November 24, 1937
2. PHP
3. *Memories and Adventures*, p. 50
4. Richardson, p. 151
5. Richardson, p. 79. An excellent read for further information about "coming out"
6. Devonshire, *Wait for Me*, p. 90
7. Bedell Smith, p. 45
8. *Sunday Times Magazine*, October 31, 1982
9. *Sunday Times Magazine*, October 31, 1982
10. *The Sketch*, June 26, 1938
11. Mitford, *Letters*, p. 431
12. Quoted in Richardson, p. 149
13. Devonshire, *Wait for Me*, p. 90
14. Devonshire, *Wait for Me*, p. 90
15. Byrne, p. 89
16. PHP
17. Kennedy Presidential Library, Kathleen Kennedy: Family Correspondence, September 10, 1943
18. McTaggart, p. 39; Goodwin, p. 543; Bedell Smith, pp. 43–4
19. Bedell Smith, p. 45
20. Eden, p. 59

4

1. RDCH 4/17
2. RDCH 4/17
3. RDCH 4/17
4. PHP
5. PHP
6. Collier and Horowitz, p. 100
7. McTaggart, p. 18
8. Evans, p. 6
9. Dallek, p. 47
10. Ogden, p. 67
11. Ogden, p. 69
12. RDCH 1/3/1
13. RDCH 1/3/1
14. *Twenty-One Years*, p. 119
15. PHP
16. PHP
17. Bedell Smith, p. 50
18. David Ormsby-Gore, quoted in *Vanity Fair*, July 1988. In 1961, Ormsby-Gore became ambassador to the United States
19. Bedell Smith, p. 41
20. PHP
21. PHP
22. Byrne, p. 135
23. Beaton, p. 13

5

1. *Memories and Adventures*, pp. 4–5
2. Bedell Smith, p. 52
3. PHP

4 *Memories and Adventures*, pp. 4–5; Leslie, p. 47; Abramson, p. 309; Roberts, p. 188
5 Letter to Violet Hammersley, October 10, 1939, Mitford, *Love from Nancy*, p. 84
6 *Memories and Adventures*, p. 7
7 RDCH 4/17
8 RDCH 1/3/6; PHP
9 PHP
10 RDCH 4/17
11 *Sunday Times Magazine*, October 31, 1982
12 PHP
13 RDCH 4/17
14 MCHL 5/1/84
15 MCHL 5/1/84
16 Mitford, *Love from Nancy*, p. 431
17 MCHL 5/1/84
18 Russell, October 1, 1939, p. 69
19 Leslie, p. 43
20 PHP
21 Ireland, p. 62

6

1 *A Daughter's Tale*, p. 180
2 *A Daughter's Tale*, p. 180
3 Abramson, p. 310
4 *Memories and Adventures*, p. 6
5 *Twenty-One Years*, p. 18
6 Ziegler, p. 94
7 Ireland, p. 179, ref *The Last Lion* pp. 310–11
8 BREN 1/11
9 Beaton, p. 13
10 PHP
11 *His Father's Son*, p. 175
12 Pamela interview, BREN 1/11
13 Ogden, p. 92
14 Colville, *The Churchillians*, p. 24
15 Ireland, p. 121
16 PHP
17 Roberts, p. 77
18 Roberts, p. 175
19 Ireland, p. 172
20 RDCH 4/17
21 *Memories and Adventures*, p. 8
22 Leslie, p. 47
23 Roberts, p. 177
24 *Memories and Adventures*, p. 11
25 *His Father's Son*, p. 175
26 PHP
27 Purnell, p. 212
28 Montague Browne, p. 115

7

1 Bedell Smith, pp. 67 and 58
2 RDCH 1/3/5
3 BREN 1/11
4 RDCH 1/3/5
5 RDCH 1/3/5
6 RDCH 1/3/5
7 PHP
8 PHP. These letters are mostly undated, but I have matched them with events as closely as possible
9 Purnell, p. 236
10 Ireland, p. 222
11 *His Father's Son*, p. 155
12 *The Second World War. Volume I*, p. 524
13 PHP
14 *Time*, July 5, 1993
15 *New York Times*, March 22, 1977
16 Lockhart, p. 56
17 Gilbert, vol. VI, p. 454
18 BREN 1/11
19 CSCT June 27, 1940
20 Channon (ed. Rhodes James), p. 314
21 Channon (ed. Heffer), June 26, 1941, p. 592
22 Colville, *The Fringes of Power*, Saturday June 29, p. 177
23 Colville, *The Fringes of Power*, p. 178
24 PHP
25 RDCH 1/3/5
26 RDCH 1/3/5
27 RDCH 1/3/5
28 Harriman, "Churchill's Dream"
29 Beaton, p. 54
30 RDCH 1/3/5
31 *A Daughter's Tale*, p. 237
32 *Memories and Adventures*, p. 1

8

1 BREN 1/11
2 Colville, *The Fringes of Power*, p. 264
3 Colville, *The Fringes of Power*, October 11, 1940, p. 262
4 Colville, *The Fringes of Power*, October 13, 1940, p. 265
5 PHP
6 PHP
7 Leslie, p. 49
8 RDCH 1/3/5
9 Gorodetsky (ed.), November 30, 1940, p. 323
10 Beaton, p. 53
11 Celia Sandys interview with author

NOTES

12 Waugh, *Letters*, November 1940, p. 145; Roberts, p. 197
13 *Memories and Adventures*, p. 16
14 Bedell Smith, p. 57, Waugh, *Letters*, February 18, 1941, p. 149
15 Waugh, *Letters*, February 18, 1941, p. 149
16 *St. Louis Post-Dispatch*, November 19, 1940
17 Ireland, p. 202
18 Quoted in Martin, p. 81
19 Robert Sherwood quoted in Abramson, p. 269
20 Kathleen Harriman Mortimer, interview with Rudy Abramson, quoted in Costigliola
21 *Life*, February 17, 1941
22 Roberts, p. 202
23 Conversions of sterling amounts to today's money taken from the Bank of England inflation calculator
24 Letter to Laura Waugh, Waugh, *Letters*, February 23, 1941, p. 150
25 Roberts, p. 201
26 PHP
27 Bedell Smith, p. 76, ref transcript of John Pearson interview with PH
28 PHP
29 PHP
30 PHP Biographies
31 Beaton, p. 49
32 Eden, p. 59
33 PHP
34 PHP
35 *Sunday Times Magazine*, October 31, 1982
36 PHP

9

1 Hemingway, p. 105
2 Salisbury, p. 183
3 *W*, November 30, 1987
4 *W*, November 30, 1987
5 Channon (ed. Heffer), January 20, 1943, p. 946
6 Olson, p. 98
7 *Washington Post*, June 12, 1987
8 Schlesinger, September 15, 1971, p. 342: Later, Pamela confirmed that "Beaverbrook engineered the whole thing in order to get something on Averell and thereby influence American policy"
9 PHP
10 PHP

11 PHP
12 Parrish, p. 239
13 For more on the geopolitical significance of her role see Costigliola
14 *Sunday Times Magazine*, October 31, 1982
15 *New York*, January 18, 1993
16 PHP
17 Ogden in *Daily Mail*, February 24, 1997
18 Colville, *Winston Churchill and His Inner Circle*, p. 120
19 Harriman and Abel, p. 167

10

1 PHP
2 Ogden in *Daily Mail*, February 24, 1997
3 Montague Browne, p. 152
4 Jones (ed.), p. 112, from Mortimer Family Papers
5 *New York*, January 18, 1993
6 AHP
7 *New York*, January 18, 1993, ref AHP
8 Brenner, in Jones (ed.), p. 126
9 Sarah Norton diary, April 28, 1941, quoted in Bedell Smith, p. 93
10 Bedell Smith, p. 94
11 Brenner, in Jones (ed.), p. 112
12 Jones (ed.), p. 125, from the Mortimer Family Papers
13 Bedell Smith, p. 91
14 Jones (ed.), p. 123
15 Ogden, p. 123
16 Ireland, p. 212
17 Roberts, p. 211
18 *A Daughter's Tale*, p. 255
19 *Memories and Adventures*, p. 19
20 Harriman and Abel, p. 58
21 CHAR 20/33/37–44, ref in Katz, p. 94
22 *His Father's Son*, p. 191
23 *Memories and Adventures*, p. 20
24 AER to JB February 4, 1945, John Boettiger Papers, Franklin Roosevelt Presidential Library
25 *Newsweek*, May 31, 1943; KLH to Marie Harriman, AHP
26 Katz, p. 120
27 Jones (ed.), p. 113
28 Jones (ed.), p. 125
29 *His Father's Son*, p. 196
30 Waugh, *Letters*, p. 154
31 Harriman and Abel, p. 75

NOTES

32 I am indebted to a fascinating analysis of their similarities by Costigliola
33 PHP
34 Costigliola
35 Harriman and Abel, p. 112; BREN 1/11; Katz, p. 94; ref Mortimer Family Papers
36 BREN 1/11

11

1 AHP
2 Lockhart, p. 159
3 Lockhart, p. 159
4 Roberts, p. 231
5 Letter May 2, 1942, *His Father's Son*, p. 206
6 MCHL 1/1/8 January 3, 1943
7 Ireland, p. 226
8 FO 954/5B/200 TNA
9 Channon (ed. Heffer), March 17, 1942, p. 749
10 Lees-Milne, p. 36
11 Channon (ed. Heffer), June 27, 1942, p. 813
12 Waugh, *Letters*, p. 160
13 FO 954/5B/203 TNA
14 Bedell Smith, p. 98
15 Schlesinger, September 15, 1971, p. 34
16 Bedell Smith, p. 101
17 CSCT April 11, 1942
18 Ireland, p. 231
19 Kathleen letter to Marie, October 4, 1942, AHP
20 Lockhart, February 8, 1943, p. 227
21 Leslie, p. 71
22 Several sources close to the Churchill family confirmed this to the author
23 Channon (ed. Heffer), January 22, 1943, p. 947
24 Channon (ed. Heffer), December 6, 1942, p. 921
25 Interview with Colville, Abramson, p. 316
26 *His Father's Son*, p. 202
27 PHP
28 *A Daughter's Tale*, p. 296
29 BBK C/92
30 *Manchester Evening News*, December 18, 1945
31 *A Daughter's Tale*, p. 297
32 MCHL 1/1/7 diary January 3, 1943
33 MCHL 1/1/7 diary July 2, 1942
34 MCHL 1/1/7 diary June 10, 1942
35 MCHL 1/1/7 diary March 20, 1943
36 MCHL 1/1/7 diary March 20, 1943
37 MCHL 1/1/7 diary September 24, 1942
38 Bedell Smith, p. 76, ref transcript of John Pearson interview with PH
39 PHP
40 Jones (ed.), p. 127
41 Pamela told Schlesinger, p. 354
42 WAH to KLH, undated, October 1943, Mortimer Family Papers, via Katz, p. 98

12

1 AHP
2 PHP
3 April 16, 1943, *His Father's Son*, p. 225
4 AHP
5 Ogden, p. 173
6 Hemingway, p. 87
7 Hemingway, p. 83
8 Ogden, p. 125
9 Bedell Smith, p. 119
10 PHP
11 PHP
12 PHP
13 *Sunday Times Magazine*, October 31, 1982
14 PHP
15 Sperber, p. 244
16 Persico, p. 217
17 Brandon, p. 19
18 Costigliola
19 Bedell Smith, p. 113
20 Visitors' book, BBK
21 Author interview with Lady Portal's niece, Jane Portal, later Lady Williams
22 PHP
23 PHP
24 PHP
25 Eden, p. 76
26 PHP
27 PHP
28 Kick to JFK, quoted in Byrne, p. 194
29 *Sunday Times Magazine*, October 31, 1982
30 Quoting from Gilbert and Arnn, p. 1311, and CHAR 1/381/35–37
31 BREN 1/11
32 BREN 1/11
33 PHP

NOTES

34 Bedell Smith, *In All His Glory*, p. 218, ref interview with Holbrooke
35 Bedell Smith, *In All His Glory*, p. 101
36 Bedell Smith, *In All His Glory*, p. 217, ref Marie Brenner interview with Paley
37 Bedell Smith, p. 121
38 Kendrick, p. 221
39 PHP
40 PHP
41 Abramson, p. 315
42 Larry Laseur, interview with Abramson, April 27, 1987, Abramson Collection, Library of Congress
43 *New York Times*, March 2, 1977
44 Olson, p. 145
45 PHP
46 Costigliola

13

1 PHP
2 Kendrick, p. 269
3 C-SPAN interview, May 3, 1994
4 PHP
5 Hackett, p. 63
6 Hemingway, p. 100
7 PHP
8 PHP
9 PHP
10 Lees-Milne, p. 100
11 PHP
12 Hemingway, p. 101
13 Ireland, p. 251, ref Macmillan, *War Diaries*, pp. 474–5
14 Lockhart, p. 352
15 PHP
16 Letter from Randolph to Clementine, July 4, 1944, RDCH 1/2/4
17 PHP
18 Kendrick, p. 263
19 Eric Sevareid quoted by Olson, p. 133
20 Bedell Smith, p. 124
21 PHP
22 PHP
23 PHP
24 Bliss (ed.), November 12, 1944, p. 89
25 Letter to Averell, PHP
26 PHP; MCHL 1/1/9
27 PHP
28 Bedell Smith, p. 120
29 Sperber, p. 246
30 CBS president Frank Stanton, Bedell Smith, p. 124
31 Ogden, p. 176
32 Persico, p. 225
33 PHP
34 *Sunday Times Magazine*, October 31, 1982
35 Abramson, p. 354
36 PHP
37 PHP
38 Katz, p. 195
39 PHP
40 The Yalta conference has been studied by many eminent names, but I am particularly grateful for the excellent analysis in Isaacson and Thomas, p. 223
41 PHP
42 PHP
43 C-SPAN interview, May 3, 1994
44 PHP
45 PHP
46 PHP
47 PHP
48 Isaacson and Thomas, p. 251
49 *New York*, January 18, 1993
50 PHP

14

1 PHP
2 PHP
3 Ogden, p. 179
4 PHP
5 Bedell Smith, p. 129
6 *New York Journal American*, March 6, 1946
7 BBK C/88
8 PHP
9 Mary Warburg interview, Bedell Smith, p. 125
10 PHP
11 PHP
12 Kendrick, p. 290
13 Private information from a Churchill family member
14 Katz, p. 302
15 Abramson, p. 676
16 Abramson, p. 676
17 Bedell Smith, p. 133
18 House of Commons Library
19 *Evening Standard*, September 3, 1946
20 PHP
21 PHP
22 PHP
23 *Memories and Adventures*, p. 39
24 *His Father's Son*, p. 279

NOTES

25 Marina Sulzberger, p. 50
26 Sperber, p. 256

15

1 *Sunday Times Magazine*, October 31, 1982
2 Slater, p. 190
3 Slater, p. 9
4 Mitford, *Letters*, October 5, 1954, p. 346
5 PHP
6 From author's interview with the late Peter Duchin, who asked Marie Harriman what Averell was like in bed
7 *Vanity Fair*, January 6, 2015
8 Interview with Peter Duchin and others
9 Private information
10 Blair and Blair, p. 558
11 Claims made by Onassis about comments that Jackie later made to him, Evans, p. 30
12 Dallek, p. 151
13 Blair and Blair, p. 558
14 Goodwin, pp. 731–2
15 Goodwin, p. 736
16 Collier and Horowitz, p. 170
17 PHP
18 PHP
19 Mitford, *Letters*, August 10, 1948, p. 105
20 DIAC 1/6/12
21 Waugh, *Letters*, October 14, 1948, p. 284
22 Leslie, p. 133

16

1 Author's interview with Rosamée de Brantes, Prince Jean-Louis's niece, who was also staying in the villa
2 Interview with author
3 PHP
4 PHP
5 Ogden, p. 209
6 Ogden, p. 210
7 Friedman, p. 11
8 Helms, p. 6
9 *Agnelli*, HBO documentary, 2017
10 Ogden, p. 212
11 Friedman, p. 36
12 DIAC 1/6/12
13 Interview with author
14 PHP
15 *New York*, January 18, 1993
16 *Churchill's Girl*, Channel 4, November 30, 2006
17 PHP
18 Interview with author
19 PHP
20 PHP
21 C. L. Sulzberger, *The Last of the Giants*, March 7, 1959, p. 454
22 C. L. Sulzberger, *The Last of the Giants*, November 23, 1954, p. 114
23 *New York*, January 18, 1993
24 Interview with author
25 Interview with author
26 Heymann, p. 301
27 PHP
28 *Churchill's Girl*, Channel 4, November 30, 2006
29 RDCH 1/3/1
30 PHP
31 RDCH 1/3/1
32 *Memories and Adventures*, p. 80
33 *Memories and Adventures*, p. 94
34 PHP

17

1 *New York*, January 18, 1993
2 Friedman, p. 14
3 Friedman, p. 50
4 Coward was noted for his combination of "cheek and chic, pose and poise." *Time*, December 26, 1969
5 PHP
6 *Agnelli*, HBO documentary, 2017
7 *Vanity Fair*, July 1991
8 *Agnelli*, HBO documentary, 2017
9 *Vanity Fair*, July 1991
10 I am most grateful to Pamela's friend David Sulzberger for tracking down the exact details of this marvelous car
11 PHP
12 From Nicholas Gerogiannis (ed.), *Ernest Hemingway: 88 Poems* (New York: Harcourt Brace Jovanovich, 1979)
13 Clarke, p. 486
14 PHP
15 PHP
16 PHP
17 Ogden, p. 226
18 Undated letter, PHP
19 RDCH 1/2/12
20 Lovell, *The Riviera Set*, p. 354
21 Sally Bedell Smith in *Vanity Fair*, July 1991

NOTES

22 *Agnelli*, HBO documentary, 2017
23 PHP
24 *Agnelli*, HBO documentary, 2017
25 Interview with author
26 *Vanity Fair*, July 1991
27 *Sunday Times Magazine*, October 31, 1982
28 PHP
29 *New York*, January 18, 1993
30 PHP
31 Interview with author
32 PHP

18

1 Bedell Smith, p. 164
2 Mitford, *Love from Nancy*, October 21, 1954, p. 348
3 Bedell Smith, pp. 173–4
4 Interview with author
5 Interview with author
6 PHP
7 Heymann, p. 302
8 Bedell Smith, p. 164
9 As relayed by Brooke Hayward on *Churchill's Girl*, Channel 4, November 30, 2006
10 Bedell Smith, p. 164
11 Interview with author
12 PHP
13 DIAC 1/6/1/26 August 11, 1954
14 Interview with author
15 Gladwyn, *Diaries*, June 21, 1956, p. 176
16 PHP
17 PHP
18 PHP
19 Gladwyn, *Diaries*, July 18, 1954, p. 164
20 Bedell Smith p. 168
21 PHP
22 Bedell Smith, p. 171
23 DIAC 1/6/1/26 August 11, 1954
24 RDCH 1/3/16
25 DIAC 1/6/1/26
26 Bedell Smith, p. 168
27 PHP
28 Interview with Shelagh Montague Browne
29 PHP
30 Letter to Ann Fleming, September 18, 1954, Fermor, p. 97
31 PHP
32 DIAC 1/6/1/26
33 Peter C. Lambert, Claudine L. Peters and Santiago A. Centurion, "Vaginal spermicides that contain Nonoxynol-9 are mutagenic in a bacterial back-mutation assay," *Carcinogenesis*, 12 (April 2004)
34 Bedell Smith, p. 188
35 RDCH 1/3/1
36 *Memories and Adventures*, p. 84
37 July 3, 1956, BBK
38 DIAC 1/6/1/26
39 DIAC 1/6/1/26

19

1 Persico, p. 401
2 Friedan, p. 24
3 Sotheby's catalogue, Pamela Harriman estate
4 Heymann, p. 302
5 Isaacson and Thomas, p. 584
6 Duchin, p. 70
7 Alsop, p. 180
8 Alsop, p. 133
9 Keith, p. 243
10 PHP
11 Keith, p. 244
12 Keith, p. 244
13 *New York*, January 18, 1993
14 Keith, p. 243
15 PHP
16 Interview with author
17 Ireland, p. 302
18 PHP
19 *New York*, January 18, 1993
20 PHP
21 PHP
22 *New York Journal-AM*, June 1, 1959
23 *New York*, January 18, 1993
24 PHP

20

1 Letter July 15, 1959, in Clarke (ed.), p. 315
2 *Memories and Adventures*, p. 98
3 *Memories and Adventures*, p. 98
4 PHP
5 PHP
6 PHP
7 PHP
8 Hayward, p. 272
9 *Churchill's Girl*, Channel 4, November 30, 2006
10 Ogden, p. 279
11 Ogden, pp. 298–9; Heymann, pp. 303–4
12 Keith, p. 253
13 Keith, p. 254

NOTES

14 Duchin, p. 320
15 Kitty Kelley, *New York Social Diary*, December 30, 2016
16 PHP
17 Hayward, p. 58
18 PHP
19 Hayward, p. 230
20 Hayward, p. 277
21 Hayward, p. 205
22 *Churchill's Girl*, Channel 4, November 30, 2006
23 PHP
24 Hayward, p. 274

21

1 Hayward, pp. 18–19
2 Ogden, p. 300
3 Ogden, p. 286
4 PHP
5 PHP
6 Mitford, *Love from Nancy*, February 18, 1965, p. 431
7 PHP
8 PHP
9 PHP
10 Bedell Smith, p. 234
11 Friedan, p. 21
12 Hayward, p. 57
13 PHP

22

1 McCann and Mollan
2 Collier and Horowitz, p. 235
3 *Sunday Times Magazine*, October 31, 1992
4 PHP
5 PHP
6 Graham, p. 290
7 Pamela's assessment, PHP
8 PHP
9 Harrison
10 DIAC 1/6/1/32 February 15, 1963
11 Letter from Bobby Kennedy, October 12, 1964, PHP
12 PHP
13 PHP
14 DIAC 1/6/1/32
15 Baldwin, p. 332
16 PHP
17 Heymann, p. 306
18 Duchin, p. 320
19 The albums are kept at the New York Public Library
20 DIAC 1/6/1/32

21 *New York Herald Tribune*, September 8, 1963
22 Ogden, p. 355
23 PHP
24 Graham, p. 353
25 Schlesinger, November 15, 1963, p. 206
26 *New York*, January 18, 1993
27 Winkler, p. 66
28 Winkler, p. 68
29 *New York*, January 18, 1993
30 PHP
31 PHP
32 PHP
33 Undated letter of thanks from Gloria Steinem to Pamela, PHP
34 PHP
35 PHP
36 Heymann, p. 314
37 Capote, p. 86
38 *Architectural Digest*, December 31, 1999
39 Clarke, p. 273
40 Schlesinger gives one example, February 27, 1976, p. 407
41 Graham, p. 392
42 *Washington Post*, November 25, 1966
43 Schlesinger recalls when Capote died on August 27, 1984, p. 577
44 Capote, p. 146
45 Capote, p. 155
46 Capote, p. 178
47 Keith, p. 238; Grafton, p. 255; Ogden, p. 309
48 Interview with Gerald Clarke, Ogden, p. 309

23

1 PHP
2 Montague Browne, p. 299
3 PHP
4 *New York Times*, July 16, 1964
5 Pam i/v BREN 1/11
6 Mitford, *Love from Nancy*, p. 431
7 PHP
8 Joy Billington for the *Sunday Times Magazine*, October 31, 1982
9 Schlesinger, March 31, 1962, p. 150
10 Leslie, p. 204

24

1 *Washington Post*, May 29, 2010
2 Ogden, p. 313
3 Private information

4 Brooke Hayward quoted in Heymann, p. 307
5 Duchin, p. 320
6 Heymann, p. 309
7 *Memories and Adventures*, p. 236
8 C. L. Sulzberger, *Seven Continents & Forty Years*, p. 463
9 Letter from Rose Kennedy to Pamela, PHP
10 Halle (ed.), p. 283

25

1 Cahan, p. 211
2 Marina Sulzberger, p. 398, interview with her son and Pamela's close friend, David Sulzberger
3 PHP
4 PHP
5 PHP
6 Ogden, p. 315
7 Bedell Smith, pp. 250–1
8 PHP
9 Bedell Smith, p. 251
10 Bedell Smith, p. 252
11 Bedell Smith, p. 252
12 PHP
13 Kaplan, p. 849
14 Shrum, p. 178
15 PHP
16 Letter to Kathleen Malley, Leland's secretary, PHP

26

1 Duchin, p. 313
2 Abramson, p. 682
3 Interview with author
4 Interview with author
5 *New York*, January 18, 1993
6 Interview with author
7 Interview with author
8 Duchin, pp. 323–4
9 Interview with author
10 Schlesinger, September 15, 1971, p. 342
11 Interview with Pamela, Abramson, p. 684
12 PHP
13 September 23, 1971, Nixon Presidential Materials Staff Conversation No. 280-1
14 Abramson, p. 685
15 Hackett, p. 198
16 Interview with author
17 PHP
18 Duchin, p. 325

27

1 PHP
2 Bedell Smith, p. 266
3 AHP
4 Interview with author
5 Abramson, p. 685
6 Clark Clifford in Frantz and McKean, p. 329
7 Baldwin, p. 334
8 Baldwin, p. 333
9 Ogden, pp. 346–7
10 *New York*, January 18, 1993
11 Brandon, p. 249
12 https://www.nixonlibrary.gov/sites/default/files/forresearchers/find/tapes/finding_aids/tapesubjectlogs/oval793.pdf; Presidential Recordings, Miller Center, University of Virginia https://prde.upress.virginia.edu/conversations/4006749
13 *New York*, January 18, 1993, quoting Berl Bernhard, a top Democrat since the Kennedy years
14 Bedell Smith, *In All His Glory*, p. 111
15 Vreeland to Pamela, April 28, 1972, PHP
16 Interview with Janet Howard
17 Interview with author
18 PHP
19 *Washington Post*, May 5, 1977
20 *New York Times*, March 2, 1977
21 Eden, p. 59
22 Equisearch, March 13, 2002
23 Interview with author
24 Interview with author
25 *New York*, January 18, 1993
26 Duchin, p. 343

28

1 *New York Times*, December 14, 1971
2 *New York Times*, December 16, 1971
3 Hackett, p. 199
4 PHP
5 Abramson, p. 687
6 *New York*, January 18, 1993
7 PHP

29

1 *New York*, January 18, 1993
2 Schlesinger, April 5, 1975, p. 401
3 Interview with author
4 *New York Times*, October 1, 1982
5 Kay to Pamela, May 16, 1974, PHP

NOTES

6 Cahan, pp. 251–2
7 Brandon, p. 133
8 Brandon, p. 133
9 PHP
10 PHP
11 Duchin, pp. 96–7
12 Interview with Sally Quinn
13 Interview with Frank Wisner
14 Mary Soames's *Clementine Churchill* and for more on Clementine Churchill's role read Purnell's *First Lady*
15 Henderson, p. 281

30

1 *New York Times*, July 22, 1976
2 PHP
3 PHP
4 *Washington Post*, September 14, 1976
5 *Washington Star*, October 21, 1976
6 PHP
7 Abramson, p. 691
8 For more on Holbrooke, read George Packer's excellent biography, *Our Man: Richard Holbrooke and the End of the American Century*
9 Interview with author
10 Interview with author
11 Brandon, p. 281
12 Schlesinger, May 31, 1978, p. 448
13 Matthews, p. 155
14 *New York*, January 18, 1993
15 *New York Times*, February 3, 1977
16 Graham, p. 611
17 PHP
18 PHP
19 *Washington Post*, May 21, 1980
20 *W*, October 24, 1980
21 *Sunday Times Magazine*, October 31, 1982
22 Albright, p. 85
23 PHP
24 Bedell Smith, p. 31
25 PHP
26 Interview with author
27 PHP
28 Shrum, pp. 171–2
29 *Women's Wear Daily*, November 30, 1976
30 *50 Plus Magazine*, March 1979

31

1 *New York Times*, March 2, 1977
2 Hayward, p. 3
3 Hayward, p. 17
4 *New York Times*, March 9, 1977
5 *New York Times*, March 9, 1977
6 *New York Daily News*, April 11, 1977
7 *New York Daily News*, April 11, 1977
8 *New York Daily News*, April 11, 1977
9 *News Tribune of Tacoma*, May 22, 1977
10 *Democrat and Chronicle* (Rochester, NY), September 4, 1977
11 *W*, October 24, 1980
12 *W*, October 24, 1980
13 PHP
14 Interview with author
15 *Churchill's Girl*, Channel 4, November 30, 2006
16 Bedell Smith, p. 275
17 PHP
18 Heymann, p. 313
19 Katz, p. 305
20 Heymann, p. 314
21 *Washington Post*, September 17, 1986

32

1 Interview with author
2 PHP
3 Ford Library NSC NSA Memcons Box 8
4 PHP
5 PHP
6 PHP
7 PHP
8 PHP
9 PHP
10 PHP
11 PHP
12 Interview with Colette Shulman
13 PHP

33

1 *W*, October 24, 1980
2 *W*, October 24, 1980
3 PHP
4 Interview with author
5 *New York*, January 18, 1993
6 Interview with Eizenstat, Bedell Smith, p. 291
7 Interview with author
8 Interview with Janet Howard
9 *New York*, January 18, 1993
10 Interview with author
11 *Washington Post*, November 6, 1992
12 *New York Times*, October 1, 1982
13 PHP

NOTES

14 *Washington Post*, November 26, 1980
15 Albright, p. 128
16 Interview with author
17 Interview with author
18 Interview with author
19 Bernstein, p. 160
20 Interview with author
21 Bill Clinton, p. 293
22 PHP
23 Interview with author
24 PHP
25 PHP
26 *Washington Post*, June 12, 1983
27 *Mail on Sunday*, June 6, 1982
28 *Sunday Times Magazine*, October 31, 1982
29 *New York Times*, February 11, 1997
30 *Sunday Times Magazine*, October 31, 1982
31 *Savvy*, October 28, 1987
32 *Sunday Times Magazine*, October 31, 1982
33 PHP
34 Note written by Pamela in 1991 sent to Alida Rockefeller Messinger entitled "To Be a Democrat Is," from Mark Steitz's personal papers
35 *Architectural Digest*, October 1982
36 Bedell Smith, p. 292
37 Interview with Sven E. Holmes
38 *New York*, January 18, 1993
39 Interview with author
40 *Washington Post*, February 11, 1981
41 Bedell Smith, p. 292
42 *Boston Globe*, May 8, 1981; *Washington Post*, November 16, 1981
43 Interview with author
44 *Boston Globe*, May 8, 1981
45 Interview with author
46 Bill Clinton, p. 294
47 PHP
48 PHP
49 *New York Times*, October 1, 1982
50 PHP
51 Interview with author

34

1 Interview with author
2 Interview with author
3 Interview with author
4 Heymann, p. 319
5 *Los Angeles Times*, April 5, 1993
6 Shrum, p. 172
7 Interview with author
8 Interview with author

9 *New York Times*, October 1, 1982
10 Bedell Smith, p. 301
11 Heymann, p. 319
12 Interview with Janet Howard
13 *W*, June 5, 1981
14 *Wall Street Journal*, October 8, 1981
15 *New York Times*, October 9, 1981
16 *New York Times*, October 21, 1981
17 *Newsweek*, November 5, 1981
18 Interview with author
19 Interview with author
20 Interview with author
21 PHP
22 Brandon, p. 254
23 Interview with Frank Wisner
24 PHP
25 *Washington Post*, June 12, 1983
26 Interview with author
27 Helms, p. 180
28 *New York Times*, May 11, 1984
29 *Washington Post*, November 6, 1992
30 PHP
31 Heymann, p. 334
32 Interview with author
33 *New York*, January 18, 1993
34 Heymann, p. 290
35 Interview with Tom O'Donnell

35

1 PHP
2 Interview with author
3 *New York Times*, November 16, 1982
4 Peter Swiers interview with Association for Diplomatic Studies and Training (ADST) Foreign Affairs Oral History Project
5 Cahan, p. 249
6 Peter Swiers ADST interview; *New York Times*, June 3, 1983
7 As recounted by Swiers in *Vanity Fair*, July 1988
8 *Vanity Fair*, July 1988
9 Interview with Janet Howard. Dmitri later came to stay with Janet in Washington
10 *Washington Post*, June 12, 1983
11 Pamela relays this account from Georgy Arbatov, director of the Institute of the United States, America and Canada, in PHP
12 Recounted by Richard Holbrooke in a letter to her July 31, in PHP
13 Bedell Smith, p. 307
14 CBS, February 14, 1984

NOTES

36

1. Interview with Holbrooke, Abramson Collection, Library of Congress
2. Interview with author
3. Bedell Smith, p. 308
4. Heymann, p. 314
5. Ogden, p. 403
6. Interview with Paul Kirk

37

1. *Chicago Tribune*, January 28, 1988
2. Shrum, p. 173
3. Heymann, p. 302
4. PHP, plus several letters of thanks
5. Interview with author
6. PHP
7. *Sunday Times Magazine*, October 31, 1982
8. *Washington Post*, November 6, 1992
9. *New York Times*, April 29, 1984
10. PHP
11. *Daily Mail*, April 13, 1984
12. *Savvy*, October 28, 1987
13. *Washington Post*, June 12, 1983
14. Interview with author
15. PHP, AHP
16. PHP

38

1. Holbrooke, p. 95
2. PHP
3. PHP
4. *New York Times*, July 27, 1986
5. Interview with author
6. PHP
7. PHP
8. Associated Press, September 19, 1986
9. *Washington Post*, September 19, 1986
10. Duchin, p. 353
11. *Chicago Tribune*, January 23, 1988
12. *Washington Post*, September 23, 1986; Heymann, p. 320; Bedell Smith, pp. 319–20
13. Helms, p. 179
14. Private information
15. *Time*, July 5, 1993
16. PHP
17. Interview with author
18. Private information
19. Heymann, p. 331
20. Heymann, p. 332
21. *Savvy*, October 28, 1987
22. PHP

39

1. *Churchill's Girl*, Channel 4, November 30, 2006
2. C-SPAN interview, May 23, 1994
3. PHP
4. Bedell Smith, p. 349
5. Interview with Artemis Cooper and Antony Beevor
6. Interview with author
7. PHP
8. Interview with author
9. PHP
10. PHP
11. *Washington Post*, October 17, 1991
12. Her introduction to Pamela's speech at the 1984 Democratic Party Convention
13. Heymann, p. 334
14. PHP
15. *Chicago Tribune*, January 28, 1988

40

1. Pamela's notes of the occasion, PHP
2. *New York Times*, December 11, 1987
3. From her notes in PHP
4. Pamela's notes, PHP
5. *Time*, December 21, 1987
6. PHP
7. PHP
8. PHP
9. PHP
10. *Women's Wear Daily*, December 8, 1987
11. Interview with author
12. *Washington Post*, April 28, 1988
13. *Washington Post*, April 28, 1988
14. Interview with Melissa Moss
15. *Washington Post*, April 28, 1988
16. *Washington Post*, April 28, 1988
17. PHP
18. Interview with author
19. Heymann, p. 332
20. Interview with author
21. *Izvestia*, October 19, 1990, translated from the Russian, PHP
22. *Washington Post*, June 12, 1983
23. PHP
24. PHP

41

1. *Chicago Tribune*, January 28, 1988
2. PHP
3. Heymann, p. 332
4. Cable sent July 16, 1987, PHP

NOTES

5 Bill Clinton, p. 335
6 Shrum, p. 211
7 PHP
8 *Savvy*, October 28, 1987
9 PHP
10 Hillary Rodham Clinton, pp. 128–9
11 Bill Clinton, p. 341
12 Bill Clinton, p. 343
13 PHP
14 *Washington Post*, November 4, 1988
15 Heymann, p. 330
16 Steven (ed.), p. 513
17 PHP
18 PHP
19 Interview with author
20 Interview with author
21 PHP
22 PHP
23 Interview with author
24 Interview with Mary's daughter, Emma Soames
25 Ogden in *Daily Mail*, February 24, 1997
26 *Washington Post*, May 25, 1986
27 PHP
28 *New York*, January 18, 1993
29 Pamela's testimony in PHP
30 Heymann, p. 333
31 PHP
32 PHP
33 *Washington Post*, June 21, 1989
34 Transcript, February 15, 2002, National Gallery Archives, quoted in Harris, p. 565
35 *Vanity Fair*, January 1995
36 *Chicago Tribune*, January 28, 1988
37 *New Yorker*, December 28, 1992
38 Kerry, p. 188
39 Interview with author
40 *Washington Post*, December 11, 1990
41 PHP
42 PHP
43 Health submission to the State Department 1993
44 Interview with author
45 *New York Times*, September 19, 1989
46 Testimony from Judith Kipper
47 Interview with author
48 Interview with author
49 Interview with author

42

1 Interview with his campaign manager Rob Stein
2 Interview with Rob Stein and others
3 *New York Times*, February 11, 1989
4 Interview with author
5 Interview with author
6 *New York*, January 18, 1993
7 Halperin, p. 24. For more on this meeting and its aftermath, read Halperin's excellent account
8 Interview with author
9 Interview with author
10 Halperin, pp. 15–26
11 Interview with author
12 Interview with author
13 Interview with author
14 WNDC dinner in December 1992
15 Interview with Rob Stein
16 *New York*, January 18, 1993
17 Schlesinger, May 30, 1991, p. 710
18 PHP
19 PHP
20 PHP
21 Hillary Rodham Clinton, p. 134
22 Interview with author
23 Interview with author
24 Interview with author
25 Bill Clinton, p. 385
26 As she privately revealed to Robert Legvold
27 *Washington Post*, November 6, 1992
28 Schlesinger, July 21, 1992, p. 724
29 *New York*, January 18, 1993
30 Interview with author
31 PHP
32 Bill Clinton, p. 287
33 *Los Angeles Times*, April 5, 1993
34 *Washington Post*, November 6, 1992
35 PHP
36 *Washington Post*, November 6, 1992
37 Testimony of Artemis Cooper
38 PHP
39 Ogden, p. 3; Bedell Smith, pp. 379–80; *Washington Post*, November 20, 1992; *Washington Post*, November 21, 1992; *New York Times*, November 21, 1992
40 Ogden, p. 5
41 PHP
42 Heymann, p. 335
43 *Washington Post*, November 20, 1992
44 PHP
45 *New York*, January 18, 1993
46 *New York Times*, June 27, 1993; Lane, p. 144
47 Interview with author
48 *Los Angeles Times*, April 5, 1993
49 From Pamela's notes, PHP
50 Interview with author

NOTES

43

1 Heymann, p. 335
2 Interview with author
3 Bernstein, p. 32
4 *New York*, January 18, 1993
5 PHP
6 *New York*, September 25, 1991
7 Letter to Thatcher, October 29, 1992, PHP
8 *Washington Post*, April 27, 1994
9 PHP
10 PHP
11 PHP and interview with Janet Howard
12 Interview with author
13 Pamela's notes from the meeting, PHP
14 PHP
15 PHP
16 PHP
17 PHP
18 Bedell Smith, p. 370
19 *Baltimore Sun*, November 24, 1996

44

1 *Providence Journal*, March 30, 1993
2 *New York Post*, March 24, 1993
3 *New York*, January 18, 1993
4 Personal Data Statement to the State Department, PHP
5 Heymann, p. 336
6 *Daily Mail*, May 7, 1993
7 Testimony from David Sulzberger
8 PHP
9 PHP
10 *Time*, July 5, 1993
11 *Time*, July 5, 1993
12 Interview with author
13 Via *Washington Post*, March 27, 1993
14 Interviews with several State Department officials
15 Associated Press, May 27, 1993
16 Bedell Smith, p. 381
17 *New York*, April 26, 1993
18 Bedell Smith, p. 18
19 Ogden, p. 455
20 Ogden, p. 456
21 Reuters, May 4, 1993
22 Ogden, p. 461
23 Blinken files, Clinton via Carter Presidential Library
24 Interview with author
25 *New York Times* international edition, January 18, 1994
26 Interview with author
27 December 7, 1992, PHP
28 PHP
29 Bernstein, p. 330
30 PHP
31 *New York Times*, international edition, January 18, 1994
32 Interview with author
33 Interview with author
34 *Vogue*, February 1994
35 PHP
36 *Vogue*, February 1994
37 *Architectural Digest*, December 31, 1999
38 *Town & Country*, February 1994
39 *Le Monde*, July 31, 1998
40 Interview with author
41 Interview with author
42 Mallaby, p. 267
43 Interview with author
44 PHP
45 Interview with Michael Jay, who came in as British ambassador in 1996
46 Mallaby, p. 267
47 *Vogue*, February 1994
48 *Vogue*, February 1994
49 Interview with author
50 Interview with author
51 ADST interview
52 Interview with author
53 *Washington Post*, February 6, 1997
54 *Wall Street Journal*, December 6, 1993
55 Bedell Smith, p. 393
56 *New York Times* international edition, January 18, 1994
57 Bedell Smith, p. 392
58 *Town & Country*, February 1994
59 Interview with author
60 Lévy, p. 464
61 *Churchill's Girl*, Channel 4, November 30, 2006
62 *Town & Country*, February 1994
63 *Time*, July 5, 1993
64 Heymann, p. 338
65 Lévy, p. 464
66 *Town & Country*, February 1994
67 *Time*, July 5, 1993
68 ADST interview
69 *Time*, July 5, 1993
70 ADST interview
71 *Town & Country*, February 1994
72 *Town & Country*, February 1994
73 PHP
74 Interview with author
75 Interview with Christiane Amanpour
76 *Fortune*, October 1993

NOTES

77 *New York Times*, May 17, 1992
78 Interview with Lord (Charles) Powell, who was on board
79 Interview with author
80 *New York Times* international edition, January 18, 1994
81 Heymann, p. 332
82 Interview with author
83 *Vogue*, February 1994
84 Private information
85 Interview with author
86 Eden, p. 60
87 *Town & Country*, February 1994
88 Interview with Frank Wisner, drawing on conversations he had with Pamela
89 Interview with author
90 Bedell Smith, p. 378
91 PHP
92 *Vogue*, February 1994
93 PHP
94 PHP
95 Quoted in *Women's Wear Daily*, February 6, 1997
96 Interview with author

45

1 *Vanity Fair*, January 1995
2 Executive Branch Public Financial Disclosure Report, March 24, 1993, State Department, PHP
3 Ogden, pp. 471–3
4 *Vanity Fair*, January 1995
5 *New York Times*, September 25, 1994
6 *Vanity Fair*, January 1995
7 *Vanity Fair*, January 1995
8 *New York Times*, June 5, 1994
9 *Independent*, April 28, 1994
10 *New York Times*, November 10, 1996
11 Holbrooke, p. 95
12 *Chicago Tribune*, June 3, 1994
13 PHP
14 *Vanity Fair*, January 1995
15 Details are laid out in her financial submissions to the State Department, PHP
16 Heymann, p. 340
17 Interview with author
18 Interview with author
19 PHP
20 Interview with author

46

1 PHP
2 Albright, p. 163
3 Heymann, p. 337
4 Heymann, p. 351
5 PHP
6 PHP
7 Lovell, *A Scandalous Life*, p. xi
8 Schlesinger, May 14, 1994, p. 767
9 Hamilton, p. 235
10 Interview with author
11 Clinton Presidential Library, White House Staff and Office Files, Box 29, 2006-04580F OA/ID: 10140
12 Private information
13 PHP
14 Bohlen, ADST interview
15 *Le Monde*, February 12, 1999
16 Interview with author
17 PHP
18 Speech script in PHP
19 *Time*, July 5, 1993
20 Interview with Avis Bohlen, ADST interview, Stuart Eizenstat interview and other sources
21 Entries in her diary, PHP; Clinton Presidential Records; Bohlen, ADST interview
22 *Town & Country*, February 1994
23 Schlesinger, July 26, 1994, p. 769
24 Schlesinger, August 3, 1994, p. 770
25 Interview with author
26 Bernstein, p. 154
27 Bernstein, p. 192
28 PHP
29 Bandler, ADST interview
30 *Boston Globe*, February 25, 1995
31 Interview with Avis Bohlen
32 *Washington Post*, February 23, 1995
33 *Vanity Fair*, January 1995
34 Bandler, ADST interview
35 *Le Monde*, March 1, 1995
36 *Le Monde*, March 1, 1995
37 *Atlantic*, May 2004
38 Shrum, pp. 275–6
39 *Le Monde*, May 14, 1995
40 *Washington Post*, June 28, 1995
41 *Independent*, May 1, 1995
42 *Independent*, April 26, 1995
43 *Guardian*, September 23, 2004
44 Ogden in *Daily Mail*, February 24, 1997, and PHP
45 PHP
46 *Wall Street Journal*, October 1, 1996
47 *Washington Post*, October 4, 1995
48 Clinton Presidential Library
49 Interview with author
50 Interview with author, name withheld

NOTES

51 Albright, p. 155
52 Richard Holbrooke in *New Yorker*, May 18, 1998
53 Interview with author
54 Interview with author
55 Talbott, p. 184
56 Interview with author
57 Interview with author
58 Clinton Presidential Library
59 Marton, p. 5
60 *Washington Post*, February 6, 1997
61 Holbrooke, p. 83
62 Chollet, in Chollet and Power (eds), p. 203
63 Interview with author
64 Holbrooke, p. 84
65 Holbrooke, p. 84
66 Bandler, ADST interview
67 Holbrooke, p. 91
68 Holbrooke, p. 97
69 Holbrooke, p. 92
70 Holbrooke, p. 95
71 Holbrooke, p. 97
72 Lévy, p. 464; Holbrooke, p. 99
73 Holbrooke, p. 95
74 *Washington Post*, February 6, 1997
75 Izetbegović interview, *Le Monde*, October 19, 2003
76 Lévy, p. 464
77 *Financial Times* quoted by Holbrooke, p. 102
78 Interview with author
79 Bill Clinton, p. 684
80 Her notes, PHP
81 Interview with Levitte
82 Declassified, Clinton Presidential Library
83 Interview with Clinton
84 Bill Clinton, p. 689
85 *Le Monde*, February 18, 2003
86 Interview with author
87 Bedell Smith, p. 435 and others
88 *New York Times*, December 30, 1995
89 Heymann, p. 341
90 Heymann, p. 340
91 Bedell Smith, p. 436
92 *Washington Post*, October 1, 1996
93 PHP
94 Interviews with author
95 Interview with author
96 Letter of thanks from Winston, PHP
97 Interview with author
98 *Le Monde*, November 3, 1996
99 Interview with author
100 Interview with author
101 Heymann, p. 333
102 *New York Times*, November 10, 1996
103 Bedell Smith, p. 389
104 Rohatyn, p. 245
105 Rohatyn, p. 251
106 Rohatyn, p. 254
107 Interview with author
108 Hillary Rodham Clinton, p. 522

47

1 State Department news conference, February 5, 1997
2 Interview with Janet Howard
3 Interview with author
4 Interview with author
5 PHP
6 Interview with author
7 *Churchill's Girl*, Channel 4, November 30, 2006
8 Bandler, ADST interview
9 Holbrooke in *Washington Post*, February 6, 1997
10 Schlesinger, February 3, 1997, p. 813
11 Bandler, ADST interview
12 Bandler, ADST interview
13 *Churchill's Girl*, Channel 4, November 30, 2006
14 Documents in the Blinken file—Clinton Presidential Records, White House Staff and Office Files, National Security Council, speechwriting Antony Blinken [OA/ID 3388]
15 Memo in Blinken files; NARA WJC-NSCSW Records of the National Security Council Speechwriting office; Antony Blinken's files
16 Schlesinger, February 5, 1997, p. 813
17 Interview with author
18 Interview with author
19 Quoted in Hastings, p. 510
20 Ogden in *Daily Mail*, February 24, 1997
21 *New York Times*, February 9, 1997
22 Interview with author
23 Interview with senior White House official
24 Shrum, p. 277
25 Interview with senior White House official
26 Interview with author
27 Private information

NOTES

28 Interview with author
29 *Washington Post*, February 16, 1997
30 *Washington Post*, March 16, 1997
31 Interview with author
32 Interview with Janet Howard
33 *Architectural Digest*, August 31, 2000
34 *New York*, May 19, 1997
35 Interview with author
36 Interview with author
37 *Washington Post*, February 6, 1997

Selected Bibliography

Abramson, Rudy, *Spanning the Century: The Life of W. Averell Harriman, 1891–1986*, William Morrow, 1992

Agnelli, Marella, *Marella Agnelli: The Last Swan*, Rizzoli, 2014

Agnelli, Susanna, *We Always Wore Sailor Suits*, Viking, 1975

Albright, Madeleine, *Madam Secretary: A Memoir*, Harper Perennial, 2013

Alsop, Susan Mary, *To Marietta from Paris, 1945–1960*, Doubleday, 1975

The American Ambassador's Residence in Paris, American Embassy, 1997

Arnold, Catharine, *Pandemic 1918: The Story of the Deadliest Influenza in History*, Michael O'Mara Books, 2018

Baldwin, Billy with Michael Gardine, *An Autobiography*, Little, Brown, 1985

Beaton, Cecil, *The Years Between 1939–44*, Sapere, 2018

Bedell Smith, Sally, *In All His Glory: The Life of William S. Paley—The Legendary Tycoon and His Brilliant Circle*, Simon & Schuster, 1990

Bedell Smith, Sally, *Reflected Glory: The Life of Pamela Churchill Harriman*, Simon & Schuster, 1996

Bernstein, Carl, *A Woman in Charge: The Life of Hillary Rodham Clinton*, Hutchinson, 2007

SELECTED BIBLIOGRAPHY

Blair, Joan and Clay Blair Jr., *The Search for JFK*, Berkley, 1976

Blanch, Lesley, *The Wilder Shores of Love*, John Murray, 1954

Bliss, Edward, ed., *In Search of Light: The Broadcasts of Edward R. Murrow 1938–1961*, Alfred A. Knopf, 1967

Brandon, Henry, *Special Relationships: A Foreign Correspondent's Memoirs from Roosevelt to Reagan*, Atheneum, 1988

Buruma, Ian, *The Churchill Complex: The Rise and Fall of the Special Relationship*, Atlantic, 2020

Byrne, Paula, *Kick*, William Collins, 2016

Cahan, William G., *No Stranger to Tears: A Surgeon's Story*, Random House, 1992

Cannadine, David, *Aspects of Aristocracy: Grandeur and Decline in Modern Britain*, Penguin, 1995

Capote, Truman, *Answered Prayers*, Random House, 1987

Channon, Henry, ed. Robert Rhodes James, *"Chips": The Diaries of Henry Channon*, Weidenfeld & Nicolson, 1967

Channon, Henry, ed. Simon Heffer, *Henry "Chips" Channon: The Diaries 1938–1943*, Hutchinson, 2021

Chisholm, Anne and Michael Davie, *Beaverbrook: A Life*, Hutchinson, 1992

Chollet, Derek and Samantha Power, eds., *The Unquiet American: Richard Holbrooke in the World*, Public Affairs, 2012

Churchill, Randolph S., *Twenty-One Years*, Weidenfeld & Nicolson, 1965

Churchill, Winston S., *His Father's Son: The Life of Randolph Churchill*, Weidenfeld & Nicolson, 1996

Churchill, Winston S., *Memories and Adventures*, Weidenfeld & Nicolson, 1989

Churchill, Winston S., *The Second World War. Volume I: The Gathering Storm*, Cassell, 1948

Clarke, Gerald, ed., *Too Brief a Treat: The Letters of Truman Capote*, Random House, 2004

SELECTED BIBLIOGRAPHY

Clarke, Gerald, *Capote: A Biography*, Hamish Hamilton, 1988
Clinton, Bill, *My Life*, Alfred A. Knopf, 2004
Clinton, Hillary Rodham, *Living History*, Simon & Schuster, 2003
Collier, Peter and David Horowitz, *The Kennedys*, Secker & Warburg, 1984
Colville, John, *The Churchillians*, Weidenfeld & Nicolson, 1981
Colville, John, *The Fringes of Power: 10 Downing Street Diaries 1939–1955*, Norton, 1986
Colville, John, *Winston Churchill and His Inner Circle*, Wyndham, 1981
Cooper, Duff, *Old Men Forget: The Autobiography of Duff Cooper (Viscount Norwich)*, Rupert Hart-Davis, 1957
Costigliola, Frank, "Pamela Churchill, Wartime London, and the Making of the Special Relationship," *Diplomatic History*, 36:4, September 2012
Dallek, Robert, *John F. Kennedy: Unfinished Life*, Penguin, 2013
Devonshire, Deborah, *Wait for Me! Memoirs of the Youngest Mitford Sister*, John Murray, 2010
Devonshire, Deborah and Patrick Leigh Fermor, ed. Charlotte Mosley, *In Tearing Haste: Letters Between Deborah Devonshire and Patrick Leigh Fermor*, John Murray, 2008
Drew, Elizabeth, *On the Edge: The Clinton Presidency*, Touchstone, 1995
Druon, Maurice, *The Film of Memory: A Novel*, Rupert Hart-Davis, 1955
Duchin, Peter with Charles Michener, *Ghost of a Chance: A Memoir*, Random House, 1996
Dunne, Dominick, *The Mansions of Limbo*, Crown, 1991
Eden, Clarissa, ed. Cate Haste, *A Memoir: From Churchill to Eden*, Weidenfeld & Nicolson, 2007
Evans, Peter, *Nemesis: Aristotle Onassis, Jackie O, and the Love Triangle That Brought Down the Kennedys*, Regan, 2004

SELECTED BIBLIOGRAPHY

Fermor, Patrick Leigh, ed. Adam Sisman, *Dashing for the Post: The Letters of Patrick Leigh Fermor*, John Murray, 2016

Fleming, Ann, ed. Mark Amory, *The Letters of Ann Fleming*, Collins Harvill, 1985

Frantz, Douglas and David McKean, *Friends in High Places: The Rise and Fall of Clark Clifford*, Little, Brown, 1995

Friedan, Betty, *The Feminine Mystique*, W. W. Norton, 1963

Friedman, Alan, *Agnelli and the Network of Italian Power*, Harrap, 1988

Gilbert, Martin, *Winston S. Churchill, Volume VI: Finest Hour, 1939–1941*, Houghton Mifflin, 1983

Gilbert, Martin and Larry P. Arnn, *The Churchill Documents, Volume 18: One Continent Redeemed, January–August 1943*, Hillsdale College Press, 2015

Gladwyn, Cynthia, *The Paris Embassy*, Collins, 1976

Gladwyn, Cynthia, ed. Miles Jebb, *The Diaries of Cynthia Gladwyn*, Constable, 1995

Goodwin, Doris Kearns, *The Fitzgeralds and the Kennedys: An American Saga*, Simon & Schuster, 1987

Gorodetsky, Gabriel, ed., *The Maisky Diaries: Red Ambassador to the Court of St. James's 1932–1943*, Yale University Press, 2015

Grafton, David, *The Sisters: The Lives and Times of the Fabulous Cushing Sisters*, Villard, 1992

Graham, Katharine, *Personal History*, Weidenfeld & Nicolson, 1997

Hackett, Mary, *William "Bill" Walton: A Charmed Life*, Branden Books, 2013

Halle, Kay, ed., *Randolph Churchill, the Young Unpretender: Essays by His Friends*, Heinemann, 1971

Halperin, Mark, *How to Beat Trump*, Regan Arts, 2019

Hamilton, Nigel, *Bill Clinton: Mastering a Presidency*, Century, 2007

Harriman, Pamela C., "Churchill's Dream," *American Heritage*, 34:6, October/November 1983

SELECTED BIBLIOGRAPHY

Harriman, W. Averell and Elie Abel, *Special Envoy to Churchill and Stalin 1941–1946*, Random House, 1975

Harris, Neil, *Capital Culture: J. Carter Brown, the National Gallery of Art, and the Reinvention of the Museum Experience*, University of Chicago Press, 2013

Harrison, Cynthia E., "A 'New Frontier' for Women: The Public Policy of the Kennedy Administration," *Journal of American History*, 67:3, December 1980

Hastings, Max, *Finest Years: Churchill as Warlord 1940–45*, Harper Press, 2009

Hayward, Brooke, *Haywire*, Alfred A. Knopf, 1977

Helms, Cynthia, *An Intriguing Life: A Memoir of War, Washington, and Marriage to an American Spymaster*, Rowman & Littlefield, 2013

Hemingway, Mary Welsh, *How It Was*, Weidenfeld & Nicolson, 1977

Henderson, Nicholas, *Mandarin: The Diaries of Nicholas Henderson*, Weidenfeld & Nicolson, 1994

Heymann, C. David, *The Georgetown Ladies' Social Club: Power, Passion, and Politics in the Nation's Capital*, Atria, 2003

Holbrooke, Richard, *To End a War*, Random House, 1998

Ireland, Josh, *Churchill & Son*, John Murray, 2021

Isaacson, Walter and Evan Thomas, *The Wise Men: Six Friends and the World They Made*, Simon & Schuster, 1986

Jenkins, Simon, *England's Thousand Best Houses*, Allen Lane, 2003

Johnson, Gill, *Love from Venice: A Golden Summer on the Grand Canal*, Hodder & Stoughton, 2024

Jones, Radhika, ed., with David Friend, *Vanity Fair's Women on Women*, Penguin, 2020

Kaplan, James, *Sinatra: The Chairman*, Doubleday, 2015

Katz, Catherine Grace, *The Daughters of Yalta: The Churchills, Roosevelts, and Harrimans: A Story of Love and War*, Houghton Mifflin Harcourt, 2020

SELECTED BIBLIOGRAPHY

Keith, Slim with Annette Tapert, *Slim: Memories of a Rich and Imperfect Life*, Simon & Schuster, 1990

Kelly, Charles J., *Tex McCrary: Wars. Women. Politics. An Adventurous Life Across the American Century*, Hamilton, 2009

Kendrick, Alexander, *Prime Time: The Life of Edward R. Murrow*, J. M. Dent, 1970

Kerr, Andrew, *Intolerably Hip*, Frontier, 2011

Kerry, John, *Every Day Is Extra*, Simon & Schuster, 2018

Knox, Tim, *The British Ambassador's Residence in Paris*, Flammarion, 2011

Lane, Kenneth Jay, *Faking It*, Harry N. Abrams, 1996

Lees-Milne, James, *Ancestral Voices and Prophesying Peace: Diaries 1942–1945*, John Murray, 1998

Leslie, Anita, *Randolph: The Biography of Winston Churchill's Son*, Beaufort, 1985

Lévy, Bernard-Henri, *Le Lys et la Cendre*, Grasset, 2014

Lockhart, Sir Robert Bruce, ed. Kenneth Young, *The Diaries of Sir Robert Bruce Lockhart 1939–1965*, Macmillan, 1981

Lovell, Mary S., *A Scandalous Life: The Biography of Jane Digby el Mezrab*, Richard Cohen, 1995

Lovell, Mary S., *The Riviera Set*, Little, Brown, 2016

Mallaby, Christopher, *Living the Cold War: Memoirs of a British Diplomat*, Amberley, 2017

Marlborough, Laura, Duchess of, *Laughter from a Cloud*, Weidenfeld & Nicolson, 1980

Martin, Ralph G., *Seeds of Destruction: Joe Kennedy and His Sons*, G. P. Putnam's Sons, 1995

Marton, Kati, *Paris: A Love Story*, Simon & Schuster, 2012

Matthews, Chris, *Hardball: How Politics Is Played, Told by One Who Knows the Game*, Free Press, 1999

SELECTED BIBLIOGRAPHY

McCann, Leo and Simon Mollan, "Placing Camelot: Cultivating Leadership and Learning in the Kennedy Presidency," *Leadership*, 18:1, February 2022

McLellan, Diana, *Ear on Washington*, Arbor House, 1982

McTaggart, Lynne, *Kick Kennedy: Her Life and Times*, Doubleday, 1983

Mitford, Nancy, ed. Charlotte Mosley, *Love from Nancy: The Letters of Nancy Mitford*, Hodder & Stoughton, 1993

Mitford, Nancy, ed. Charlotte Mosley, *The Letters of Nancy Mitford & Evelyn Waugh*, Hodder & Stoughton, 1996

Mondale, Walter F., *The Good Fight: A Life in Liberal Politics*, Scribner, 2010

Montague Brown, Anthony, *Long Sunset: Memoirs of Winston Churchill's Private Secretary*, Podkin, 2009

Moon, Vicky, *The Middleburg Mystique: A Peek Inside the Gates of Middleburg, Virginia*, Waverly Lee Media, 2016

Nicolson, Harold, ed. Nigel Nicolson, *The Harold Nicolson Diaries 1907–1963*, Weidenfeld & Nicolson, 2004

Ogden, Christopher, *Life of the Party: The Biography of Pamela Digby Churchill Hayward Harriman*, London, Little, Brown, 1994

Olson, Lynne, *Citizens of London: The Americans Who Stood with Britain in Its Darkest, Finest Hour*, Scribe, 2015

Packer, George, *Our Man: Richard Holbrooke and the End of the American Century*, Cape, 2019

Pardew, James W., *Peacemakers: American Leadership and the End of Genocide in the Balkans*, University Press of Kentucky, 2018

Parrish, Thomas, *To Keep the British Isles Afloat: FDR's Men in Churchill's London*, HarperCollins, 2009

Persico, Joseph E., *Edward R. Murrow: An American Original*, McGraw-Hill, 1998

Purnell, Sonia, *First Lady: The Life and Wars of Clementine Churchill*, Aurum, 2015

SELECTED BIBLIOGRAPHY

Radziwill, Lee, *Happy Times*, Assouline, 2000

Richardson, Kristen, *The Season: A Social History of the Debutante*, W. W. Norton, 2020

Roberts, Brian, *Randolph: A Study of Churchill's Son*, Hamish Hamilton, 1984

Rohatyn, Felix, *Dealings: A Political and Financial Life*, Simon & Schuster, 2010

Rounding, Virginia, *Grandes Horizontales: The Lives and Legends of Marie Duplessis, Cora Pearl, La Païva and La Présidente*, Bloomsbury, 2003

Russell, Maud, *A Constant Heart: The War Diaries of Maud Russell, 1938–1945*, Dovecote, 2017

Salisbury, Harrison E., *A Journey for Our Times*, Harper & Row, 1983

Schlesinger, Arthur Jr., *Journals 1952–2000*, Penguin, 2007

Sebba, Anne, *That Woman: The Life of Wallis Simpson, Duchess of Windsor*, Phoenix, 2012

Shrum, Robert, *No Excuses: Concessions of a Serial Campaigner*, Simon & Schuster, 2007

Slater, Leonard, *Aly: A Biography*, W. H. Allen, 1966

Soames, Emma, ed., *Mary Churchill's War: The Wartime Diaries of Churchill's Youngest Daughter*, John Murray, 2021

Soames, Mary, *Clementine Churchill*, Cassell, 1979

Soames, Mary, *A Daughter's Tale: The Memoir of Winston and Clementine Churchill's Youngest Child*, Doubleday, 2011

Sperber, A. M., *Murrow: His Life and Times*, Freundlich, 1986

Spinney, Laura, *Pale Rider: The Spanish Flu of 1918 and How It Changed the World*, Vintage, 2017

Steinem, Gloria, *My Life on the Road*, Oneworld, 2015

Sulzberger, C. L., *Seven Continents and Forty Years: A Concentration of Memoirs*, Quadrangle/New York Times Book Co., 1977

SELECTED BIBLIOGRAPHY

Sulzberger, C. L., *The Last of the Giants*, Weidenfeld & Nicolson, 1970

Sulzberger, Marina, *Marina: Letters and Diaries of Marina Sulzberger*, Crown, 1978

Talbott, Strobe, *The Russia Hand: A Memoir of Presidential Diplomacy*, Random House, 2002

Taylor, A. J. P., *Beaverbrook*, Hamish Hamilton, 1972

Thomas, Evan, *The Man to See: The Bestselling Biography of Legendary Trial Lawyer Edward Bennett Williams*, Touchstone, 1991

Thomas, Helen, *Front Row at the White House: My Life and Times*, Scribner, 1999

Waugh, Evelyn, ed. Mark Amory, *The Letters of Evelyn Waugh*, Phoenix, 1995

Waugh, Evelyn, ed. Michael Davie, *The Diaries of Evelyn Waugh*, Phoenix, 2010

Weisman, Steven R., ed., *Daniel Patrick Moynihan: A Portrait in Letters of an American Visionary*, Public Affairs, 2010

Winkler, Peter L., *Dennis Hopper: The Wild Ride of a Hollywood Rebel*, Robson Press, 2012

Ziegler, Philip, *Diana Cooper*, Hamish Hamilton, 1981

Picture Credits

PLATE SECTION 1

p. 1
top: Pamela Digby Churchill Hayward Harriman Papers, Library of Congress
middle: Central Press/Getty Images
bottom: Wikipedia

p. 2
top: ANL/Shutterstock
bottom: John F. Kennedy Presidential Library and Museum, Boston

p. 3
top: Fred Ramage/Getty Images
bottom: Churchill Archives Centre, The Papers of Lady Soames, MCHL 6/2/19

p. 4
top: ANL/Shutterstock
bottom: © Estate of Nancy Sandys Walker/Mary Evans Picture Library

p. 5
top: PA Images/Alamy Stock Photo
bottom: Fremantle/Alamy Stock Photo

p. 6
top: J. Wilds/Getty Images
bottom: Bettmann/Getty Images

p. 7
top: John Rawlings/Condé Nast/Shutterstock
bottom: Rue des Archives/GRANGER

PICTURE CREDITS

p. 8
top left: Douglas Miller/Getty Images
top right: Associated Press/Alamy Stock Photo
bottom: Benno Graziani/Photo12

PLATE SECTION 2

p. 9
top: adoc-photos/Getty Images
bottom: © André Ostier/Association des Amis d'André Ostier

p. 10
top left: John Swope/Getty Images
top right: Anthony Wallace/ANL/Shutterstock
bottom: Abbie Rowe. White House Photographs. John F. Kennedy Presidential Library and Museum, Boston

p. 11
top: Bettmann/Getty Images
middle: Slim Aarons/Getty Images
bottom: Ron Galella/Getty Images

p. 12
all images: WWD/Getty Images

p. 13
top: CHRIS WILKINS/Getty Images
middle: WILFREDO LEE/Getty Images
bottom: Associated Press/Alamy Stock Photo

p. 14
top: Diana Walker/Getty Images
bottom: Alain Nogues/Getty Images

p. 15
both images: JOYCE NALTCHAYAN/Getty Images

p. 16
Annie Leibovitz/Trunk Archive

Index

Abel, Elie, 123
abortion issue, 279, 288, 331
Abramson, Rudy, 246
Abzug, Bella, 252, 267–69, 300
Acheson, Dean, 139
Acland, Antony, 321, 402
Admiralty House, 52, 56, 57–59
Aga Khan, 152, 154
Agnelli, Gianni, 160–63, 169, 172–74, 175–78, 232, 347; adultery after marriage to Marella, 186–87; continued friendship with PCH, 179–80, 187, 201, 211, 223, 276–77, 327–28, 428–29; PCH ends affair with, 179–80, 181; and PCH's death, 437, 440; seriously injured in car crash, 178–79; suffers heart attack, 428
Agnelli, Giorgio, 179
Agnelli, Marella, 180, 181, 182, 186–87, 220, 277, 429
Albright, Madeleine, 3, 275, 402, 415, 433, 434, 438, 440, 441
Amanpour, Christiane, 383, 392, 395, 418, 420, 433, 437
Ames, Charles, 397, 398
Anderson, Major General Fred, 115–16, 125, 126, 127, 136
Andropov, Yuri, 310–12, 313, 314–15, 335, 337, 338

art collection, Harriman: auctioned at Sotheby's after PCH's death, 444; and Carter Brown, 328, 348–49; Degas works, 248, 276, 348; and Marie Harriman, 107, 243, 248; and Kathleen Harriman, 323, 326, 349, 412; Harriman transfers to PCH (1982), 323; informally pledged to the National Gallery, 323, 326, 348, 412, 444; Kuhn works, 383; Matisse works, 412; at Paris embassy residence, 382, 422; Picasso works, 248, 294, 383, 412; Renoir works, 248, 294, 383, 412; Romney's *Lady Hamilton as a Vestal*, 244, 306, 445; sales from, 348–49, 412; shown to Mandela, 367–68; Van Gogh's *White Roses*, 248–49, 261, 294, 301, 305, 328, 338, 348, 365, 382, 412, 422, 444
Astaire, Adele, 83, 96
Aston, Dr. Sherrell, 327
Astor, Brooke, 232, 411
Astor, Nancy, 151
astrology, 189
Atlantic Council, 332, 333
Attlee, Clement, 60, 357–58
Australia, 3

INDEX

Bacall, Lauren, 196, 220, 232, 385
Baillie, Lady (Olive), 23–24, 29, 33–34, 35–36, 37, 41, 96, 176
Baillie, Sir Adrian, 36
Baldwin, Billy, 215–16, 247, 251
Baldwin, Stanley, 68
Balladur, Édouard, 390, 409, 411
Balzac, Honore de, 16
Bandler, Donald, 386, 391, 411, 436–37, 442
Bank of Commerce and Credit International (BCCI), 349
Barbados, 316, 317
Bardot, Brigitte, 193
Baring, Rowley, 31
Barry, Marion, 284
Beaton, Cecil, 44, 49, 72–73, 76, 80, 96, 200, 248
Beatty, Warren, 261
Beaverbrook, Lord (Max Aitken), 48–49, 52, 57, 60, 62, 78–79, 83, 105–6, 110, 139, 187; offers PCH job at *Evening Standard*, 145, 147; as PCH's "control officer," 86, 90, 92–93, 115, 116; sends PCH to New York and Montego Bay (1946), 148
Bedell Smith, Sally, *Reflected Glory* (1996), 5, 371, 372, 431–32, 442
Beevor, Antony, 389
Belton House, Lincolnshire, 47
Bennett, John Wheeler, 131
Bentsen, Lloyd, 341–42, 378
Berger, Sandy, 292, 332, 339, 340, 342, 366, 378, 380, 433, 441, 442
Berger, Susan, 292, 380, 401, 431, 441
Berlin, Irving, 212
Berlin, Isaiah, 217
Bernhard, Berl, 297
Bernstein, Carl, 380, 409
Berry, Seymour, 47

Bertrand, Sandy, 395
Bestegui, Charlie de, 165
Beverley, East Yorkshire, 49–52
Bevin, Ernest, 62
Biden, Jill, 330
Biden, Joe, 82*, 273, 300, 329–30, 331, 344, 365–66, 376, 377, 378, 415
Big Apple (dance craze), 22
Black, Conrad, 403
Black Hawk Down fiasco (October 1993), 415
Blanch, Lesley, *The Wilder Shores of Love* (1954), 185, 229
Blass, Bill, 396
Bohlen, Avis, 381, 383, 389, 391, 393, 401, 402, 406, 410, 436
Bohlen, Avis (mother of Avis Bohlen), 402
Borghese, Pauline, 385
Bosnian war, 414–26, 432, 442
Boudin, Stéphane, 33, 177, 211, 216–17
Bracken, Brendan, 65, 113, 122, 139
Braden, Joan, 319
Bradlee, Ben, 264, 304
Bradley, Bill, 305
Branca, Marina, 179
Brandon, Henry, 262
Braniff Airlines, 274
Brantes, Rosamée de, 159
Brezhnev, Leonid, 272
Brinkley, David, 313, 405
Broadwater House, Chailey Common, 224
Brokaw, Tom, 280
Bronfman, Edgar, 267
Brookings Institution, 332
Brown, Carter, 278, 328, 332, 340, 348, 350, 360, 393
Brown, Ron, 355–56, 357, 358–59, 365, 385, 428

INDEX

Brown Brothers Harriman bank, 185, 413
Browne, Anthony Montague, 90, 223
Bruce, David, 167
Bruce, Evangeline, 184, 330, 392
Brzezinski, Zbigniew, 273
Burge, Christopher, 412
Bush, Barbara, 336
Bush, George, 305, 336, 343, 345, 350, 352, 357–58, 359, 379
Byrd, Robert, 300

Cahan, Dr. William, 231–32, 262, 295, 311
Calhoun, Jesse, 290, 297
Callaghan, Audrey, 280
Callaghan, Jim, 262
Canada, 22, 48
Capote, Truman, 175, 200, 219–22
Carter, Jimmy, 269, 272–73, 274–75, 281, 284, 289–90, 306
Carter, Lillian, 274–75
Carter, Rosalynn, 274, 289
Cassini, Oleg, 183, 193
Castle, Barbara, 250
Catholicism, 16, 23, 28, 224, 231, 243; of the Kennedys, 32, 144, 156, 157, 210; PCH as disillusioned with, 331; PCH converts to, 175–76, 179–80, 198, 207, 224; and Sir Everard Digby, 16, 42
Cavendish, Lord Charles, 83
Cerf, Bennett, 215
Cerne Abbas giant, 17
Cerne Abbey, 285, 286
Cézanne, Paul, 385
Chamberlain, Neville, 24, 30, 31, 38, 47, 56, 59, 68
Chancellor, John, 316
Chanel, Coco, 31

Channon, Chips, 63
Charteris, Laura, 50–51, 52, 93
Chartwell, 35, 42, 157, 169
Chatsworth House, 32, 251
Chequers, 63, 66–68, 70, 82, 84, 117, 127, 128–29, 133
Cherkley Court, 48, 81, 86, 92, 101, 115, 116, 129
Chernenko, Konstantin, 315
China, 332–33
Chirac, Bernadette, 384–85
Chirac, Jacques, 3, 407, 411, 414–19, 425, 430, 437; acknowledges French role in the Holocaust, 426–27; speaks at PCH's memorial ceremony in Paris, 439–40
Christie, Father, 175–76, 179, 243
Christopher, Warren, 425
Church, Frank, 264, 292, 298
Churchill, Clementine (née Hozier), 4; at Churchill's state funeral, 225; death of (1977), 286; in Downing Street during Blitz, 65; "electrical storms" of, 62; family background, 89; and grandson Winston, 169, 224, 242, 286; and Hopkins's visit to London, 76, 82; knowledge of PCH-Harriman affair, 89–90; loathing for Beaverbrook, 48; low opinion of Randolph, 35, 58–59, 63; PCH stands in for during war, 62–63; and PCH's loathing for Randolph, 102; and PCH's pregnancy, 55–56; PCH's ties with loosen, 133; prevents PCH from becoming pilot, 122; Randolph's girlfriends look like, 44, 93; and Randolph's wedding to PCH, 43, 46, 47; relationship with PCH, 52–53, 57–58, 68, 119, 128, 189, 197–98, 201–2,

INDEX

Churchill, Clementine (*cont.*) 207, 226, 266, 286; strength of influence on Churchill, 53, 61, 213; troubled relationship with Randolph, 35, 44–45, 53, 54, 101, 105, 129, 191; at wartime Chequers, 63, 99, 117

Churchill, Diana, 53, 66, 72, 73, 96, 135, 191; suicide of (1963), 226

Churchill, Jennie Jerome, 89

Churchill, Marina, 391

Churchill, Lord Randolph, 435

Churchill, Randolph (first husband of PCH): accepts Churchill's honorary U.S. citizenship (1963), 213; adultery, 50–51, 52, 64, 70, 93, 95; alcohol consumption, 34, 41, 43, 49, 63–64, 77, 93–94, 95, 101, 105, 110, 129, 158; alimony obligations, 146; as arrogant and ill-mannered, 34, 45, 48–49, 53, 73, 93–94, 95, 116; attitude to women, 35, 41–42, 48–49, 50–51, 55, 157, 158; at Churchill's state funeral, 225; as crushed by the Churchill name, 227; death of (June 1968), 230; debts of, 51, 52, 55, 60, 71, 73, 75, 77–78, 80; disintegration of by mid-1960s, 227; engagement to PCH, 40–45; honeymoon night with PCH, 47–48; as hugely unpopular in society, 34–35, 41; jealousy of PCH's wartime role, 58–59, 63, 65; June files for divorce (1956), 191; learns of PCH-Harriman affair, 105–6, 108; lives in Downing Street, 59–60, 63–66; married life with PCH, 48–54, 55, 57, 61, 63–66, 71, 73; marries June Osborne (1948), 158; marries PCH (October 4, 1939), 46–48; military career, 40, 49, 55, 58–59, 71, 73–75, 77–78, 81, 92–97, 100–105; mother's low opinion of, 35, 58–59, 63; as object of disdain in army, 51–52, 71, 77–78, 93–94, 102; and PCH after Churchill's death, 226; PCH avoids on the Riviera (1948), 160–61; PCH seeks annulment of marriage, 176, 179–80, 347; PCH's dislike/ loathing of, 73, 77–78, 102, 104–5; PCH's pre-emptive peace offering (1944), 130; political career, 64–65, 73, 100, 101, 149, 157; positive comments about Nazi Germany, 70; relationship with his father, 34–35, 54, 55–56, 63, 101–2, 105–6, 129–30, 157, 170, 191, 223; sense of grievance, 49, 59, 64–65, 101–2, 105–6, 119, 129, 149, 157–58, 224; sexual technique, 48, 153; sexually abused at boarding school, 48; and son Winston, 96–97, 110, 117, 149, 160–61, 170, 190, 201, 223–24, 347; threatens to go public over Harriman affair, 105–6; trial weekend with PCH at Stinchcombe (1948), 158; troubled relationship with his mother, 35, 44–45, 53, 54, 101–2, 105–6, 129, 130, 191; violent/ abusive behavior, 49–50, 105, 129, 158, 191, 223, 230; walks to York and back, 51–52; as wartime security risk, 64, 92–93, 94, 105–6; as Winston's best man, 223

Churchill, Randolph (PCH's grandson), 225, 320, 442

Churchill, Sarah, 53, 90, 104, 106, 129, 136, 191, 226

490

INDEX

Churchill, Winston, 4, 5; and Gianni Agnelli, 163–64, 173, 175, 177; appointed prime minister (May 19, 1940), 59; at Atlantic Conference (August 1941), 97–98; awarded honorary American citizenship (1963), 213; death of (January 24, 1965), 224; as descended from Digbys, 16; despises Joseph Kennedy, 260; distrust of Stalin, 137; failing health in later years of war, 100, 129, 136; and fall of France (June 1940), 60; as First Lord of the Admiralty (1939-40), 40, 43, 47, 52–57; and Gallipoli campaign, 58; and grandson Winston, 68, 70, 117–18, 170–71, 224; and Averell Harriman, 82–83, 84; and Hopkins's visit to London, 76, 82, 388; "Iron Curtain" speech in Fulton (March 5, 1946), 167, 272, 347; knowledge of PCH-Harriman affair, 89–90, 103; letter to Roosevelt, 74, 75; life in Downing Street/Annexe during war, 65, 74, 103, 128–29, 133; need to draw USA into war, 74; "never in the field of human conflict" speech, 64; orders destruction of French fleet at Oran, 61; and PCH, 53–54, 58, 102–7, 110, 117, 126, 130, 163–64, 197–98, 207, 266; PCH as bearer of the flame, 227, 249; PCH compared to by Democrats, 302–3; PCH meets at Chartwell (1939), 42; PCH's ties with loosen, 133–34, 136; as peacetime prime minister (1951-55), 289; and Pearl Harbor attack (December 7, 1941), 99; at RAF Uxbridge (September 15, 1940), 67; and Randolph's debts, 52, 60, 71; and Randolph's wedding to PCH, 43; receives Médaille Militaire in Paris, 150; relationship with son Randolph, 35, 53–54, 63, 101-2, 104–5, 129–30, 157, 170, 191, 223–24; resigns as prime minister (April 1955), 198; Roosevelt's view of, 75; sale of papers of by his grandson, 412–13; shows *That Hamilton Woman*, 89, 244; and Special Relationship concept, 167, 193; strength of Clementine's influence on, 53, 61, 213; on surrender of Singapore (February 1942), 100; "terrible scene" with Randolph (June 1944), 129, 130; "Victory at all costs" speech (May 13, 1940), 59; warnings in 1930s over Nazi threat, 20, 30, 42; *The Dream* (1947), 435; *A History of the English-Speaking Peoples*, 246; *Jug with Bottles* (painting), 382; "Thoughts and Adventures" (1932 essay), 442

Churchill, Winston Spencer (son of PCH), 5; accepts Churchill's honorary U.S. citizenship (1963), 213; affair with Soraya Khashoggi, 287; and Averell's death, 324, 325; as a baby, 70, 73, 76, 78; birth of during air-raid, 69, 70; Bobbie (nanny of), 117, 127, 135; childhood of, 96–97, 101, 105–6, 110, 117, 127, 143, 148–49, 156, 159–60, 169–71, 174, 177–78; and the Cresta Run, 177; denigrates PCH in public,

INDEX

Churchill, Winston Spencer (*cont.*) 321; deserts Minnie, 413, 444; and father Randolph, 96–97, 110, 117, 149, 159–60, 170, 190, 200–201, 223–24, 347; and grandmother Clementine, 286; and Leland Hayward, 200–202, 218, 233–34; higher education of, 198, 201, 218; holiday at Sun Valley with PCH (1991), 351; and La Colombiere ski chalet, 286–87, 348; loses money as a Lloyd's Name, 413; married life, 235, 245–46; marries Minnie d'Erlanger (1964), 223–24; new partner Luce Engelen, 429–30, 446; PCH sees Randolph in, 287; PCH/Averell's transfers of wealth to, 245–46, 254, 286–87, 294, 320, 323, 348; and PCH's altered will, 444, 445–46; and PCH's death, 437, 438, 440; and PCH's financial problems, 349; PCH's parenting of, 117, 130, 135, 143, 148–49, 158, 159–60, 168–71, 174, 177–78, 186, 187, 188; at PCH's swearing-in ceremony (1993), 379; as pilot, 245; plays tennis with Ethel Kennedy, 211; political career, 229, 262, 274, 284–85, 285*, 320, 444; and racial issues, 284–85, 285*; sale of his grandfather's papers, 412–13; schooling of, 146, 149, 169–71; sees himself as rightful tribune of Churchill legacy, 346; teenage years of, 186, 187, 191; troubled relationship with mother, 223–24, 245, 320–21, 347–48, 429–30; as unpopular with his mother's staff, 346; *Defending the West* (1981), 309; *Memories and Adventures* (autobiography, 1989), 347

Clark, General Wesley, 422, 423

Clark, Kenneth (art historian), 15

Clarke, Gerald, 222

Clifford, Clark, 287, 290, 302, 303–4, 323, 349, 366, 398, 401, 412, 414, 428

Clinton, Bill, 1, 3; 1982 campaign for governorship, 293, 306; administration appointments (1992), 366, 368; administration's problems, 380, 408–9, 415; appoints PCH ambassador to France (March 1993), 374–80, 403, 443; background of, 358; and Bosnian war, 414–26, 432; and Chirac, 414–19, 425; energy and resilience of, 306–7, 358, 361–62; in France for D-Day commemorations (1994), 406–9; friendship with PCH, 292–93, 321, 340, 346, 354, 358–68, 388, 408–9, 416, 430, 432–33, 446; at Middleburg Meeting (June 1991), 356, 362–63; in the N Street paddock, 321; and PamPAC, 291–93, 298, 299, 306, 345; PCH introduces to Washington, 292–93, 306–7, 360–61; and PCH's death, 438; PCH's role in 1992 election, 360–68, 379–80, 443; proposes to award Presidential Medal of Freedom to PCH, 438, 446; and racial issues, 355; reelected president (1996), 432; says no to 1988 presidential run, 343–44; sex life of, 343–44, 359, 360–61, 369; speech at PCH's memorial service, 442–43; *Tonight Show* appearance (1988), 344–45;

INDEX

Vietnam draft and marijuana controversies, 361, 404; weaknesses/flaws of, 361, 409; Whitewater affair, 398, 404; wins 1992 election, 363–68, 443
Clinton, Hillary Rodham, 293, 343, 344, 360, 361, 363–64, 390, 409, 430; in France for D-Day commemorations (1994), 404–9; and PCH, 369–70, 380, 408, 433, 438, 441, 443
CNN, 418
Coelho, Tony, 329
Cold War: Berlin blockade/airlift, 167; building of Berlin Wall (August 1961), 212; Churchill's "Iron Curtain" speech (March 5, 1946), 167, 272, 347; end of, 339, 426; PCH's personal part in rapprochement, 312–15, 334, 336–39; period of détente with Moscow in 1970s, 271–73; and politics of Vietnam War, 257, 271–72; Reagan-Gorbachev summit (Reykjavík, 1987), 312; Soviet occupation of Eastern Europe, 136, 167, 272; Stanislav Petrov false alarm incident (1983), 314; tensions of early 1980s, 309–12, 314; U.S. focus shifts toward Soviets, 135–37, 154
Collingwood, Charles, 91, 114
Columbia University, 309, 374
Colville, Jock, 63, 70, 86, 87, 117
Commission on Presidential Debates, 332
Conservative Party, 15, 20, 114, 229, 284, 285*, 285
Cooper, Artemis, 364
Cooper, Duff, 72, 149, 164, 166
Cooper, Lady Diana, 40, 48, 72–73, 163, 187, 213, 215, 242; PCH stays with in Paris embassy, 149, 159, 164, 166; on PCH's "courtesanship" in Paris, 184; on PCH's marriage to Hayward, 216; Randolph at fortieth birthday party of (1932), 34–35; and Randolph's violence, 191
HMS *Cossack*, 56
Council on Foreign Relations, 332, 333
Couric, Katie, 405
Coward, Noël, 173
Crespi, Count Rudi, 161
Crowe, Admiral William, 336
Cuomo, Mario, 325, 357
Curley, Walter, 375, 376
Cutler, Lloyd, 398, 399, 400, 401, 442

Damascus, 403
Davids, Jules, 300
Davis, Sir Daniel, 156
Day Lewis, Cecil, 123
de Gaulle, General Charles, 61–62, 194, 393
de Klerk, F. W., 367
Democratic Party: Brown chairs DNC, 355–56, 357, 358–59; Carter administration, 272–74, 281, 284; *Democratic Fact Book*, 308; Harriman Communications Center, 308; Kennedy's campaign for nomination (1960), 200–201; losses in November 1994 midterms, 409; Middleburg Meeting (June 1991), 356–60; midterm victories (1982), 300; midterm victories (1986), 329, 332; PamPAC counter-ads against NCPAC, 298; PCH as Democratic Woman of the Year (1980), 274; PCH backs Carter

INDEX

Democratic Party (*cont.*)
(1976), 269; PCH backs Muskie as candidate (1972), 257–58; PCH drawn to ideas of, 114, 154, 214, 295–96; PCH in Mango Bay, 317; PCH makes N Street a Democratic hub, 263, 264; PCH's allegiance to, 256; PCH's Democrats for the Eighties (PamPAC), 291–300, 301–8, 329–30, 345–46; PCH's marriage to Averell, 242, 243, 327; PCH's National Polling Project, 345–46; PCH's search for a suitable candidate (1980-92), 281, 290, 291, 292, 297, 301–3, 305–8, 322, 343–45, 350, 356–63; PCH's speech at National Convention (1984), 322; PCH's support for Bella Abzug (1976), 267–69, 300; presidential election (1980), 281, 289–90; presidential election (1992), 360–68, 443; and Reagan's control of political narrative, 298, 317; and selection of 1992 presidential candidate, 356, 358, 359–61; son Winston as liability for PCH, 284; and Marietta Tree, 192–93. *See also entries for individual politicians*
Devonshire, Mary Cavendish, Duchess of, 103
Diana, Princess, 2, 384
Dickey, Christopher, 389
Didion, Joan, 280
Dietrich, Marlene, 131, 193
Digby, Constance (Pansy, née Bruce, mother of PCH), 9–14, 43, 47, 71, 175, 275; death of (March 1978), 286; Jewish blood of, 19–20; in New York and Toronto (1937), 21–22; pacifism of, 20; PCH aids financially, 285–86; quest to get PCH married, 23, 26, 31–32
Digby, Constance Sheila (sister of PCH), 10, 11, 12, 18, 25, 243, 372; coming out/the Season (1939), 33, 36
Digby, Edward, 12th Baron Digby (Eddie, brother of PCH), 14–15, 178, 233, 285–86, 342, 444
Digby, Edward Kenelm, 11th Baron Digby (Kenny, father of PCH), 9–10, 12–13, 15–16, 20, 24, 29, 71, 175, 177; as military secretary in Australia, 11; in New York and Toronto (1937), 21–22; quest to get PCH married, 31–32; and son-in-law Randolph, 43, 47, 102
Digby, Sir Everard, 16
Digby, Jane (1807-81), 16–17, 20, 152, 185, 229, 403–4
Dior, Christian, 149–50, 164, 166, 229
Ditchley Park, Oxfordshire, 70, 76
Dobrynin, Anatoly, 310
Dole, Bob, 378
Downham School, Hertfordshire, 18–19, 28, 158, 374
Druon, Madeleine, 394
Druon, Maurice, 165*, 165, 276, 384, 390, 440
Duchin, Cheray, 240–41, 247, 255
Duchin, Eddy, 107
Duchin, Peter, 229, 239, 240–42, 247, 251, 347, 442; carries Averell's coffin, 324–25; and Marie Harriman, 107, 243–44, 253–54; hatred of PCH, 253–54, 323, 325–26, 371, 398–99, 434; marries Brooke Hayward, 323; as society bandleader, 216, 220

INDEX

Dukakis, Michael, 305, 306, 344–45
Dulles, Allen, 109
Dunn, Lady Mary, 34, 39–40, 46–47, 121
Dunn, Sir Philip, 39

Eaker, Ira, 111, 116
Easy Rider (Dennis Hopper film, 1969), 228
Eden, Anthony, 36, 62, 194, 261–62
Eden, Clarissa (née Spencer-Churchill), 18, 26, 28, 79–80, 85, 117, 253, 262, 394
Egypt, 194
Eisenhower, Dwight, 3, 111, 121, 123, 193, 225, 383
Eizenstat, Fran, 405
Eizenstat, Stuart, 289–90, 291, 295, 304, 307, 330, 354, 363, 405, 426; on Middleburg Meeting (June 1991), 358; on PCH's Issues Evenings, 301, 302; on PCH's Samuel D. Berger Memorial Lecture, 339, 340
Ekberg, Anita, 186–87
Eliot, T. S., 123
Elizabeth, Queen (Queen Mother), 184–85
Elizabeth II, Queen, 262–63, 406
Elkann, Ginevra, 163
el Mezrab, Sheikh Abdul Medjuel, 17
Ely-Raphel, Nancy, 346, 386
Embiricos, André, 176
Engelen, Luce, 429–30, 446
environmental issues, 256, 268
d'Erlanger, Minnie, 223, 224–25, 235, 246, 287, 413, 444, 446
d'Estainville, Anne-Marie, 178
Eton College, 170–71
European Coal and Steel Community, 168

European Union, 387, 405
Evans, Harold, 371

Fairbanks, Douglas, Jr., 34
Fairlie, Henry, 341, 370
Falklands War (1982), 320–21
Farrow, Mia, 220, 234
Faucigny-Lucinge, Prince Jean-Louis de, 159, 160
Feinstein, Dianne, 331, 365–66
Fellowes, Daisy, 30
Fellowes, Rosamond, 30
feminism, 219–20, 252, 265, 267–68, 279, 330, 332, 369–70, 390–91
Fenn, Peter, 282, 292, 294, 297, 298–99, 300, 303, 304, 358; blames PCH's death on lawsuits, 439
Fermor, Patrick Leigh, 188
Ferraro, Geraldine, 322
Fiat corporation, 160, 161–62, 173–75, 276
First World War, 9, 20, 58, 84, 97
Fisk, Averell, 282–83, 401, 428
Fisk, Robert, 326
Fitzwilliam, Earl (Peter), 151, 156–57
Flowers, Gennifer, 360–61
Flynn, Errol, 163
Foley, Tom, 296, 318, 380, 442
Fonda, Jane, 218
Fonda, Peter, 228
Foot, Michael, 55
Forbes, Robert, 405
Ford, Gerald, 3, 262, 269
France: British destruction of fleet at Oran, 61; Cap Martin, 30; Château de Balleroy, Normandy, 405; Clintons in for D-Day commemorations (1994), 404–9; Colleville-sur-Mer military

495

INDEX

France (*cont.*)
  cemetery, 406; fall of (June 1940), 60; film industry, 387; Franco-American relations, 376, 386–87, 389, 390, 410–11, 414–19, 425, 426–27, 430, 440; Free French exile administration, 61; and Marshall Plan, 154, 168; PCH appointed ambassador to (March 1993), 374–80, 443; PCH in (1938–39), 30–31; PCH's working life as ambassador in, 383–88, 389–94, 404–9, 410–11, 414–25, 426–27, 430–31, 434–35, 436; Riviera, 30–31, 152–54, 159–61, 163, 172–75, 177–79, 187, 211; spying accusations against U.S. (1995), 410; and Suez fiasco (1956), 194, 261–62; Villa Léopolda, Cap Ferrat, 177, 178, 187, 211. *See also* Paris
Franklin, Aretha, 445
Fraser, Hugh, 28
Friedan, Betty, 208, 252
Friendly, Alfred/Arthur, 292, 442
Friendly, Pie, 264, 276, 316, 330, 346
Fritchley, Polly, 265
Frost, David, 219

Gable, Clark, 34, 123
Galbraith, Evan, 389
Galitzine, Princess, 172
Galliher, John, 165
Gamsakhurdia, Zviad, 353
Garbo, Greta, 173, 193
Gates, Bill, 392
GATT world trade negotiations, 387, 410
gay rights, 268, 404
Geashill Castle (near Dublin), 10
Gellhorn, Martha, 119, 261, 428
Geoffrey, Georges, 165

George VI, King, 24–25
Georgia (country), 353
Germany, 19–21, 24, 29–30, 59, 60–61, 94, 139; Nazi expansion in 1930s, 19–21, 24, 29–30, 31
Gibbs, Betty, 118
Giscard d'Estaing, Valéry, 263, 389
Givenchy, 396
Goldberg, Whoopi, 445
Goldwater, Barry, 438
Good Friday Agreement, Northern Ireland (1998), 427
Goodwin, Doris Kearns, 370
Gorbachev, Mikhail, 3, 312, 315, 334–39, 340, 351–52
Gorbachev, Raisa, 3, 334, 336–39
Gore, Al, 300, 321, 344, 359, 361–62, 364, 379, 380, 442
Gore, Tipper, 344, 364, 380, 441
The Governor (horse), 253
Graham, Donald, 366
Graham, Kay, 239–40, 261, 265–66, 336, 337, 366, 379, 403, 441; Capote's Ball in honor of (1966), 220; on Jimmy Carter, 272–73; on the Kennedy men, 211; runs sham burial story, 325–26
Gray, Hannah, 337
Greenwood, Arthur, 60
Guinness, Gloria, 210, 219–20, 235
Guinness, Loel, 210, 235
Gulf War (1991), 350, 357–58
Gunpowder Plot (1605), 16, 42

Haiti, 415
Hamilton, Lady Emma, 89, 244*, 244
Hamilton, Nigel, 404
Hammerstein, Oscar, 203
Hampton, Mark, 382
Hardy, Thomas, *The Woodlanders*, 12
Harrach, Countess von, 19–20

INDEX

Harriman, Averell (third husband of PCH): affair with PCH (from April 1941), 85–88, 89–90, 92, 103–8; as American ambassador to the Soviet Union, 108, 109, 135–36, 137, 271; arrival in London (March 1941), 82; as Assistant Secretary of State, 213; at Atlantic Conference (August 1941), 97–98; background of, 83–84, 92, 294, 295; biological grandchildren, 282–83, 326, 399, 401, 427; breaks off affair with PCH (October 1943), 108, 109; brief resumption of affair with PCH, 147–48; as briefly American ambassador to UK, 147; buys ten-seater Westwind jet, 318; at Capote's Black & White Ball (1966), 220–21; as champion of Britain, 82, 84, 87; changes imposed on life/properties of by PCH, 247–55; character of, 84, 101, 107, 148, 168, 242, 244, 264–66, 273, 297, 313, 316; at Cherkley with PCH and Randolph, 101; and Clinton, 306; death and funeral of (1986), 324–25; death of wife Marie (1970), 239, 243, 254; diagnosed with prostate cancer, 254–55, 275; eminence and authority in 1970s Washington, 260–66, 267; final trip to Moscow (1983), 310–11, 335; flies across Atlantic with PCH (1965), 225; as governor of New York, 193–94, 258, 259; ignores PCH at El Morocco nightclub, 146–47; increasing infirmity of, 266, 275–76, 294, 302, 308, 311, 316–17, 320; management of estate, 323, 326, 348–50, 395–96, 397–99, 400, 427–28; mansion at Arden, upstate New York, 84, 107–8, 239, 250–51, 283, 325, 398; married life with PCH, 247–55, 264–66, 270–71, 275–76, 282, 313; marries PCH (September 1971), 243–44; as Marshall Plan's representative in Paris, 168; meetings with PCH near Haywire, 229; meets PCH (March 1941), 82–83; and nuclear disarmament issue, 272–73; obsession with ousting Nixon, 256, 257–59; as one of Six Wise Men, 194; and PamPAC, 291, 296–97; patrician image of, 114, 294, 295; PCH and biological grandchildren of, 282–83, 326, 401, 427; PCH at Sands Point with (1971), 240–42; PCH follows career from afar, 193–94; PCH shares apartment on Grosvenor Square with, 102–3; PCH's correspondence with in Moscow, 130, 131, 132, 133–34, 135–36, 138; PCH's reunion with (1971), 240–41; and PCH's son Winston, 229, 320; PCH's strategy to charm, 83, 84–88, 89–90, 275; and Pearl Harbor attack, 99; and presidential election (1972), 257–59; and relations with Soviet Union, 271–73, 309–12, 335, 339; return to U.S. at end of war, 138; revived political ambition in 1970s, 249–50; as Secretary of Commerce, 148; sees PCH at Kay Graham's party (1971), 239–40; seriously ill with paratyphoid (1942), 103–4; sham

INDEX

Harriman, Averell (*cont.*)
burial story, 325–26; signs new will (1984), 323; as statesman not politician, 258, 259; transfers art collection to PCH (1982), 323; and transfers of wealth to Winston (1970s), 245–46, 254, 286–87, 320, 323, 324; trip to Egypt (1941), 94–95; at Vietnam peace talks in Paris (1968), 239, 270, 419; view of women's role in politics, 264–66, 267; at Yalta (1945), 136, 137

Harriman, Marie, 83, 107, 135, 137, 220, 241, 247, 249–50, 282–83, 325; art expertise, 107, 165, 243, 248–49; and Averell's political career, 193; death of (September 1970), 239, 243, 254, 283; and Peter Duchin, 107, 241, 253–54; on husband Averell, 92, 107; PCH erases every trace of, 247, 254; and PCH's affair with Averell, 107–8, 146–47

Harriman, Pamela Churchill (PCH) FINANCES: alters will (January 1997), 430, 444; auction of effects at Sotheby's, New York, 444–46; cost of running Paris embassy, 376, 382, 386, 394, 395–96; crisis at end of Hayward's life, 228–29, 232–34, 235; crisis of 1993-95 period, 399–401, 412, 413–14; death blamed on lawsuits, 439; Harriman lawsuits settled, 427–28; Harrimans file lawsuit (September 1994), 401, 403–4, 412, 427–28; joint case against Clifford and Rich, 428; left a wealthy widow, 326; legal costs of Ogden case, 373; management of, 323, 326, 349, 396, 397–99, 400, 427–28; problems in late 1980s, 348–49; sales from art collection, 348–49, 412; sues Brown Brothers Harriman bank, 413; sues Clifford and Warnke, 413–14; tax-free sums from Churchills, 101; Union Pacific stock, 245, 282, 323, 398, 400; and Linda Wachner, 392–93

Harriman, Pamela Churchill (PCH) PHYSICAL APPEARANCE: Beaton's portraits, 72–73, 76–77, 96, 248; beauty regime in Paris (1950s), 182–83; beauty regime in Washington, 277, 327; has facelift (1988), 1, 327; Brooke Hayward on, 202; in her childhood/teens, 14, 18, 25–26, 27, 37, 40; in her seventies, 1, 2, 389–90, 428–29, 432–33; *maquillage*, 1, 26, 46, 153, 396; mesmerizing eyes, 2, 62, 72, 160; milky skin, 30, 62, 114–15, 219; red hair, 26, 30, 62, 160, 202, 219; wardrobe in childhood/teenage years, 21, 25–26; white streak in hair, 14

Harriman, Pamela Churchill (PCH) POLITICAL/DIPLOMATIC LIFE, 1, 2; addresses Joint Session of Congress (1982), 294; admiration for Thatcher, 370; appointed ambassador to France (March 1993), 374–80, 443; belief in America's sacred destiny, 212, 407, 423, 442–43; and Carter White House, 269, 272–74, 281; celebration supper at 3038 N Street (November 1992), 364–66;

INDEX

and Jacques Chirac, 411, 413–19, 430; Clinton fundraiser at Willow Oaks (September 1992), 362–63; Conservatism of her parents, 15, 19; control of two Harriman foundations, 332; correspondence with Dmitri, 312; and D-Day commemorations in France (1994), 404–8; as Democratic Woman of the Year (1980), 274; Democrats for the Eighties (PamPAC), 289–300, 301–8, 329–30, 345–46; deployed to charm de Gaulle, 61–62; disbands PamPAC (1990), 350; eggnog party before Christmas in Washington, 261; eminence and authority in 1970s Washington, 260–66, 267–74, 281–82; first exposure to non-Tory worldview, 21–22; friendship with Bill Clinton, 292–93, 321, 340, 346, 354, 358–68, 387–88, 416–17, 430, 432–33, 446; galvanized by 1980 election disaster, 288–300, 301–8; gives Samuel D. Berger Memorial Lecture (April 1988), 339–40; and the Gorbachevs in Washington (1987), 334, 336–39; greets the *Cossack* at Leith (February 1940), 56; has tea with Hitler (1937), 20–21, 36, 260; high-level overseas trips in late 1980s, 332–33; introduces Clinton to Washington, 306–7, 360–61; Issues Evenings at 3038 N Street, 301–4, 306–7, 322, 432; and Labour politicians, 60, 138; lifelong mission of self-education, 21, 33, 36, 165–67, 215–16, 272, 302–3, 309; lives in Downing Street, 3–4, 59–65; and Nelson Mandela, 367–68, 430; Middleburg Meeting (June 1991), 356–59; National Polling Project, 345–46; nuclear disarmament issue, 272–73; nurtures Preston constituency, 80, 101; personal attacks on during PamPAC period, 304, 319–20, 341–42, 345; political education at Lady Baillie's salon, 33, 36; as political hostess in Washington, 250–54, 260–66, 274, 281; political worldview shifts leftward, 114, 138, 139; posthumous award of Grand Croix of the Légion d'Honneur, 437, 440; presidential election (1972), 257–59; Republican contacts, 192–93, 262–63, 307; revived political ambition in 1970s, 249–50, 256–59, 260–66, 267–74; role over peace in Bosnia, 414–26, 432, 443; and Roosevelt, 99; runs Churchill Club at Ashburnham House, 122–23, 128, 132, 138, 165; soirées with Americans at 49 Grosvenor Square (the Attic), 110–12, 120–22; and the Soviet Union, 72, 136–37, 272–73, 309–15, 334, 335, 336–39, 340–41, 351–54; style of entertaining while ambassador in Paris, 394–95; tactical retreat over women in politics, 279; toys with political career in UK, 139, 147; tributes to over 1992 success, 363–64, 443; and U.S. elections in 1980s, 321–23, 329–30, 332, 343–45; views impact of Allied mass bombing, 138–39; and

INDEX

Harriman, Pamela Churchill (*cont.*)
Washington art elite, 277–78;
wish to leave ambassadorial post
(1996), 431; working life as
ambassador in Paris, 383–87,
388–94, 402–3, 404–8, 413,
414–25, 426–27, 430–31, 434–35,
436. *See also under* Democratic
Party; women *and entries for
associated people and places*
Harriman, Pamela Churchill
(PCH) PRIVATE LIFE:
Giorgio Agnelli shoots at, 179;
American citizenship, 244, 256;
attempts to buy son Winston's
love, 246, 254, 286, 320, 323,
348; behavior toward Peter
Duchin, 254–55, 323, 324–25;
birth of (March 20, 1920), 9, 10;
birth of son Winston during air-
raid, 69, 70; board positions after
Averell's death, 332; cars driven/
owned by, 24, 29, 106, 171, 174,
251; childhood, 10, 11–16, 18–19;
and Winston Churchill, 53–54,
55–57, 59–60, 105–7, 112,
119–20, 126, 129–30, 164, 198,
207, 266; Clarissa Churchill on,
18, 28; Churchillian pedigree/
name, 145, 150, 197, 247, 272,
284, 292, 321, 346–47, 388; at
Churchill's state funeral, 225;
coming out/the Season (1938),
24–27; continued friendship with
Agnelli, 181, 187, 201, 211, 223,
276–77, 327–28, 428–29;
conversion to Catholicism, 175–76,
179–80, 198, 207, 224; death of,
1, 437–39; desire to live a life on
her own terms, 121–22, 180–81,
446; directorship at Braniff
Airlines, 274; in Downing Street
during Blitz, 65–66; education
of, 15, 18–19, 158, 374; erases
every trace of Marie Harriman,
247, 254; as *Evening Standard*
columnist, 147–48; family
background, 9, 10–11, 15–17,
19–20; fascination for power,
3–5, 11, 21, 48–49, 92, 193, 259;
features on cover of *Life*
magazine, 76–77, 91; and
feminism/women's liberation,
219, 220, 252, 266, 267–69, 332,
369, 390–91; gambling debts, 29,
37; with Kathy Harriman in
Beare Green, 95–96; and
Harriman sham burial story,
325–26; has abortion in
Switzerland, 176; has
hysterectomy (1955), 189; horse
riding, 14, 22, 253, 436; ill
health, 116–17, 130, 187, 189–90,
275–76, 350–51, 354, 378; jewels
of, 78, 163–64, 184, 188, 195,
198, 209, 228, 229, 250, 277,
280, 295, 446; at Kennedy
compound in Palm Beach (1945),
144–45; and Bobby Kennedy's
assassination (1968), 230; and
Jack Kennedy, 144, 154–56, 210,
211, 212–14, 217; on Joe
Kennedy, 33; and Kick Kennedy,
26–27, 32–33, 119, 144, 151–52,
154–55, 156–57, 296; lack of
interest in children, 169;
memorial service in Washington,
441–43; miscarriage of second
pregnancy, 79; Murrow chooses
Janet over, 145–46; in New York
and Toronto with her parents
(1937), 21–22; *noblesse oblige*/
philanthropy, 253, 295–96; opens
shop on East 57th Street, 216–17;

INDEX

ostrich family crest, 12, 14, 175, 247, 368; and parenting of son Winston, 117–18, 130, 135, 143, 148–49, 159, 160, 168–71, 174, 177–78, 187, 188; parents' attempts to marry off, 23, 25, 31; pregnancy, 55–56, 57–58, 61, 63, 68–69; privileges Winston over Leland's children, 233–34, 246, 254; at RAF Uxbridge (September 15, 1940), 67; relationship with Clementine, 52–53, 57–59, 71, 119, 130, 189, 197–98, 201–2, 207, 226, 266, 286; relationship with her adult son, 224, 226, 245, 320–21, 346–50, 429–30; renews friendship with Murrow (mid-1950s), 192, 213; reputation of not liking other women, 118–19, 261, 303, 381; Rothschilds close ranks on, 198, 382; row over Brooke Hayward's *Haywire* (1977), 280–82; ruthless streak, 12, 24, 184, 384–85, 433; Mary Soames's dislike of, 46–47, 106–7, 225, 346–47; and son Winston's wedding, 223, 224; spoken voice of, 393; ties with Churchills loosen, 133–34, 136; and transfers of wealth to Winston (1970s), 245–46, 254, 286–87, 294, 320, 323, 348; tributes to on her death, 437–39; uncontested divorce granted (1945), 143; wartime translation work, 39. *See also under entries for associated people and places*

Harriman, Pamela Churchill (PCH) RESIDENCES/ PROPERTIES: 3034 N Street, Georgetown, Washington, 263, 270, 271, 290, 308, 400; 3038 N Street, Georgetown, Washington, 246–49, 254–55, 260–62, 294–95, 297, 301–7, 329–30, 337, 343–44, 364–66, 368, 400, 412, 446; 49 Grosvenor Square (the Attic), 106, 110–12, 118, 120–22, 123, 127, 128, 135, 149; apartment at 1020 Fifth Avenue, 207–8, 228; in Beekman Building on Park Avenue, 228; Carlos Place, Mayfair, 24, 27–28; Harriman mansion on 81st Street, 243, 252, 254; Haywire country home (later Birchgrove, Westchester County), 215–16, 229, 232–33, 234, 279, 286–87, 295, 313, 324; at Hobe Sound, Florida, 239, 254, 381; house on rue Delabordere, Paris, 164; at Ickleford, 65, 71, 72, 73, 78–79; lives at Admiralty House, 56, 57; lives at Dorchester Hotel, 79, 83; Mango Bay (house in Barbados), 317, 318, 373; Paris apartment at 4 avenue de New York, 174, 175, 181, 194–95, 196–97, 198; rents Chateau de la Garoupe, 172–74, 176–77; ski lodge in Sun Valley, Idaho, 261, 327, 351, 383; at Villa Léopolda, Cap Ferrat, 176–77, 178, 211; Willow Oaks, Middleburg, Virginia, 252–53, 270–71, 328, 331, 356–59, 362–63, 375, 427, 434

Harriman, Pamela Churchill (PCH) SEXUAL BEHAVIOR/ RELATIONSHIPS: affair with Élie de Rothschild, 183–84, 185–86, 187, 188, 197, 198, 382, 393–94, 440; affair with Gianni

INDEX

Harriman, Pamela Churchill (*cont.*)
Agnelli, 160–64, 169, 172–74, 175–81, 347; affair with Harriman (from April 1941), 83–88, 89–90, 91–92, 103–6; affair with Murrow, 112–15, 116, 118, 134, 143–44, 146, 192, 226; affair with Prince Aly Khan, 151–54, 165, 170; affair with Whitney, 109–10, 115, 122; Capote's "La Cote Basque 1965," 221; deal with Beaverbrook, 78–79, 80, 83, 86, 87, 92; diplomatic use of sex, 1, 4, 76, 78–79, 82–88, 89–90, 103–4, 109–17, 120–24; "fast" reputation of, 37–38; flings after D-Day, 132; flirtation with McCullagh, 22, 23–24, 48, 111; as full-time *grande horizontale* in 1950s, 183–89, 198; gold-digger reputation, 4, 165, 179, 351, 399; Aly Khan's prowess, 151–54, 241; power as an aphrodisiac, 92; preferred type of man, 113; scholarly recognition of strategic sex life, 123; seeks new rich man in New York, 146–47; Frank Sinatra rumors, 234–35; society reaction against wartime erotic escapades, 165; as "that red-headed tart," 2, 184; trip to Paris with Fulkie (1939), 37–38

Harriman Fisk, Mary, 282, 325, 326, 349, 397–98; death of, 428; files lawsuit over finances (September 1994), 401, 404, 412, 427–28

Harriman Mortimer, Kathleen, 90–91, 94, 108, 146–47, 225, 243, 282–83, 297, 326; confronts PCH in Paris (December 1993), 397–98; and father's art collection, 323, 326, 348–49, 412; files lawsuit over finances (September 1994), 401, 404, 412, 427–28; and Harriman sham burial story, 325–26; knowledge of PCH-Harriman affair, 92, 147; married life, 282–83; in Moscow with Harriman, 109; with PCH in Beare Green, 95–96; at PCH's memorial service, 442; settles lawsuit with PCH, 427–28; at Yalta (1945), 136, 137

Hart, Gary, 259, 343

Hart, Kitty Carlisle, 215, 248, 267, 318, 398–99, 442

Hart, Moss, 215

Hartington, Billy Cavendish, Marquess of, 32, 119

Hayward, Billy, 204, 205, 209, 217, 228, 233–34, 254, 281

Hayward, Bridget, 204, 209

Hayward, Brooke, 202, 205, 209, 215, 217–18, 229, 232–34, 254, 442; *Haywire* (1977), 279–83, 347; marries Peter Duchin, 323; on PCH's death, 439

Hayward, Leland (second husband of PCH), 195–99, 200–202, 203–5, 206–9, 210, 212, 214–16, 218–19; and Brooke Hayward's *Haywire* (1977), 279–83, 347; death of (February 1971), 232–33, 243; lives with PCH in New York, 203–5, 206–7; married life with PCH, 206–8, 210, 212, 214–16, 218–19; marries PCH in Carson City (May 1960), 207; PCH and children of, 201–2, 204–5, 209, 215, 218, 229, 233–34, 254, 279–83, 347; PCH and musical career of, 203–4, 208, 216; PCH

in Las Vegas with, 206–7; PCH's pursuit of, 195–99, 200, 201–2, 205; serious ill health of, 228–29; *The Trial of the Catonsville Nine* (play), 231–32; works on *That Was the Week That Was*, 218–19
Hayward, Slim, 195–97, 199, 200, 202–4, 206–7, 221
Hayworth, Rita, 160
Hearst, William Randolph, 127
Helleu, Paul, 382, 445
Helms, Cynthia, 306, 327
Helms, Jesse, 299, 377, 378
Hemingway, Ernest, 131, 174–75, 196
Hepburn, Katharine, 76, 193, 195, 232
Heuvel, William van den, 402
Hill, Anita, 331–32
Hitler, Adolf, 19, 20–21, 24, 29–30, 31, 33, 36, 49, 260
Holbrooke, Richard, 121, 263, 318, 332–33, 366, 399, 401, 433, 442; as Assistant Secretary of State for Europe, 386; and Bosnian war, 419–24, 425, 426; character of, 270, 420; and death of Averell, 324, 325; and PamPAC, 290; on PCH's ambassadorship, 5, 420, 423, 447; and tour of Soviet Union (1991), 353–54
Hollywood, 34, 37, 123, 160, 173, 193, 195, 261, 387–88, 442
Holm, Richard, 410, 413
Holmes, Sven, 297
Hopkins, Harry, 75–76, 82, 83, 87–88, 94, 97–98, 108, 388
Hopper, Dennis, 218, 228, 234
Hornblow, Leonora, 196, 198–99
Howard, Janet, 297, 318, 320, 321, 330–31, 342, 362, 364, 371, 377, 442; arranges Averell's funeral, 324–25; blames PCH's death on lawsuits, 439; on Carter Brown, 350; as a director of PamPAC, 330, 346; as divisive character, 291–92; estrangement with PCH, 429, 436, 441, 444; as executive assistant in Paris, 381, 391, 393, 394, 396, 401, 402–3, 428, 429; at Middleburg Meeting (June 1991), 356, 362–63; and PAC idea, 290–91; returns to USA from Paris, 436
Hozier, Lady Blanche, 89
Hudson, Sam (butler), 149
Huffington, Arianna, 403
Hungarian uprising (1956), 311
Hunnicutt, Gayle, 375
Hunt, Very Reverend Ernest, 442
hunting, 14, 22, 190, 253

Institute for the Advanced Study of Russian-American Affairs, Columbia University, 309
International Ladies' Garments Workers' Union, 21
Iraq War (2003), 426
Ireland, 10, 97, 154–55
Ismay, General Hastings "Pug," 62, 127
Italy, 160–62, 173–74, 179–81, 277
Izetbegović, Alija, 421, 422–24, 425

Jackson, Reverend Jesse, 344, 365
James, Jacquetta (née Digby, sister of PCH), 15, 175, 372, 375
Janklow, Morton, 370
Japan, 87, 99, 100, 115, 139, 333
Jay, Michael, 429, 434–35, 440, 444
Jay, Sylvia, 429, 435, 444
Jebb, Cynthia, 184–85, 384
Jebb, Sir Gladwyn, 166

INDEX

Jews, 19–20, 121, 164, 198, 426–27
Johnson, Lyndon, 225
Johnson, Snakehips, 81
Jones, Paula, 404
Jordan, Ann, 380
Jordan, Vernon, 365, 380, 442
Jospin, Lionel, 411
Juppé, Alain, 384
Jurassic Park (film), 387

Kantor, Mickey, 363, 387–88
Kaplan, James, 235
Karimov, Islam, 353
Karsh (photographer), 224
Kassebaum, Nancy, 337
Kazakhstan, 353–54
Kelly, Sharon Pratt, 365
Kemp, Gerald van der, 278
Kemsley, Lord, 50
Kennedy, Edward, 289, 301
Kennedy, Ethel, 211, 217, 243, 256
Kennedy, Jackie, 155, 192–93, 207, 211, 212, 213, 230, 233, 267, 349, 375, 376, 395, 445–46
Kennedy, John Fitzgerald (Jack), 3, 32–33, 192, 207, 294, 371; assassination of (November 22, 1963), 217; attitude to women, 155, 211, 213; awards Churchill honorary American citizenship (1963), 213; campaign for Democratic nomination (1960), 200–201; diagnosed with Addison's disease, 156; friendship with Gianni Agnelli, 173, 211; on his father, 226–27; inaugurated as U.S. president (January 1961), 210; PCH accompanies to New Ross in Ireland, 155; PCH and presidency of, 211, 212–14; run for Congress in Massachusetts, 144, 154–55; visit to Paris (1961), 376
Kennedy, Joseph, 26–27, 38, 64, 74, 75, 144, 157, 207; allegations over sexual conduct, 32–33, 220–21; Churchill despises, 260–61; Jack Kennedy on, 226–27; secretly meets Nazi officials, 33
Kennedy, Kathleen "Kick": affair with Earl Fitzwilliam, 151, 156–57; dies in plane crash (1948), 157; house in Smith Square, 151; and London society, 27; marries Billy Hartington, 119; and PCH, 27, 31–32, 119, 144, 151–52, 154–55, 156–57, 296
Kennedy, Robert, 211–12, 214, 216; assassination of (June 1968), 230
Kennedy, Rose, 27, 32, 144–45, 156, 157, 230
Kennedy, Joe, Jr., 119
Kerrey, Bob, 357, 359
Kerry, John, 295, 300, 301, 349
Khan, Prince Aly, 151–54, 159–60, 165, 170, 241, 371
Khashoggi, Adnan, 287
Kierkegaard, Søren, 5
King, Larry, 385
King, Martin Luther, Jr., 230
Kinnock, Neil, 344
Kipper, Judith, 340, 345–46, 351, 353, 442
Kirk, Paul, 329
Kirkpatrick, Jeane, 319*, 322
Kissinger, Henry, 172, 249, 251, 263, 285
Klein, Joe, 361
Klosters, 188, 348
Knickerbocker, Red, 63
Korda, Alexander, 89, 244

Labour Party, 60, 138, 139, 147, 413
Lagarde, Christine, 391

INDEX

Lagerfeld, Karl, 396
Lane, David, 261
Lane, Kenneth Jay, 367
Lanza, Prince Raimondo, 160
Largs, Scotland, 72, 73
Las Vegas, 206–7
Laycock, Colonel Robert, 71
Le Rosey school, Switzerland, 169–70
Leeds Castle, Kent, 23, 34, 36–37
Legvold, Robert, 309, 338, 351, 353, 354
Leslie, Anita, 52, 227
Levitte, Jean-David, 414, 416, 420, 424, 426
Lévy, Bernard-Henri, 389, 422–23, 424
Levy, Moses, 19
L'Horizon, Chateau de (French Riviera), 152–54, 156, 158, 159–60
Lilly, Doris, 345
Lismore Castle, Northern Ireland, 103, 154
Lloyd, Geoffrey, 36
London: Blitz, 65–66, 69, 75, 81–82, 85–86, 90–91, 121–22; Churchill Club at Ashburnham House, 122–23, 128, 132, 138, 165; Dorchester Hotel, Park Lane, 79–80, 83, 85–86, 91, 92, 100, 275–76; Four Hundred Club, Leicester Square, 26, 40; the Season, 23, 24–28, 33, 36; sex in during war, 81
Lopez-Willshaw, Arturo, 165
Lovell, Mary, 403
Luce, Claire, 50–51, 52, 64
Luce, Harry, 132
Ludinghausen, Baroness Hélène de, 172
Lytton, Pamela Plowden, Countess of, 42

Macintyre, Ben, 399
Maisky, Ivan, 72
Major, John, 285*, 379, 417
Mallaby, Sir Christopher, 383–84, 385, 389
Manchester, William, 327, 345
Mandela, Nelson, 367–68, 430
Manzullo, Don, 439
Marcus Aurelius, 114
Margesson, David, 36, 39, 41, 147, 176
Margrethe, Queen of Denmark, 278
Marlborough, John Spencer-Churchill, 10th Duke of, 66
Marlborough, Mary, Duchess of, 66
Marriott, Maud (Momo), 93, 95
Marshall, General George C., 111, 120
Martin, Marion (housekeeper), 135, 156, 174, 201, 285
Marton, Kati, 419
Mason, Christopher, 346
McCrary, Tex, 87, 92
McCullagh, George, 22, 23–24, 48, 111
McCurry, Mike, 437
McGovern, George, 257, 258–59
McLean, Kiki, 302
McNamara, Robert, 256
Menzies, Robert, 3, 79
Messel, Oliver, 317
Mikulski, Barbara, 331, 337, 341
Milošević, Slobodan, 425–26, 437
Minnelli, Liza, 204
Minterne, mansion of (Dorset), 10, 11, 12–17, 21, 31, 43, 143, 235
Mitchell, George, 300, 329, 341, 380
Mitford, Clementine, 43–44
Mitford, Deborah (Duchess of Devonshire), 25, 26–27, 103, 251

INDEX

Mitford, Nancy, 26, 152, 182, 207, 225
Mitford, Unity, 20
Mitterrand, François, 388–89, 407, 416
Mladić, Ratko, 418
Moffett, Charles, 382–83
Monahan, Katie, 253
Mondale, Walter, 274–75, 321–22
Monroe, Marilyn, 193
Montego Bay, Jamaica, 148
Montgomery, Field Marshal Bernard, 126, 127, 133, 170
Moore, Bishop Paul, 325
Morgan, Alida, 282
Morgan Stanley investment bank, 297
Mortimer, Averell, 282–83
Mortimer, David, 333, 427
Mortimer, Stanley, 146
Moss, Melissa, 340, 355, 356–57, 362
Mountbatten, Edwina, 112
Mountbatten, Lord Louis, 24
Moynihan, Daniel Patrick, 267–68, 345, 377
Moynihan, Pat, 217
Munich, 19–20
Munich crisis (1938), 30–31
Murrow, Casey, 143, 145
Murrow, Ed: affair with PCH, 113–15, 118, 134–35, 143–44, 145, 189–90, 226; background of, 113–14; on the Blitz, 121–22; character of, 113–14, 115–16, 118, 144; chooses Janet over PCH, 145–46; death of (1965), 226; as head of United States Information Agency, 213; in liberated Paris (1944), 131–32; PCH commits to life with in USA, 143–44, 145; on postwar Britain, 149; radical politics of, 113, 114, 192; renews friendship with PCH (mid-1950s), 192, 213; Second World War broadcasting from London, 91, 112–13, 115, 125, 133, 146
Murrow, Janet, 111, 114–15, 122, 134–35, 143, 144, 145
Muskie, Edmund, 257–58, 259, 307, 339
Mussolini, Benito, 160

Nelson, Admiral Lord, 244*
New York, 21–22, 107, 189–90; apartment at 1020 Fifth Avenue, 207–9, 228; Capote's writing, 219–22; Century Club, Manhattan, 345; El Morocco nightclub, 146–47; Metropolitan Museum of Art, 208, 278; PCH as *Evening Standard* columnist in (1946), 147; PCH in (Christmas 1945), 143–44, 146–47; PCH lives in (1959), 198–99, 200–202; PCH opens shop on East 57th Street, 216–17; radical politics in 1930s, 21–22; St. Thomas's Episcopal Church on Fifth Avenue, 324; the Swans of Fifth Avenue, 219–20
Newick, Ben, 394
Niarchos, Stavros, 187, 188, 428
Nicholas II, Tsar, 271
Nicholson, Jack, 228, 261
Nigra, Dr. Thomas, 446
Niven, David, 123
Nixon, Richard, 3, 249, 256–59, 262, 271
Nizari Ismailis, 152
Noailles, Marie-Laure de, 190
Norfolk, Lavinia, Duchess of, 23, 28

INDEX

North Atlantic Treaty Organization (NATO), 168, 314, 424–25
Norton, Sarah, 24, 27, 29, 36–37, 50, 91
nuclear weapons, 167–68, 239, 257, 272, 310, 314; atom bomb developed in Los Alamos, 136; atom bombs dropped on Japan, 139; Reagan-Gorbachev treaty (1987), 335, 336–37

O'Connor, Sandra, 337
O'Donnell, Tom, 305–6, 345
Ogden, Christopher, 275, 370, 442; *Life of the Party* (1994), 5, 370–73, 399–400, 404, 431–32
Oliver, Vic, 90
Onassis, Aristotle, 163, 177, 187, 188, 223, 233
Osborne, June, 158, 191

Palewski, Gaston, 182
Paley, Babe, 146, 195, 197, 203, 219
Paley, Bill, 120–21, 134, 146, 173, 195, 197, 243, 276
Paris: British residence, 383–84, 385; Christian Dior's New Look, 149–50; Élysée Palace, 414, 425; glass pyramid at the Louvre, 407; Harriman's Marshall Plan role in, 168; Hôtel de Pontalba (ambassadorial residence), 381–82, 385, 393, 395–96, 398, 406–7, 419, 420–23, 425, 440, 444; Hôtel Ritz, 1, 2, 131, 174, 196, 402–3, 436–37; the Kennedys visit (1961), 376; liberation of (August 1944), 131; NATO headquarters in, 168; Marie-Laure de Noailles's costume ball, 190; PCH in (1938), 30; PCH in after liberation (September 1944), 131; PCH leaves for USA (1959), 198–99; PCH's arrival in (May 1993), 380–82; PCH's "finishing" in (1936), 19; PCH's "finishing" in (1936–37), 19–21; PCH's life in (late 1940s and 1950s), 90, 149–50, 159, 164–68, 174–75, 181, 182–85, 194–99, 430–31; PCH's trip to with Fulkie (1939), 37; racing at Longchamp, 151–52; Travellers Club, 391
Pasqua, Charles, 409–11
Patten, Susan Mary, 169, 194
Paul, Henri, 2
Pavlovich, Grand Duke Dimitri, 31
Peck, Gregory, 442
Pei, I. M., 407
Perón, Eva, 189
Perot, Ross, 363, 374
Perroots, Leonard, 314
Petrov, Stanislav, 314
Philip, Prince, 24, 31
Pickering, Tom, 384, 388, 420, 431
Podesta, Tony, 260, 302
Poland, 49, 136
Pompadour, Madame de, 414
Portal, Charles "Peter," 116, 136, 137
Portal, Jane, 164, 169
Powell, Charles, 393
Powell, Enoch, 284
Powell, Lewis, 438
Presley, Elvis, 190
Primakov, Yevgeny, 340
Prospect (horse), 253
Putin, Vladimir, 311

Quinn, Sally, 264–65, 266, 268, 304, 441
Quinn, Thomas, 351, 390

INDEX

racism, 152, 284, 358
Rainier, Prince, 390
Random House, 370–71
Reagan, Nancy, 3, 307, 335–36, 337
Reagan, Ronald: control of political narrative, 298, 317; disapproval of women in politics, 319; fails to attend Andropov's funeral, 314; and Franco-American relations, 389; homelessness under, 317; low-tax low-spend Reaganomics, 296, 304, 308, 317; nuclear treaty with Gorbachev (1987), 335–36; PCH's view of, 269, 289–90, 296, 314, 317, 322; and presidential election (1984), 321–22, 323; Reykjavík summit (1987), 312; "Star Wars" Strategic Defense Initiative, 310; tribute to Averell Harriman, 324; wins 1980 election, 289–90
Reardon, Roy, 427
Red Brigade in Italy, 276
Redford, Robert, 261
Renwick, Sir Robin, 328, 379, 392
Repard, Arabella, 435
Republican Party: culture warriors of, 369; female politicians, 319, 322, 337, 350; and Leland Hayward, 214, 256; loss of 1992 election, 363; low-tax low-spend Reaganomics, 296, 304, 308, 317; move right of, 269, 289; NCPAC attack advertisements, 298; PCH's contacts with, 192–93, 262, 307; and PCH's nomination as French ambassador, 377, 378; trickle-down theory of, 296; wins Congress (1994), 409; wins presidential election (1980), 288–90. *See also entries for individual politicians*

Ribbentrop, Joachim von, 68
Rice, Donna, 343
Rich, William, 287, 323, 349, 397–98, 399, 401, 428
Richardson, Tom, 399
Rivers, Joan, 446
Robb, Charles, 332, 377
Rockefeller, Jay, 297, 357, 359
Rodgers, Richard, 203
Rohatyn, Elizabeth, 432
Rohatyn, Felix, 303–4, 400, 432, 442
Romney, George, 244, 306, 445
Roosevelt, Anna, 136
Roosevelt, Eleanor, 213
Roosevelt, Franklin Delano, 3, 33, 38, 67, 74, 75, 83–84, 97, 114; Atlantic Conference (Newfoundland, August 1941), 97–98; centennial of (1982), 294; Churchill's letter to, 74–75; decision to privilege the war against Hitler, 115; failing health of, 136; Hopkins as envoy to London, 75–76, 82–83, 87, 388; and PCH, 98; and Pearl Harbor attack (December 7, 1941), 99; sends Harriman to Moscow (1943), 108; at Yalta (1945), 136–37
Roosevelt, Franklin, Jr., 173
Rosebery, Eva, Countess of, 23, 186
Rosenfeld, Dr. Isadore, 318, 410–11, 428, 437
Rosnay, Stella de, 166, 183, 184, 395
Ross, Gill, 179
Rothschild, David de, 436
Rothschild, Élie de, 183, 185–86, 187–88, 197, 198, 382, 393, 440
Rothschild, Jacob, 171
Rothschild, Liliane de, 184, 185, 186, 393–94

INDEX

Russell, Maud, 44
Russell, Sir John, 32
Russian Revolution, 11
Russo-Ukraine War (from 2022), 4, 82*

Sačirbey, Muhamed, 422
Salinger, Nicole, 390
Sandys, Celia, 73, 183, 197, 251
Sandys, Duncan, 105
Sarajevo marketplace atrocity (1995), 421
Sarbanes, Paul, 298, 341, 377–78
Sarkozy, Nicolas, 393
Sawyer, Diane, 270, 314
Schiaparelli, Elsa, 30
Schiaparelli, Gogo, 30
Schlafly, Phyllis, 279
Schlesinger, Arthur, 226, 241–42, 248, 260, 318, 332, 408–9, 436, 439
Second World War, 4; Allied landings in Sicily (July 1943), 119–20; Anglo-American dispute on tactics ahead of D-Day, 116, 119–20; Atlantic Charter, 98, 137; Atlantic Conference (Newfoundland, August 1941), 97–98; Atlantic War, 49, 74, 94; Battle of Britain (1940), 64–67; bombing of Britain's cities, 65–67, 68–69, 74, 75, 81, 85–86, 90; Café de Paris bombing, 81; D-Day (June 6, 1944), 125–26; destruction of French fleet at Oran, 61; dissent over Chamberlain's conduct of, 56, 59; division of Poland, 49; Dunkirk evacuation (1940), 60; Eastern front, 97, 133, 271; fall of France (June 1940), 60; fiftieth anniversary of D-Day (1994), 404–9; first mass casualties of, 43; German invasion of Crete (May 1941), 94; German invasion of Western Europe (May 1940), 59, 60; Guards' Chapel V-1 bombing, 128; the Holocaust, 426–27; Hopkins as FDR's envoy to London, 75, 82–83, 87, 388; impact of Allied mass bombing, 138–39; Lend-Lease military aid program, 82–83; liberation of Paris (August 1944), 131; London Blitz, 65–67, 69, 75, 81, 85, 90, 121; Normandy landings, 116, 126–27; North Africa campaign, 74–75, 81, 100, 104; Norway campaign, 56–58; Operation Market Garden (September 1944), 133; outbreak of, 38; Pacific war, 99, 100, 112–13, 115, 136; Pearl Harbor attack (December 7, 1941), 99; "phoney war" period, 40, 49; RAF victory of September 15, 1940, 67; sinking of the *Altmark* (February 1940), 56; surrender of Singapore (February 1942), 100; tensions over U.S. strategy, 112, 115; V-1 flying bomb raids, 127–28; V-2 rocket attacks, 133; VE Day celebrations, 138; Yalta Conference (February 1945), 135–37

Seitz, Ray, 384
Shaw, Irwin, 165
Sherman, Wendy, 377
Shorenstein, Walter, 400
Shrum, Bob, 292, 302, 318, 339, 367, 386, 392, 410, 434, 441, 443
Shrum, Marylouise, 434
Shulman, Colette, 270–71, 310, 317, 318, 351

Shulman, Marshall, 270, 310, 317
Shultz, George, 313, 389
Simon, Paul (senator), 377
Sinatra, Frank, 196, 215, 220, 233, 234–35
Soames, Christopher, 149, 157
Soames, Emma, 168, 253
Soames, Mary (née Spencer-Churchill), 52, 53, 55, 66–67, 94, 106–7, 133, 191; biography of her mother, Clementine, 266, 347; dislike of PCH, 47, 106–7, 225, 347; marries Christopher Soames (1947), 149, 157; on PCH, 46–47, 107; on Randolph, 102, 106
Somalia, 415
Sorensen, Theodore, 371, 372, 374
The Sound of Music (stage musical), 197, 200, 203, 206, 214, 234
South Africa, 368, 427, 430
Soviet Union, 97, 133, 270, 309, 340–41; collapse/breakup of, 352–54; the Gorbachevs in Washington (1987), 334–39; Harriman and relations with, 271–73, 310–13, 335, 339; Harriman as ambassador in Moscow, 108, 136–37, 271; invasion of Afghanistan (1979), 271, 289; nuclear arms race of 1980s, 310–12; as nuclear power, 167–68; occupation of Eastern Europe, 136, 167, 272; PCH's trip to Moscow (May 1991), 351–52; U.S. focus shifts toward, 136–37, 154
Spaak, Paul-Henri, 148
Spanish flu pandemic, 9*, 9, 97
Special Air Service, 104
St. Moritz, 177, 187, 428
Stalin, Joseph, 49, 109, 136–37, 271
Stanley, Edward, 40, 41, 43–44, 93

Stark, Admiral Harold, 116
Stein, Robert, 301, 303, 355, 357, 442
Steinem, Gloria, 219, 220, 252, 267, 332
Steitz, Mark, 356, 357, 358
Stephanopoulos, George, 361
Stevens, Liz, 240
Stevenson, Adlai, 193
Stewart, Jimmy, 34, 123
Stinchcombe, Gloucestershire, 158
stock market crash (1987), 348, 397
Strauss, Robert, 259, 273–74, 281, 290, 291, 294, 299, 302, 305, 349
Streisand, Barbra, 267, 362, 377
Suez fiasco (1956), 194, 261–62
Sullavan, Margaret, 204, 206, 209
Sulzberger, Cy, 166–67, 230
Sulzberger, David, 390, 393, 403, 428–29
Sulzberger, Marina, 183, 232
Swiers, Peter, 310, 311, 312, 377

Talbott, Strobe, 351, 417
Tarnoff, Peter, 368
Tauber, Diana, 70
Tauber, Richard, 36
Taylor, Elizabeth, 267
Terra Museum of Modern Art, Chicago, 400
That Hamilton Woman (Alexander Korda film, 1941), 89, 244
That Was the Week That Was (U.S. TV show), 218–19
Thatcher, Margaret, 250, 285, 287, 330–31, 335, 341, 370*, 370
Thomas, Clarence, 331–32, 377
Thompson, "Tommy," 99
Thurmond, Strom, 374
Tito, Josip, 272, 274, 414
Trapp, Baroness Maria von, 197
Tree, Marietta, 193
Trotsky, Leon, 271

INDEX

Truman, Harry S., 148, 250
Trump, Donald, 336, 392, 442
Tudjman, Franjo, 425
Tully, Paul, 357–58
Turin, 161–62, 163–64, 169, 180
Turkey, 333

Ukraine, 4, 82*, 353
United Kingdom: allegation over help for Bush, 379; attitudes to PCH as ambassador in Paris, 384, 389; Chamberlain's appeasement policy, 24, 30, 31, 33; end of Pax Britannica, 154; fading power in later years of war, 125–26; female politicians, 147, 250; general election (1945), 138, 139–40, 147, 321, 357–58; Home Guard, 61; media attacks on PCH (1990s), 375, 404; postwar austerity/exhaustion, 149, 154; postwar reconstruction, 139; power of press barons, 48; Special Relationship concept, 167, 193, 194, 379; Suez fiasco (1956), 194, 261–62. *See also* London
United Nations, 148
United States, 21–22; 82nd Airborne Division, 126; African Americans, 21–22; Anglo-American relationship in early war years, 74, 75, 82, 83, 86–88, 97–98; atom bombs dropped on Japan, 139; Bay of Pigs invasion (April 1961), 211, 212; Central Intelligence Agency (CIA), 173–74, 410; Equal Rights Amendment (1971), 252; global leadership role concept, 194, 212, 257, 407, 414–15, 417–18, 424–26, 443; Grosvenor Square Embassy, 23; growing focus on Soviet Union, 136–37, 154; Iranian hostage crisis (1979–81), 289; Irish Americans, 97; Joseph Kennedy as ambassador in London, 26–27, 32–33, 38, 64, 144, 260; Kent State University killings (1970), 257; lack of female politicians, 213, 250, 267, 303, 322, 337, 350; Lend-Lease military aid program, 82–83; Marshall Plan, 154, 168; Office of Strategic Services, 109; PCH appointed ambassador to France (March 1993), 374–80, 443; PCH takes interest in affairs of state (1950s), 192–93; PCH's arrival in (1959), 198, 199; Pearl Harbor attack (December 7, 1941), 99; postwar attraction of for PCH, 140, 143–45; and postwar reconstruction, 139; presidential election (1972), 257–59; presidential election (1976), 269–70; presidential election (1980), 288–90; presidential election (1984), 321–23; presidential election (1988), 343–45; presidential election (1992), 360–68, 443; presidential election (1996), 432; racial justice issue in, 114, 256–57, 284, 322, 358, 366; rise of conservatism in 1970s/80s, 279, 288–90, 319; Second World War neutrality, 74, 75, 97; social and political turbulence of early 1970s, 256–57; Special Relationship concept, 167, 193, 194, 379; tensions with Britain over war strategy, 112, 115; wealthy Americans in wartime London, 103

INDEX

Vance, Cyrus, 269–70
Verveer, Melanne, 360, 368, 369, 386, 407, 431
Vestal Virgins, 244*
Viertel, Peter, 187–88
Vietnam War, 214, 228, 231, 249, 257, 264, 268; Clinton and the draft, 361, 379, 404; impact on future U.S. foreign policy, 231, 271–72, 415, 419; peace talks in Paris (1968), 239, 270, 419
Vilmorin, Louise de, 166, 444
Vreeland, Diana, 205, 250, 277
Vreeland, Frank, 174

Wachner, Linda, 393, 429, 434, 436, 444
Wahl, Nicholas, 376, 403, 406
Walker, Mallory, 327
Walters, Barbara, 263, 392
Walton, Bill, 91, 116, 123, 126, 211, 217, 239, 248, 257, 261; on the Churchill Club at Ashburnham House, 122–23; death of (1994), 428; in liberated Paris (1944), 132; pieces on PCH in *Architectural Digest*, 296
Warhol, Andy, 220
Warnke, Paul, 287, 398, 401, 413–14
Warwick, 7th Earl of (Fulkie), 37
Washington, DC: becomes political capital of the world, 192; as "a cauldron of biting nastiness," 249–50, 261–62, 265, 319; Georgetown, 213, 240, 246–49, 252, 261–66, 289, 400; Jockey Club, 367; National Gallery, 248, 278, 323, 326, 328, 348–49, 350, 382–83, 412, 444; PCH as political hostess, 250–54, 260–66, 274, 281
Watergate scandal, 257, 262, 264

Waters, Maxine, 365
Waugh, Evelyn, 71, 73, 77, 97, 102, 158, 182
Weiller, Paul-Louis, 164
Welsh, Mary, 81, 118–19, 126
Weymouth, Lally, 239–40
Whistler, Rex, 44
Whitney, Betsey, 146, 190, 195, 197, 371
Whitney, Colonel Jock, 115, 143, 173, 190, 197, 201, 232–33, 243; allowance to PCH, 110, 146; as ambassador to Britain, 193, 195; PCH's affair with, 109–10, 121, 371
Whitney, Craig, 431
Wick, Charles, 337
Williams, Carol, 274, 292
Williams, Edward Bennett, 281–82
Williams, Mona Harrison, 44, 52
Winant, Gil, 90, 99
Windsor, Duke and Duchess of, 160, 164–65, 172–73, 185, 220–21, 251
Winn, Popsy, 23, 24
Wintour, Charles, 147
Wisner, Frank, 246, 265, 378, 432, 442
women: Averell's view of role in politics, 263–66, 267–68; banned from wearing trousers in Reagan White House, 319; birth control issue, 38, 118, 176, 279, 331; Carter's 51.3 Percent Committee, 269; Randolph Churchill's attitude to, 34–35, 41–42, 48, 49, 55, 157, 158; conservative backlash against feminism, 279; contraction of lives at end of war, 138, 151, 165, 168; Equal Rights Amendment (1971), 252; female politicians in UK, 147, 250;

Ferraro as first female vice-presidential candidate, 322; Raisa Gorbachev meets in Washington, 337–38; and higher education, 19; Jack Kennedy's attitude to, 154, 211, 213; lack of bathrooms at Senate, 350; lack of female politicians in USA, 213, 250, 267, 303, 322, 337, 350; as liberated by the war, 80, 81, 122, 138; and life in 1950s America, 193, 208–9; *Madame l'ambassadeur* form of address, 383, 394; Pasqua's sexism over spying issue, 409–11; PCH addresses Joint Session of Congress (1982), 294; PCH's admiration of success/strength in, 119, 220–21, 250, 270–71, 330–31; PCH's blind spot on sexual harassment, 331; PCH's "real man" comment, 303, 330; PCH's reputation of not liking, 119, 261, 303, 381; PCH's support for Abzug (1976), 267–69, 300; and political ambition in 1970s Washington, 265–66; in postwar Parisian society, 166, 168, 183; in powerful jobs in France, 390; primogeniture, 14; *Roe v. Wade*, 279; role of in politics, 264–66, 267–69, 270–71, 303, 306, 319, 322, 330–31, 345–46, 381; roles of at Yalta, 136; sexist attacks on Hillary Clinton, 390; silence over domestic abuse, 105, 230; the Swans of Fifth Avenue, 219–20; upper-class custom of leaving the room after dinner, 214, 264–66; wearing of trousers in New York restaurants, 252

Woodward, Elsie, 21, 24
Woolsey, James, 360, 366
Wrightsman, Charles, 189

Yeltsin, Boris, 352
York races, 29